# IN THE NAME OF
# THE VOLK

# IN THE NAME OF
# THE VOLK

*Political Justice in Hitler's Germany*

H.W. Koch

St. Martin's Press
New York

© H. W. Koch, 1989

First published in the United States of America in 1989

Printed in Great Britain

ISBN 0–312–03205–6

Library of Congress Cataloging-in-Publication Data

Koch, H. W. (Hannsjoachim Wolfgang), 1933–
    In the name of the Volk : political justice in Hitler's Germany /
H. W. Koch.
        p.    cm.
    Bibliography: p.
    Includes index.
    ISBN 0–312–03205–6
    1. Criminal justice, Administration of—Germany—History.
2.  Germany. Volksgerichtshof—History.  3.  Treason—Germany—
History.  I.  Title.
KK9430.A65K63   1989
345.43'05—dc20
[344.3055]                    89–31746
                        CIP

# Contents

*Dem Gedächtnis*
*von*
Karla Zapf
1908–1984
and

with deepest gratitude to my teachers of 25 years ago: P.J.V. Rolo, D.K. Adams, F. Field and W.S. Cole, at the University of Maryland, to whom, apart from my family, I owe everything. But above all, I am grateful for two things: first, for a level of teaching at the University of Keele I have not encountered elsewhere since; and secondly, for a degree of intellectual tolerance on controversial issues unthinkable in any institution of higher education in my own country – 'the freest state in our history' (*dem freiesten Staat unserer Geschichte*), as Helmut Kohl calls it.

# Introduction

In 1978, while working on study leave in Germany, I became increasingly fascinated by the history of the German judiciary during the twelve years of Hitler's rule. It seemed to embody one of the most chilling aspects of the Third Reich: the use of legal, even constitutional, means to thwart, imperceptibly at first, the course of justice and impose in specific areas of the law its own definitions of right and wrong. In the hands of Hitler's judges, an important portion of the courts became a virtual arm of the state and its instrument of terror. In contrast to other aspects of the Third Reich, moreover, the German judiciary had been rather neglected. Apart from a few books, the number of which could be counted on one hand, there was very little historical treatment, and what there was was full of polemic and relatively little analysis. Hence I allowed myself to look more closely at the judiciary, and in particular at the National Socialist People's Court, or Volksgerichtshof (VGH), the court exclusively concerned with all cases of treason.

The VGH epitomizes the use of the judiciary under Hitler. Armed with the German public law principle of *Treu und Glauben*, of loyalty and good faith, the VGH pursued its treason cases with a ferocity hitherto unseen in the German courts. At heart, it was the legal weapon in Hitler's battle to 'purify' the nation, and it performed this function by uniting the concepts of loyalty to one's country and loyalty to a particular ruler. 'Those not with me are against me' became its motto – a definition of loyalty in which virtually any doubting of authority became an act of treason, and under which it sentenced tens of thousands of Germans and citizens of occupied countries to hard labour, imprisonment and death. The history of the VGH provides us with frightening evidence of the ease with which the instruments of a state based on law can be transformed into the means of its destruction.

A dangerous misconception about the VGH is that it began and ended with Hitler. Institutionally, of course, it spanned the years of

National Socialist domination, from 1934 to 1945. But its roots lay
in the Weimar Republic, when the judiciary had become politicized
and the precedent for depriving an accused of his or her legal rights
had been established. In 1922, and under a Social Democrat Reich
President and Minister of Justice, the Law Protecting the Constitution
broke for the first time with the hallowed principle of *nulla poena
sine lege* ('no punishment without law'). The door was opened for
the National Socialists to take this precedent to its logical conclusion.

The VGH's ascendancy in German legal and political history was
determined by three main features of the country's history. These
deserve serious consideration, because without them the VGH's rise
to power is incomprehensible.

The first was the conviction of a large part, if not the majority, of
German people, including both Hitler and his opponents, that
Germany had lost the Great War primarily as a result of treason and
revolution. The soldiers at the front had been betrayed by those at
the rear; Germany had been 'stabbed in the back'. This unshakeable
belief, as well as the conviction, especially after 1939, that '1918'
should under no circumstances be repeated, shaped both the policy
and the practice of the VGH. And, indeed, '1918' found no
repetition. The consequences of that defeat, of course, are a different
matter.

The second factor was the Enabling Law of 23 March 1933,
Article 2 of which explicitly empowered the government to enact
legislation deviating from the constitution and to do so without the
sanction of the Reichstag. Incredibly, the Enabling Law was passed
by secret ballot by the last democratically elected Reichstag; with the
exception of the Social Democrats, all Reichstag representatives
voted for it. The new government was thus handed vast legislative
possibilities which it was quick to put to use.

The third and final formative element in the VGH's history was the
National Socialist *Führerprinzip* ('leadership principle'), the belief in
the absolute primacy of the leader, whether of the family or of the
state. Unquestioning loyalty was the order of the day, a principle
which was nowhere applied within the German judiciary with greater
rigour than in the senates of the VGH. Roland Freisler, the VGH
president during its crucial final years, argued for the application of
the 'leadership principle' with lethal fanaticism.

I must admit to having approached this study not without
preconceived ideas. As a child in Munich, I lived through Hitler's

twelve years of power, and Freisler's temperamental outbursts are still strong in my memory, even though I only saw them as a boy on the cinema newsreels. Equally strong in my memory are the pink posters on Munich's billboards of the late war years: headed by the phrase 'In the Name of the Volk' in bold black letters, they announced the death sentences pronounced by the VGH against 'traitors' and 'defeatists'.

It would be untrue, therefore, to say that I began my research for this book from the very outset *sine ira et studio*. Nevertheless, my tendency is towards the *Historismus* tradition and to seek objectivity rather than an historical interpretation tied to a specific political point of view. However difficult they may be to achieve, Ranke's postulates about the ethical norms of historians are, in my opinion, superior to the dogmatic approach which characterizes much of present-day historiography. It is the task of the historian to give back to the dead their voices irrespective of whether those voices are sublime and principled, or, as in the case of the Third Reich's judiciary, distasteful and even evil.

The more one delves into the past, the more one realizes that history is more rich in nuance than one remembers. This is not to say that what has been written about the Third Reich is largely misleading, but that within the framework established so far, there is room for greater qualification, subtlety and a more careful weighing of factors hitherto ignored. This trend is perhaps best demonstrated by the different schools of interpretation that have developed over the last two decades – the 'intentionalists' (represented, for example, by K.D. Bracher) and the 'functionalists' (represented by H. Mommsen and M. Broszat). These schools of thought have newly defined the structures, interests and aims (or lack thereof) of the Third Reich, with the result that the scholarly debate is no longer bound by the status quo established at Nuremburg. Serious historiography can no longer be satisfied with mere clichés.

Indeed, it is essential that historians reject these clichés. With forty years between us and the Nuremburg trials – at which the German judiciary as a whole, not the VGH itself, was tried – it is far too easy to relegate the horrors of the Third Reich and its instruments to the distant world of history, and to comfort ourselves with the thought that only a few individuals were responsible. In his first years after being appointed chancellor, Hitler rested less on an ideological indoctrination of his mass base than on the fact that almost half of the German electorate saw in him, as the historian Martin Broszat puts it, 'a middle way between democracy and [an] obsolete constitutional authoritarian state.' Likewise, the origins of the VGH go far beyond Hitler and his conception of the law to encompass substantial popular support and precedents which reach into the Weimar Republic. Yet the disturbing proclivity for facile, easy answers remains. 'The morality of dismay and perplexity about the NS past,' Broszat writes,

> has ... exhausted itself. It has lost much of its singularity through our experience of world historical acts of force and catastrophes and has meanwhile degenerated into an accepted set of vague lip-service confessions, devoid of moral strength. The dictum, 'National Socialist rule of force', can only be morally rejuvenated by a greater, keener historical insight. Therefore the relationship between morality and historical understanding – a relationship which has changed and will probably continue to change – appears to be ... the crux of the question, how much has National Socialism become the part of the past, how historical has it become.

Those who have not forgotten the NS past, but who are looking for a justification of much that took place in Germany between 1933 and 1945 and have failed to learn anything from the events which pushed Germany and most of Europe to the abyss, will be disappointed by this book. Equally disappointed will be those seeking to find in the VGH's victims evidence of a broad 'German resistance', particularly in the 20 July 1944 bomb plotters. The conspirators' ideas bore little resemblance to 'the changed self-perception of the Federal Republic,' as Broszat comments, and their views of 'the Jewish problem' differed from Hitler's more in method than in principle.

There is no nation that does not live without its myths, and, taking a purely pragmatic viewpoint, it is understandable that the 'resistance' has stood at the cradle of the two states which share a common nationality. Many Germans, as individuals or in small groups, did oppose the NS regime from its beginning to its, or their own, end. But to invoke the myth of a widespread, élite-led resistance forty years later, in the light of all we know and should know, is to transform it into the existential lie of the Federal Republic.

As to this study, two points must be made, one regarding the structure of this study, the other regarding some of the sources. As far as the structure is concerned, my initial intention was to relegate

tables and statistics to an appendix. But since the figures and details
which these supply are an integral part of my argument, they could
not be separated from the text. For the British version of this book,
however, I have substantially reduced the level of detail, leaving out,
for example, the fairly exhaustive account of the VGH cases given in
the German version and referring to identical cases in the Notes. The
German version also contains an almost complete transcript of the
first trial of the plotters of 20 July 1944, included there because it is
so selectively cited but appearing here in summary. While scholars
may wish to refer to the more detailed of the two, the analysis in
both books is the same.

The sources for this book present a peculiar difficulty. When I
conducted my first interviews in the second half of 1978 and early
1979, the information came readily. In the spring of 1979, the
Federal Parliament decided to revoke the Statute of Limitations (not
without considerable pressure from abroad), however, and while my
sources did not dry up, no one who had been interviewed or who
had supplied me with information wished to be mentioned by name
– especially as Berlin's *Landgericht* I (Land Court, the equivalent of a
county court) had initiated proceedings against former VGH
professional and lay judges as accessories to murder. (What gave
these investigations a particularly sour flavour was that the state
prosecutor accepted, without reservation, evidence supplied by East
Germany, where VGH judges had joined the judiciary in the
country's early years.) Between 1979 and 1986, there existed the very
real possibility of men the youngest of whom was 75 being accused
or being called as witness to these investigations. One of the accused
committed suicide.

For these reasons, I have not named some of my sources. Members
of the VGH should have been tried, but not more than forty years
after the event. Whenever in the Notes there is a reference to the
archive of the author, this means that the material is in my
possession. This also applies to Freisler's correspondence, which,
apart from the passages I have quoted, contains details about specific
cases before the VGH as well as the lower courts, particularly the
*Sondergerichte*, the Special Courts established by Hitler's regime, and
with it evidence which might well incriminate others still alive. All
these sources will be handed over to the archive of the Institut für
Zeitgeschichte in Munich, but the files will remain closed until 2010
so that the children of those convicted of NS crimes will be
protected. Nothing justifies the exposure of these children to an

ordeal for actions for which they bear not the slightest responsibility.

On the judiciary as a whole, Herman Weinkauff's *Die Deutsche Justiz und der Nationalsozialismus* (The German Judiciary and National Socialism) and Walter Wagner's *Der Volksgerichtshof im nationalsozialistischen Staat* (The People's Court in the National Socialist State) offer a usable collection of materials, but are sadly lacking in analysis. Files on the VGH itself – those that have survived the war – are fragmentary and in the main held at the Federal Archive in Koblenz. Additional documentation can be found at the Ministry of Justice in Bonn, the Berlin Document Center, and the Institut für Zeitgeschichte in Munich. However, personal files of members of the German judiciary are only accessible thirty years after their death. Freisler's file, unfortunately, shows signs of being incomplete, for reasons that cannot be ascertained.

I am in great debt to all the archives and their staff mentioned in the Notes. Great assistance was given to me by Professor Dr Thomas Nipperdey, and by Martin Broszat and Helmut Aucherbach of the Institut für Zeitgeschichte, who made a room available to me at the institute in which I could work without disturbance. Dr Wilhelm Lotz of Soest clarified a good many judicial problems and saved me from many pitfalls into which I as an historian without legal expertise might well have stumbled. Heinz Höhne of *Der Spiegel* and Dr Karl-Heinz Janssen of *Die Zeit* were kind enough to supply me with documents and publications.

Particular gratitude is due to my former teacher, Professor P.J.V. Rolo, and to my colleague J.W.D. Trythal, who assisted me in every stage of the production of the manuscript as well as making sure that the syntax did not contain excessive 'Germanicisms'. Professors J.A.S. Greenville, at the University of Birmingham, and W. Carr, University of Sheffield, read the manuscript critically and offered many helpful suggestions. However, I alone am responsible for the contents of this study and the judgements and opinions expressed within it.

My thanks are equally due to those who helped to strengthen my moral backbone and who assisted me in many a difficult moment while I was writing this book. In this connection, I am deeply indebted to the unstinting support given to me by Frau Karla Zapf, to whom this book is dedicated. I am also grateful to Dr Georg Maier and to Herr Willi and Frau Eleonore Hess, Herr Helmut Buchenberger and Frau Marianne, friends of times long past, when air raids shattered our home town and later when we lived through the turbulent post-war years, years of friendship which have survived both time and distance. Last but not least, I wish to thank Frau Magdelana Sailer and the Grainer and Eib families, who deserve more than a mere mention for their assistance, and the Morell Library of the University of York, particularly Mr David Griffith.

Hannsjoachim W. Koch
Munich, Kirchdorf and York, 1988

# 1

# The Background

Berlin, Tuesday, 24 April 1934. A day like any other in the heart of Germany's capital. The weather was typical of April – rain and sleet, accompanied by bitterly cold winds, swept through the city streets. One might have felt that winter rather than spring was approaching.

In the city's Prinz-Albrecht Strasse, a street rich in large houses with elegant Jugendstil façades, a crowd was forming. The neighbourhood, substantial and wealthy, dated back to the bustling 1870s when the German Empire had been founded and its bubble of prosperity, created by the war reparations paid by the French after the Treaty of Frankfurt, had burst. When France paid its last installment in 1873, the German economy went into decline, putting an end to the wave of speculative ventures and sparking bankruptcies and unemployment. In Prussia the government had intervened in an early example of what we might call deficit financing by 'priming the pump', including the subsidizing of extensive building projects. The Prinz-Albrecht Strasse was one of those streets which had benefited from the programme and looked the better for it.

On that Tuesday in April 1934 the street's residents were suddenly surprised as limousine after limousine pulled up before the seat of the former Prussian Diet. For some time the building had stood empty, and only in recent weeks had workmen started to get busy. The crowd quickly began to rally – old and young women and a few pensioners. Most of the men were still at work, and the children were at school. Held back by the green uniformed police, the crowd could see the men emerging from the cars. Formally dressed in black coats and top hats, they were followed by uniformed members of the NSDAP's paramilitary units, the SA in their brown uniforms, the SS in black. Then came army and navy officers; the Luftwaffe did not as yet officially exist.

For the bulk of the onlookers, the faces of these obviously prominent men were unfamiliar. These were the anonymous, faceless men of the bureaucracy and armed forces. Franz Gürtner, the stocky

1

Bavarian Reich Minister of Justice, for example, was unknown despite the fact that he had already served as Justice Minister in two previous cabinets headed by Franz von Papen and General von Schleicher. But who could remember all the faces of the frequently changing cabinets of the Weimar Republic? Perhaps the only readily recognizable person was Dr Wilhelm Frick, Reich Minister of the Interior and a member of Hitler's cabinet from its inception. Though in civilian attire, he strode into the building at a military pace, his closely cropped head standing out among the many top hats and military caps. His colleague Gürtner stumbled as he mounted the steps to the building, a sign for superstitious minds of an ominous future.

Among the crowd hopes began to rise that perhaps they would see 'their Führer'. Their hopes were disappointed, for the German chancellor was away that day in his mountain refuge on the Obersalzberg high above the German-Austrian border. From his home above Berchtesgaden he could see into his native country as far as Salzburg.

Inside the hall of the house on the Prinz-Albrecht Strasse the visitors divested themselves of their coats. The civilians left their hats in the entry way, and donned robes and squarish caps. They were judges and state prosecutors, members of the German judiciary, that much-maligned profession. In the days of the Empire, they had been accused by the Conservatives of being 'soft on the Reds' and criticized by the Social Democrats for carrying out a biased 'class justice'. The transformation from Empire to Republic had not changed the vulnerability of the judiciary to attack, nor, as we shall see, did it change in Hitler's Germany.

The visitors were ushered up the stairs to the first floor and into a hall with a seating capacity of two to three hundred. Within, chairs were arranged to the left and right with a narrow corridor in the middle leading to a platform on which a further row of chairs was arrayed just behind a speaker's desk. As the visitors took their seats, they saw before them, spreading from ceiling to floor, an enormous swastika flag.

When all had settled, the large, winged double doors were shut. Gürtner stood up in his gown and cap and from the speaker's desk delivered a short address to his audience. Only his concluding phrase has been recorded: 'I herewith open the National Socialist People's Court,' he proclaimed. His speech was followed by a few short words from Frick, as well as from a few other party dignitaries. Then all stood up and, raising their right arms in the National Socialist 'German salute', sang the German national anthem. The meeting concluded with the song which was to be Germany's second national anthem for the next twelve years, the Horst-Wessel song: '. . . comrades killed by Red Front and the forces of reaction march in spirit with us.' Gürtner, Frick and the other dignitaries left the platform and the hall while the audience remained standing, leaving only after the last of the leaders had stepped through the door.[1]

The entire ceremony had lasted less than an hour. A new but disastrous and extremely bloody chapter of German legal history had begun, although few of those present, perhaps not even Gürtner or Frick, could foresee it at the time. The media took scarce note of it. The opening of the National Socialist People's Court was neither a news item on the radio nor a feature in the newsreels. In the press, the new VGH merited only one or two paragraphs tucked away in the inside pages. The German public was hardly aware of its existence. Unexamined and largely unremarked by press or public, the opening of the VGH marked the beginning of an era in which the treason laws and the aims of National Socialism became one and the same.

The National Socialist People's Court was an élite court system with virtually exclusive jurisdiction over cases of treason. Operating within the penal code, it resembled the criminal courts in structure, although its hierarchy was expressed in a series of senates (two at the outset, a number which later expanded to six), the first of which, headed by the VGH president, claimed the most important cases. Its judges, numbering only a dozen at its inception and over 200 at its demise in 1945, were both professional and lay; like their counterparts in other courts, they wore the traditional robes of the judiciary, and sat in judgment in their courtrooms in Berlin, and occasionally elsewhere in the country. The VGH was not alone in meting out political justice: the lower courts and the 'Special Courts', another National Socialist innovation, also heard political cases.

On the surface, little had changed. True, the creation of a separate and largely autonomous court to try treason cases represented a marked elevation of the issue – a fact in part reflecting both popular and judicial belief that in the wake of the 'stab in the back' of the First World War, the treason laws needed to be tightened up. Yet neither the legal basis for, nor the legal procedure of, the VGH differed significantly from treason trials of the past.

Both before and after 1934, an individual suspected of treason would be prosecuted by the police, often acting on information provided by informants. The prosecuting authority would then decide whether to bring a formal indictment, in which case the prosecuting counsel – a civil servant under instruction from his superiors at the Ministry of Justice – would be brought forward. Because of the 1922 amendments to the law in the aftermath of Rathenau's assassination, the accused would be tried without a right of appeal, and would be found guilty or innocent according to the law.

The legal basis of VGH judgments also remained essentially intact. Along with the 1871 penal code, its twin pillars were the two forms of treason defined in German law since the late Middle Ages. High treason (*Hochverrat*) covered acts of treason against the state from within the country: attacks violating the Constitution, for example, or against the head of state or against the state's security. *Landesverrat*, or treason against the country, was that directed against the external security of the state and its position *vis-à-vis* other states.[2] Thus passing on state secrets, espionage or unintentionally communicating state secrets to a foreign power constituted Landesverrat.[3] These definitions of treason, without substantial amendment, were the legal justifications under which the victims of the VGH were sentenced.

What did change was the judiciary's interpretation of law and the harshness of the sentences. This reflected both its shrinking independence from the state and the aims of the VGH as conceived by its leaders. While the individual prosecuted for treason prior to 1934 would have been reasonably certain of being tried by a judge free from the political considerations of the day, after 1934 he or she would have been judged by a man who had been appointed expressly because of his loyalty to the National Socialist state. The NS People's Court had been created to further the aims of National Socialism, and it was this responsibility which made it unique among Hitler's judiciary. As Goebbels told an audience of VGH judges in 1942, the judiciary had to recognize its political task. Whether a judgment was just or unjust was unimportant; what mattered was that it fulfilled its purpose.

The two men to whom this task was entrusted were Otto Georg Thierack, a political opportunist whose policies during his 1934–42 presidency laid the ground work for the radicalization of the VGH's sentencing policy, and Roland Freisler, an absolutely convinced and fanatical National Socialist who continued Thierack's line and applied those policies with renewed vigour in the crucial years 1942–5. In his capacity as Ministerial Director in the Prussian Ministry of Justice in 1933 and Secretary of State in the Reich Ministry of Justice since 1934, Freisler had been one of the VGH's most fervent advocates and the author of a plethora of academic papers arguing its case. Killed in a bombing raid towards the end of the war, he provided a convenient scapegoat after 1945, and has thus been held up as the ultimate expression of National Socialist 'justice' in a way which has partially distorted the important and widespread collusion of the rest of the judiciary.

The VGH's principal jurisdiction covered the 70 million citizens in Germany, whose loyalty was seen as paramount importance. But the judgments of the VGH also applied to the entire population of Czechia, the so-called 'protectorate' of Bohemia and Moravia, Poles in the annexed territories, Germans in Alsace-Lorraine and Eupen-Malmedy, and, after 1941, to non-German 'terrorists' in occupied France, Belgium, Norway and Holland, who were deported to Germany to stand trial in the VGH courts. For obvious reasons, many of the German citizens brought before the VGH were Communists, trade unionists, Social Democrats and other dissenters from National Socialism. The accused in the VGH trial of Hitler's would-be assassins – the 20 July 1944 Wehrmacht bomb plotters – were, by contrast, élite members of the armed forces and the civil service. Middle class professionals, blue collar factory workers, artisans, members of the aristocracy and the military, Catholics and Confession Christians all came within the VGH's ambit. Only Jews were not subject to its jurisdiction after 1943; as 'inferior people', they were not worthy of the rule of law.

The crimes for which those appearing before the VGH could be convicted ranged from the most serious to the apparently trivial – from assassination attempts on Hitler to sabotage to listening to foreign radio broadcasts. For such acts the accused could expect one of three penalties: imprisonment, forced labour or death. Between 1934 and 1944, almost 13,000 individuals (including foreign nationals) were sentenced to death. In the early years of the VGH, death sentences were relatively rare, but their number rose sharply as the war progressed and as the definition of treason became increasingly elastic. A world-famous pianist was sentenced to death for criticizing National Socialism; a doctor, himself a former NSDAP member, received the same penalty for voicing doubts about Germany's eventual victory over the Allies; others died for telling political jokes – an ideological mistake which ten years earlier would have been punished by a few years' imprisonment.

Interestingly, the VGH acquitted many more people than is generally believed, although the figures we have, produced by the VGH judges themselves, are not entirely reliable. The acquittal rate was a sign of the uncertain accuracy of the denunciations which led people into VGH courtrooms, and of the judiciary's adherence to some notion of the rule of law – the remnants, perhaps, of their previous standards of objectivity and impartiality under the Empire. After 1936, however, these acquittals became largely irrelevant. With open access to VGH files, the Gestapo adopted the practice – the norm during the war – of re-arresting individuals just acquitted or released from prison and interning them in concentration camps; if the law did not suffice, force would. But if the power of the VGH was exercised more subtly than that of the SS, it was no less effective an instrument of terror. By 1944, Freisler could fairly accurately write that the VGH had become 'a truly revolutionary tribunal to purify the nation.'[4]

What distinguished the VGH from its legal antecedents, then, was the intimate relationship between its aims and those of the political powers of the day. In most countries, as in pre-National Socialist Germany, the law is meant to stand above politics; here, the law was unabashedly and wholeheartedly meant to further the aspirations of the Third Reich. As Thierack wrote to his successor on the advent of Freisler's assuming the VGH presidency: 'the judge of the VGH must become accustomed to seeing primarily the ideas and intentions of the leadership of the state, while the human fate which depends on it is only secondary. . . . The accused before the VGH are only little figures in a much greater circle . . . which fights the Reich.'[5]

So much for the rule of law; so much for citizens' legal rights. The accused before the VGH had no right of appeal and no trial by a jury of peers. They were tried by professional and lay judges specially picked for the strength of their commitment to NS ideals and their expertise, in the case of the lay judges, many of whom came from the Wehrmacht, in matters of espionage and national security. Coupled with the ever-widening scope of the definition of treason, this judicial system represented a perversion of justice so profound that it hardly merited the name. For the next eleven years, even citizens of the type surrounding the luminaries on the Prinz-Albrecht Strasse would be subject to its tests of loyalty to the Volk.

# 2

# A Political Judiciary

The proper functioning of the National Socialist People's Courts required that a substantial minority, if not the majority, of judges embrace National Socialist ideology as an appropriate instrument of the courtroom. Staunch monarchists under Bismarck, loyal (if unenthusiastic) servants of the law under the Weimar Republic, these men, known for their integrity and strict adherence to the letter of the law, continued their careers under the Third Reich with scarcely a murmur of protest. One astonishing feature of this apparent volte-face was that prior to 1933 virtually no judges had been members of the NSDAP. Weimar, quite simply, thrust the judiciary into a political position. Personally disenchanted with the Republic, exhausted by the constant criticism, the judiciary welcomed the Reichstag's constitutional amendments which released them from their uncomfortable position as arbitrators of political cases. The changes under Weimar provided both motivation and opportunity to a disoriented judiciary ready to spread its political wings, and by the time Hitler came to power the political pump had already been primed. It was a short step from the politicized courts of the Republic to those of the Third Reich.

Bismarck's Second Empire had laid the foundations for a strong, nationally cohesive judiciary. One of the central problems brought about by the re-unification of Germany in 1871 had been that of producing a unified code of law; under Bismarck's leadership, such a legal code began to take shape. In 1877, the law determining judicial procedure, the Gerichtsverfassungsgesetz, or GVG, and the law determining procedure in criminal cases, the Strafprozessordnung, or StPO, were enacted, resulting in the civil code of 1896. This came into force as the German legal code (Bürgerliches Gesetzbuch, or BGB) in 1900.[1] The penal code (Strafgesetzbuch, or StGB) – under which the VGH was later to function so contentedly – was enacted in 1871.[2] At the same time, a nation-wide judicial structure was established, made up of local, district, appeal and supreme courts.

There were, of course, regional variations, but for the most part the courts, for the first time in Germany's history, functioned as a cohesive whole (see Appendix for a fuller explanation of the judiciary). With both a consistent legal procedure and structure, the keynotes of the judiciary's existence were stability, consistency and a peaceful pursuit of the normal course of civil and criminal cases.

It is often asserted that, after 1878, when Bismarck took a more conservative path, the German judiciary, and the Prussian one in particular, experienced a major crisis. In the face of the advancing tide of liberalism and socialism, it is argued, Bismarck removed from the Prussian judiciary almost the entire generation of judges which had opposed him during the constitutional conflict in Prussia between 1862 and 1866. He then refused, as part of a policy of fostering judicial, social and ideological conformity, to fill the resulting vacancies with new appointees. The judiciary thus became a conservative, even reactionary, bulwark of the state.[3]

In fact, a strong case can be made that the judiciary remained independent throughout the life of the Empire. While it was loyal to the Crown, it displayed, for example, a marked degree of liberalism in such vexed questions as the rights of Polish minority, which from 1880 onwards was subjected to repeated attempts at 'Germanization'. At a time when neither labour nor liberals were in favour, moreover, the Prussian judiciary, the most important in the German federal system, defended the right to organize and the right of Social Democrats to freedom of assembly. And however much Bismarck may have wished to control the judiciary, there are few signs that he succeeded. The so-called purge of the Prussian judges actually took place during Bismarck's 'culture struggle' (*Kulturkampf*) – a development backed by German liberals – and those who retired after 1878 would have done so in any event, the majority having long since celebrated their fiftieth anniversary in public office. During the Second Empire, moreover, advocates and lawyers gained their autonomy from the Ministry of Justice and were thus able to set up practices free from the confines of the state bureaucracy – a sign of growing, not shrinking, legal independence.[4]

Yet there is no doubt that the judiciary was severely shaken by the collapse of the Empire and the subsequent departure of the Emperor into exile. Nor did it ever fully recover from the shock of the Weimar Republic and its failure to attain any real stability. Loyal to *Kaiser und Reich*, they were accustomed to a stable environment in which they could preside over routine civil and criminal cases, and in which they could retain their self-perception as apolitical. Weimar threw this relatively tranquil – at least known and understood – situation into chaos.

After 1920 it was increasingly impossible to form a government based on the majority support of the Reichstag. Minority governments were the order of the day. The average duration of governments between 1919 and 1928 was a mere seven months. A spate of politically inspired violence developed, putting the judiciary under a pressure of which it had so far encountered very little. Suddenly judges were called upon to adjudicate in cases of crimes committed by revolutionaries who claimed their acts as sacred rights of the revolution, but which for a judge was a crime to be dealt with by the traditional norms as set out in the German penal code. It was a conflict in the interpretation of the law which neither side fully understood, with which the judiciary was unprepared to cope, and which added to the tension of the judiciary's position *vis-à-vis* the government and to the vociferousness of public criticism.

Compounding the problem was the fact that in the years immediately before and during the First World War, the primacy of an attitude of service to the Crown had been replaced by a dispassionate professionalism. While this shift applied mainly to civil servants, it also extended to the legal profession. As those who believed in the monarchy and an absolute loyalty to the state retired, their places were filled by younger members of the judiciary who lacked a firm, fixed point which demanded loyalty and to which loyalty would be unquestioningly given. By 1918, the judiciary was too anchored in its professional ethos – or in its political apathy – to be transplanted into the shallow sands of the highly fragile Republic. In fact, it seems a gross error to speak of the dissolution of the Republic from 1930 onwards. From its very beginning, the Weimar Republic did not have the strength to mobilize almost anyone on its behalf, and this discontented majority included the judiciary.

This is not to say that the judiciary, along with the other representatives of the pillars of the state, the bureaucracy and the army, acted against or even subverted the Republic. They fulfilled their 'duty to the fatherland' as their training had led them to.[5] Some defended the Republic, although this was an unpopular and defensive position for which its proponents came under attack from monarchists, the extreme left and right, and those essentially indifferent to the Republic. The judiciary was losing its traditional image and was in search of a new one. Some eminent jurists, such as Gustav

Radbruch, Ernst Frankel and Hugo Sinzheimer, sought to establish an alternative political banner for the judiciary. But their Republikanischer Richterbund was basically a socialist organization and failed to attract the majority of judges.[6] Most judges continued to view with attitudes ranging from skepticism to outright alarm all that which called itself the political process in the Weimar Republic.

Their fears were confirmed by two distinct developments: the erosion of their living standards, and the plunging of the judicial system into a political quagmire. Already underpaid – certainly paid less than top civil servants – their salaries were reduced by as much as 20 per cent, first by inflation and then by the deflation of the Weimar period and by government economic measures. It was a poverty even more acutely felt because of the judges' high social standing. The plight of the young men trying to enter the legal profession, the Assessors, was also worrisome. Having completed their university studies, they were then obligated to work for an indefinite period of time in the courts until such time as a place on the judge's bench became vacant. The Assessors were very badly paid and were forced to rely for financial assistance on their families, who themselves, ruined by inflation and deflation, were increasingly unable to provide it. We do not know the extent to which these young men later became victims of National Socialism propaganda, but it is clear that both judges and aspirants to the judiciary were sufficiently disillusioned with the Republic to at least entertain the notion of a political alternative.

Equally destabilizing was the surge of political unrest. The early years of the Republic were rocked by a series of profound, mostly left-wing, upheavals. Beginning with the revolution of November-December 1918, the insurgencies continued with the Berlin risings of January and March 1919; the founding of a 'Soviet Republic' in Munich in April of that year; the rising in the Ruhr of a Red Army in March and April 1920; and risings in central Germany in 1921 and in central Germany and Hamburg in 1923. From the right came two main actions: the Kapp-Lüttwitz putsch of 1920, and Hitler's unsuccessful political revolt of 1923.

The court cases which these events engendered put the judiciary straight into the firing line. First of all, the penal code held no solutions to the question of how to deal with political crime. Was a bomb-thrower a revolutionary or a common criminal? Should he be tried and sentenced according to the standards laid down by the criminal law, or were these standards inadequate to the task? How should treason be treated, especially if the alleged traitor had sought to enforce Germany's adherence to the terms of the Versailles treaty and armistice? By using the criminal law, judges hoped to find their way through the jungle of the times; instead they lost themselves more and more.

A second factor was the almost complete lack of self-protective action on the part of the country's elected representatives. One of the great deficiencies of the Weimar Constitution was that it contained no provision which directed itself against those forces whose explicit aim was to do away with the Republic. Civil servants, for example, were constitutionally guaranteed the right to political freedom, which meant that they could join the Communist Party or any other revolutionary party with impunity. (Significantly, the NSDAP, despite its frequent violence, did not question the existence of the German state *per se*. Hitler's expressed intention of obtaining power by constitutional means, of which more will be said later, put around the NSDAP a cloak, albeit a tattered one, of respectability.) In plain terms, it was not unconstitutional to overthrow the Republic, providing it was done with the assent of the necessary two-thirds majority of the Reichstag as stipulated in Article 76 of the Constitution. This constitutional omission transferred the problem of a conflict between would-be revolutionaries, left or right, to the judicial system. If the government would not take preventive action, the judiciary would deal with the consequences in the courts.

The result was a barrage of criticism from all sides. With left-wing insurgencies pre-dating and outnumbering by six to two those of the right, the left inevitably suffered more victims than its right-wing opponents. From the left came easily levelled charges of militarism, class justice and political bias. When it came time for the right to stand trial, however, the judiciary was just as harsh as it had been with Communists. It was thus placed in the impossible position of pleasing neither left nor right – and certainly not the general public.

In 1928 there appeared before the Berlin Landgericht I (the county court) one of a series of the judiciary's most highly politically charged cases. These were the trials of the members of the armed forces responsible for the Feme murders. The term itself, meaning 'condemnation' and referring to lawless individuals against whom any kind of punishment can be meted out, is derived from ancient practice among Germanic tribes. In Weimar Germany it applied to right-wing political murders committed in secret, without recourse to trial, for allegedly treasonable activities.

After 1921 the army had encouraged the formation of various quasi-official military and intelligence units.[7] Under the direction of the counter-intelligence Abwehr, these units sprang up around the country to defend the nation. The Organisation Consul operated in Upper Silesia and those parts of Germany occupied by the Allies; the Selbstschutz Oberschlesien protected German citizens from the violence of the irridentist Polish bands led by the former deputy of the Reichstag, the Pole Korfanty; in the Ruhr, the Truppenamt fought against the separatist governments established after the French and Belgian invasions of 1923; and the Black Reichswehr, also under the direction of the Abwehr, among other activities, defended parts of central and eastern Germany.[8]

In terms of the Versailles peace treaty, however, these military and intelligence units were illegal: any German military build-up was strictly forbidden. The government, therefore, had to pretend to know nothing about them. But the clandestine units were subject to frequent infiltration by members of the left, seeking to expose their operations and to publicize the creation of the illegal military reserves in the press. Because the units themselves operated outside the legal system, any infiltrator who was caught could not be turned over to the courts, but was summarily executed.[9] When the murders came to light in the late 1920s, the perpetrators were arraigned before the courts, although the Reichswehr held its protecting hand over those who were convicted, and often made arrangements for others to escape prior to their arrest and trial.

First Lieutenant Reim was one of those unfortunates who was not so well protected.[10] A member of the Black Reichswehr, he had assisted in the execution of a suspected infiltrator, a Sergeant Legner, in 1923. Legner's crime had been to inform on the illegal Black Reichswehr at a time when to many Germans it appeared a national duty to evade the provisions of the Versailles treaty. When Reim came to trial in late 1928 he was sentenced by the jury to three years' hard labour. Until then, as we have seen, most political trials had been of left-wing activists. Now the right exploded in anger of what it saw as the judiciary's persecution of patriots defending the fatherland against traitors and foreign occupation.

The verdict illustrated that the urgency of the emergency situation had not yet overrun either the judiciary's or the ordinary jurist's sense of the proper application of the law. Legally speaking, the provisions of the Versailles treaty had become part of German law. But how many honestly motivated German patriots were prepared to accept this? This strongly felt sentiment was a sign of things to come – presaged, not least, by the sophisticated analysis of the trial offered by Dr Luetgebrune, one of the NSDAP's leading legal lights, and a famous defence lawyer during the Empire. His view was undoubtedly coloured by his role as defence counsel for a number of Feme murderers, but that it gained currency was a significant straw in the wind.

Luetgebrune noted that several factors could have excused Reim's action. First, although the Black Reichswehr was not formally within the army structure (and could not be because of the restrictions of the Versailles treaty), previous judicial decisions had considered such 'saviours of the state from revolutionary activities' as part of the armed forces. Therefore Reim could have legitimately argued that he was acting under orders, and was not responsible. Secondly, the claim that the murdered man could, as an infiltrator, have been brought to trial was only applicable under 'normal circumstances' – a description hardly appropriate to Germany in 1923. Finally, and most importantly, there was the issue of treason. Were individuals such as Legner, the murdered man, 'informers pointing to transgressions of the Versailles treaty, and disclosing information about German illegal troop formation' committing treason? Or were they the true patriots, adhering to international law? The question of treason, Luetgebrune continued, related to

> the most significant justification of the Feme actions insofar as the Black Reichswehr can claim to have acted in an emergency against infiltrated informers. When the jury court in Berlin holds that the concept of emergency would not apply, that self-defence can be committed only on behalf of individuals but not of such valuable goods as the system of defence of the country, then this is rather peculiar. When the Black Reichswehr – a secretly built defence system ... built up secretly by the state – was threatened by treason, then this attack on the state is an attack on the state as a person in law.[11]

In other words, where treason was involved, the application of the law was of dubious value. Luetgebrune's criticism signalled a growing ambivalence among some legal circles about the strict adherence to the law in the face of a national security crisis. For the judiciary, his criticism was one more blow to an already fragile institution. The result of the Feme murder trials was that the smallest Reich Ministry, that of Justice, was subjected to the heaviest public attack. The urge to escape this situation – in which the judiciary was in the position of the permanently accused – profoundly influenced the judiciary towards the end of the Republic.

One key event allowed the judiciary to break for the first time with the formality of the law. The issue was the devaluation of the Mark. According to the letter of the law, judges were tied to the principle that one Mark equalled one Mark, irrespective of whether it was tendered in gold or paper currency. Because of ethical considerations – by 1923 paper currency had become worthless, and anyone receiving paper rather than gold Marks was instantly the poorer for it – the judiciary overturned the law. Debts of any kind, including longstanding ones, could no longer be paid in paper currency.

This was essentially a judicial encroachment on the legislature's terrain. Never before had the judiciary sought to do anything more than interpret the law; now it had actually abolished one. The judges began to interpret the law in this light, a development which led to a general discussion about the function of the judiciary and the scope of its powers. The government heavily criticized the assumption of such far-reaching powers, but it refrained from intervention.[12]

After that, the extension of the judiciary's power into the legislative sphere was no longer questioned, and in practice judges now began to treat the law with greater regard for expediency than had ever before been the case. They were no longer servants of the law, but formulated it themselves. This dangerous tendency continued to accelerate the more the national and regional parliaments failed in their functions as legislators. Other governmental bodies moved in – the country had to be run somehow – and the vacuum was occupied by the civil service and judiciary. Their consciences somewhat released by an end to the severe constraints of the law, and no doubt relieved to have the go-ahead for greater freedom in handling difficult and political cases, the judiciary found its legal scruples reduced to an extent impossible to foresee in the days of the Empire. The change in the apparently trivial technicality of the treatment of the Mark set the judiciary, like so much else in Weimar Germany, on a slippery downward slope, the full results of which were only seen in the Third Reich.[13]

The Reichstag, meanwhile, set a similar precedent in legislative terms by applying Article 48 of the Constitution, which granted the president emergency powers. Carl Schmitt, one of the foremost legal thinkers of the time, argued vigorously against the use of this article on the grounds that through it the Weimar Republic would deprive itself of its liberty and open the back door to tyranny.[14] After Hitler came to power, Schmitt drew the logical conclusion. Once dictatorship had been admitted and permitted in a parliamentary and democratic manner, in Schmitt's view, there was no longer any need for a strictly National Socialist civil law. The general clauses established by the judiciary over the 1920s and early 1930s required only their infusion with the new ideology in order for the existing law to be applied in accordance with National Socialist principles.[15] The legal code, developed with such care during the Second Empire, was becoming increasingly obsolete, particularly in political cases. The application of nationalist and National Socialist principles met little opposition.

The National Socialists might not have had such an easy task if the judiciary had not been allowed to arrogate such extensive powers to itself. The question of conscience raised over the monetary revaluation could equally have provided food for thought about the role of the judiciary in a parliamentary democracy. But this never happened. The new legislation devaluing the Mark brought about the crucial opening break between the judiciary and the written law, and a blurring of the division between the judiciary and the legislature. It was a development which was welcomed by most judges, but it did not help them to create a new self-image, nor did they ever debate the question of their new-found freedom. The authority under which the judiciary acted remained vague and ill-defined. But if the judges themselves had become amenable to wielding political power, the other side of the coin – a politicized penal system in which they could operate – also had to be put in place.

The People's Court was not Hitler's invention. It was, in fact, the inspiration of Kurt Eisner, the first Prime Minister of the 'Free State of Bavaria,' who introduced his People's Court on 16 November 1918.[16] Such courts were to try cases that had arisen in the confusion of the revolution: murder, manslaughter, arson, plunder and theft. On 21 February 1919, after Eisner's assassination, their jurisdiction was extended to try cases of resistance to the forces of the state, breaches of peace, and the forming of gangs.[17] And on 12 July 1919, more than two months after the Soviet Republic in Munich and Bavaria had been quashed, the Bavarian government, in order to do away with drum-head courts martial, passed a law extending the scope of the People's Courts still further to cases of attempted revolution, including the trial of treasonable activities.[18]

When the Weimar Constitution came into force on 14 August 1919, the People's Courts became illegal under Article 105. Nevertheless they remained active in Bavaria. These courts were widely renowned for the scanty protection they offered to the accused, and for their vast powers of arrest, search and confiscation. A written indictment was considered unnecessary; nor did the accused, once sentenced, have the right of appeal.[19]

The NSDAP was hardly a collection of innovators; it was simply adept at putting the Republic's legal tools to good use. After all, Hitler himself had been sentenced by a People's Court in 1924. That the sentence was in the event rather light had less to do with Hitler's guilt or innocence than with the fact that important members of the Bavarian government had been implicated in the preparation of the November 1923 putsch, and that the Bavarian People's Court was therefore more concerned to sweep the unsavoury evidence under the carpet than to pronounce a stiff sentence against Hitler.[20]

The courts of the 'Free State of Bavaria' set the example; the Reichstag made it possible for this example to be extended under the tutelage of the Third Reich to the whole of Germany. In 1922 the Reichstag passed the Law for the Protection of the Republic with a two-thirds majority. Its justification was the wave of terrorism sweeping the country, specifically the murders of Mathias Erzberger in 1921 and Walter Rathenau in 1922. Gustav Radbruch, then Minister of Justice, explicitly stated during the debate in the Reichstag that the law was to be used against the right, not the left.[21] No one, apparently, foresaw the purposes to which it would be put.

The law politicized penal laws to an unprecedented degree. It abrogated a whole range of the basic rights of the individual as set out in the Constitution.[22] For the first time in German legal history, the judiciary was authorized to depart from the principle of *nulla poena sine lege* ('no punishment without law'). Thus the accused in the Rathenau trial (the actual assassins were dead) had no right of appeal. Later, of course, the NSDAP would be quick to capitalize on this precedent in passing its emergency legislation of 1933 (the Lex van der Lubbe, named after the man who set fire to the Reichstag), and in offering it as a perfectly constitutional rationale for its Special Courts and the National Socialist People's Court. In the meantime, however, the law heightened the judiciary's political role, and gave those who wished to use it greater autonomy in pursuing political cases.

The politicization of the penal laws was viewed with considerable disgust by many judges, especially as it was the work of centre to left parties in the Reichstag, and it helped fan the flames of controversy. Whatever verdict the highest court of the country, the Reichsgericht, reached, for instance, whatever sentence it imposed, it was subject to criticism – from Communists, Social Democrats and National Socialists alike. Once again the government's elected representatives had passed to the judiciary the burden of handling the political crisis. It is arguable that the judiciary under the Republic was overloaded with political trials, that it had dealt with them too tamely, and that in this sense it therefore failed.

In its personnel policy the judiciary remained as demanding as before. Even Martin Hirsch, now a retired constitutional judge of the Federal German Constitutional Supreme Court, a man inclined towards the left rather than the right, attested that the judges who trained him during the Weimar Republic did so with great competence and integrity.[23] The Ministry of Justice was an expressly elitist body, from which first-rate administrators for other ministries were detached and first-rate judges trained. Its ministerial continuity was preserved through the Permanent Secretary of State of the Ministry of Justice, Curl Joël, a former Minister of Justice in Brüning's second cabinet, who, unlike the heads of ministries, did not step down at each new government. Of Jewish descent, Joël retired in 1933, probably assuming that the anti-Semitic aspects of National Socialism would disappear once the party took the responsibilities of government. (In his own case he was correct: Joël was one of a handful of Jewish individuals to be protected by Hitler.)[24] The judiciary's relationship to the NSDAP was remote; until 30 January 1933, the party claimed almost no judicial members.[25]

For this reason it is all the more surprising that the transition from Republic to dictatorship was carried out so smoothly and without great changes in the personnel of the judiciary. One reason, perhaps, is that the end of the Weimar Republic came about by perfectly legal means. Weimar became the victim of its own constitutional law, while Carl Schmitt's warning that constitutional change should never be confused with the destruction of the Constitution was ignored. This may well have been the reason why Hitler at no time during his rule ever considered the formal abolition of the Weimar Constitution; those who advocated a specifically National Socialist Constitution met with his scant support.

At the top of the judicial pyramid, continuity was preserved. Franz

Gürtner, the Reich Minister of Justice and Bavaria's Minister of Justice at the time of Hitler's trial in 1924, retained his ministerial post until his death in 1941. Erwin Bumke, the president of the Reichsgericht, did the same. Max Schlegelberger, a jurist in the true Wilhelmine tradition, served as Curt Joël's successor and after Gürtner's death took on the additional responsibility of administering the Ministry of Justice that same year. Freisler, of course, served as a second Secretary of State from 1934 to 1942, although his political inclinations seem to have been somewhat curbed by Schlegelberger.

A picture of how the judiciary felt on the eve of the Third Reich is best gained by looking at the judges' official journal, the *Deutsche Richterzeitung*.[26] In its first issue of 1932, it raised a whole list of complaints. First was the terrible economic plight of the members of the judiciary, who had been, it complained, the first to be affected by the government's economic measures. Second came the problem for would-be judges, the Assessors, and their families. Last was the continuous public and party criticism, and on this topic the paper was particularly bitter.

At a time, the paper argued, when famous criminals received obituaries several columns long in the daily press, the ordinary judge who simply did his duty was exposed to the full blast of public criticism. Whoever lost in a trial or a civil suit could always expect to find a newspaper which, in order to boost its own circulation but motivated only by a 'burning concern for justice,' would indict the unpardonable sins of the judiciary. In contrast, one would be hard put to find a newspaper which would be prepared to print articles amicably disposed towards the judiciary.

> But he who walks upright through life, continuously fulfilling his duty, without deviating from the straight and narrow path, despite pressures from the world, can today no longer expect due recognition. He will rub everyone the wrong way and acquire a reputation for unpleasantness because the times have dimmed the light for conditions that were once considered normal and instead the product is spiritual confusion.

Thus the judiciary, criticized from all sides, largely politically apathetic, economically underprivileged, was bound to put its hopes, however cautiously, in a new party and a new regime. Things could hardly get worse.

# 3

# The NSDAP and the Law

No other event in German history was as destructive as the conclusion of the First World War. Forced to relinquish land, bound by the vindictive terms of the armistice, Germany felt itself betrayed by its former enemies and by the enemies within – but most of all by those within. The 'trauma of Versailles' was a genuine one for most Germans, cutting across party lines and, along with other factors, playing a crucial role in Hitler's rise to power. Nor did it end in 1933. Just as the judiciary had come to accept the need for a new way of conducting the courtroom, so the German population came to accept that traitors, however they were defined, should be forever removed from the Reich.

It was a sentiment which corresponded neatly with Hitler's own messianic conception of the law: purify the nation, eliminate enemies, and ensure the ever-growing glory of National Socialism. For a person who despised the legal profession, with its squalid concern for the rights of the individual, Hitler's use of the law was remarkably thorough and astute. However much Hitler proclaimed his intention to abolish parliamentary democracy, he recognized the important protection it offered him and his party. With the emotional underpinning of the 'stab in the back' legend, he was able by 1933 to turn the Constitution and Germany's parliamentary democracy into the means of his consolidation of power.

The 'stab in the back' legend had two versions.[1] The first was a question of fact: because of the revolution at home, the German army was compelled to relinquish territory while it still occupied the lands of its opponents. The upheaval at home, moreover, meant that it was unable to build up a firm defensive line on the frontiers of the Reich, a development which, at least in Winston Churchill's opinion, would have resulted in a negotiated peace.[2] The German government was so concerned with internal strife that it could not tend properly to the peace settlement. Thus its former enemies were free to impose whatever conditions suited them and to ignore as far as Germany and Austria were concerned all the promises made in Wilson's Fourteen Points.[3]

The second version begins where the argument leaves off: but for the 'stab in the back', it asserts, Germany could have won the war. By September 1918 neither Hindenburg nor Ludendorff believed that Germany could actually win the war.[4] The German offensives from March to June 1918 in the west had clearly demonstrated that the German army was at the point of exhaustion, that at best a temporary defence could be held, and that even this could not be done indefinitely.

In contrast to German press policy of the Second World War, that of the First World War had provided rosy pictures of victory being just around the corner.[5] Censorship became extremely stringent after the military reverses in the west from July 1918 onwards.[6] The German people, and for that matter German soldiers, could not explain to themselves how from one day to another they had been vanquished while still deep in enemy territory. Psychologically unprepared for the defeat, many people, lacking reliable information, took recourse in conspiracy theories.

Germany's attempted revolutions of 1918 and 1919 provided ample raw material for these theories.[7] The war's end, military defeat and revolutionary upheaval at home formed, in the popular mind, a direct causal connection. Into this situation entered new demands for changes in Germany's social and political structure. The whole bundle of reasons and motivations did not concern themselves with a sober stock-taking and analysis of a lost war, but defined the attitude to 'the revolution' and to the social and political legacy of the past. The reasons were morally weighted and emotionally loaded. The search was on for a scapegoat.

In the weeks immediately following the armistice, the prevailing slogan which greeted the returning German army was 'Unconquered in the Field!'. It was a phrase used even by Friedrich Ebert, the Republic's first head of government and president. 'Your sacrifices and your deeds are unexampled,' he told the returned Berlin garrison. 'No enemy has overcome you. Only when the superior power of the enemy in men and material became ever more overpowering did *we* give up the struggle.'[8] Obviously the interpretation hinges on what Ebert meant by *we*. It could all too easily be applied to the home front only, and so it was.

The phrase 'stab in the back' did not originate in Germany, but was coined by the British general Sir Frederic Maurice, who saw in the German army's failure the apathy of the German civilian population and the treason of German revolutionaries.[9] The slogan was further brought home with the publication of the Versailles peace terms in May 1919. The war guilt clause and the blanket condemnation of Germany's history, together with the demand for the extradition of the Kaiser, Hindenburg, Ludendorff and others as war criminals, touched a point of honour among many Germans. The 'imposed lie of Germany's sole guilt' established emotional barriers, making it virtually impossible to analyse the past critically. As Ernst Nolte once put it, Germany's disappointed hopes at Versailles were as much a grave-digger of the young republic as was the 'stab in the back' legend.[10]

The Reichstag established a parliamentary committee to investigate the question of responsibility for the defeat. On 18 November 1919 Hindenburg and Ludendorff appeared before the committee. Hindenburg, refusing to be questioned, simply read out a statement:

In spite of the immense demands on troops and leadership, in spite of the numerical superiority of the enemy we could have ended the unequal struggle in our favour, if a close and unified cooperation between army and home front had existed. In that we had seen the means for the German cause. But what happened? While among the enemy in spite of the superiority of manpower and material all layers of society consolidated themselves in their will to victory . . . among us where such consolidation in view of our inferiority would have been all the more necessary, party interests spread far and wide and these circumstances led very soon to the loosening and splitting of our will to victory. . . . At that time began the systematic and secret dissolution of our navy and army as continuation of similar appearances in peacetime. . . . Thus our operations were bound to fail, the collapse had to come, and the revolution represents only the final milestone. An English general stated with justification: 'The German army has been stabbed in the back.' The good core of our army is not to blame. Its achievements and those of the officer corps are equally as admirable. Where the guilt lies has been clearly established. If further proof is needed then it can be found in the statement of the English general cited and in the astonishment of our opponents about their victory.[11]

This statement ensured the enormously wide popularity of the stab in the back legend throughout the coming decades until the end of the Second World War.

There cannot be the slightest doubt that the German nation had been psychically and physically deformed by the experience of the Great War. It was, in the most literal and medical meaning of the term, a traumatic experience for all the participants in the slaughter. What separates the Germans from their opponents, however, was that they were not seen to have lost. More important was that they had given up in good faith in response to Wilson's Fourteen Points. Versailles then came to the Germans not only as a rude awakening, but as a great betrayal, a betrayal that cut straight across party lines.[12]

American military psychologists have in recent years coined the term: 'post-traumatic stress symptoms', meaning psychological disorders among ex-combatants often manifesting themselves years after the event. This author believes that this term can also be applied to a collective, in this case the German nation, for the issue of Versailles was a wound which never healed; its crust broke open time and again. As any close analysis of party-political agitation, of public speeches, of the politics of the cabinets of the Weimar Republic will show, Versailles always stood in the centre. Even in Hitler's speeches, both before and after he came to power, Versailles occupied a much more prominent place that his virulent anti-Semitism. From 1919 to 1945 the German nation as a whole manifested to a virtually excessive degree 'post-traumatic stress symptoms'.

As far as the NSDAP was concerned, the stab in the back was not a slogan to be manipulated, but an article of faith which determined their action in many fields. The whole concept of the *Volksgemein-schaft*, the racial national community, was permeated by the determination not to return to a situation in which one part of the nation would rise against the other. Social classes were to be 'racially purified' and class conflict was to be eliminated by the racially homogeneous 'national community'.[13] Among many NS leaders, including Hitler himself, the collapse and the revolution of 1918 had been the formative experience, and once in power the question was never far from Hitler's mind as to how to pursue a course of domestic policy that would consolidate his and his party's position within Germany on the basis of the broadest possible consensus. This policy embraced among its practical consequences a disparate collection of actions, including the creation of concentration camps for political dissidents,[14] progressive social welfare measures and the founding of the armed field units of the SS (later the Waffen-SS), which Hitler explicitly viewed over the long term as a highly armed and experienced police force to be used in the case of internal upheavals for which the Wehrmacht could not be deployed.[15]

Hitler's analysis of the German collapse moved along two parallel tracks. On the one hand he viewed it as an inevitable consequence of excessive urbanization, the decay of ethical standards, the growth of materialism, the arrogance of the upper classes, the influence of the Jews, and a weak degenerating political leadership. On the other hand Germany's collapse was due to the cowards in the rear areas of the front and in Germany itself, to corrupt party politicians and Jewish-Marxist behind the scene manipulators. The party functionaries of an essentially corrupt and decadent political system had stabbed Germany and the German army in the back. Once in power Hitler combined strong repressive measures with the perverted ideological idealism of his concept of the 'national community' and thus mobilized within Germany a nationalist idealism of an intensity never before experienced. Even before it came to power the widely proclaimed aim of the NSDAP was to provide a reckoning with the traitors of 1918. After 1933 the Marxist organizations, and for that matter all political organizations other than the NSDAP, were smashed.[16]

Hitler and the NSDAP became the sole representatives of the 'national community'; their legislation, their institutions, like the German Labour Front, were directed towards integrating the German working class into the German nation, a task which the Empire had achieved only in part.[17] Prior to 1933, Hitler and the NSDAP had made few inroads into the voters of SPD and the KPD. Hitler won his battle for the support of the German working class between 1933 and 1939.[18] He could never fully eliminate resistance groups, but up to 1939 resistance to the regime from the left was a problem easily handled by the police. Much more serious as a potential threat was the opposition that emerged from 1937 onwards from among Hitler's erstwhile conservative 'entente' partners.[19] But they in no way managed to erode the degree of national integration which Hitler had achieved.

After 1941 the threat from Russia and the round-the-clock bombardments by the Allied air forces produced among the German population as a whole a kind of fortress or trench mentality, a mentality that endured until every square mile of Germany was occupied by its enemies,[20] a mentality that may in a different form have survived the disaster and defeat of 1945 and lie at the roots of the economic miracle of both German states.

Hence the NS attitude to the law was that, irrespective of whether any changes would have to be made to it, its primary purpose was to serve the NS 'national community'; the individual would come second.

In *Mein Kampf* Hitler had railed against the prosecution of small-time traitors when the real traitors, the republicans and capitalists 'on whose conscience rests the deaths of two million', were left untouched. 'On the whole,' Hitler wrote, 'my attitude is that one should not hang little thieves and let the big ones roam about freely, but that a German National Court will have to deal with several tens of thousands of organized and thus responsible criminals of the November (1918) treason . . . in order to sentence and execute them.'[21] What Hitler meant by a 'German National Court', as we shall see, ultimately emerged in the form of the VGH, but its function had been defined years before.

Similarly, the criteria for those who would run such a court system had long since been decided. The party programme, promulgated in 1920, stipulated that all public office holders (a category which included the judiciary) would be Aryans.[22] Only a *Volksgenosse* (a racial comrade) could be a citizen; and only citizens could hold public office. (Jews, of course, were not *Volksgenossen* by dint of their supposed non-German blood.) Thereafter the judiciary and all other public office bearers would be part of the quest for racial purity.

Within the NSDAP in its pre-1933 days, three legal minds stood out. The first was Dr Otto Luetgebrune, whose analysis of treason we saw in Chapter 1. A well established and highly reputed defence lawyer in the days of the Empire,[23] he became a foremost NSDAP defence counsel. In 1922 he defended the youths accused of involvement in the Rathenau murder; in 1924 he successfully defended Ludendorff who, jointly with Hitler and others, was accused of high treason as a result of the November putsch of 1923.[24] He then acted as defence counsel for a number of Feme murderers, and for the leaders of the *Landvolk* movement in Schleswig-Holstein who rose in protest against excessive taxation.[25] In 1930, after Ernst Röhm had returned from Bolivia and become chief of staff of the SA, Luetgebrune became chief legal advisor of the SA, courtesy of Röhm's appointment, with the rank of an Obergruppenführer, although Luetgebrune had never been a member of the NSDAP.[26]

He escaped death by a hair's breadth during the 'Röhm purge' and received severe ill-treatment at the hands of the SS. Those who met him at the time thought he was a totally broken man; the man who had once vigorously and cleverly defended SA, SS and NSDAP members appeared only a shadow of his former self.[27] Nevertheless he rallied and had disciplinary proceedings initiated against himself by the Court of Honour of the SA. In spite of Göring's explicit demand for a conviction he was fully exonerated.

After this Luetgebrune resumed his interrupted work on a new 'Germanic Law'. In his view, once the revolution had been liquidated, Hitler as the 'Supreme Judge' had to create a new law. But the more Luetgebrune got involved in this task and in analysing Roman law, the more he realized that as far as he was concerned there was nothing better than the Roman law itself. He let his opinion be known and then retired into the background from which, until his death after the Second World War, he was never to emerge.[28]

By far the greatest driving force for the creation of a new 'Germanic Law' was the lawyer Hans Frank.[29] As a student in 1919 Frank had belonged to the Bavarian voluntary army unit, the Freikorps Epp, which participated in liquidating the Soviet Republic in Bavaria. In September 1923, while serving his apprenticeship in the Bavarian judiciary, he joined the NSDAP, and participated in the November putsch. He subsequently became a lawyer and the star defence counsel of the NSDAP; of its over 40,000 cases between 1924 and 1933, he represented over 2,400. He clashed with Hitler in 1926 over the question of the German Southern Tyrol, which Hitler was willing to sacrifice to Mussolini. In 1927 he rejoined the NSDAP, but in 1929 he considered entering a university career which would have meant cutting his ties with the NSDAP once again; Hitler's personal intervention changed his mind.[30]

That same year Frank became head of the Rechtsamt der NSDAP, the legal office of the NS party; in 1933 he was made the first NS Minister of Justice in Bavaria; and shortly thereafter he became Reich Commissioner for the Coordination of the Judiciary in the Lands and for the Renewal of the Legal Order. At a national level he also became Minister without Portfolio, but this was hardly a significant promotion once Hitler ceased to call cabinet meetings.

Of somewhat unstable character, Frank was, nevertheless, less pliable an instrument than Hitler would personally have wished. He protested loudly against the legal aspects of the Röhm purge, and vehemently objected to the campaigns against jurists and the judiciary launched by official NSDAP papers. And although in his 'Guidelines for German Judges' in 1936 he stated that against 'Führer-decisions', in the form of law, decree or verbal order, no German judge could take a stand, he nevertheless added that judges would have to be fully independent in order to fulfill their duty to the 'national community', an assertion which did not make him a favourite with Hitler. Indeed, in spite of being an 'old fighter' and associate of Hitler, he never entered Hitler's inner circle. However, his leadership of the Bund Nationalsozialistischer Juristen (the League of National Socialist Jurists), the membership of which after Hitler's assumption of power climbed quickly to 80,000, gave him, on the surface at least, something of a power base.[31]

Frank did not shun military service. As lieutenant of the reserve after 1933, he served in the Potsdam infantry regiment No. 9, popularly known as '*Graf Neun*', 'Count Nine', because of the predominance of the scions of the old Prussian aristocracy within it. From that regiment were to emerge ardent supporters as well as fanatical opponents of Hitler. The discussion in the mess was unrestrained and unfettered by political considerations. According to Frank himself: 'I for my part found these Potsdam men absolutely splendid. Although they had not one good word to say about the Third Reich, they fulfilled their duty towards the state and also to Hitler just as painstakingly as they had over the centuries gone by.'[32]

Despite his tolerance of political differences in the mess, Frank was convinced that the existing law in Germany was fundamentally alien to the German people, that what they required was a return to some form of 'Germanic common law' at the centre of which stood the Volk. Not without some justification, he criticized Germany's excessive legal formalism, the degeneration of the law into legal technical routine.[33] What he failed to see was that Hitler's own attitude was hostile to any law, and deeply suspicious of any lawyer and jurist. Still, between 1933 and 1939 Frank threw his entire energy behind creating a new law, while Hitler saw in the law nothing but tripwires. But in spite of his low estimate of the legal profession, Hitler never allowed Frank to fall; he always held out a saving hand. This may have had to do with the generally highly developed sense of loyalty which Hitler had had for all his old comrades, even when they had become obvious liabilities like the Jew-baiter Julius Streicher, or for that matter Hermann Göring, who was after 1940 totally incompetent.[34]

Probably Hitler's loyalty had also more to do with the unique opportunity with which Frank provided him in 1930.[35] Two Reichswehr lieutenants on active service in Ulm and one who had left the Reichswehr were accused of high treason for spreading NS propaganda among their comrades. The NSDAP and SA declined to support them.[36] When the affair became public knowledge the officers concerned were dismissed from the army and arraigned before the Reichsgericht in Leipzig. Among the defence counsels was Hans Frank and he had the brilliant idea of calling Hitler as a witness. Hitler was called to testify 25 September 1930, only a few days after the NSDAP had achieved its national breakthrough at the Reichstag elections, increasing its number of seats from 12 to 107.[37] In his evidence, Hitler rejected any notion of a conspiracy between the NSDAP and the SA on one side and members of the Reichswehr on the other, adding, however, that once he came to power he would try to infuse the National Socialist spirit into the army.[38]

The presiding judge asked a number of further questions, for instance concerning a remark attributed to Hitler that if the NSDAP should come to power, 'heads will roll in the sand.' Hitler replied: 'May I assure you that when our movement in the course of a legal struggle comes to power then a German State Court will come, November 1918 will find its revenge and then heads will roll.' A little later the presiding judge asked him: 'How do you imagine the establishment of the Third Reich?' to which Hitler replied: 'The National Socialist movement will endeavour to attain its aims by constitutional means. The Constitution prescribes for us the methods, but not the aims. In a constitutional manner we shall obtain decisive majorities in the legislative bodies in order that from the very moment of our success we may cast the state in the form which corresponds with our ideas.' The judge once again asked Hitler, 'You mean by constitutional means?', to which Hitler simply replied 'Jawohl!'[39]

Thus Hitler had been provided with the unique opportunity to state before the highest court of the country and to the German nation at large his two aims: first, to achieve office by constitutional and not revolutionary means; secondly, to change the entire state according to his ideas once he had gained power. No one can say that, as far as Germany's political institutions were concerned, Hitler had tricked anybody or had maintained an ambivalent attitude. As far as his domestic policy was concerned he had stated his aims quite clearly, not only in 1930 but from that point until his Reichstag speech of 23 March 1933, when he left the deputies of the various parties in no doubt that by voting for the Enabling Bill they would, for the most part, also vote themselves out of political existence.[40] Still Hitler received more than the necessary two-thirds majority, which he would have had even if the Communist deputies had been present as well and voted with the SPD against the Bill.

If Luetgebrune and Frank were for a time the legal luminaries on the NS horizon, there was also one man of whom, except in the inner circles of the party, the general public had heard very little, but who was well on the way to making his name and whose personality and actions are at the centre of this study, Dr Roland Freisler.

Freisler was born on 30 October 1893 and baptized in the reformed Protestant faith on 13 December of the same year in the city of his birth, Celle.[41] Two years later his brother Oswald followed. Their father was Julius Freisler, who had originated from Klantendorf in Moravia and then moved into the Reich, where he married Charlotte Auguste Florentine Schwerdtfeger in Celle.[42] The fact that Freisler's father came from Moravia has given rise to idle speculation that Freisler was of Jewish extraction, because Klantendorf is alleged to have been a centre of Jewish settlement.[43] The evidence points entirely in the opposite direction, Klantendorf until 1945 being an almost exclusively Protestant domain.[44] Freisler's Jewish extraction is also alleged to be 'evidently' supported by his 'typically Jewish' appearance, although what is meant by this term is obscure. Freisler was well above medium height, slim, with a sharply chiselled face dominated by eyes that could charm as much as they could look ice-cold in the course of uttering a sardonic remark or reprimand during a trial. Some even called him handsome.[45]

In December 1893 the Freisler family moved to Hanover and then Hamelin, where Freisler's brother Oswald was born. Julius Freisler, père, a qualified engineer, moved to Duisburg in January 1896 where he found employment in the harbour offices. In 1901 he was appointed professor at the Royal Mining School. In 1903, at the age of ten, Roland Freisler entered Kaiser Wilhelm grammar school (today called the Einhard grammar school). Freisler quickly established a reputation for academic thoroughness and a readiness to engage in debate.[46] In the autumn of 1908 the family settled in Kassel in Hesse where in 1912 he took his *Abitur*, finishing first in his class.[47] He then matriculated at the University of Kiel to read law, but interrupted his studies at the outbreak of war to enter 167th Infantry Regiment in Kassel as an ensign.[48]

After a relatively short period of training, his regiment, attached to 26th Reserve Corps on 10 November 1914, attacked Langemarck in Flanders, the great graveyard of Germany's youth. Freisler was wounded, returned home for convalescence and in the spring of 1915 rejoined his regiment which was then transferred to the northern sector of the Russian front. Shortly after being promoted lieutenant and awarded the Iron Cross of both classes, he led a reconnaisance patrol which fell into a Russian ambush and was captured.[49] Freisler spent the rest of the war as prisoner in an officers' camp north of Moscow. After the Bolshevik Revolution and the Treaty of Brest-Litovsk, this camp, like many others in Russia, was handed over to German administration; Freisler was appointed its commissar in charge of food supplies. Contrary to many post-war assertions, the title was purely functional and not political.[50] Freisler was never a Communist, though in the early days of his NS career, like most NSDAP members north of the river Main, he belonged to its left wing.[51]

Freisler finally returned from Russia on 17 July 1920 and was given the option of remaining in the Reichswehr – an offer unlikely to be made to one who was or had been a Communist.[52] But he had decided on a law career and immediately matriculated in the Law Faculty of the University of Jena where within the remarkably short period of one year he took his doctorate, the subject of his thesis being 'Fundamental Factors in Industrial Organization',[53] published by the University of Jena in 1922. He then moved to Berlin where in 1923 he successfully took the final bar examination which allowed him to practise as lawyer.[54] The period between completing his doctorate and the bar exam he occupied by serving first as a *Referendar* and then as *Assessor* at the Celle local court.[55]

From the moment he had returned from Russia Freisler had joined the temporary volunteers of the University of Jena and became a member of the extreme right-wing Völkisch-Sozialer Bund.[56] A few months after Hitler refounded the NSDAP in Munich, Freisler became an NSDAP member, membership No. 9,679.[57] From 1924 on he was a member of the Kassel Assembly of Citizens Deputies, and in that capacity was elected into the Prussian Diet; after 1932 he was a member of the Reichstag.[58] On 24 March 1928 he had married Marion Russegger, the daughter of a fairly wealthy merchant.[59] This marriage produced two sons, Harald, born on 1 November 1937, and Roland, born on 12 October 1939; both were baptized as reformed Protestants in Berlin.[60] Neither Freisler nor his wife ever abandoned their religious affiliation at a time when many considered it more opportune to leave the Church to become 'German Christians' or to become simply *gottgläubig*, a nonde-nominational 'believer in God', as the NS phrase went.[61]

Besides pursuing his lawyer's practice, in which he was soon joined by his brother, Freisler as Deputy Gauleiter (district leader) of the NSDAP was fully occupied by party business, in many cases standing in as defence counsel on behalf of Dr Luetgebrune.[62] His aspiration was to become Gauleiter of Hesse-Nassau-North. But this could only be achieved if the present incumbent, Dr Schultz, could be replaced.[63] All this resulted in an internal intrigue in which Freisler was accused as administratively incompetent. But his later career shows that whatever else may be said about Freisler, it cannot be said that he was anything other than an extremely competent and conscientious administrator.

This period of Freisler's career was marked by frequent clashes with his political opponents, whether in Kassel or Berlin, the Prussian Diet and the Reichstag, or on the streets. The general atmosphere was no longer that of latent unrest but had approached civil war.[64] One such incident in Freisler's political history illustrates the extreme climate of the times, and his own staunch commitment to the NSDAP.

In his capacity as party activist, Freisler had organized four NSDAP speeches, to be given at different restaurants in the city of Kassel on 18 June 1930.[65] Tensions were high: the KPD planned to give a public rally on the same day, at which the Social Democrats' paramilitary force, the Reichsbanner, was to be present, and the city government had banned the wearing of uniforms. With NSDAP publicity posters being torn down by its left-wing opponents, the police first defended the party's property and then, under orders from the police president to direct actions only against the National Socialists, abandoned all effort to protect the NSDAP. In the mêlée that followed, sixteen National Socialists were injured and one was knifed to death by angry left-wing crowds.

At the City Deputies' assembly on 23 June 1930, Freisler attacked the police as well as the chief of the police. He said: 'the witnesses had formed the firm conviction that blood would flow; the present police president, the Jewish former lawyer Dr Hohenstein, is not in a position to be above party when National Socialists are involved. It is not the misguided *Volksgenossen* who carry the main burden of guilt, but the Jewish police president and the Social Democratic Lt-

Colonel Schulz [the police commander].' Freisler's interpolation led
to a trial at which he was acquitted on the charges concerning Schulz
but fined 300 Marks for defaming Dr Hohenstein and another 100
Marks for the breach of the peace.

In his law practice Freisler concentrated on criminal and political
cases.[66] In political trials, as was to be expected, he fought for his
political ideas and the interests of his party without pulling any
punches, while in non-political cases he proved considerate and a
pleasant defence counsel.[67] His working capacity was immense;
while working for the NSDAP he never missed a court session. Next
to Luetgebrune and Frank, Freisler now emerged as one of the star
counsels of the NSDAP; with Hesse being one of the main centres of
Germany's Social Democracy, Freisler's own stand must have been
anything but easy. The city's police, administration and judiciary
were loaded against the NSDAP in general and Freisler in particular,
one more reason to transform him into an uncompromising fanatic.
He was the subject of a number of press feuds in which the charges
ranged from embezzlement to personal enrichment, but in each case
when Freisler sued he won hands down.[68]

What is surprising in retrospect was that within the NSDAP he did
not have a more meteoric and greater career. In spite of Frank's legal
brilliance, Freisler certainly was more than a match for him;
moreover, once engaged in a course of action he saw it through
systematically and, if necessary, ruthlessly. He made up his mind
quickly and acted accordingly. He had a good brain for abstract
thought, but at the same time was able to revert quickly to political
and legal practice. Yet he too never managed to enter into the inner
circle of the NSDAP leadership. Perhaps Kassel was too far removed
from the centre of power; perhaps his friendship with Gregor
Strasser, the man regarded as representing the socialist wing of the
NSDAP, damaged his reputation.[69] But Freisler forever remained on
the fringe of the NSDAP leadership. It could be that in his early years
in the NSDAP he was not radical enough in one important aspect,
anti-Semitism. Of course he paid lip-service to it, but in his speeches
his references to the Jews are few and marginal,[70] and on the
evidence in print he appears not to have been as radical as Hitler,
Streicher, Goebbels or Himmler. Or perhaps the reason why Freisler
stayed on the edges was that, as far as Hitler was concerned, Freisler
was just one lawyer too many.

Hitler detested the legal profession.[71] Lawyers, legal experts and ministerial bureaucrats – and more often than not they were identical – were a nightmare for Hitler; he intuitively felt that they acted as a brake on his more fantastic plans. On the other hand, he was a great admirer of Frederick the Great's *Landrat* administration, all of whom were fully trained in the law.[72] No doubt part of Hitler's dislike of the legal profession originated during the Weimar Republic when, for instance, it was possible in Berlin for criminal gangs to establish their headquarters in restaurants between the Alexanderplatz and Friedrichshain, where they held their annual balls, undisturbed by the police and the judiciary, the executive condemned to inaction because of legal technicalities.[73]

Hitler could explode into paroxysms of hate against the judiciary when he came across light sentences against traitors and the murderers of women and children and this was one reason why, for instance, Fritz Lang's film 'M', in which Peter Lorre played a demented child murderer, was immediately withdrawn from circulation in 1933.[74] Sometimes he accused the judiciary of pettiness, for example when a case came to his ears in which the will of an elderly woman was declared invalid who, because of her infirmity, could no longer sign the will and instead had her name typed in.[75] The only jurist he really respected was Dr Heinrich Lammers, since 1922 Ministerial Counsellor in the Ministry of the Interior and from 1933 to 1945 Chief of the Reich Chancellery, first as Secretary of State and then as Reich Minister. In Hitler's view, Lammers knew that his task was to produce legal foundations for measures he judged necessary in the interest of state; he did not confuse legal abstractions with practical life.[76] In Hitler's eyes, Lammers had not lost his sound common sense in spite of his doctorate in law, which of course in practice meant that Lammers was not troubled by any scruples when weaving veils of legality over manifestly illegal acts.

On one occasion Hitler stated that Ribbentrop was quite right in urging the reorganization of the German Foreign Service, because every German Foreign Office member active abroad represented the Reich. If he made an error or simply a bad impression, then this would damage the whole of the Reich. A civil servant of the judiciary, however, could be completely mad and cause heaven knows what nonsense, and no cock would crow after him, except when the Reich suffered an obvious irreparable damage. Hitler summed up his general opinion on the legal profession: they were as international as criminals, but not half as clever.[77]

Nevertheless, Hitler was always anxious to have his actions legally secured. As already stated, the Weimar Constitution contained nothing which made it illegal to change the Constitution or even abolish it, provided there was the necessary two-thirds majority in the Reichstag. The Weimar Constitution also contained elements of direct democracy such as the referendum and the plebiscite, and the possibility of unlimited constitutional change by way of legislation according to Article 76.[78] Hence Hitler's appointment as Chancellor was well within the framework of the Constitution and in fact was rather more constitutional than any of the governments that had come and gone since the break-up of the Great Coalition of 1930. According to the letter of the Constitution, Hitler's appointment meant a return of government into normal parliamentary channels, i.e. as outlined in Articles 54 and 32 of the Constitution, which stated that the Chancellor and his ministers required the confidence of the Reichstag to conduct their office. That confidence was expressed by the majority vote of the Reichstag. Up to that point everything was normal; the abnormal situation arose only after 23 March 1933 when Hitler succeeded in having his Enabling Bill enacted as law.[79]

In the meantime, however, there were to be new elections: the Reichstag was dissolved on 1 February 1933. Given the civil war climate in which the two presidential and two Reichstag elections of 1932 were carried out, it was not unnatural that emergency decrees were introduced in order to curb and to contain excesses, a precedent being Groener's legislation of 1932 – revoked by Papen later in the year – prohibiting the NSDAP's paramilitary formations. In his role as Deputy Commissar for Prussia, Göring had already on 30 January and again on 2 February introduced a decree prohibiting Communist public demonstrations.[80] On 4 February followed national emergency legislation based on Article 48 of the Constitution which subjected all public assemblies to prior police approval and prohibited all assemblies in the open air which could pose a potential threat to public order and security. The freedom of the press was constrained and a ban was placed on publications 'whose content is likely to endanger public security and order.'[81]

As will be shown in the next chapter, the National Socialists did not expect to hold to power uncontested and anticipated some sort of left-wing uprising. They expected that they would be called upon to fight it out in the streets. Because in Prussia the police force had over the past thirteen years been heavily infiltrated by Social Democrats, Göring took the SA and SS as an 'auxiliary force' into the Prussian police;[82] it was inevitable that in the process of their 'executive duties' some old scores were settled. However, the point of culmination was reached when the Dutchman Marinus van der Lubbe set fire to the Reichstag, destroying its entire interior.[83] The subsequent emergency legislation enacted on 28 February 1933, also based on Article 48 of the Constitution, was the product of *ad hoc* improvisation, and not the result of long-term planning.[84]

Among Hitler and his entourage the conviction was firm that the Reichstag fire was the signal for a Communist uprising or at least a general strike.[85] The emergency legislation suspended all the basic rights of the Constitution[86] and was supplemented on 21 March 1933 by a law directed against 'treacherous attacks against the Government of the National Revolution'[87] (supplemented a year later by a law against treacherous attacks upon party and state and for the protection of party uniforms, the so-called *Heimtücke Gesetz*, the Law against Deliberate Malice).[88] Although the Communist uprising never materialized, this legislation remained in force until the end of the Third Reich.

In spite of this, the KPD was not officially prohibited until June 1933,[89] although such a course was advocated by Hugenberg in cabinet prior to the Reichstag fire but opposed by Hitler. Though numerous Communists were arrested, many of them put in improvised SA concentration camps, they were still allowed to participate in the election held on 5 March 1933. For the NSDAP the election proved a disappointment. It did not gain its hoped-for absolute majority but received 43.9 per cent of all the votes. Thanks only to its allies in the German National People's Party (DNVP) could the NSDAP state that 56 per cent of the German population supported the 'Government of the National Revolution'.[90]

The election results nonetheless offered the party a position of strength. At the first meeting of the Reichstag, Hitler introduced his Enabling Bill, which was to give him unlimited powers for the 'Recovery of Germany' for a period of four years. Hitler's aim was to gain unlimited power in Germany. He had said so often enough. 'We National Socialists,' he proclaimed, 'have never asserted ourselves representatives of the democratic point of view, but have openly declared that we take recourse to democratic means only to win power and that after our seizure of power we shall decline without any hesitation to afford to our opponents all those means which were put at our disposal in times of opposition.'[91] And in the same year he declared: '. . . for us parliament is not an end in itself, but a means to an end. In principle we are not a parliamentary party, that would contradict our entire concept. Under duress we are a parliamentary party and what forces us to use such means is the Constitution.'[92]

Hitler was quite aware that over the long term Article 48 of the Constitution would be entirely inadequate. What Hitler needed was a blank cheque. Only Article 76 of the Weimar Constitution could provide him with that. Article 76 stipulated that the Constitution could only be changed by way of legislation, and any such change required the assent of two-thirds of the quorum of Reichstag deputies, the quorum itself being two-thirds of the total number of Reichstag deputies. In the event, the Social Democrats alone voted against it; even the full Communist presence would have made no difference.

All Reichstag members who voted, even those not belonging to the NSDAP, knew that Hitler would break with the parliamentary system. They also knew what the Enabling Bill, called The Law for the Recovery of People and Reich from Suffering, which was released the following day, meant. Article 1 stated bluntly: 'Notwithstanding the procedure laid down in the Reich Constitution laws may be passed by the Reich government.'[93] The principle of the separation of powers was blatantly broken, the opinion of the Reichstag ignored, and those who were to be ignored sanctioned this action. Article 2 stated that laws enacted under Article 1 might also deviate from the Constitution. In this way the Executive gained full powers over the Legislature and all by constitutional means.

Much has been said and written about the intimidation of Reichstag deputies, about the alleged atmosphere of terror.[94] Even if these allegations are true, the question remains as to why the SPD voted *en bloc* against the Enabling Bill while 82 per cent of Germany's full-time parliamentarians endowed Hitler with powers about the purpose and use of which there could be no doubt. Hitler was quite forthright and honest in his speech advocating the acceptance of the law. As regards Germany's legal system he said: 'The security of tenure of the judges on the one side must correspond on the other with an elasticity for the benefit of the community when reaching judgements. The centre of legal concern is not the individual but the Volk.' He continued:

It would contradict the spirit of the National Revolution and not suffice for the intended purpose if to enact its measures the government had for each case to request the agreement of the

Reichstag. The government is not motivated by the intention of abolishing the Reichstag as such. On the contrary it reserves for itself the right to inform the Reichstag from time to time about its measures. . . . Since the government as such has a clear majority, the number of cases in which it has to take recourse to this law is in itself a limited one. All the more, however, the government of the National Revolution insists upon passing this law. In any case it prefers a clear decision. It offers the parties the possibility of peace and quiet and from that a way forward towards understanding in the future, but it is equally as decided and ready to accept the confirmation of rejection and thus the proclamation of resistance. May you now, my honourable deputies (*meine Herren Abgeordneten*), make your own decision – peace or war![95]

This was clear enough; if more clarification was needed, SPD deputy Otto Wels in his speech defending his party's attitude pointed to all the implications of the bill. After that no deputy could maintain that his eyes had not been opened. Wels stated that the government had indeed obtained a clear majority in the elections but with the Enabling Bill the National Socialists intended nothing other than to take the final step in the direction of the dissolution of parliamentary democracy in Germany. For this purpose his party and the parliamentary part of the SPD could not be won over.[96]

In other words, the parties of the Weimar Republic were not deceitfully removed or even smashed; they removed themselves. Hjalmar Schacht, Hitler's economic minister and president of the Reichsbank until 1938, remarked that the democratic parties unnecessarily relinquished their parliamentary influence, 'an act of political self-emasculation unknown in the history of modern democracy.'[97] The parties themselves had put the Constitution out of operation on those issues decisive for a democratic structure. They had thus voluntarily voted for their own dissolution.

Weimar did not die because of its enemies, but because it possessed no genuine friends, not even among the Socialists. It did not have parties that unreservedly supported the state, only pall bearers that carried the coffin. Its trenchant left-wing critics, as the writer Kurt Tucholsky himself admitted shortly thereafter, lacked any sense of the boundaries between change and destruction.[98] The Republic was managed by parties whose democratic loyalty was limited to their own party programme, and on occasion not even that. What the acceptance of the Enabling Bill proves is that the parties of the Weimar Republic were almost at one in their opinion that the liberal system on whose existence their own continuance depended, contained no possibilities for any political life in the future. The last act had ended, the curtains were drawn. Hitler kept his promise in his fashion; he did not abolish the Reichstag as such, but merely changed its composition to form an acclamatory assembly of the NSDAP which from time to time was called together to be informed about 'the measures of the government'. He even had the Enabling Law renewed, twice before the war, and once during it.[99]

But even before the Enabling Bill was passed, the process of 'coordination' (*Gleichschaltung*) – institutional, political and psychological – had begun throughout Germany. The *Lands* were 'coordinated' into the Reich, each under a *Reichsstatthalter*, an official acting on behalf of central government.[100] Despite this centralization of power, Hitler still expressed himself in favour of some degree of decentralization, and allowed his Gauleiters considerable freedom of operation. The Third Reich, far from being a firm monolith, was very much a polycratic structure, in which, however, Hitler had the last say. By July 1933 all political parties other than the NSDAP had disappeared. All this had become possible because of the Reichstag's action.

# 4

# The National Socialist State and the Law

The foundation of National Socialist rule in all aspects of German life was the NS *Führerprinzip*, the leadership principle. Hitler had emphasized its importance in *Mein Kampf*, but the leadership principle was probably not so much an NS invention as a characteristic of hierarchical societies. Its establishment in Germany after 1933 proceeded almost unnoticed; even before the days of the Weimar Republic the idea of an authoritarian leader had gained fairly wide currency.[1] If anything, the Weimar Republic had furthered the popularization of the *Führerprinzip* through its actions, or rather the lack of them.[2]

Hitler never anchored the leadership principle institutionally or legally. It was not contained in the party programme of 1920 nor in any piece of legislation after 1933.[3] Instead it could build upon the mental militarization of the German people which ranged from the Conservatives to the Communists, from the non-party Youth Leagues to the Hitler Youth.[4] By making reference to the leadership principle the National Socialists struck a chord already in existence. They immediately adapted its external trappings, the ritual of the leader and followers as exemplified in NS public ceremonies with their pseudo-religious and liturgical features. After all, the leader was not to provide a solution but salvation,[5] or, as one lawyer of the period put it in an official journal: 'The German people are united in the opinion that because of their disunity they require a Führer'.[6]

The leadership principle was vague, ambivalent, unlimited and therefore extremely flexible: the power of the Führer was devoid of any legal constraint. The leadership principle became an undefined absolute.[7] Not only, therefore, did *Führerbefehle* (Führer orders) have to be unconditionally obeyed but the will of the Führer became the guideline, the yardstick, for all actions.[8] Some National Socialists tried to derive the leadership principle from traditional historical sources, to see it as part of the development of political ideas since the French Revolution of 1789.[9] But this apparently rational justification was soon swept away by slogans like the 'feeling' of the Volk, 'intuition' and so forth.[10]

Existing German constitutional law was replaced by slogans, postulates and general clauses. The Führer's powers could be understood only 'intuitively'; legal considerations were swept away because they contradicted the 'depth and width' of the leadership principle.[11] Liberal 'abstract' systems of thought were dismissed, and into their place stepped the 'concrete' values of the 'community' (*Gemeinschaft*). What underlay these values remained undefined. The NSDAP spoke of the *völkische Gesamtordnung*, the racial all-embracing order,[12] but what this meant in terms of law remained an open question. It also spoke of a *völkische Verfassung*,[13] a constitution, but that constitution never materialized, perhaps because whichever way it might have been formulated, it would have contained rights and duties, thus erecting constraints on the exercise of power, and it was precisely in order to be free from such constraints that Hitler had needed the Enabling Act.

The leadership principle was to be carried out within the judiciary in its most absolute form. In the early years of the Third Reich, the principle of judicial independence was not formally thrown overboard; instead its independence was to be reshaped in the NS spirit. As early as 1933 Carl Schmitt had published an article in which he stated that the independence of the judges rested on their tie with the law, and the law of the state. Without that connection their independence would amount to arbitrary action.[14] The Third Reich's cautious approach was an attempt to reconcile the independence of the judges with the leadership principle, but it met with quick opposition even from NS judges, who insisted on the continuance of their independence, while on the other hand linking it with the will of the Führer. 'The Führer is the highest German judge, he is the German judge.'[15]

Article 1 of the Law for Securing the Unity of Party and State of 1 December 1933 stated: 'Since the victory of the National Socialist revolution the NSDAP is the carrier of the idea of the German state and thus indissolubly united with the state.'[16] Hence Hitler and the NSDAP claimed virtual infallibility in all their actions and in all spheres of life in Germany.[17] Institutionally, therefore, political leadership, administrative leadership and judicial leadership were inextricably intertwined: at the top sat the *Führer und Reichskanzler*, the merged posts of president and chancellor; at the lower level the offices of *Landrat* and *Kreisleiter*.[18] The *Führerbefehl* became the decisive instrument. Hitler normally entrusted one of his 'old fighters' with the task of seeing that it was carried out.[19] They could demand that the existing bureaucracy assist them, but they could also go over their heads.[20]

Organizationally the NSDAP's dominance over the state was established through a whole host of offices which duplicated already existing institutions of the state.[21] The NSDAP stated clearly that the German state took second place to the NSDAP and the NS ideology,[22] a demand reflected, for instance, in the German Civil Service Law of 1937 in which the civil servant is defined as the executor of the will of the state embodied in the NSDAP.[23] The civil servant owed loyalty to the Führer unto death. His entire behaviour must be guided by the fact that the NSDAP, indissolubly tied to the Volk, is the carrier of the idea of the German state.[24] In the judiciary, Germany's highest court, the Reichgericht, stated in 1939 that not the state but the Volk was the decisive criterion.[25] Thus the NSDAP became the primary element of all *völkisch* life, the example for the as yet undeveloped state; the existing state in its present form was considered temporary. Appointment and promotions within the bureaucracy and judiciary were subject to the agreement of the NSDAP.[26]

The degree to which the personnel policy of the German judiciary was affected by the application of the leadership principle remains uncertain. At present it appears that a certain continuity was preserved, certainly at the top.[27] Insofar as any changes can be registered, they took place in the Oberlandesgerichte, but even here the shifts in personnel were not dramatic.[28] Rather more Ministry of Justice civil servants than judges or prosecutors seem to have been moved or retired. One can tentatively conclude that in essence the judges retained their professional as well as social homogeneity.[29] Yet in spite of this homogeneity there were no official or unofficial protests when Jewish colleagues were removed,[30] or against the murders of June 1934, which were legalized post factum on 3 July 1934.[31] However, although the evidence is slender, there are indications that between March 1933 and June 1934 the judiciary was investigating various SA leaders, among them Karl Ernst, for illegal arrest, manslaughter and even murder committed in their unofficial, 'wild' concentration camps. All those under investigation were liquidated on or shortly after 30 June 1934.[32]

National Socialism understood itself as the ultimate form of the expression of the *Volksgemeinschaft*, the 'racial national community', which it claimed to lead. This was a blanket rejection of the liberal legal system, individual liberties and the rights contained in the Weimar Constitution. What was subject to endless argument until the outbreak of war was whether the Weimar Constitution ceased to be in force after 30 January 1933 or whether parts of it were suspended through NS legislation that was tantamount to constitutional change.[33] Such legislation, for instance, was the suspension of the basic rights in the wake of the Reichstag fire. The National Socialists left no doubt about their viewpoint: 'The present legislation has only for the sake of order ... used the formal procedures laid down in the Weimar Constitution, but does not derive its justification from it.'[34]

The Constitution and the legal principles based on it had been overcome by the *Volksgemeinschaft* and the National Socialist *Weltanschauung*. Thus in 1935 in a trial of Jehovah's Witnesses in Hamburg the continuation of the Weimar Constitution was negated by the judges and declared irreconcilable with the National Socialist concept of state.[35] The breaking and changing of the Constitution by the judiciary was declared as admissable.[36] Some judges went so far as to consider the NSDAP party programme as the legal basis of their arguments,[37] something which even Hitler was personally rather reluctant to do. And Carl Schmitt noted in 1934 that 'it is quite evident that any discussion concerning the constitutional structure must begin with the simple sentence: "The Weimar Reich Constitution is no longer valid." '[38]

This was in fact correct. The law establishing the VGH was already outside the framework of the Constitution[39] and so of course was the *post factum* legal justification of the Röhm purge,[40] and subsequent legislation which forbade German lawyers to represent 'non-Aryans', including gypsies, before German courts.[41] Once the war against Poland had begun and Poland was occupied, this prohibition was not formally applied to Poles but lawyers were advised 'to consider the interests of the national community and to impose upon themselves great self-restraint.'[42] The NS leadership principle superseded and replaced any legal constraints and if the Third Reich had lasted longer than it did, it would ultimately have produced complete chaos in all spheres of the law.

These developments could not be foreseen on 30 January 1933 when Hitler and his cabinet were sworn in. On the surface the cabinet seemed to preserve continuity and this no more so than in the judiciary.

A genuinely new appointment within the Prussian Ministry of Justice under Dr Hans Kerrl was that of Freisler, who in February 1933 was made *Ministerialdirektor*.[43] At this time Freisler was more preoccupied with the process of *Gleichschaltung* in Kassel than with his civil servant's duties in Berlin. Together with the local members of the NSDAP he took over Kassel's town hall, an action he intended to repeat at Kassel's Oberlandesgericht.[44] Its president, Dr Anz, however, persuaded Freisler to desist since it would hardly be in the interest of the reputation of a Prussian *Ministerialdirektor* to participate in mob actions. Freisler took the point and limited his action to having the swastika flag put up over the court's entrance.

Despite their differences of opinion, mainly of a political nature, there existed a bond of mutual respect between Anz and Freisler. While Freisler respected Anz's utter integrity and impartiality, even in matters where impartiality was difficult to maintain, Anz respected Freisler's intellectual ability. When Freisler was promoted Secretary of State on 1 July 1933 he applied all his influence to have Anz transferred to Berlin. But the newly appointed Secretary of State's powers were as yet not influential enough to overcome the NSDAP's objections to having at the head of the Berlin Kammergericht a man who was not a member of the NSDAP or any of its formations.[45] Less than a year later, on 1 April 1934, Freisler was promoted Secretary of State in the Reich Ministry of Justice, obviously to keep an eye on Schlegelberger and to act as a brake on what was considered the latter's excessive legalism.[46]

In 1928 Hitler had decided to infiltrate the organizations of the legal profession and recruit members for the NSDAP from it. In October 1928 he had approved the founding of the *Bund Nationalsozialistischer Deutscher Juristen* (BNSDJ), the 'League of NS Jurists', led by Hans Frank.[47] But reputable lawyers, let alone judges, were difficult to recruit. Within the first year of its existence it had only thirty members, though by the end of 1930 the number had increased to 233. But the depression, too, left its mark and by 1932–3 the BNSDJ counted 1,347 members, mainly young lawyers.[48] Judges still kept their distance as far as membership was concerned,[49] but this does not allow any conclusions as to where the political sympathies of many lay. The great rush for membership set in after the March elections of 1933 and by December 1933 the BNSDJ counted over 80,000 members.[50]

When Frank was put in charge of the *Gleichschaltung* of the judiciary on 22 April 1933 he rapidly subordinated existing professional organizations of the judiciary and lawyers to the BNSDJ. The Law Concerning the Restoration of a National Professional Civil Service of 7 April 1933[51] removed Jewish judges by way of forcible retirement, and also limited the access of Jewish lawyers to German courts. In part, as far as the lawyers were concerned, this was allegedly due to the excess numbers of lawyers that had begun to build up between 1931 and 1933.[52] In Prussia alone, there were a total of 18,038 advocates and notaries, which by way of the Aryan paragraph and other legislation discriminating against Jews, was reduced by 5,424 by the end of 1935.[53] Such Jewish lawyers as were still left could appear only on behalf of Jewish clients before court. Those Jewish judges who were retained were transferred by Freisler from large urban centres to rural areas[54] until the Nuremberg Laws of 1935 put an end to their service.

Within the context of the establishment of the VGH, however, the most decisive event was the Reichstag fire. The historiographical controversy surrounding it need not interest us here; what is important are the consequences: the suspension of the basic rights of the Constitution such as the liberty of the person, the inviolability of one's dwelling, the secrecy of the mail, the right of free opinion and assembly, the right to form associations and the inviolability of personal property.[55] The death sentence was introduced for offences hitherto punishable only by imprisonment, notably in cases of high treason and Landesverrat.

The so-called Law van der Lubbe was made retroactive – an act for which the Weimar Republic in its Law for the Protection of the Republic in 1922 had set a precedent – because only in this way could van der Lubbe be sentenced to death.[56] It had been introduced on 28 February 1933 in the form of the presidential decree 'against Treason on the German People and Activities of High Treason' which, if widely interpreted, allowed mass arrests, mass sentences and collective threats. On 29 March 1933 there followed the Law concerning the Sentence and Execution of the Death Penalty[57] which imposed the death sentence threatened in the presidential decree 'for the Protection of the German People'. It applied retroactively to all capital crimes committed between 31 January 1933 and 28 February 1933, and authorized hanging instead of decapitation.[58]

The legislation against treason also met the requirements of the Reichswehr.[59] The occupation of the Rhineland and the activities of Allied Control Commissions had left their traces in Germany. Active espionage inside Germany emanated principally from three countries:

France, Poland and Czechoslovakia.[60] The legislation allowed the German Abwehr a more active and forward role, while the harsher sentences were meant to provide an active deterrent. The German armed forces had long ago considered existing legislation in the case of threatened or actual war as quite inadequate. First drafts for the purpose of amending existing legislation and introducing new laws had begun as early as 1928. But it was to take more than ten years until legislation had been framed to satisfy the chiefs of the three services, the Ministry of Justice, that of Economics, as well as that of the Interior.

What the government had still to face was the trial of those accused of having set fire to the Reichstag. Government and Communists were at one in their conviction that Marinus van der Lubbe could not have set fire to the Reichstag without accomplices. Along with van der Lubbe, therefore, Ernst Torgler, the leader of the parliamentary party of the KPD, and Georgi Dimitroff, the head of the Western European Office of the Comintern, had been arrested as well as two of Dimitroff's Bulgarian associates. The trial, as far as the National Socialists were concerned, proved one big embarrassment at home and abroad.[61] All but van der Lubbe were acquitted; van der Lubbe himself was sentenced to death.[62] The judgment announced on 23 December 1933 showed that however embarrassing the trial may have been for the government, the Supreme Court of the Reich, the Reichsgericht, had still retained its integrity and had closed its ears to National Socialist propaganda and pressure.

The criticism expected by the members of the Reichsgericht from the NSDAP was not long in coming. None other than Hans Frank's journal *Deutsches Recht: Zentralorgan des Bundes National-sozialistischer Deutscher Juristen* (German Law: The Central Organ of the League of National Socialist German Jurists) denounced the judgment as a *glattes Fehlurteil*, a plainly faulty judgment.[63] Hitler himself stated in 1942 that the Reichstag fire could have seriously damaged the NSDAP's reputation in the eyes of the German public. For that reason on 28 February 1933 he had immediately driven to editorial offices of the party's daily paper, the *Völkischer Beobachter* (VB), at 2 o'clock in the morning only to find that the morning edition was to contain a mere ten-line news item on the subject. Together with Goebbels he had got to work and written articles and reports on the fire to cover the whole front page. But what he had secured was undone before the judges of the Reichsgericht. The trial had dragged on for weeks on end; the bench he described as 'senile judges'.[64]

At party and cabinet level thoughts began to occur about a special court which would deal exclusively with cases of treason; and these culminated in a cabinet meeting of 23 March 1934 in which Hitler, Minister of the Interior Dr Wilhelm Frick, Gürtner, Göring and Minister without Portfolio Ernst Röhm participated.[65] 'The conversations produced agreement that trials for *Hoch- und Landesverrat* should be handed over to a special People's Court. The court should consist of two professional and three lay judges. The latter should be appointed for a longer period. The Reich Minister of Justice will submit a correspondingly amended draft for the necessary law.'[66] In regards to the Reichsgericht, Germany's final court of appeal, the meeting decided it fulfilled functions which were separate from those envisaged for the People's Court and should therefore no longer have to deal with cases of treason. On 24 April 1934 the Volksgerichtshof was formally founded.[67] More than a year later the editor-in-chief of the *VB* Wilhelm Weiss commented:

> For good reasons the National Socialist state, after the seizure of power, has created a special court for the trial of the most serious crimes that exist in political matters. Whoever is familiar with the sentencing policy of German courts especially before the NSDAP seizure of power can fully appreciate the necessity for such a court of law. One could object by saying that before 30 January 1933 high treason and Landesverrat were matters for the Reichsgericht in Leipzig. The trials which were pending or dealt with there could not lead to a satisfactory solution in the National Socialist sense, because the Reichsgericht in its work and tendency was dependent on the general political and spiritual basic attitude which dominated in the democratic state of Weimar. Any trial for treason in Leipzig was as a rule an affair which led to confrontations in parliament and produced a shameless agitation by the gutter press against all who made a modest attempt to protect the Reich at least from the most blatant acts of treason.
>
> The legal uncertainty which dominated before the National Socialist seizure of power is furthermore evidence of the fact that a state cannot be protected solely by the letter of the law, if the law is not in accord with a clear political idea. In this sense then the Volksgerichtshof for the German Reich is an organic creation of the National Socialist state. It is a form of expression of National Socialist basic concepts in the field of the application of the law.[68]

However, as another NS commentator insisted, it was not be a revolutionary tribunal.[69]

The law founding the VGH specified Berlin as its seat. Like the Reichsgericht, it was to have five judges, and in minor trials three, inclusive of a presiding judge. However, the cabinet decided that only the presiding judge and one assisting judge should be professional judges; a third assisting judge as well as the three lay judges were to be appointed on an honorary basis and were not required to have any formal training in law. All appointments were to be suggested by the Minister of Justice and confirmed for a period of five years by the Chancellor.[70] (In the case of the Reichsgericht, the practice had been that judges were proposed by the Reichsrat, an institution which had dissolved itself in 1934.)[71] Investigating judges were to be appointed for a term of office of one year. Of how, or by whom, the investigating judges were to be appointed the law said nothing and very often in practice the investigating judges were seconded by the Reichsgericht to the VGH.[72] No judge could reject his nomination to the VGH, and this applied to all judges at all levels of the judiciary.[73]

The president of the VGH was to divide the court into separate senates, distribute the court's business over the senates and staff them with professional and lay judges.[74] The Minister of Justice was also to appoint a permanent deputy for the president of the VGH, a rule which in 1938 led to establishment of a vice-president.[75] Subsequent decrees empowered the president of the VGH to call VGH court sessions in other parts of Germany, and in order to leave no doubts about the importance of the VGH, all VGH judges after 1936 were allowed to wear the red robe, a privilege hitherto accorded only to the judges of the Reichsgericht.[76] The VGH's first home was the building of the defunct Prussian Diet in Berlin's Prinz-Albrecht Strasse, but in May 1935 it moved to the Bellevue-Str. 15 where it remained until February 1945, when the building was bombed and the VGH was forced to move to Potsdam and ultimately to Bayreuth.[77]

On 14 July 1934 the VGH was formally opened. Gürtner administered the oath to the judges, and the first sessions were held on 1 August 1934.[78] At first, however, there was no place in the budget for the VGH which meant that every one of its judges had been seconded from another court, and received the same salary as before. There was an intensive struggle by the Ministry of Justice to claim regular funds for the VGH, but it was turned down time and again by the Ministry of Finance.[79] This caused Gürtner to rethink the original law founding the VGH, and after some manoeuvring the rules were changed to favour the VGH judiciary. Its judges were not, as was originally stipulated, to be appointed for five years, but for life. In that position they were also interchangeable with judges of the Reichsgericht. Hence on 16 April 1936 a new law concerning the VGH was enacted, which transformed the VGH into a permanent institution with a president, senate presidents and professional judges.[80] All permanent members of the VGH had to be professional judges of at least 35 years of age; only the honorary lay judges were appointed for terms of five years.[81]

Within the Ministry of Justice, Secretary of State Roland Freisler provided the driving force behind the consolidation of the VGH.[82] His objective was not merely to establish the VGH as a parallel institution of the Reichsgericht but to make it Germany's Supreme Court.[83] Hence he was not entirely satisfied by the arrangement of 1936. In one of his many articles he emphasized the need to change basic attitudes to fundamental questions concerning the German people. Only after such attitudes had been changed could one begin a fundamental renewal of German law with any chance of success. With the NS assumption of power such changes could be carried out; collegiate decisions and majority votes in court could be replaced by NS concepts of law, with their clearly defined principles and assigned responsibility for decision-making. The spirit of 'responsibility through the leadership principle' would inform every judicial decision.[84]

Freisler then went on to discuss the VGH's work to date, underlining its speed and efficiency, and the immense benefits accruing to the VGH from the fact that against its sentences there was no appeal. It was the court of the first and last instance.[85] He heavily criticized the VGH's omission from the government's budget, and dismissed the notion of the VGH being a purely temporary institution.[86] As yet, no clear decision had been made as to which of the two was the superior court, the Reichsgericht or the VGH; Freisler argued that one could do away with the Reichsgericht altogether if within the VGH an appeal and review senate were created. This would then lead the VGH into the highest position it could reach, namely to be the Reichsstrafgericht, the Reich Penal Court.[87] The pattern of evolution pointed in this direction, the only objection was that the courts dealing with criminal cases had not yet fully followed the way pointed out to them by the Volksgerichtshof.[88]

The first president of the VGH was Dr Fritz Rehn, who, however, died on 18 September 1934.[89] Then for almost two years the post of president remained vacant, this office being run by the oldest serving senate president. Only on 1 June 1936 was Dr Georg Thierack appointed president of the VGH. Thierack, born in 1889, had begun his legal career as a prosecutor in Saxony in 1921. He was one of the very few established members of the judiciary to join the NSDAP prior to 1933; after 30 January 1933 he had become Minister of Justice in Saxony. In 1935 he was appointed vice-president of the Reichsgericht, a post which he held for a year prior to joining the VGH.[90] Gürtner felt ill at ease with him because he was anything but straightforward,[91] and even Freisler had his reservations.[92] While Freisler had no qualms about interpreting the law in the strictest and widest National Socialist sense and bringing it to bear with extreme severity, he was always anxious never to be seen to depart from the basis of the law; Thierack, by contrast, as will be seen in the Eliáš affair, did not shrink from leaving the procedure of the law altogether and acting with callous brutality in the pursuit of his own personal ambitions.[93]

Lay judges were appointed from among the higher functionaries of the NSDAP and its formations and officers of the three services of the Wehrmacht. It was desirable that they possess expert knowledge and experience in dealing with subversive attacks directed against the state or any of its institutions. The number of lay judges exceeded that of the professional judges considerably. When the VGH was established it had only 19 lay judges, but by 1935 there were 43 and by 1939, 95. Of these thirty were officers of the armed forces, four were police officers, and the rest were SS, SA, NSKK and NSDAP leaders.

National Socialist criminal justice classified the political criminal into the lowest category of criminal. The concept of 'political criminality' was new in German criminal justice and helped to obscure the boundaries between various crimes; what remained was 'the enemy' whose political aims and ideological principles stood in direct opposition to National Socialism, to the NS regime, and thus by definition to Germany as a whole. Freisler personally appealed incessantly for the emergency legislation of February and March 1933 to be used relentlessly against political opponents. By means of oral instructions to state prosecutors, he emphasised that it was the judiciary's task to 'secure formally and irrevocably the guarantee of the National Socialist revolution and evolution.'[94] He placed great importance on the close cooperation between the prosecutor's office and the agencies of the NSDAP. His aim, and here the VGH was to serve as the model, was to punish quickly, sharp as lightning. 'Within 24 hours the indictment must be drawn up, within 24 hours the sentence must be passed, to be carried out immediately . . . the time for extenuating circumstances is past.'[95] Although between 1933 and 1939 the rate of criminality in Germany declined, in 1932 in Prussia for instance, 52 death sentences were pronounced, in 1933 78. Sentences of hard labour in Prussia in 1932 totalled to 6,345; in 1933 there were 9,661.[96]

No other court in Germany between 1934 and 1945 appears to have practised the maxim coined by Hitler in his Reichstag speech of 23 March 1933 quite as relentlessy as the VGH: 'Not the individual, but the Volk, should be the centre of legal concern. *Landes- und Hochverrat* must henceforth be expurgated ruthlessly.'[97]

In assessing this maxim one is struck by its callous inhumanity, magnified many times over by the 'tyranny of hindsight' and our knowledge of where it led one people and what terrifying price it extracted from it and from others. Nor did the process end there: as events were to show, Hitler himself was quite prepared to transgress his own maxim and to sacrifice his own Volk on the altar of his Social-Darwinian beliefs simply because by 1945 it had, in his view, not withstood 'the struggle for survival, the survival of the fittest'. Its extinction therefore followed the biological law of nature.

As to the relationship between individual and community, no doubt one will have to differentiate between legal maxim and actual practice. The *cause célèbre* of Captain Dreyfus, for instance, does not impress this writer as an illustration of the dominance of liberal, humanitarian traditions; rather it gives rise to speculation about the unknown number of those without legal defence, who in the course of history have been sacrificed in the interest of communities and institutions. But this is and must remain a speculation. Injustice is a fact of life, but still this remains a different thing from injustice being institutionalized and embodied in what is – or ought to be – the fountain of justice, the law. However, the law in the service of totalitarian claims is virtually by definition arbitrary, irrespective of the brand of totalitarianism.

In Germany after 1933 law became preventive law. It often struck before it had been broken. It then no longer took account of the personality of the accused or his or her human and personal requirements. It struck blindly. After 1939 the liberal traditions of the German judiciary were largely abandoned, on the justification of a superficial reference to the emergencies of war, to make way for the extensive use of 'preventive detention', the collective identification of groups as 'criminals' such as Jews, gypsies and other minorities, and the complete hopelessness of the case of any individual caught up in the machinery of what was called the law.

# 5

# The National Socialist People's Court 1934–1939

The legal basis on which the VGH operated was the existing penal code, the Strafgesetzbuch (StGB), an extremely wide interpretation of its provisions, and other laws enacted on the basis of the Enabling Act and *Führerbefehle* which further extended the scope of the penal code.

The provisions defining high treason in National Socialist Germany were contained in the first portion of the special part of the penal code.[1] In paragraph 81 high treason was defined as an action attempting to change the Constitution or the territory of one of the federal states. This was not changed, although in the process of *Gleichschaltung* the Reich and its authorities were centralized and the federal structure abolished. Paragraphs 83 and 84 dealt with conspiracies to commit high treason – in other words, cases in which individuals planned to commit high treason but had not had the opportunity to carry it out. Paragraph 86 made preparation for high treason a punishable offence. Up to 1933 the sentences for these crimes were hard labour, imprisonment and the confiscation of property; after 1933, the death penalty was added to the list.[2]

The provisions concerning Landesverrat were only in part contained in the penal code, where they were dealt with in the same section as high treason. Up to 30 January 1933 paragraph 87 defined conspiracy to commit Landesverrat in much the same way as paragraph 84 did for high treason. Landesverrat was committed where a German in concert with a foreign power tried to damage its interests. Paragraph 88 made it an offence for a German subject to serve in the army of an enemy. Support of Landesverrat to the disadvantage of Germany or its allies was made a punishable offence by paragraph 89. Paragraph 90 listed in detail acts constituting Landesverrat: the destruction or sabotage of war *matériel*, fortresses or means of communication, the recruitment of Germans for enemy powers, incitement to desertion, spying or supporting spies, betrayal of operational plans or the plans of fortresses and finally incitement to mutiny in Germany's armed forces. These paragraphs applied both to Germans and to foreigners living in Germany.[3]

Even before the turn of the century it was thought that the existing law had too many gaps. For instance, while communicating state secrets to foreign powers was punishable, the agent of that same foreign government could not be prosecuted. In 1893 harsher provisions were introduced[4] which were then replaced by the Law concerning the Betrayal of Military Secrets of 3 June 1914.[5] The betrayal of official papers or drawings and the handing on of other secret information were made punishable, but in spite of stricter legislation, the death penalty was not introduced for any violations.

The National Socialists had from the beginning, under the impact of '1918', heavily criticized the 'soft' line of the treason laws, condemning them as the product of a corrupt liberal age (although Hitler himself in 1924 had profited from this liberal line).[6] Point 18 of the NSDAP programme demanded the death sentence for usury and black marketeering, and this was soon extended to high treason and Landesverrat.[7] National Socialists, notably Freisler, rejected the notion that criminal acts were different when committed out of political conviction.

With the Emergency Decree of 4 February 1933, based as it was on Article 48 of the Constitution, provisions had already been made for the confiscation of printed matter or newspapers whose content was judged treasonable.[8] But the real watershed was the presidential decree of 28 February 1933, which, as already mentioned, suspended all the most important basic rights contained in the Constitution.[9] High treason as well as a range of other offences were now to be punished by death, while an attack on the President or a member of the government was punishable by death or hard labour.[10] The law of 29 March 1933, as we have seen, retroactively introduced the death sentence through hanging or decapitation for offences committed between 31 January and 28 February 1933.[11]

On 28 February 1933 a second presidential decree was published. Directed against 'Treason against the German People and actions of High Treason',[12] it made the death sentence mandatory for Landesverrat, for instance for the betrayal of military secrets.[13] The fabrication and communication of faked state secrets was made punishable as was the stocking and distribution of printed matter containing treasonable material;[14] here, however, the punishment ranged from imprisonment to hard labour. High treason was also committed if an attempt was made to spread hostile propaganda within the police or the armed forces.[15] (This had already been a crime during the Weimar Republic when in 1930 in the trial of the three lieutenants of the Ulm garrison they were found guilty of *Zersetzung des Reichsheers*, the undermining of the army.[16] Hence *Wehrkraftzerseztung*, too, had its Weimar precedent.) Actions by Germans against their country when abroad were equally made punishable, the ultimate punishment for such actions being death.[17]

However great the confusion caused initially by these numerous changes and amendments to the law, the basic intention was to put high treason and Landesverrat into a coherent context in order to deal with them promptly and thoroughly.[18] Threatening to commit treason was to be punished as severely as having committed an act of treason. The admission of mitigating circumstances into evidence was barred. Treason was the lowest form of common criminality, and the perpetrator of such a crime, if he was not sentenced to death, could be detained without any time limit. Furthermore, any traitor was automatically excluded from any amnesty.[19] Between 1933 and 1939 legislation based on the Enabling Act largely replaced the emergency decrees of 28 February 1933.

On 17 August 1938 a *Kriegssonderstrafrecht* decree, a special legal code applying to war time (KSSVO), was introduced. It redefined espionage and partisans.[20] Any spy was to be sentenced to death who, on German or German occupied territory, gathered information in order to make it available to the enemy. A partisan was defined as a non-combatant who was armed and participated in war actions. The most serious aspect of this decree was, however, paragraph 5, which broadened the scope of the crime for which the Ulm garrison lieutenants had been sentenced, the undermining of the defensive power of the Reich. What distinguished this new formulation was its extreme flexibility, a fact which was to play a major role in VGH trials once the war had broken out.[21] The war itself, as will be seen, added considerably to the legislation existing in 1939.

The scope of the VGH's jurisdiction was defined in its founding law of 24 April 1934.[22] It was restricted to matters of treason of any kind and to those offences as listed in the Decree for the Protection of the German People and State of 28 February 1933.[23] In principle, each senate of the VGH was to decide on a collegiate basis,[24] though the president of each senate was to act as the Führer. The investigating judge had the exclusive right of investigation.[25]

The scope of jurisdiction of the VGH was not exclusive. The

Oberreichsanwalt, the Supreme Prosecuting Counsel, could decide that certain trials for treason, particularly for preparation of treason, could be handed over to the next lower court, the Oberlandesgericht, to be dealt with. This rule was maintained throughout in order not to overburden the VGH. But by way of the Supreme Prosecuting Counsel, himself a civil servant of the Ministry of Justice, an eye could be kept on the cases dealt with by lower courts. Freisler himself tended to look at the lower courts as branches of the VGH.[26] In the course of time the jurisdiction of the VGH was extended considerably; damage to arms and armaments or any defence *matériel* was made punishable in 1935 and treated as treason,[27] as was the failure to denounce anyone who had planned or committed such an act was made punishable. On 1 December 1936 a new law concerning economic sabotage[28] was created to prosecute those who transferred their assets in Germany abroad illegally or who, without official permission, maintained assets abroad – a further amplification and extension of legislation introduced by Brüning in 1931.[29] Needless to say, Germany's territorial expansion between 1936 and 1939 also extended the VGH's area of operation.[30]

This expansion almost by definition increased the range of charges and the number of the accused. Even an action committed by a non-German, for instance a Czech, against Germany before the dissolution of the Czech state during the period of 30 September 1938 to 15 March 1939, could now be prosecuted. But this required the assent of the Minister of Justice. As will be seen, after the outbreak of the Second World War, when within a matter of months large parts of Western Europe fell into German hands, German émigrés, when caught, could be arrested, indicted and tried before the VGH.[31]

The VGH considered itself as a primarily political court. No attempt was made to disguise this fact, but in its early days it did not impose excessive sentences. Thus, in 1934, the First Senate sentenced a man convicted of carrying arms and distributing illegal literature among the police – thus committing preparation for high treason and keeping an unlicensed weapon – to two-and-a-half years of imprisonment minus seven months spent on remand. The Second Senate sentenced a man who had committed much the same action among the Reichswehr to nine months' hard labour minus seven months on remand.[32] These were extremely mild sentences in view of the fact that the decrees of 28 February 1933 demanded in principle long hard-labour sentences for offences of this kind. In Kassel,

Freisler's pre-1933 main area of activity, a former Communist functionary who had continued illegal KPD activities was sentenced to a year and a half of imprisonment, including the period spent in custody.[33]

According to German law, when sentences of imprisonment are given, the *bürgerlichen Ehrenrechte*, the citizen's civic right, which includes the active and passive franchise, can be suspended.[34] When in November 1934 two VGH senates in two cases of treasonable activities refused to suspend these rights, the Ministry of Justice expressed its serious annoyance.[35]

The cases mentioned so far concerned aspects of high treason. However, for Landesverrat the yardstick was rather more severe, primarily because past NS criticism had directed itself mainly against the mildness of sentences for that offence.[36] Although the sentences in this area became much harsher, the Reich Ministry of Justice in 1936 compiled a list of eighteen cases dealt with by the VGH between 1935 and 1936 and criticized the lack of the severity of the sentences.[37] As far as death sentences were concerned, four were passed in 1934, nine in 1935.[38]

With Thierack's appointment as president of the VGH a profound change occurred. Thierack held the view that judges should take as their guideline the views of the NS leadership and on that basis only should political justice be imposed. Protecting the security of the Reich and of the NS regime were to be the main functions of the VGH.[39] As Thierack later wrote to Freisler:

> In no other court as in the VGH is it so clearly apparent that the application of the law of the highest political court must be in accord with the leadership of the state. Therefore it will, for the most part, fall to you to lead the judges into this direction. You must therefore look at every indictment and recognize where it is necessary in confidential and convincing consultation to convince the judges concerned what is essential for the state. I want to emphasise again, that this must take place in a manner which convinces and does not order the judges. . . .[40]

One major issue which began to preoccupy the VGH is what the Reich Ministry of Justice defined as 'political Catholicism', cases in which members of the Roman Catholic clergy criticized the NSDAP from the pulpit. In a circular to state prosecutors as well as to the VGH on 20 July 1935, Secretary of State Schlegelberger, acting on

Gürtner's directive, emphasised that the judicial authorities in close cooperation with the Gestapo and other administrative authorities should act against attempts at undermining the state, the bringing about of divisions within the *Volksgemeinschaft* by 'political Catholicism.'[41]

Wherever political Catholicism, or Christianity for that matter, showed itself, irrespective of person and position, it was to be fought relentlessly but with great circumspection.[42] Schlegelberger then invoked all the paragraphs of the penal code that had been in existence since 1879 plus the legislation introduced since 1933. He went on to stress that speed was of the essence; punishment had to immediately follow the deed. In the trials themselves sentences should be demanded and passed which would make it clear to the German population how dangerous such activities were. However, prior to drawing up an indictment the Ministry of Justice was to be consulted.[43]

Despite these precautions, no case involving a Catholic or Protestant clergyman or a nun reached the VGH before the outbreak of war, though at local level, mainly at the initiative of the local NS leadership, 1936 and 1937 were marked by numerous cases against clergymen and nuns for charges ranging from homosexuality to illegal currency dealings.[44] However, as Germany moved further into international crisis, these trials drastically declined. Although no evidence can be found of a government directive to stop them, it seems a fair assumption that for the sake of maintaining internal unity in the face of crisis trials of this kind were officially stopped.[45]

Meanwhile, the foundations were being laid for a close collaboration between the Ministry of Justice, the state prosecutors and the VGH judges on the one side and the Gestapo on the other. On 13 June 1936 the principal officers of each organization were invited to a conference to be held in Berlin for the purpose of discussing issues arising out of treason.[46] The conference took place on 11 and 12 November 1936;[47] Freisler made the introductory speech, and was followed by lectures by Gestapo and other officials on the Comintern and Communist activities in Germany, Social Democracy and Otto Strasser's 'Black Front'. The conference reconvened the following day to listen to talks on 'The Communist and Police Investigations' and 'The Position of the Gestapo in Court Trials'. After a detailed discussion and Freisler's final speech the conference ended. The official conference report records the expression of mutual agreement and the necessity of close cooperation between the judiciary and the

Gestapo. It was the thin end of Himmler's wedge: two months later, the Gestapo, the prosecutors and the investigating judges of the VGH were regularly exchanging files on treason cases.[48] The compliance of the judiciary with this order demonstrates the extent of Himmler's power. Although as Chief of the German Police he was still nominally the subordinate of the Minister of the Interior, there is no evidence that in this case Frick had been consulted. Nor for that matter did the Ministry possess any powers of supervision or intervention in Himmler's 'concentration camp state'.

How far the VGH in particular, and its prosecutors in general, had become a direct tool of the state executive was shown in 1939 at a meeting in the Reich Ministry of Justice, held between 23 and 25 January.[49] At issue were some of the consequences of the anti-Semitic pogrom of 9–10 November 1938. The prosecutors complained that they were unable to try the perpetrators of the pogrom; their hands were tied by a ministerial directive which demanded that all cases be handed over to the Gestapo. Freisler bluntly argued that prosecution should really lie within the hands of the judiciary, and that the Führer himself should decide the cases for which no prosecution should be carried out. Even members of the party and its formations should be prosecuted, albeit quickly; if necessary such persons should be expelled from the NSDAP.

Gürtner argued that only the most blatant cases should be prosecuted; the rest would best be forgotten. Oberstaatsanwalt Joel, however, said that the cases should be prosecuted by the Gestapo as Göring had originally ordered. Therefore all the files should be handed over to the Gestapo and the Chief of Security Police, Reinhard Heydrich, and from there they should be forwarded to the Court of Honour of the NSDAP and to the Ministry of Justice. However, he went on to say, the problem was that the pogrom was considered by the majority of the participants to have been allowed, even ordered, by the government. Hence if any penalties were to be meted out they should only be small fines. The problem was that any 'action' committed after 11 November 1938 should in theory be severely punished since by that date counter-orders were known everywhere. Gürtner tried to tone down the discussion by suggesting that if there were trials the public should be excluded and any 'small plundering' should be ignored. In the end he decided to keep the judiciary out of the pogrom affair and to hand the files to Gestapo as requested.

One point raised at this conference affected the VGH directly. This was the Gestapo practice, unofficial since 1936, of re-arresting persons acquitted by the VGH or political criminals who had completed sentences. They would then be taken into 'protective custody' and transferred to a concentration camp. Freisler appears to have felt some misgivings about this practice but stated that nothing could be done about it, except that proper regulations would have to be drafted to provide it with a legal foundation. In other words, as long as overtly illegal and unethical actions by the state were sanctioned by the normative force of the law there were no objections from him.

A few days before Thierack had given an interview to the *Völkischer Beobachter* in which he underlined the identity of views between the Italian and the German judiciaries. The danger of Bolshevism presented a particular challenge to the authoritarian states; Fascist Italy had created its own VGH, the Tribunale Speciale per la difesa della Stato, to meet the challenge. The VGH was now almost five years old and had more than justified its existence, Thierack said. A few months later the president of the Second Senate, Engert, who was also the VGH's vice-president, stressed that the court's task was exclusively to deal with those crimes such as treason and economic sabotage which could destroy the foundations of the state.[50]

Of the many treason cases, one in particular preoccupied the army and the VGH. On 27 January 1937 the Reichskriegsgericht, the Military Court, had sentenced the gunner Paul Kompalla to death for Landesverrat.[51] His brother Ludwig Kompalla, a civilian, had participated in the act and was tried before the VGH, which sentenced him to eight years' hard labour.[52] The army intervened in order to revise Paul Kompalla's sentence from death to imprisonment, a proposal which Hitler personally turned down and instead demanded that the VGH have another look at the sentence.[53] The result was that both were sentenced to death, but in the wake of this case extensive correspondence and deliberations took place with the aim of bringing the sentencing policy of the Reichskriegsgericht and the VGH into line. Freisler personally introduced some minor but nevertheless stringent paragraphs into the penal code, which allowed the VGH to act as a Court of Review but only to the detriment of the accused.[54]

Between August 1934 and September 1939 cases of high treason clearly outnumbered those of Landesverrat. The NS regime was determined to consolidate its position and never again part with the power it held. Hence virtually any action against the state and/or the NSDAP was by definition high treason. The VGH acted as one of the major guarantors of this sole claim to power. Though it tried individuals, the accused in VGH courtrooms were immediately labelled as groups, whether 'Communists' or 'reactionaries'. The definition of treason was all-embracing, including collecting money on behalf of political prisoners or their dependants, 'word-of-mouth' propaganda, distributing illegal literature and pamphlets. These offences were all the more serious when aimed at members of the state or party institutions, the police or the army.[55] But even before the war, public criticism of the regime could lead those who uttered it before the VGH, though there are several cases of acquittals where it could be proven that the accused had acted in an angry mood, had a general tendency to argue or was simply intoxicated.[56]

As far as high treason was concerned, paragraph 83, part 3 of the StGB comprised four sections which were widely used. First, it outlawed any form of political organization outside the NSDAP. Such organizations could only be directed against the NSDAP and therefore constituted the organizational preparation of high treason.[57]

Secondly, any attempt to infiltrate the army and police forces constituted high treason. It need not actually have been carried out; the intention sufficed. Criticism of party and government to members of 'the protectors of the Reich' counted as 'infiltration', as of course did the spreading of rumours and the distribution of illegal literature.[58]

The third area of offence was the production and publication of material, written or audio-visual, directed against the NSDAP and the state. By means of publications, recordings and illustrations a small group might exercise influence quite out of proportion to its actual size. Mass influence operated concentrically from small groups to larger ones. Thus any form of opposition to the NSDAP amounted to a treasonable and therefore punishable action.[59]

The fourth area was really a corollary of the third and applied to listening to illegal Communist or Soviet broadcasting stations. Although prior to the outbreak of the Second World War no law existed in Germany prohibiting a wireless owner from tuning into foreign stations, communicating the contents of these broadcasts to others constituted a treasonable offence, since 'the KPD and the Comintern have shifted their major emphasis upon propaganda by broadcasts, to fortify the morale of the Communists in Germany, to widen their knowledge of revolutionary tactics and strengthen their revolutionary impact.'[60]

Another important tool in the wide range of legal instruments available to the VGH was paragraph 139 of the penal code. Ominously, it stipulated that anyone who knew of treasonable activities or their preparation and failed to report them was guilty either of high treason or Landesverrat.[61] Even the Reichsgericht in 1934 had agreed to this reformulation.[62] The VGH further sharpened this paragraph by arguing that he who planned treason was also prepared to carry it out and therefore failure to denounce such a person was tantamount to treason[63] – an interpretation, as will be seen, which gained its full weight in the trial of the bomb-plotters of 20 July 1944.

Sections 3 and 4 of paragraph 139 of the StGB applied to Germans living abroad who committed treasonable acts against Germany. The VGH saw the KPD as the exponent of world communism and world revolution, its major agency being the Comintern. Whoever supported the KPD supported the Comintern, world revolution and the domination of Germany by Bolshevism. None of these aims could be attained without the prior overthrow of the NS regime.[64] Any pro-Soviet activity by Germans in Russia or elsewhere was thus treasonable and those who returned to Germany immediately ran the risk of prosecution for treasonable actions. However, as late as 1936 the VGH prosecutor's office was prepared to state that membership in a foreign Communist Party did not necessarily fall within this definition of treason, only where the foreign organization aimed at revolution in Germany.[65]

The outbreak of the Spanish Civil War in 1936 caused initial uncertainty in the Ministry of Justice. As late as 27 December 1937 Gürtner was still declaring that entry into the 'Red Spanish' army or recruitment for it constituted high treason only if it could be proven that the accused also indirectly supported revolutionary action against the German government.[66] Yet on 18 February 1937 a law had been passed making it illegal to participate in the Spanish Civil War[67] – despite the fact that by this time the Legion Condor was fighting with Franco. The law thereby served two purposes: it provided a window dressing for the Committee of Non-Intervention of which Germany was a member; and it offered a weapon to be used exclusively against German participants on the Republican side.

But confusion still continued. When after the outbreak of the Second

World War and the fall of France large numbers of former German members of the International Brigades were handed over to Germany[68] the German Armistice Commission assured many of them that if they returned to Germany they would not be prosecuted (whereupon the Armistice Commission was asked no longer to give such assurances). But as late as 1942 the VGH prosecutor's office issued instructions according to which no prosecutions should be raised against individuals who had returned to Germany on the basis of assurances given by the Armistice Commission. If, however, a Communist had also been active in any other way against the German Reich, he should be prosecuted; his membership in the International Brigade, however, would not be included in the indictment. The number of former Brigadists who were handed over to the Gestapo and SD for execution is still a matter of debate, although probably fewer than is commonly supposed were killed.[69]

From the moment of its inception the VGH's activities were directed against the Communists, since theirs was the only party prepared to advocate the overthrow of the NS regime. Conversely it was the NSDAP's declared aim to demonstrate publicly that it would deal with the Communists rather differently and more decisively than the Weimar Republic.[70] The Reichstag fire had provided the occasion for mass arrests of KPD members, though the majority were released again after a few months and remained unmolested as long as they refrained from any political activity other than on behalf of the NSDAP.

Those who did not were exposed to the full force of vengeance. Mathias Thesen and Robert Siewert had been KPD members of the Reichstag and in August 1933 Thesen was arrested, accused of high treason and sentenced to three-and-a-half years of hard labour. After he had completed his sentence he was re-arrested and transferred to a concentration camp, where he again agitated against the NS state with the result that he came before the VGH. There he was sentenced to four years' hard labour, to be served in Sachsenhausen concentration camp, where in October 1944 he was shot on Himmler's orders. Siewert's fate was identical.[71] Walter Duddin, a former KPD member of the Prussian Diet, was sentenced on 10 August 1934 to three years' hard labour for preparation of high treason because he had acted as leader of the illegal KPD in Thuringia.[72] The same punishment was meted out to Willi Melhorn, another former KPD member of the Reichstag, on 17 November 1934.[73] A long list of other prominent Communists and of those less prominent could be added. Many perished; some, like the former Reichstag deputy of the KPD, Fritz Selbmann, who was to become a Minister in the DDR government, survived.[74]

The VGH's reasoning in trials of Communists is made quite clear in a judgment of 5 February 1936:

> Already before the National Rising the KPD was pursuing the overthrow of the government and the Constitution by force. These aims are well known from numerous trials before the Reichsgericht and the Volksgerichtshof.
>
> After the organization of the KPD and its subsidiary organizations were smashed by the National Socialist government, every KPD activity was prohibited. From that point the KPD began illegal attempts to reconstruct the party organization, its subsidiary organizations like the Rote Hilfe (RHD) and the Revolutionary Trade Union Opposition (RGO). Preparations for this illegal work had already been made in the autumn of 1933. The aims of the KPD, as their pamphlets show, remained the same. Now as then – and after the National Rising in increased measure – the KPD aims at the overthrow by force of the German Reich and at the establishment of a Workers' and Peasants' Republic according to the pattern of Soviet Russia.
>
> Since the prohibition of its organization and of the activities which made open recruitment possible, the KPD initially publicized ideas with pamphlets which had been produced abroad and were brought in considerable quantities across the frontier to be distributed in Germany. Partly, though in smaller numbers, these pamphlets were also produced in Germany illegally. Partly also the printing plates were produced abroad, secretly transported into Germany and used for the production of pamphlets. Providing, producing and distributing of the pamphlets lay in the hands of technical leaders and agitation and propaganda leaders in the Reich, its districts and sub-districts. Besides the endeavour to circulate their ideas in printed form among the masses and thus influence them ideologically, the aim of the KPD since the beginning of its illegality was to reconstruct its organization. . . . The whole of Germany is divided into districts and sub-districts headed by political leaders who follow the instruction of the *Land* leadership which is located inside Germany and which in turn is subordinate to a Reich leadership, whose seat is abroad, where the greater part of the leading men of the KPD have escaped to. Also the Reich leadership of the so-called 'Technical *Apparat*' which is concerned mainly with propaganda by pamphlets has its seat abroad.
>
> The illegal organization of the KPD is widespread. It is aware that the number of its followers who have remained in Germany is too small in order to realize its aims. Therefore it endeavours to cooperate

with other Marxist parties pre-dating the National Rising in Germany, such as the SPD and the SAP, who have been equally prohibited and operate in exile, i.e. from alien territory. . . . The aim is the overthrow of the government . . . to create a united front to overthrow by force the common deadly enemy: the National Socialist government and its constitution (*sic!*). Within the frame of the illegal reconstruction of its party apparatus the KPD also aims at the reconstruction of free trade unions under its leadership. In the pursuit of this aim it is mainly interested in creating cells at the factory level.[75]

Despite its tedious repetitiveness, the VGH's assessment of Communist activities in Germany was, broadly speaking, correct and was vindicated by subsequent cases among which that of the former KPD deputies in the Reichstag Robert Stamm and Max Maddalena in 1937 were probably the most prominent. The appointment of Thierack as president of the VGH in 1936 meant also stiffer sentences. Stamm was sentenced to death; Maddalena received life imprisonment for their underground activities on behalf of the KPD.[76] Former NSDAP members who had become Communists could expect no leniency and in such cases the death sentence seems to have been the rule.[77] Splinter groups of the KPD were persecuted with equal fervour:[78] 'in spite of their relatively small numbers they must not be underestimated.'[79]

Social Democrats and trade unionists, in other words non-Communist organizations of the left, were as much a target of the VGH as Communists. The SPD had been officially prohibited by decree on 22 June 1933,[80] by formal law on 14 July 1933.[81] Violations of this law attracted penalties of hard labour or imprisonment of up to four years, but these provisions were largely ignored by the VGH especially after 1936. It considered sign of the SPD and the trade unions and their activities as preparation for high treason. Indeed the VGH could fall back on a judgment of the Reichsgericht of 1934 in which it declared that the SPD had now become a revolutionary party.[82] Equally affected were the SPD's subsidiary organizations such as the Reichsbanner Black-Red-Gold, several members of which were sentenced to various terms of hard labour on 21 August 1935.[83]

Former NSDAP members fared just as badly. A number of members of Otto Strasser's Black Front, for example, met their deaths by VGH decision. Strasser had broken with Hitler in 1930 with the slogan 'The Socialists are leaving the Party!'[84] His brother

Gregor stayed – to become one of the victims of the Röhm purge of 1934. It is difficult to take Otto Strasser seriously politically; theoretical consistency was not his strength. It seems more appropriate to describe him as a national-revolutionary maverick, and his close confidants around him appear of the same mould, like Major Buchrucker, one of the former commanders of the Black Reichswehr and the initiator of the short-lived Küstrin putsch of 1923.[85]

In a judgment of 20 February 1935, the VGH condemned the Black Front as highly treasonable.[86] Two years later the first Black Front member was sentenced to death, a Jewish student by the name of Helmut Hirsch, who after 30 January 1933 had fled to Prague where he later joined Strasser. He was assigned the mission to assassinate National Socialist leaders with the aid of explosives, if possible kill Hitler himself. He managed to cross the German frontier but was arrested in Stuttgart where he was to receive the explosives. Put on trial before the VGH he was sentenced to death and executed on 4 June 1937.[87] On 20 November of that year, several more members of the Black Front faced the VGH; all were sentenced to varying terms of hard labour.[88] Strasser's doctor was acquitted in July 1938 because the VGH accepted his argument that his relationship with Strasser had been purely personal and social and he had not been a member of the Black Front, and no evidence of any treasonable activity could be produced.[89] Subsequently two further members of the Black Front received hard labour and prison sentences respectively.[90]

The 'National Bolsheviks' were a typical product of Berlin of the late 1920s. Their leader, Ernst Niekisch, a Bavarian and former primary school teacher, had already been once convicted for his participation in the Bavarian Soviet Republic in 1919. Subsequently he joined and departed from several nationalist fringe groups on the left until, in 1929, he founded his own publishing house in Berlin in which he published his journal *Der Widerstand*. Like Strasser, he supported a pro-Soviet, anti-West German foreign policy. At various times he collaborated with Hans Zehrer's neo-conservative 'Tat Circle', which took its name from *Tat*, 'the deed', and national revolutionaries such as Ernst Jünger and Ernst von Salomon.[91]

Niekisch continued publishing his journal until it was forbidden in December 1934. In March 1937 he and 71 of his associates were arrested. However, it took until 10 January 1939 for Niekisch and two of his associates to come to trial before the VGH (Thierack presided). The court defined Niekisch's group as a political party and thus in violation of the law of 14 July 1935, a party whose aims were in direct conflict with those of the NSDAP. Niekisch's own published words provided ample evidence and he received a life sentence. Niekisch's wife and eighteen other members of the group were tried on 18 February. Four, including his wife, were acquitted; the others were sentenced to terms of imprisonment or hard labour.[92]

Besides these groups there was also an anarcho-syndicalist group inspired by the ideas of Proudhon, Bakunin and Prince Kropotkin. Most gave up their activities in January 1933, although a few 'loners' continued, of whom several were convicted before the war broke out. None received the death sentence.[93] Other 'loners' motivated by personal rather political grievances gave cause for the VGH to intervene, and here, too, the sentences were harsh: a sentence of eight years of hard labour could be received even by someone obviously mentally deranged.[94]

Until 1936, the VGH tended, while applying the existing law widely and with extreme flexibility, to sentence individuals relatively mildly. Thierack's appointment as president represents a watershed as does the growing influence of Himmler. From 1936 onwards the sentences would be markedly more severe.

To conclude from these pre-war examples of the VGH's practice that Germany was already a fully fledged totalitarian state, its population exposed to the full brunt of NS terror, would be a mistake. We must, at least at this stage, differentiate between totalitarian claims and totalitarian reality. In contrast to the war years, the VGH's sentences were not widely published, and were mostly to be found in legal journals or those intended for the NS leadership corps. The population at large was unaware of the treason courts. Hitler was still reluctant to apply the maxim of 'he who is not for me, is against me' with its full vigour. The individual was as yet not forcefully integrated into the 'new state'; he could still stay aloof from it. Membership figures of the NSDAP signify very little in this context, since after 1933 opportunism or simply the question of economic survival played a large role.

There were many corners which the process of *Gleischschaltung* had not reached. Within some of these corners developed the circles of potential resistance to Hitler; equally they harboured the 'inner immigration' of those who had little desire to be publicly associated with National Socialism. Gottfried Benn, disillusioned after his initial flirtation with National Socialism, Ernst Jünger and Ernst von Salomon are but three examples.

Though the German press was gagged, those who could afford it could buy British, French and Swiss newspapers at the newsstands – at least until September 1939. If one wished to inform oneself via the new medium, the wireless, then even with a simple and cheap *Volksempfänger*, the People's Radio, one could tune in to Radio Beromünster, to Paris or London.[95]

True, many emigrated, some because they had to, some because they believed they had to and some because they wanted to. The apostle of political Dadaism, the artist George Grosz, emigrated, although twenty years later he renounced his former 'stupid, pseudo-scientific Marxist and Freudian views. . . .'[96] On the other hand his fellow artist Otto Dix stayed, and though not allowed to exhibit publicly he could continue to paint and sell his works privately. One of his best customers was Germany's Foreign Minister, Joachim von Ribbentrop, who had his children painted by him. He was arrested and imprisoned only once – by the French in 1945 who took him prisoner as a member of the Volkssturm, Germany's last-ditch homeguard.[97]

Between 1933 and 1939, and to some extent to 1945 and beyond, Germany exhibited a split consciousness determined by totalitarian claims on the one hand, and by day-to-day reality on the other, a theme most recently and incisively explored in Hans Dieter Schäfer's *Das gespaltene Bewusstsein* (The Split Consciousness).[98]

However, where the individual, or groups of individuals, moved out of their 'corner' into active resistance to the NS state, then the full power of a perverted law met him. It was all the more sinister and deadly because behind the power and force of the law no longer stood *Justicia* but the nascent SS state of Himmler and Heydrich and all that these two names imply.

# 6

# Freisler as Publicist

Between 1936 and early 1938 Freisler himself was exposed to criticism from a dangerous source – none other than the Reich Minister for Propaganda and Popular Enlightenment (indeed this was his full title!), Dr Joseph Goebbels. From the moment the NSDAP had come to power Hans Frank had envisaged not only the reform of the German penal code, but the replacement of the existing one by a new Germanic common law. While the plan never came to fruition, it had proponents other than Frank, and the VGH was pressed to prepare a new penal code. Various drafts were in circulation and even those were very slow in coming. When one such draft reached his desk in August 1936, Goebbels noted: 'Vexation with the Ministry of Justice. There the old spirit still dominates and Freisler is a man of big words but no action.'[1] When in December he saw a new version of the draft, he wrote: 'Have studied the new draft for new German penal code. Quite good. Some of it is still too verbose, this is Freisler's hand.' But then in the same diary entry he seems to have had second thoughts. 'Looking at the draft for a new German penal code closer I still find much to object to. In some points rather old-fashioned.'[2] Throughout his life Goebbels tended to be critical of men whose stylistic quality was equal to his own, and was especially scathing when they were not from his ministry.

This, however, was not the issue which caused Goebbels to direct his full wrath against Freisler. The cause rose out of the measures directed against some sections of the Catholic Youth Movement, as a result of which the leader of the Catholic Peace Union Chaplain Joseph Roussaint had been in 1937 arraigned before the VGH. The Catholic Peace Union was alleged to have been offered Communist support and said to have taken it. Roussaint was found guilty and sentenced to fifteen years' hard labour.[3] What caused Goebbels' wrath was that Freisler's brother Oswald was defending the accused. He pressed Freisler to exert pressure upon his brother,[4] compelled Gürtner to call the two brothers to order,[5] and on the following day indicated that the NSDAP's own court might initiate proceedings against Freisler's brother.[6] A few days later Goebbels received material with which to finish off Oswald Freisler.[7] On 30 April 1937 he noted with satisfaction: '[Oswald] Freisler expelled from the party by the Führer.'[8] By mid-May 1937 he was describing Roland Freisler as 'an absolute failure.'[9] On this charge he was to change his mind by the end of the war.

Goebbels' judgement sounded less harsh after Freisler had discussed with him the problems of the judiciary in September, but he still insisted that the judiciary's independence and full tenure in office should be abolished. 'These stupid jurists think they are the masters of the state. One must throw them out.'[10] In the beginning of 1938 the U-boat ace of the First World War, the Protestant Pastor Niemöller, was tried and in the proceedings immediately took the initiative – a public embarrassment. 'I speak with Freisler and brutally tell him my opinion. He is quite frightened and admits serious mistakes. The presiding judge is a reactionary.'[11] Niemöller spent his time, until 1945, in a concentration camp.[12]

No doubt interventions such as this were bound to be sources of personal and political disquiet. Freisler's work load was considerable and there can be no doubt that as Secretary of State he was a very busy man. He not only had his fill of work, but also travelled extensively during the pre-war period. He delivered lectures in Italy, where he was decorated with the Grand Cross of Italy. To this was then added the Medal for the Commemoration of the 13 March 1938 (the *Anschluss* of Austria), the Commemoration of 1 October 1938 (the *Anschluss* of the Sudetenland) and the NSDAP Long Service Medal, which he held in all three classes, bronze, silver and gold.[13]

Besides being a meticulous administrator and a prolific letter writer, Freisler published on a massive scale from 1934 until his appointment as president of the VGH. His articles covered several broad areas which are best dealt with thematically.

The discussion of the nature of the state had, of course, been a central topic of German philosophers and legal thinkers from Hegel to Carl Schmitt.

In Hegel's view, the state stands above society; the individual's role within it is that of a member rather than that of a private person and civil society compared with the state is inferior both in an historical and moral sense. The state stands above the individual, party and sectional interests as the supreme arbiter and judge. By means of its institutional framework, it absorbs all internal conflicts. Therefore, however, it is all the more important it be a state based on the firm foundation of law, a *Rechtsstaat*.[14]

Less than a century later other criteria had begun to intrude into the definition of the state. Tonnies posited the 'community',[15] Herder the Volk,[16] although the latter was increasingly racially defined and perverted. Max Weber tried to counter this approach by defining the national state as 'the secular organization of the nation.'[17] To him the state was principally a political association based on the subjective decision of the members of the nation which, of course, corresponds in this respect with Renan's definition of the nation state as the *plébiscite de tous les jours*, the daily voluntary decision of the individual in favour of his nation and state.[18]

For National Socialism there could be no such voluntary subjective decision. The individual was born within the racially defined *Volksgemeinschaft* and, therefore, belonged to it and owed it total loyalty. The corollary to this was that anyone making the subjective choice to stand outside the Volk committed treason. In other words, the allegedly organically grown *Volksgemeinschaft* took priority over the institution of the state; the NSDAP as the Volk's representative organ claimed, as we have already seen, primacy over the state.

These ideas never fully took hold in the legal sphere. Since National Socialism at no stage ever produced a fully coherent ideology, old concepts continued to exist, though in the course of twelve years many of them were eroded and deprived of their original content. The civil and criminal law code stayed intact, although the penal laws were substantially amended and penalties for violations drastically sharpened to serve NS ends.

Yet as far as Freisler was concerned, and that goes for many others within and without the German judiciary, the fiction of the *Rechtsstaat*, the state based on law, was upheld. One may even wonder whether most of them were aware of this fiction, whether they did not privately deny that they served and lived in a *Rechtsstaat*. But this speculation cannot apply to Freisler; he was a firm believer apparently without private doubt:

> The *Rechtsstaat* is the organized form of the life of the Volk, which combines the entire vitality of the Volk to secure the right of the Volk domestically as well as against threats from abroad. . . . For only this concentrated *völkisch* force will do, as only a concentrated charge was

capable of taming the tank threatening the Front. This organized form of bringing into action the concentrated charge of the *völkisch* force for the protection of the Volk is our concept of the *Rechtsstaat*.[19]

Apart from the fact that military similes and historical analogies (while not always correct) came easily to Freisler, what is notable about this quote is its racially defined concept of a Volk whose interests are to be served by the *Rechtsstaat*. This postulate can now barely be found in the mainstream of German legal thought, but apart from its racial connotation, it shows the influence of Carl Schmitt's 'friend-enemy image' (*Freund-Feind*) theory.[20] The state is the sum of the Volk, a conclusion which at first sight could be described as liberal and democratic. On closer examination it shows three major NS perversions: first, the Volk is defined in exclusively racial terms, with the *Rechtsstaat* as a subordinate force, a formulation which has little to do with Herder's originally formulated concept which was devoid of any qualitative valuations.[21] Secondly, it negates the individual's subjective choice as to whether he wants to belong to the Volk.[22] Thirdly, it implicitly draws on the *Führerprinzip*,[23] which effectively deprived any member of the *Volksgemeinschaft* of any active and positive participation in the political and institutional decision-making process.

Nevertheless, Freisler spoke out against the 'total state'. This was not in order to defend the rights of the individual, but because of the danger that the state could become an end in itself and not a means to an end, the end not being the individual but the Volk, the German race itself. For National Socialism the state was not a mere instrument but rather the institution which was organically linked via the NSDAP to the Volk. In consequence the state's institutions would have to be permeated by the NS spirit, which would provide the wisdom and the catalyst for NS action.[24]

Implicit in this argument, then, is not the totalitarian state as such, but the totalitarianism of National Socialism and its ideology. The state is no more than a mirror image of the ideology which permeates it. Apparently unable to define a coherent National Socialist ideology, Freisler circumvents this dilemma by blandly asserting that the organic worldview would defeat any attempt to define and categorize the NS state. But in doing so he attempts to square the circle, because at no point does Freisler ever state what this ideology is in any detail; all he asserts is that National Socialism is a total ideology, yet the NS state is not a totalitarian state.[25]

The unity of leadership and Volk had been established by various legislative measures, eliminating from the Reichstag the rule of the 'irresponsible dead number'[26] through the process of *Gleichschaltung* which destroyed the centrifugal forces of particularism, and by all civil servants being bound personally to Hitler by way of their oath. Leadership, responsibility, loyalty, obedience, 'these are in the life of our state legal concepts and they are its foundation because each of them contains a task which will never be fully accomplished, a task that will always remain a task.'[27] This allegedly existing external challenge is one side of the coin of which the other is Hitler's Social-Darwinian notion of life as an eternal struggle which, irrespective of the victories Germans would achieve, would continue, and would have to continue as part of the eternal cleansing process by which the race would retain its purity and vigour.[28]

For Freisler this process is an organic one which defies rational categorization and analysis and can only be understood intuitively. That understanding is an essentially rational capacity and therefore in contradiction to intuition, Freisler failed to see. Volk, Race and Blood are the pillars of the NS *Rechtsstaat*,[29] he asserts categorically; that this brand of *Rechtsstaat* may defy and contradict hitherto universal and traditional notions of fundamental justice, he seems readily to accept. The principles of justice are thereby subordinated to NS claims, whatever they may be.[30]

There is no room in this concept of the state for the separation of powers. Freisler considers this an obsolete legacy of the past, of a time of distrust between the people and its political leadership. Since under NS leadership this distrust has been overcome, so claims Freisler, there is no longer any need for the separation of powers. Into its place steps the organic unity between leader and followers and 'confidence in the healthy unity of the Volk, confidence in the strength of the Volk and the challenge to maintain this attitude throughout its history. . . .'[31]

Fundamental to the maintenance of NS state is the attitude of its judiciary and its lawyers who must not be constrained by any notion of an essentially static natural law. Under no circumstances must the law ever ignore the biological laws of nature. Law, in order to secure Volk and state, must forever be organic and developing, adaptable to changing circumstances, 'for the law which today is good can be bad tomorrow', but at all times its primary consideration has to be to maintain the health of Volk and state and the protection of its interests.[32] Thus, Freisler implies, the law is no longer a normative absolute but an instrument of political expediency.

The Volk by way of the intuitive wisdom of its Führer expresses its will through the institutions of NSDAP and from there through the institutions of the state, and this will in its manifold expressions at all times must serve its own survival. Hence, once Germany under Hitler's leadership had stepped beyond its territorial and ethnically defined boundaries, the law and with it the application of justice applied to Germans only. Peoples under German domination, particularly those of the east, may then live under their own laws but only in so far as this corresponds to Germany's interests, so Freisler argues. Special legislation would administer the law for 'inferior races' such as Jews and Poles, though not to dispense justice, but to assert Germany's superior dominance (*Oberherrschaft*) and to ensure Germany's racial purity.[33] It is no overstatement, therefore, to conclude that Freisler's concept of state was of one based on brute force expressed and contained not by moral considerations but by expediency.

Freisler published his first lengthy excursus on the *Führerprinzip* in the aftermath of the Röhm purge notwithstanding the fact that one of his close associates of earlier years, Gregor Strasser, was among its victims. The Führer had acted and it was the duty of all Germans to follow him.[34] What Freisler may have thought privately, we do not know: for this period there are no sources available to us. On the other hand Hans Frank did raise a personal protest about the manner of the proceedings which hardly endeared him to Hitler.[35]

Freisler argues that Hitler had acted in a state emergency and therefore what he did was not only necessary but legal. Behind this argument there obviously lay the weight of a congratulatory telegram from the Reich President;[36] in addition, Hitler's claim to have acted in this hour as 'the executor of the Supreme Law'[37] was post factum 'legally' endorsed by Gürtner's decree of 3 July 1934.[38] According to Freisler, the German people had no option but to close ranks and follow its leader unconditionally, come what may. Emergencies especially would provide the great testing ground of the *Führerprinzip*. Legal limitations which apply to the individual German do not, in Freisler's view, apply to the NS leadership, since in its actions it fuses the legal functions of the state in all its aspects. An individual's emergency action carried out without the explicit order from the Führer would be acceptable only if it was fully in accord with the leadership of the Volk.[39]

To turn the *Führerprinzip* into a constituent part not only of Germany's leadership but also of the judiciary should have alerted many inside and outside the legal profession. However, with the exception of Hans Frank, no voice of protest was raised. On the contrary, it seems that the belief prevailed that with the elimination of Röhm and the effective neutralization of the SA, political radicalism within the NSDAP had been silenced and from then on an essentially moderate and reasonable Hitler would prevail. Admittedly, so many may have thought, it was a nasty business, but one could hardly make omelettes without breaking eggs.

But the *Führerprinzip* still represented one of Freisler's favourite leading themes in his publications, so much so that in one particular instance he falsified an important quote. Tracing back the *Führerprinzip* to Charlemagne, he quotes the Carolingian Emperor's advisor, the English monk Alcuin in the original Latin:

> *Dum dignitas imperialis a Deo ordinata ad nil aliud exaltata esse videtur nis populo praesse, proinde datur a Deo electis potestas et sapientia; potestas ut superbos apprimat et defendat ab improbis humiles; sapienta, ut regat et doceat pia sollicitudine sujectos.*

Freisler then supplies his own translation:

> Since the dignity of rule, established by God, is obviously elevated to no other purpose than to lead the people and to further it, for this purpose God gives *the chosen one* (my emphasis) power and wisdom in order to restrain the mighty and protect the weak against the wicked wisdom so that with pious solicitude he may lead and teach his subjects.

Where in fact the Latin original refers in the plural to 'the chosen ones', Freisler reduces it to the singular in order to make it applicable to Hitler alone.[40]

Freisler places great emphasis on the value of the application of the *Führerprinzip* in the courtroom. At all times it is the judge who is the presiding 'leader' of a trial; his leadership is more important than the dusty files containing the evidence. Freisler even demands that fellow judges and lay judges give preference to the leading role of the judge rather than to the law.[41]

(Though Freisler takes this admonition to the point of excess, in actual substance the role which a presiding judge plays in a trial to this day in Germany actually favours this development. In an English court, the courtroom drama is concentrated on the battle, sometimes extremely sharp, between the prosecution and the defence, while the presiding judge plays a relatively passive role, directing questions to the defendant in the dock or on the witness stand only in order to clarify points. In his summing up he essentially directs the jury on points of law. By contrast, in a German court the role of a presiding judge is also that of an investigator, which even today, depending on the judge's temperament, can become also that of an inquisitor. His role is not confined to clarifying points and the final summing up to direct the jury: his role is as active as is that of the prosecution and defence. Excesses have happened in the past and no doubt will happen in the future; the problem lies in the judicial system and the temperament of the judge concerned. But it is quite a different matter when such behaviour is elevated to represent the norm, sanctioned by the *Führerprinzip*. And in no other court was the role of the judge as the 'leader' more pronounced than in the VGH.)

In a state governed by the *Führerprinzip*, loyalty in the sense of *Treue* or the old Anglo-Saxon *trewe* was a corollary. Indeed as we shall see in later chapters it found its way frequently into Freisler's judgments when he was president of the VGH, and he used it frequently in the course of a trial.

> Loyalty can be sworn only to one man. Loyalty is sworn by every official of the movement to the Führer. Loyalty is being sworn by every civil servant to the Führer. Loyalty is being sworn by every soldier to the Führer. Everyone, irrespective of the position he holds – and however long the line of superiors to him may be – everyone swears loyalty to the Führer. Only to him![42]

As this quote, and for that matter his other invocations of loyalty during court trials, shows, Freisler appears to have held a very crude and unreflective concept of loyalty, the entire range of which is exemplified by his invoking the story of how the last of the Ostrogoths rallied round their king Teja in the battle on the foot of Mount Vesuvius in 522 against the Byzantines under Narses.[43] The source of his concept of Germanic 'loyalty' is easy to detect. It owes little to any deep study of old Germanic legal concepts and much to a highly popular and immensely readable novel by the late nineteenth-century German historian and writer Felix Dahn, *Ein*

*Kampf um Rom* (A Struggle for Rome), which describes the fate of the Ostrogoths from the death of Theoderic the Great to the death of Teja, their last king. Freisler himself often embellished on the novel by asserting that the Goths fought with their king to the last man, whereas Dahn remains faithful to his main source, Procopius, according to which after the death of their king, Narses allowed the remaining Goths, with the dead king on their shoulders, free passage north 'until we/ in the cool blue sea/ find the Isle of Thule' (*bis wir/ im kühlen blauen Meer/ die Insel Thule finden*).[44]

The true nature of Germanic loyalty, of *Treue*, is to this day a controversial subject among scholars.[45] However, whatever the controversies on other points, a consensus exists over the conclusion that an all-embracing, specifically Germanic concept of *Treue* has never existed except in historiography. Tacitus in his *Germania* was probably the first to point to such a concept, but he saw his major task as posing as a warning contrast between decadent Roman society and the virility of the unspoilt Germanic tribes.[46] We also have the example of the *Anglo-Saxon Chronicle* of how the death of King Cynewulf (757) is being avenged by his followers.[47] But this tells us very little about the origins and complexity of Germanic *Treue*. Instead of an unconditional loyalty, there was a contractual relationship binding both: *Treue um Treue*, loyalty for loyalty, with a legal character, though this relationship was not specifically Germanic. Under the Carolingians this relationship found a new definition which no longer allowed a distinction between loyalty and obedience.[48]

The notion of a specifically Germanic concept of loyalty emerged around the turn of the fifteenth to the sixteenth century among German humanists in the region of the upper Rhine. After the invention of the printing press it gained wide popularity, especially among the rebellious German peasantry who in their pamphlets argued that the law was divinely ordained and that man could not make law, at best he could discover old law or 'find' it. The law, of which the contractual relationship of *Treue* was an essential ingredient, was in essence static and indestructable. A thousand years of 'un-law' could not invalidate eternal existing law, divinely ordained and framed in a spirit of liberty. Law stands above states, kings and princes; royalty could not make new law but merely apply existing law, to which they were as much subject as was the humblest peasant.[49]

However, a breach of *Treue*, and thus the law, had taken place when formerly free peasants became unfree serfs. This was the belief firmly held among the peasants who rebelled against their lords. It was a revolt against the emerging territorial state whose aim it was to maximize its efficiency by a common administration and a common legal code. For this process old Germanic law seemed singularly unsuited, not least because of its regional diversity. The alternative was codified Roman law; all that was required was its adoption for the entire territory to have a law book, systematically structured and unified.[50]

But for the peasants this law was 'Un-law', written in a language they did not understand. They rose on behalf of the old common law; far from being lawbreakers they perceived themselves as the defenders of the law against their territorial lords. The nascent territorial state was the lawbreaker, not they, the peasants. In a pamphlet addressed to the Emperor they accused their lords of having broken loyalty, *die Treu gebrochen*, and appealed to him to restore the law as they had known it since time immemorial.[51]

Leaving aside the question of the practicability of application of old laws to a modern and highly complex environment, even the application of the complex arrangement summarized under 'Germanic' *Treue* would have caused havoc in Hitler's Germany. It would have contradicted the very notion of the *Führerprinzip* as formulated by the National Socialists because it would have introduced *Treue um Treue*, loyalty in return for loyalty, a contractual relationship between leader and followers, equally binding them both, both being under the law. Considering the utter abuse and perversion of the concept of loyalty in and by the NS state, how it was invoked and what crimes it was used to justify, this digression seems not only justified but necessary.

Whether Freisler was aware of the intrinsic complexities of the concept he frequently used seems more than doubtful; what he invoked was a highly romanticized version of something of which in principle he knew very little. Irrespective of this, however, any breach of loyalty he immediately branded as treason, though here again he was dealing with a problem whose complexity in an age of ideologies could not have eluded him, but which he chose to ignore in order to transform and apply from the narrow and perverse perspective of National Socialism as he interpreted it.

Given Freisler's simplistic interpretation of loyalty, it followed that his view of treason was equally crude. Indeed he argued that where genuine change of attitude towards high treason and Landesverrat had not taken place (that is, where treason was not punishable by death), no genuine revolution had occurred. As an example he was never tired of citing '1918' and the creation of the Weimar Republic; in his view the Republic had made only cosmetic changes as far as high treason was concerned, while it had actually reduced the penalties for Landesverrat.[52]

Just as the NS concept of Volk and state differed from the concept of liberalism and this again from the concept of absolutism, he argued, so National Socialism had its own specific character. The Enlightenment in Prussia had ensured that the ruler was coterminous with the state; the ruler was the first servant of the state.[53] What Freisler forgot to add was that since the advent of the Prussian General Legal Code (*Allgemeine Preussisches Landrecht*) the king was also subject to the law.[54]

What in the age of absolutism was a crime against the state was divided into high treason and Landesverrat and so it had remained throughout the liberal and liberal-democratic period. Freisler considered this division 'a-national' and posed two questions regarding high treason. Could high treason be really condemned? And could the individual through a conflict of duties be driven into committing high treason? The first question he answered with a wide and generous interpretation of what constituted high treason, specifically the actions taken by National Socialists between 1919 and 1933. The second question he answered negatively, because accepting a higher moral and supranational duty over and above the duty of loyalty of the citizen to the NS state, putting for instance humanity above the Volk, would deprive both high treason as well as Landesverrat of their very basis. Hence, in order to return to a 'normal pattern of development' it was necessary to abolish the distinction between high treason and Landesverrat.[55] Though separate crimes, then were nevertheless identical, since they attacked the very life of the Volk.

Political amnesties up to 1933, Freisler reasoned, were little but the liberation of prisoners of the political struggle.[56] The state had been far too generous; repeatedly granted amnesties indicated that the crime was not taken seriously by the state. The same tendencies, Freisler thought, were observable in the case of Landesverrat. Moreover the concept of the Magna Carta, of the protection of the individual against the state, appeared to Freisler as a barrier against any prosecution for Landesverrat. The destructive force of liberalism, internationalism and pacifism had already eroded the basis of

Landesverrat. Therefore the new NS state of the future, the new NS penal code would have to be determined by one maxim: 'My country – right or wrong!'[57] Of the ambiguity inherent in this maxim Freisler seems not to have been aware.

Freisler discerned the forces at work which were eroding the traditional concept of treason. But his nationalist blinkers prevented him from seeing the extent to which this erosion had already taken place and from recognizing the complexities inherent in the 'internationalization' of treason in an age of ideologies[58] which no longer respected national boundaries.

The definition of treason may vary from country to country and over time, but it has always been and still is a breach of loyalty. Upon loyalty rests the life of human communities, irrespective of their form and expression. But loyalty is a mutually obligatory relationship; what if one of the partners, in our case the state and its leaders, is the first to violate the mutuality of this relationship? Freisler evaded this question, proceeding instead from the a priori assumption that a breach of loyalty could only be carried out by an individual, or a group of individuals against the state, or more specifically against the NS state. In so doing he ignored Hitler's justification, in *Mein Kampf*, of tyrannicide if the leader of the people was leading it into disaster,[59] and his words before the NSDAP Reichstag deputies: 'If any one of you believes that my actions are determined by anything else but my love for Germany, then I give him the right to shoot me down.'[60]

Treason, however, as so much else, is part of the historical development of politically organized communities. Each profound change within them very often begins with an act of treason. For centuries in European history loyalty was the relationship of person to person. The Germanic word *Rat* related to the care of God, or to his secular representative on earth, the king, and his obligations to the community. *Raten*, or to counsel, embraced everything which a king owed to those whose loyalty he enjoyed and to whom he in turn owed loyalty and hence protection, care, and leadership.[61] *Verraten*, treason, is tantamount to a deliberate departure from this community of the protected, whether by a member of it or by its king. The relationship was a direct and personal one. Within the feudal system vassals governed their territory with the same powers and constraints, which bound them to king or prince. As long as central and western Europe acknowledged only one God and one Church, however, as long as it was accepted that all secular power derived from the grace of God, treason as such did not exist. Heresy served much the same function: as a breach of loyalty against the king, heresy was a breach against the divine ordained order.

After the Reformation the concept of loyalty became secularized, although nowhere was the change institutionalized. Only with the French Revolution, which abolished both God and the king, did a new relationship between loyalty and treason emerge. For the first time, the notion of popular sovereignty, within the context of the nation, was recognized in parliament and public opinion. The crime against the state as well as against society replaced the crime committed against the Crown. But as the ideas of the French Revolution, with their universal claims, transcended the French nation, the age of ideology was born.

Loyalty began to decrease in the same measure as it became depersonalized. Our own century has witnessed the dramatic progression of treason from an individual act to an act of groups or even masses. Freisler was by no means an exception in shutting his eyes to the consequences of this development. No legal code makes provision for it to this day, and it seems more than doubtful that one can make adequate provisions without at the same time destroying the fabric of the state.

What is significant for our own age is that virtually overnight whole groups can become traitors, or at least be considered potential ones.[62] Marshal Pétain became head of the French state in 1940 with an overwhelming vote of the French National Assembly which also endowed him with far-reaching dictatorial powers. It was General de Gaulle and his group in London who were the traitors while both acted, Pétain in Vichy, de Gaulle in London, in the interest of France as they interpreted it. Four years later, Pétain and all who had followed him had become traitors. Who can clearly tell whether the early atomic traitors did not act in the belief that it was too dangerous for one power to hold a monopoly over the atomic bomb?[63] In other words, loyalty, obedience and the values of past centuries have become highly problematic. They have been replaced by impersonal institutions whose only provision for the protection of their citizens is the passport, while the concepts of treason and patriotism have become increasingly fluid and relative.

Freisler's elastic definition of treason is therefore by no means unique; what is unique and barbaric is the extent to which he felt treason should be prosecuted. For Freisler the greatest national security threat was posed by acts of high treason and Landesverrat.

To him, as to many of his contemporaries, these acts were of such gravity that any consideration of their motivation became irrelevant. The memory of '1918' was never erased. In his view, in all criminal offences, but especially in treason cases, the *will* and the *intention* were as dangerous as the actual crime and should therefore be punished with equal force.[64] This alone would ensure that the law was returning to ethics of the Volk. Only the Führer could determine the character of the Reich; anyone committing a crime with the alleged aim of improving the Reich was as much a traitor as any other perpetrator of treason.

In one of his articles Freisler compiled a formidable list of crimes. This list included offences that had as yet, i.e. in 1938, not formally entered the German penal code, but for which he found ample legal justification by broadening the scope of existing laws. To stamp out criticism from the church, for example, he proposed strengthening the legislation Bismarck had introduced during the *Kulturkampf*, which had never fully disappeared from the German penal code.[65]

The most important of these crimes was 'racial defilement', the violation of the Law Protecting the Blood.[66] In his 1933–4 proposals to reform the penal code, he had argued that 'blood and soil' were the most sacred German values of which a racially pure marriage and protection of the family are basic components.[67] A few years later he explicitly stated that National Socialism was characterized 'by its biological point of view, that it looks at the Volk biologically, because its history and future development were and are biologically determined. Therefore the law also can be conceived biologically.'[68] Previously held notions of law, whether based on 'natural law', on the 'contract theory' or the notion of 'the general will', had all ignored the biological order of things. The new German law would have at its core the concept of the biological substance of the Volk in order to ensure the purity of the race. It was the task of the state 'to stop the racial mixture in Germany which had been going on for centuries' and to aim at restoring and restocking the 'Nordic blood' which alone was decisive for Germany.[69]

This process could be endangered by three major offences against the law: 'racial defilement', that is to say sexual intercourse or marriage between Germans and Jews; 'offences against racial honour', which in effect meant the association in public between Germans and Jews; and 'endangering the race', which amounted to a blanket provision covering any possible violation of the 1935 Nuremberg Laws, including such actions as counter-propaganda against 'the measures for the enlightenment of the German people.' The protection of the race was a paramount task not only for the government but for the German judiciary. The duty of the German nation and every German citizen was to practise 'racial hygiene'. Its violation was tantamount to treason.[70]

Interestingly, Freisler himself never explicitly occupied himself with the alleged 'Jewish problem' and, as will be seen later, even evinced doubts about the existence of a 'Jewish world conspiracy'.[71] His true mission was establishing the VGH at the apex of the judiciary and replacing the Reichsgericht. This, not anti-Semitism, was the principal aim of Freisler's writing career.

The problem of the judiciary up to 1933, Freisler told his readers, was that it had lacked a leader. It was the same as Germany's confusion without the Führer. 'A great strong man who would have embraced everything by the force of his personality did not exist. The ideas which circulated were certainly good, there were sufficient for two generations; ideas are excellent, but men are better'[72] – with these words Freisler characterized Wilhelmine Germany, conveniently plagiarizing the by then exiled Veit Valentin's study of the revolution of 1848–49 in Germany.[73]

The solution, of course, was for the VGH to become the Führer of the judiciary. Through its unswerving adherence to the leadership principle, it would lead both the judiciary and Germany itself to rejuvenation. The participation of the Volk would be ensured through its lay judges, while the senate presidents would be the Führers whose directives would be followed unquestioningly by professional and lay judges. Thus the judiciary would return to the true 'Germanic' form of a trial, this is to say to the romanticized visions Freisler entertained about a 'Germanic' trial.[74] Next to the prosecution it would be the judge's task to see to it that everything at issue would be cleared up swiftly and thoroughly. He was to lead and to decide; fellow professional as well as lay judges representing the Volk could advise but not decide. Responsibility lay with the presiding judge alone. Freisler hammered home this message time and again, especially after the outbreak of war. From the judges of the VGH down to the lowliest lawyer, everyone had to be 'a Soldier of the Law.'[75]

A secondary aim was reforming the penal code. This was nothing short of a crusade to make it correspond with NS ideology. Although his proposals ultimately failed, two of Freisler's notions gained general acceptance in the VGH. The first was 'the intuitive feeling of

the Volk', meaning that acts violating this nebulous notion could
lead to a death sentence, the second that the intention to commit
treason was tantamount to having committed it.[76] Freisler argued
that within generally stated NS propositions (the precise nature of
which he did not define) the judge 'will have much greater freedom
of movement, and will therefore confront with much greater success
the great variety of life, instead of being confined by narrowly
phrased legal paragraphs'.[77] The law could at best provide
guidelines; only as such could it be successful and provide full
protection and justice within the context of the Volk.[78]

What this really amounts to is an admission on Freisler's part of
his failure to achieve a thorough overhaul of the penal code. In lieu
of consistency, he advocated an arbitrary legal anarchy within which
the existing law was to play the role of the handmaiden, its
provisions being no more than *Gummiparagraphen*, rubber paragraphs, which could be expanded or contracted as the situation
required. Sentences should be severe, hard labour should mean what
it said.[79] As will be shown in our final summing up, the VGH
imposed a roughly equal number of death sentences and sentences of
imprisonment, although the death penalty was favoured. The death
sentence as such inspired Freisler's more fanciful imaginings. While
rejecting public executions, he advocated self-execution, such as the
'poison bowl' by which the condemned person would administer
poison to himself – another return to an alleged 'Germanic'
practice.[80]

To administer 'justice' quickly also entailed the overhaul of court
proceedings. Freisler therefore cut down on the reviews of cases. Not
only, in his view, did reviews waste time but they 'would shake the
faith of the public in the judiciary'[81]; an occasional miscarriage of
justice was well worth the public faith in the infallibility of the
judiciary. Basically there were only valid two reasons for a re-
hearing. The first was when a judge grossly violated existing rules,
the second if new and conclusive evidence was found. If a re-hearing
would revise the judgment only marginally it should not be held.[82]
Again it was within the realm of the VGH that these maxims
dominated the proceedings.

The problem of the recruitment of future members of the judiciary,
i.e. reform of recruitment procedures, had been one of long standing.
Freisler's suggested radical cure was that it should no longer be the
judiciary itself which selected its recruits, but the institutions of the
NSDAP. Reform in this area could not be carried out overnight, all

that could be done at the moment was to ensure that *Referendare* and *Assessoren* qualifying to become judges would no longer, as had been the practice for centuries, work for nothing, but would be paid adequately, so that recruits could come from all sectors of the *Volksgemeinschaft* and not only from those families which could afford to finance their sons for an indefinite period of time.

However, three major criteria should determine selection. Firstly they should be of good health, considering the heavy burden resting on a judge. Health standards would find further improvement by the recruit showing himself active in one of the NS formations, and, of course, sound health was also equated with coming from racially sound stock. Secondly, a recruit in the judiciary should have to provide evidence of his leadership qualities, which he would initially obtain in the Hitler Youth and then within other NS formations. Thirdly, he should provide evidence of his predisposition to find full satisfaction in the work of the community. This would show itself in his behaviour at school, and such predisposition would bring a potential candidate face to face with biological questions. The study of history alone would inevitably lead him into this direction. This in turn would produce an awareness of the needs of the Volk and of the factors essential for its existence.[83]

After the campaign in Poland, Freisler considered the 'German East' as the great testing ground that would separate the wheat from the chaff. There was to be found not only the testing ground for 'Germanic' reconstruction, but also an area in which the future judge would have to deal with such 'inferior' races such as Poles and Jews, for whom special legislation such as the Polenstrafrecht, a penal code applicable to Poles only, existed. Its application did not allow for any sentimentality; all that mattered was the interest of the German Volk. A new generation of colonizers would have to emerge who would take up the task which the Teutonic knights had let slip out of their hands. 'All who have proved themselves in the east will place their stamp on the judiciary in its totality.'[84]

According to Freisler, the judiciary's role was not that of a controller of the executive, but that of a faithful follower of the leadership.[85] The law, while no doubt inadequate, was still binding insofar as it could be adapted by National Socialism, but for the judiciary as for everyone else the principle of the separation of powers no longer existed. Such a separation, based as it was on distrust, had been overcome by the Führer and the NSDAP and replaced 'by the healthy unity of the Volk'.[86] Unity was also

demonstrated by the fact that judges in general were appointed on
the recommendations of the Gauleiters to the Ministry of Justice,
while judges for the VGH were directly appointed by Hitler or his
deputy. 'Hence the German judiciary has every reason to be proud to
be the first institution to have implemented the unity of the National
Socialist Movement and Volk and state.'[87]

With this assertion Freisler implicitly negated the independence of
the judiciary. Within the context of an organic unity such as
National Socialism claimed to be, the independence of the judiciary
had, in Freisler's view, become obsolete. The independence of the
judiciary had to be ignored as much as individualistic tendencies,
because National Socialism derived its very strength from the ever-
flowing fountain of the Volk; one of the major tasks of the judiciary
was to keep its water clean.[88] It was not up to the judges to make the
law; this was the task of the Volk represented within the NSDAP and
led by the Führer. All the judiciary had to do was to apply it in the
interest of the Volk, not in that of the individual.[89] Or, to put it
crudely, and crudeness is after all the essence of this message, the first
and foremost task of the judiciary was to subordinate itself to the
totalitarian will of National Socialism.

Freisler amplified on these points after 1939, when a total of
eleven new decrees were imposed for the duration of the war.[90] One
of them – the Extraordinary Measure for Wireless Owners – drew
Freisler's particular attention. The decree prohibited Germans from
intentionally listening to enemy and neutral broadcasting stations
and forbade the spreading of news derived from these sources.
According to Freisler what should be punished was not curiosity as
such, but the deliberate self-emasculation of a German's soul, which
if added to the damage caused when the news was spread could have
a defeatist effect.[91] The fear of a repetition of November 1918 was
forever in the background.

As far as the role of the German judiciary was concerned in
territories returned to Germany by annexation or occupation, the
same maxim applied: 'Harshness against the enemy of the Volk
means the well-being of the Volk. Once it had been lacking and then
the consequences followed – 1918!'[92]

That harshness reigned supreme is not simply shown by the
practice of the VGH which in the main operated inside Germany, but
by the practice of special courts in occupied territories and the
activities of the Einsatzgruppen.[93] This topic is outside the scope of
this study, but it is worth noting by way of example that the penal

code for Poles and Jews in 1941 deprived these groups of any, even merely formal, protection of the law.[94]

While looking at eastern nationality groups as inferior races (*Untermenschen*), Freisler in one of his last published articles examined the German judiciary in the Netherlands. He emphasised the 'comradely' collaboration between the German and Dutch judiciaries, 'comradely help' given in a 'comradely task'.[95] That this was not just mere wishful thinking, international research has firmly established. Collaboration in the Netherlands – as elsewhere in western Europe – flourished, the Dutch for example, providing proportionately the largest contingent of volunteers for the Waffen-SS forces fighting in the Soviet Union.[96] Of course, today it is more convenient to cherish the memory of Anne Frank.

Perusing Freisler's publications as a whole, the reader is at first sight impressed by the clarity of their style and exposition. Freisler, at least in this instance, practised what he demanded from the German judiciary: 'The German Law Preserver thinks, speaks and writes in German!'[97] His articles are free from the complicated, often confusing language that marks the legal profession. Each article appears as a cogently argued piece of work – although they are not devoid of the hallmarks of an ambitious charlatan.

However, this positive impression is quickly dispelled when one analyses them thematically and realizes what they actually spell out. Then the message is reduced to the crude claims of NS totalitarianism for which Freisler in his articles endeavoured persuasively to supply nothing less than legal sanction – even if this explicitly demanded the gross deviation and perversion of existing law in order to proclaim the naked and unbridled doctrine of uncontrolled power.

In early 1942 Freisler suddenly curtailed his stream of publications. With the death of the Reich Minister of Justice, Gürtner, an interregnum set in, in which the Secretary of State, Schlegelberger, acted as temporary head of the Ministry. This increased the administrative burdens on Freisler considerably, so that it is more than well-inspired speculation to say that time was no longer available to him to pour out his flood of articles. In less than two years after Gürtner's death Freisler himself was in a position to practise remorselessly the maxims he had so far called upon the German judiciary to apply.

# 7

# Judiciary in Crisis 1939–42

Given Hitler's endemic distrust and express loathing of the legal profession, a sentiment shared, as we have seen, by Goebbels and many others of Hitler's close circle, the German judiciary operated in a permanent atmosphere of crisis.

One example which Hitler never tired of citing to his secretaries to illustrate the 'idiocy' of the judiciary was how he, as 'Führer and Chancellor', found himself nearly arraigned in court and lost the case without a hearing ever taking place. The case had arisen out of the Röhm purge, in the course of which one of Franz von Papen's close associates, Dr Erich Klausener, Ministerial Director in the Ministry of Traffic and Director of the Catholic Action Group, was murdered. Less than a year later, in March 1935, his widow sued Hitler, charging him with involvement in a murder plot, and demanding damages. As accessories to the act she also charged Göring, Frick and Gürtner. Within two weeks of raising the charge, her lawyers were arrested by the Gestapo. They expected the worst, but Klausener's widow argued that she had acted on the advice and instruction of an SS-Oberführer by the name of Breithaupt, who had pointed out to her that on 13 December 1934 a law dealing with compensation claims specifically relating to the events of 30 June 1934 had been enacted. Under this law, charges had to be pressed before compensation could be considered. Her lawyers were freed and although Hitler did not have to make a court appearance an undisclosed but substantial sum was paid to her in compensation for her husband's death. For Hitler the affair was a constant embarrassment.[1]

After the war broke out in September 1939, the law became harsher as well as quicker in its execution. The Kriegsstrafrecht, the War Penal Code, was applied with draconian severity against anyone who was found guilty of having infringed it. Yet as late as 1941, after Gürtner's death, the Secretary of State, Schlegelberger, was still complaining about the mildness with which German courts were treating offenders and thus endangering the whole German people.[2] There existed a large degree of cooperation between the judiciary, the Gestapo and the SD, but up to 1938–9 the judiciary still restrained to some extent the extra-legal activities of these services, although there were individual cases in which the police 'corrected' in the most drastic form what it considered judicial errors.[3] During the course of 1939 the number of cases increased in which those acquitted by the VGH were re-arrested by the Gestapo and interned in a concentration camp.[4]

On 27 March 1937 the Reich Ministry of Justice had accepted this practice in the case of two Jehovah's Witnesses. It had no reservations about their transfer to a concentration camp, the Ministry said, and this applied to other political cases in which the accused had been acquitted or completed their sentences.[5] Whenever such individuals were acquitted or about to be released from prison, the Gestapo received prior notice from the Reich Ministry of Justice so that policemen could be present to re-arrest them. The VGH had initially expressed qualms about this practice. In a letter of 21 January 1938, Thierack was still declaring that in his opinion and that of all other members of the VGH, it was insufferable to think that after an acquittal those concerned should be taken into 'protective custody' by the police.[6] But just over a year later one of the chief prosecutors of the VGH informed Gürtner on 29 July 1939:

> I have discussed with the president of the VGH the issue of whether people accused of activities hostile to the state should be handed over to the Gestapo when their arrest can no longer be maintained by the VGH. Until further order I shall proceed in future as follows: in agreement with the president of the VGH, when acquittal has occurred, or the sentence is already covered by the period which the accused has spent remanded in custody, I shall in principle hand over such persons to the Gestapo except when the Gestapo has expressly stated it is unnecessary to do so. If an acquittal, because of proven innocence, is likely to occur, I shall ask the Gestapo whether a transfer is required or not. Should the Gestapo declare that it would be necessary to carry out protective custody, I shall initiate the transfer.[7]

Leaving aside the question of its obvious illegality, what this decision amounted to was a complete capitulation of the judiciary in general and the VGH in particular to Himmler's SS state. In the meantime, on 26 July 1939, Hitler had personally ordered that all persons in the 'protective custody' of the judiciary should immediately be handed over to the Reichsführer-SS for transfer to concentration camps.[8] The reason for this, as indicated in one of Freisler's articles, was the demand for labour for the Four Year Plan.[9] As a celebration of Hitler's fiftieth birthday on 20 April 1939 it had been planned to release a great number of concentration camp inmates. Himmler opposed this measure on the grounds that he had insufficient labour in the camps and that there was a shortage of labour in the prisons themselves.[10] But more important was the increased labour needed to achieve the targets set by the Four Year Plan.[11] Some of those in custody were occupied with useless work:

> At an inspection of the hard-labour prison of Brandenburg-Goehrden by the Chief of the Clemency Office of the Führer's Chancellery, it was noticed that a large proportion of those in protective custody are occupied making or painting cardboard soldiers on behalf of private firms. In view of the far more important, and, from the standpoint of the Four Year Plan, more urgent work, such as is concentrated on the brick manufacturing section of Sachsenhausen concentration camp, the Führer has ordered that all those subject to preventive and protective custody be transferred and be made available immediately to the Reichsführer-SS.[12]

During the first few months of the war a tendency emerged for courts other than the VGH to attempt to try cases of treason and similar offences. Freisler immediately counteracted this trend with a circular letter to all Oberlandesgerichte in which he excluded the following crimes from their immediate jurisdiction:

(a) malicious violations of the Law for State and Party and for the Protection of the Party Uniform of 20 December 1934;
(b) all cases of high treason and Landesverrat;
(c) violations of the Law for the Protection of People and State of 28 February 1933; and
(d) economic treason.[13]

Since there were no means of appeal against a VGH judgment, Gürtner considered some kind of appeal court necessary and on 4 November 1939 he established one by creating within the VGH a special senate to examine a VGH judgment against which an appeal was raised.[14] However, this new senate, consisting like any other VGH senate of both professional and lay judges, tended to favour the objections of the prosecutor who would consider a judgment too mild over those of a defence counsel who would consider it too harsh. Nor could the defence counsel appeal directly. He could appeal only via the prosecutor.[15]

A further issue was the treatment of Poles living in the territories annexed from Poland by Germany, as well as of Russians yet to be annexed. On 24 June 1941 Freisler addressed a letter to the Reichsstatthalter and Gauleiter Greiser, head of the Warthe district of German-annexed Poland, in which he summarized a previous verbal agreement on the establishment of drum-head courts martial and the use of judicial prisoners as hostages, an agreement which also extended to the SS Security Service (SD). The letter expressed agreement to the establishment of such 'courts' and stated that these would be incorporated into the new penal code for Poles. The powers of clemency and the decision to carry out executions by hanging would also be delegated to Greiser and the respective SS authorities.

In addition the letter gave Greiser the right in the territory for which he was responsible, the Wartheland, to mount trials on his own initiative, that is to say courts martial against Poles accused of having committed serious offences against the 'German Task of Reconstruction'. The courts were to hand down only two sentences, imprisonment in concentration camps or the death penalty. Poles were given the 'privilege' of being defended by Polish lawyers, of which 718 were admitted in 1940. Of these, 635 expressed their 'great gratitude' to the German authorities that no Jews had been admitted and that 'at long last Jewish influence had been eliminated in the Polish judiciary.' However, there was also agreement that there was little purpose in granting clemency in any event. The death sentence was to be carried out by hanging, and hostages would be taken from among the remand prisoners. This decision would counter public criticism as well as Hitler's own criticism of the mildness of the judiciary.[16]

What could never be completely eliminated was what had already caused Gürtner to complain in September 1939, namely the clash of jurisdiction between the VGH, the Wehrmacht judiciary and the police's drum-head courts martial.[17] The VGH tried to come to a clearly defined arrangement with the SS on matters regarding the penal code for Poles and Jews, but Himmler rejected any attempt by the VGH to take the place of the SS courts; normal conditions, Himmler said, as they existed in the Altreich (Germany within the frontiers of 1937) 'had not yet been achieved . . . and could not be expected in the near future.' While the introduction of the German penal code in the East was accepted, the operation of 'Special Penal Directives' continued, under which Himmler carried out his own so-called judicial proceedings.[18]

By the end of 1941 the VGH consisted of six senates, the first of which was presided over by the president of the VGH, Thierack. The senates occupied a total of 78 professional judges and 74 prose-cutors. Except for three judges and two prosecutors, all were members of the NSDAP, but most had joined the party after March 1933 in 'the landslide of change of mind' as Freisler had called it.[19] In addition there were 81 lay judges.[20] Of these, 71 were higher functionaries of the NSDAP and its formations and the rest Wehrmacht officers of the rank of colonel and above in the three services. None of the Wehrmacht lay judges was an NSDAP member.[21]

As a result of the Russo-German Non-Aggression Pact of 23 August 1939, the Russians handed over a substantial number of German Communists to the German authorities as an unsolicited 'gesture of good will'. The majority of them appear to have been transferred immediately to concentration camps.[22] But in spite of the pact the outbreak of war heralded heightened activity by the VGH against the illegal KPD, a trend which accelerated after the German invasion of the Soviet Union. From then on, any Communist activity was judged not only as high treason, but also as an offence furthering the aims of the enemy within the meaning of paragraph 91b of the StGB. Many former Communist officials were immediately arrested on suspicion of espionage. Moreover the charges listed on indict-ments against them shifted from high treason to Landesverrat, because any offender was considered an agent of 'World Bolshevism' and of the Soviet Union.[23] The boundaries between high treason and Landesverrat became increasingly blurred.

Penalties were drastically stiffened. On 28 May 1942 the Oberreichsanwalt, the Supreme Prosecutor, reported to his ministry that the Austrian general prosecutors and the Gestapo in Vienna had pleaded with him to stiffen sentences against Communists and argued that even for Communists in subordinate positions the death sentence should be mandatory.[24] Schlegelberger, then temporarily administering the Reich Ministry of Justice, stated in a *Führer-information* (a short special report submitted on important issues to Hitler) that while the war lasted Communist high treason was to be punished more severely than formerly, without exception by death, since all Communist actions represented Landesverrat.[25] From 7 July 1942 the VGH passed the death sentence on all Communists, including those accused of being former members of the KPD or of one of its subsidiary organizations.[26]

That the Communists themselves remained active in Germany is reflected in the Situation Reports of the Oberreichsanwalt[27] which frequently refer to discoveries of Communist cells and organizations. Moreover, of course, the persistent attempts by the Communists to reorganize themselves under cover inside Germany, especially after Germany's attack on the Soviet Union, are reflected in numerous VGH judgments.

Postal workers in the Frankfurt Central Post Office had begun before the war to organize themselves because of allegedly bad working conditions and low pay. Once war had broken out Communists took over the leadership of the postal workers' group and the group began to distribute illegal anti-war propaganda and revolutionary material. They published leaflets and collected the addresses of soldiers serving in the field to whom they addressed their propaganda material. This, however, caused their discovery and on 24 June 1942 three Communist leaders and another cell member from Frankfurt were sentenced to death on the charge of high treason.[28]

This case must, within the context of this study, stand as representative for many others concerning Communists condemned by the VGH up to 1945 though the reasoning of the VGH in pronouncing a death sentence is illustrative of its general attitude:

> Anyone who creates the first preconditions for the Communist rats to gnaw at us . . . acts in the interest of Communism. Communist activity . . . is at the same time treacherous and favours our enemies who know that they cannot overcome our soldiers. . . . They are dependent upon finding traitors within our midst to erode us from within. Everybody knows that. . . .[29]

The accused, a 72-year-old Berlin carpenter,[30] was sentenced to death.[31] In another case concerning Communists active since 1942 but discovered only in 1944 the judgment stated:

> Anyone who in the fourth year of the war disseminates . . . leaflets among German armaments workers, and does so persistently and on such a scale, knows that he is wilfully undermining our internal

cohesion and our iron readiness to sacrifice everything for victory and
that in the midst of our society he is carrying on the business of the
enemy. The Communist B. has known that clearly. Thus he has become
a traitor to our Volk in its struggle for life, and has become an
honourless serf of our enemies. His attitude aimed directly at a
repetition of the year 1918 and he is therefore in the highest measure
dangerous. The requirements of cleanliness of our Volk and the
protection of the fighting Reich therefore demand the death sentence
for this traitor. Even though he may now regret what he has done . . .
the remorse of the traitor cannot be accepted, and what he has done is
quite sufficient to exclude him forever from our midst.[32]

Subsequent trials were occupied with other left-wing activities in
the same factory in which this condemned man worked, the Borsig
A.G. in Berlin, but those found guilty were sentenced only to stiff
terms of hard labour and one accused was acquitted.[33] However,
Berlin remained a fairly fertile field of Communist activities
throughout the war.[34]

Before the war Communist activity was also directed against the
Reich from outside Germany, notably from France, Holland,
Czechoslovakia and Scandinavia. The units were operated in the
main by German exiles who established contacts with their comrades
inside Germany.[35] After the outbreak of war and the German
occupation of parts of Scandinavia and western Europe many of
them were caught and condemned. It was irrelevant that the accused
had already been deprived of their German citizenship:

The accused has committed highly treasonable acts favouring the
enemy both from abroad and from within Germany. Attempts, as for
instance infiltrating two instructors into Berlin, took place. But apart
from those, he has, while a German abroad, also committed acts
favouring the enemy. It is not only citizens of the Reich who are
Germans within the meaning of the paragraph of the penal code
concerning acts favouring the enemy, but everyone of German blood
and any former German citizen who because of his activities has been
deprived of German citizenship – at least as long as he has not
obtained another citizenship.[36]

The main centre of Communist activity against Germany was, of
course, Moscow. After the German invasion, the Russians dropped
German agents behind German lines and in Germany itself. In May

1942, for instance, German Communist agents were dropped into East Prussia, followed a month later by two more in West Prussia. The first two were caught as soon as they touched ground, the other two, whose task it was to make contact with the 'Red Orchestra' in Berlin, were not caught until later in the year. All were sentenced to death.[37]

The discovery of the Communist espionage Red Orchestra group, which had operated clandestinely in Göring's intelligence centre,[38] raised the issue of which court should try the total of 117 accused. Göring and the Luftwaffe judiciary favoured the Reichskriegsgericht, because most of the accused were serving members of the Luftwaffe or civilians in its employ. Hitler favoured the VGH, although Göring won his point. But the sentences were such as to cause Hitler's enraged protest and he categorically demanded the review of several of the sentences and the imposition of the death penalty.[39] The case also seemed to justify Hitler's public diatribe against the German judiciary.

Charges of 'favouring the enemy' (*Feindbegünstigung*) and 'undermining Germany's defensive power' (*Wehrkraftzersetzung*) could mean anything from harbouring an enemy prisoner to maintaining social contact with him or simply giving him a piece of bread; from spreading propaganda among the German population and armed forces to telling a political joke.

Thus a Berlin artisan was sentenced to death because he had described Hitler as the greatest butcher in all history. The judgment read: 'Everybody knows that the Führer has done everything to avoid this war and, when the enemy imposed it upon him, at least to localize it. A German who makes such an utterance propagates Communist ideas in a particularly dangerous manner, he is laying the groundwork for Communist high treason by *Feindbegünstigung* and *Wehrkraftzersetzung*.'[40]

A Wiesbaden interior decorator, a former fee-paying member of the SS and still a member of the German Labour Front (DAF) and the NS People's Welfare (NSV), had in 1942 stated that Hitler's real name was 'Schüttelgruber'. This together with other criticisms of the NS regime sufficed to cause his death sentence, although in the early 1920s he had fought against the separatists in the Rhineland and had been imprisoned by the French.[41]

A German miner who had shown a British leaflet to a tram-conductress, saying that what it contained was the truth, was sentenced to death on 7 January 1943. As the court's opinion stated:

The defence is of the opinion that the defendant was an eternal complainer. With this the VGH cannot agree. Anyone with enemy leaflets in his hands who states that the people should revolt, dangerously erodes our home front at a time when the German soldier is risking his life in heavy fighting. This can amount to a stab in the back of our army. It is highly dangerous – as was shown in 1917–18 – even when the first, the second and additional stabs do not hit their target. And everybody knows that, even the somewhat mentally limited defendant. He is therefore no mere complainer, but a dangerous enemy of our fighting Volk. He does exactly what the English are banking on when they drop their mixed load of bombs and leaflets: to erode the Volk, to weaken its defensive power in a total war and to favour the enemy.[42]

A more prominent case was that of Professor Dr Robert Havemann. A pharmacologist and lecturer in the Friedrich Wilhelm University of Berlin, Havemann had gained international renown for his scientific discoveries. He created the European Union to which he recruited other intellectuals. He demanded that the Union's programme should contain no NS principles and should include both Bolshevik and Anglo-Saxon elements. By September 1943 Havemann and three of his associates had been arrested. They faced the VGH on 15 December 1943; all four were sentenced to death. However, Havemann had been conducting research for the army for a number of years, and the date of his execution was therefore postponed time and again until he was liberated in 1945. A number of other members of the European Union were acquitted.[43]

Earlier in the year a young war widow was sentenced to death because she had told political jokes. One of them featured Göring and Hitler sitting on top of the Berlin broadcasting tower. Göring asked Hitler to do the German people a favour – to jump off.[44]

The 'Erosion of Germany's Defensive Will' paragraph was also applied to illegal youth organizations. Those youth leagues which had existed before 1933 and which tried to reorganize themselves after 1933 were subject to the same persecution as political parties.[45] Although some of their leaders emigrated, they were unable to organize themselves effectively underground in Germany.[46] Many of these groups were little more than bands of teenage criminals.

The Rhineland saw the termination of the Edelweiss Pirates, for instance, a group of sixty, which was smashed in 1943.[47] Among other things they were accused of *Wehrkraftzersetzung* because they had encouraged other youths not to attend to their Hitler Youth

wartime duties and had attacked Hitler Youth members. Furthermore they had burgled homes and plundered the possessions of those
bombed out. After the 1944 capture of Aachen by the Americans
when Cologne was declared a 'war zone', a new Edelweiss group
formed itself, acting much in the same way as their predecessors. A
dozen of its members, aged between 15 and 16, were caught, and
after drum-head courts martial, were publicly hanged.[48]

All of these cases were based on the paragraphs of the penal code
dealing with attempted high treason, or on provisions of the law
associated with those paragraphs. Landesverrat was still a separate
issue, however much Freisler tried to equate them. Before the war
there had been a number of spectacular cases involving a Polish
officer who as a spy had derived his information from three
secretaries in the Reichwehr Ministry. The Polish officer received a
life sentence which, however, he did not serve as he was exchanged
for a German spy sentenced in Poland. Two of the secretaries were
sentenced to death, a third received a life sentence.[49] In the course of
the pre-war years the laws, as we have seen, had been substantially
tightened and extended and sentences severely stiffened. Landesverrat
and obtaining state secrets by espionage were dealt with under
paragraphs 89 and 90 of the StGB, while during the war the category
of acts favouring the enemy, *Feindbegünstigung*, was extended to a
previously unforeseen degree. The application of paragraphs 89 and
90 depended very much on how the term 'state secret' was
interpreted. The practice of the VGH was to exclude from its scope
matters which were kept secret only for domestic reasons, as well as
matters that were purely confidential and not explicitly secret. For
the VGH, in its initial phase, a crime was committed only when the
objective was to damage the external security of the Reich.[50]

On 26 May 1933, espionage was extended from military secrets to
cover all state secrets, and to that end paragraph 92a was added to
the StGB.[51] This allowed the VGH to convict anyone caught in the
preparation of Landesverrat rather than actually committing the act.
The Landesverrat section of the StGB also covered purely criminal
acts because they represented a breach of the loyalty every German
owed to the Reich. Even asking someone to commit Landesverrat
now carried the death sentence. During the war the planning of
Landesverrat was punished by death in particularly serious cases,
even if that planning had taken place years before the war.

This retroactive legislation had been occasioned by the trial of Leo

Sklarek, an emigrant.[52] Together with his brother, who had in the meantime died, Sklarek had figured in one of the most prominent corruption cases of the Weimar Republic and had already served four years of hard labour. After his release he had moved to Prague and was arrested there when Germany occupied Bohemia and Moravia. In the autumn of 1941 he was brought before the VGH charged with Landesverrat. He received a sentence of eight years of hard labour, but this was too mild for Hitler's taste, so Schlegelberger issued a backdated demand for the death sentence. Although Sklarek himself was not sentenced to death, he was handed over to the Gestapo, sent to concentration camp and duly murdered.[53]

On 6 May 1940, paragraphs 3 and 4 of StGB were amended to include all acts committed abroad by Germans against Germany as well as acts committed by foreigners.[54] However, the prosecution of a foreigner required the prior assent of the Reich Ministry of Justice.[55] Moreover, foreigners had a greater chance of receiving a life rather than a death sentence.

With the extension of German power in Europe the scope for catching former emigrants had become extremely wide. Czech and Polish files, particularly, yielded unexpected results both in quantity and quality. Much the same was the case with the files of French, Belgian and Dutch intelligence services. On 30 July 1940, the Oberreichsanwalt reported that during the occupation of the Netherlands a whole series of cases of Landesverrat had been discovered and that a connection between the Dutch and British intelligence services had also been uncovered. Similar reports were submitted on Belgium and France. By June 1940, 77 cases of Landesverrat had been discovered in Polish files.[56]

Naturally the question arose as to whether foreign officers, officials and the like could be prosecuted along with agents who were Germans. During a conference in the Reich Ministry of Justice on 16 February 1940 it had been argued that such a prosecution, especially of the Polish intelligence service, was possible in principle, but not obligatory insofar as the person concerned had acted abroad, except when he had used very despicable methods.[57] It was agreed that Polish intelligence operatives should be prosecuted only if they had committed their criminal acts on German territory, or were 'racial Germans' or 'private collaborators'. The same ruling applied to occupied western territories.[58] But the OKW, the supreme command of the armed forces, and the RSHA, the SS Reich Security Main Office, clashed over the issue. While the Wehrmacht advocated a generous handling of such cases the RSHA argued for a more rigorous course. Agreement was finally reached between them on the basis that the Wehrmacht would undertake to keep the RSHA informed of all cases.[59]

This sudden increase of Landesverrat cases increased the VGH's work to such an extent that Thierack on 18 December 1941 complained about the excessive and ever growing burden.[60] In spite of the Russo-German Pact, Soviet espionage in Germany had continued as strongly as ever, but their networks failed to elude German counter-intelligence, which kept them under observation until the period after 1941 when a number of Russian spy networks were broken up and their members arrested, especially in East Prussia.[61]

On 15 September 1942 a Jewish merchant from Brussels by the name of Blumberg was sentenced to death for espionage. The accused was actually an Italian subject who had lived for a long time in Austria-Hungary, Romania, Canada and France before settling in Brussels in the spring of 1930. In Brussels he was recruited by French intelligence and travelled to Germany several times before the war to spy on military garrisons and installations. The Germans discovered the relevant files, arrested Blumberg, tried and executed him.[62] It seems plausible to conclude that had he been a Belgian national and not a Jew he would most likely not have been indicted at all, or at the worst would have received a hard labour sentence.

In a similar case, a former Communist from Bremen who had been acquitted of high treason in Germany had emigrated to Antwerp in 1937 and been enrolled as an agent in Belgian and French intelligence. He supplied his employers with details of German harbours and shipyards, and hired another German as his associate. Together with several others, the two men were arrested. The German Communist in Antwerp escaped; of the others two were sentenced to death and the rest to long terms of imprisonment.[63]

More fully documented are the cases involving espionage on behalf of Poland. Thus a former member of the Reichswehr had, between 1924 and 1928, served Polish intelligence in Upper Silesia. He received his information from a serving NCO of the Reichswehr. Both were arrested and sentenced to death on 9 March 1943.[64]

Another case involved the Swedish military attaché and three Poles. In 1942, one of the Poles had informed the Swede that in Warsaw the Germans were printing general staff maps of Sweden. During the First World War the Pole had served with great distinction as an officer in the Austro-Hungarian army. He cited another Polish officer as his source, but the latter denied all knowledge. The matter could not be satisfactorily cleared up by the VGH and it acquitted the two officers accused on the original charge. The first accused, however, who had handed on the information to the Swede, was then tried on another charge and was sentenced to five years' imprisonment for negligently endangering the welfare of the German Reich. But the court acknowledged that he had not been motivated by an attitude hostile to Germany.[65] Similar cases arose in Bohemia and Moravia.[66]

In the west a case took place involving Landesverrat, the supply of arms to and otherwise favouring the enemy (Feindbegünstigung) as well as undermining the defence effort (Wehrkraftzersetzung). An Austrian had gone to France in 1929 in order to find work. However, after the Anschluss, at the request of his father he opted for German citizenship although he had in the meantime married a French girl. When war broke out he was temporarily interned, and when he was released he re-applied for French naturalization. At the same time he volunteered for the French army and served in the Foreign Legion until demobilized in southern France in the summer of 1941. He stayed on in France as a farm worker but in January 1943 was arrested by the German police and ultimately tried before the VGH. The judgment stated that the accused had been under the obligation to register for service in the German armed forces. He had evaded this duty and thus violated paragraph 5 of the KSSVO. At the same time he had committed Landesverrat by serving as a German citizen in the French army. Hence he was a traitor to his blood and Volk. His allegiance to Germany was no more than lip-service and 'the healthy intuition' of the Volk demanded his extermination. On 15 July 1943 he was sentenced to death.[67]

Under paragraph 91b of the StGB, Landesverrat included any activity on behalf of the enemy, including working in an enemy factory, recruiting and assisting volunteers to serve in the enemy's forces, obtaining and passing military information (even if not secret), assisting agents dropped from the air, freeing prisoners of war or assisting their escape, handing on enemy leaflets or using faked ration cards. The paragraph's provision that it was illegal to recruit volunteers to serve in the enemy's forces was applied with full severity to the population of annexed or occupied territories, where in many cases individuals or groups tried to reach allied territory to join, for instance, the Czech or Polish Legions.[68]

Even Germans who out of compassion aided the most underprivileged group of POWs, the Russians, or the so-called Eastern workers with food or food coupons risked the charge of *Wehrkraftzersetzung*. An official report of 1 August 1942 revealed that numerous trials were pending in which Germans were charged with aiding the escape of a total of 600–800 French POWs.[69]

During the night of 29 January 1941 the Reich Minister for Justice, Franz Gürtner, suffered a stroke and died. Whether with his death the last defence of the Rechtsstaat fell is more than doubtful, because in the course of his career he had moved so closely to the NS that, to all intents and purposes, all barriers between the judiciary (especially the VGH) and the NSDAP had disappeared. All he may have intended was to preserve the outward forms of the Rechtsstaat. Be that as it may, Gürtner's death caused an interregnum in the Reich Ministry of Justice. The chief of the SD and RSHA, Reinhard Heydrich, immediately endeavoured to fill the vacuum.

After the occupation of Bohemia and Moravia in March 1939, the Germans at first pursued a moderate line. Reich Protector Konstantin Franz von Neurath, until 1938 Germany's Foreign Minister, was essentially a man of moderation. But as early as 1940 important sections and members of the Czech resistance, the Obrana Národna (National Defence Struggle), were discovered and arrested. Hitler objected to the proposed trial and ordered the drawing up of an indictment.[70] As the number of Czechs filling the prisons increased, the VGH Oberreichsanwalt, Lautz, appealed again to Hitler's headquarters for leave to try these cases. Lautz received the permission, but it was coupled with Hitler's instruction that there be no death sentences. On Hitler's orders, death sentences already pronounced were to be suspended.[71]

Heydrich looked at all this with considerable suspicion, and so did Bormann and Goebbels.[72] Another who felt rather uncomfortable was Neurath's Secretary of State, Karl-Hermann Frank, himself a Sudeten German, who considered Neurath too soft for the job.[73] Considerable student unrest in Prague, in the course of which all institutions of higher education were closed, and the general unrest in the protectorate enabled Frank, Heydrich, Bormann and Goebbels to convince Hitler that a display of firmness was necessary to bring the Czechs to heel.

On 23 September 1941 Neurath was ordered to Hitler's presence and informed that the Führer had decided on sharper measures in the protectorate. Reinhard Heydrich was to be sent to Prague, ostensibly to deputize for Neurath, who for 'reasons of health' was to take extended leave. In fact he only returned to Prague to collect his belongings.[74]

Heydrich moved into Hradshin castle with a policy of 'carrot and stick'. Insofar as German relations with the Czech labour force were concerned, he was not unsuccessful. Nor did it take him very long to identify as the source of all unrest the 'autonomous government' of the protectorate headed by General Alois Eliáš, whose case was one of the most prominent in German-occupied Europe.[75]

Eliáš had fought on the Austro-Hungarian side during the First World War and after the founding of the Czechoslovak state he had continued his military career. In 1938 he was appointed commander of the 5th Czech Army Corps, and after the Munich agreement, he became Defence Minister, then Transport Minister and, after 28 April 1939, Prime Minister. When Paris fell in 1940, the SD found French files which provided evidence that Eliáš had personally maintained shortwave radio contact with Czech emigrants abroad.[76] The SD continued in its search for evidence against Eliáš and was apparently successful. Heydrich, then still in Berlin, suggested Eliáš's arrest but was stopped short by Neurath's intervention. Once Neurath was removed there were no more barriers to Heydrich's plans. His accusations against Eliáš can in essence be summarized in six points:

First, towards the end of April 1939, the Czech General Ingre had called upon Eliáš to assist in building up an underground organization and participate in its work. Apparently Eliáš had declined, but at the same time he had failed to report the approach to the German 'protecting' power.

Secondly, in the course of 1939, the Czech General Neumann had organized a military resistance group. Though Neumann was able to escape, one of his members was caught and implicated Eliáš, whom he said had been duly informed of the setting up of his organization.

Thirdly, also in 1939, a senior Czech civil servant, Schmoranz, had infiltrated into the newly established Czech Censorship Office former Czech intelligence officers whose task it was to collect information on German troop movements. This operation was discovered in August 1939 and the matter was handed on first to the Reichskriegsgericht and from there to the VGH prosecutor. Heydrich accused Eliáš of being fully aware of what had been going on; because of his former prominent military position it was unlikely that he was ignorant of the activities of former members of Czech military intelligence.

Fourthly, Eliáš was alleged to have transferred 50,000 Crowns to the head of another intelligence organization, Lt-Colonel Trebicky.

Fifthly, at the turn of 1939–40, the Czech Ministers Necas, Feierabend, General Gihak, as well as others, had escaped across the Slovak frontier disguised as locomotive engine drivers; Eliáš was suspected of having supported this venture.

Finally, from the spring of 1939 until the summer of 1940, the Lord Mayor of Prague, Klapka, assisted by the Prague City Treasurer, Professor Wenig, had given financial support from public funds to members of the Czech Legion and their dependants. They had also given financial support to prisoners of the Gestapo and further funds had been spent assisting former Czech officers to escape abroad and join the Czech Legion. Not only had Klapka informed Eliáš of these transactions, but Eliáš himself had made utterances throwing serious doubts on his loyalty to the German cause. As far as Eliáš was concerned, the prevailing situation in the protectorate was only a temporary one. Czechoslovakia, he was alleged to have said, would ultimately regain its liberty through the war. The German Luftwaffe was quite deficient in quantity and quality and the same applied to its communications. Klapka asserted that these remarks further encouraged him in the pursuit of his anti-German activities.[77]

Heydrich was determined to have the RSHA bring the case against Eliáš. On 25 September 1941 he visited Thierack in Berlin to inform him of the measures he intended to take in the protectorate and to ask how far the VGH had progressed in drawing up the indictment against Klapka. Thierack replied that he would have to be briefed. Heydrich agreed to this, while at the same time imposing the strictest secrecy on him; Thierack should not utter a single word on the subject. Thierack then went to see Lautz and told him that all the Czech cases which had been deferred so far were soon to come to trial. Lautz said he needed another three or four weeks to complete the investigations and indictments.[78]

On the following day Thierack invited the investigating judge to a locality where he had some other business to attend to. He was briefed on the Czech question and then returned to Berlin. On the morning of Saturday 27 September he called Heydrich and arranged a meeting. At this, Heydrich mentioned the name Eliáš to Thierack for the first time and said that his interest extended far beyond the

Czech Prime Minister himself.[79] Precisely what his interest was he did not spell out. One cannot exclude the possibility that Heydrich, after Gürtner's death, was endeavouring to subordinate completely the German judiciary to the SS.

There is no evidence that Heydrich's intention was to remove Eliáš by drum-head court martial; indeed such an action would have run contrary to his entire policy in the protectorate. Both Heydrich and Thierack decided that Eliáš would have to be tried before the VGH, and as quickly as possible. Heydrich expressed concern about the investigations in the Klapka case lasting another three or four weeks. In the case of Eliáš Heydrich demanded short, sharp action. To this end, both apparently agreed – though here the evidence is both inconclusive and ambivalent – to circumvent Oberreichsanwalt Lautz and put the case of the prosecution directly into Heydrich's hands – the thin end of the wedge if it was Heydrich's bid for power over the judiciary.

In any case the procedure was a gross violation of the VGH Constitution. But Thierack seemed pleased at the outcome, as he was always aware of Hitler's low opinion of the legal profession, and no doubt cognizant of the fact that the vacancy at the top of the Ministry had yet to be filled. By acting a loyal man of the NSDAP, Thierack may have seen himself in this top position by virtue of his close collaboration with Heydrich, whose backing was not to be underestimated. Thierack could at any time have had Lautz initiate the proceedings within 24 hours, but that would have moved Heydrich, and all he stood for, into the background and Heydrich was not willing to let control of the case slip out of his hands.[80]

So Thierack, without giving his reasons, demanded the Klapka file from Lautz and, having studied it, handed it over to Ministerialrat Joel, who on the same day travelled with Heydrich to Prague. Joel was a man of moderate intelligence and considerable ambition. Like most of his colleagues he had joined the NSDAP only on 1 May 1933, but he was given the opportunity of a key post when he was put in charge of liaison between the Reich Ministry of Justice and the SS, SD and the Gestapo. He then transferred to the Reich Security Head Office (RSHA) and quickly climbed the SS ladder; his uncompromising attitude against all elements allegedly hostile to the state brought him quick prominence within the SS. Joel's role in the Eliáš case involved him in a clear contradiction of loyalties. On the one hand, as member of the Ministry of Justice, he had to keep an eye on what was going on between Thierack and Heydrich; on the other he had to ignore his own Ministry.

The day of Thierack's meeting with Heydrich was also the day on which Hitler had dated Neurath's 'extended leave' and Heydrich's appointment. Lautz, unaware of what was going on, left for Vienna after he had handed over the Klapka file to Thierack. On the following day, Sunday 28 September 1941, Thierack received news from Prague that Eliáš had been arrested and had made a full confession.

On Monday the *Völkischer Beobachter* published the news that Eliáš would be put on trial before the VGH. Naturally the Reich Ministry of Justice was surprised. Freisler tried to find out more details, but was unsuccessful. Then Lautz was told by the Ministry to make himself available to prosecute the two cases of Klapka and Eliáš in Prague. Lautz asked for the date of the trial and was informed that this would be given to him shortly. It never came, because it was Heydrich's firm intention to control the prosecution personally. Suddenly Joel telephoned from Prague, mentioning as an aside that on the following day, Tuesday, Eliáš's trial would take place before the VGH.

There was utter confusion within the Ministry of Justice. Thierack was telephoned and pretended to be ignorant: had not Joel already formally informed the Ministry? Thierack was ordered to return to Berlin immediately, where Schlegelberger did not hold back with his criticism. Did he, Thierack, not know that the name Heydrich was a programme in itself? But Thierack, convinced that with Heydrich by his side he was closer to power than Schlegelberger, took little notice of him and his attempts to mobilize the Ministry of the Interior and the Reich Chancellery (which, in any event, failed to produce results). Only Stuckart, Secretary of State in the Ministry of the Interior, telephoned Heydrich in Prague to get Lautz to undertake the prosecution. Heydrich rejected the idea outright, basing his claims on the extraordinary powers with which the Führer had endowed him. For Schlegelberger there was, in the end, no choice but to agree with steps that had been, or were to be taken.[80]

Thierack received the indictment drawn up by the Gestapo, while Lautz vainly tried to reassert his position as Supreme Prosecutor of the VGH. He was extremely bitter because he had waited near Vienna for further instructions that never came. He looked at the whole affair as a conspiracy directed against him personally.[81]

The Reich Ministry of Justice in Berlin was seriously alienated, but irrespective of that the First Senate of the VGH, presided over by Thierack, boarded the plane for Prague on Tuesday 30 September and were met there by Joel. The very next day the trial of the Czech Prime Minister, General Eliáš, began. In place of the Ober-reichsanwalt Lautz in his red robe, there appeared the black uniform of SS-Obersturmbannführer Dr Geschke. The accused faced a selected audience of about 200, among them Karl-Hermann Frank, who not so long ago had submitted rather favourable opinions about Eliáš. The trial took place in German. An interpreter, though present, was unnecessary because Eliáš spoke flawless German.[82]

The charge was attempted high treason and Landesverrat. One of the counts of the indictment had to be dropped, namely Eliáš's aid to Trebicky, which he admitted, stating, however, that only 7,000 Crowns had been involved and that the money had been paid to Trebicky's sick wife; Trebicky himself had died in the meantime. The escape of the Czech ministers was also discussed but produced no conclusive results. On the Neumann charge, Eliáš protested his innocence, and the witness produced from the Gestapo prison declared that his previous statement had been merely expressions of his private opinion, so this count also had to be dropped for lack of evidence. However, to the charges regarding Ingre and Schmoranz the accused pleaded partially guilty. But, according to Eliáš, he had refused to cooperate and had informed Czech President Hacha of the whole affair. He had warned Schmoranz not to do anything stupid. He had burnt the information and reports which he had received from Schmoranz and had instructed the Minister of the Interior to isolate him. Dr Geschke nevertheless insisted that a serious offence had been committed because in both cases Eliáš had failed to inform the German authorities. Still, from the point of view of the law, matters were far from conclusive until the Klapka charge was added. This was sufficient to support the charge of Landesverrat and *Feindbegünstigung* because it was only fifteen months old and reached well into the war, while all the other charges were two years old or more.[83]

Eliáš readily admitted that he knew of the acts of financial support. He justified his attitude by pointing to the dilemma he faced between the demands of humanity and the interests of the Reich, adding that in this case he had decided to damage the latter. But he disputed the statements which Klapka had put into his mouth and denied encouraging him. On the contrary, Eliáš said that since 1939 he had seen the future welfare of the Czech people as lying in close cooperation with the Reich and the restoration of the geopolitical, social and economic conditions as they had existed during the Hapsburg Empire. On this issue there was a direct conflict of evidence between Klapka and Eliáš. The SS prosecution described Eliáš as a 'fanatical Czech' and called Klapka as a witness who, in the witness stand, insisted on the truth of his version; the VGH judges obviously believed him.[84]

The court then withdrew to formulate its judgment, which covered 27 pages and contained references as to the validity of the entire proceedings, in itself evidence that the First Senate of VGH must have had doubts about its role in the whole affair. It was admitted that according to paragraph 7 of the law establishing the VGH only the Supreme Prosecutor of the Reich had the right to initiate and conduct prosecutions, and that according to a further paragraph he must continuously be present throughout the trial. However, it was argued, the present trial took place in the protectorate of Bohemia and Moravia, in which, by order of the Führer, Heydrich exercised extraordinary powers. Moreover, Heydrich had proclaimed a state of emergency in the protectorate and the Reich Protector had the power to change autonomous laws by decree if it was in the public interest and could issue any kind of decree in the event of immediate danger. Eliáš was sentenced to death for attempted high treason and *Feindbegünstigung*.

The next day the Klapka case took the stage. If Klapka had hoped to save his life by giving evidence against Eliáš, he was to be disappointed. After a trial lasting little more than two hours, Klapka too was sentenced to death.[85] In the wake of these trials a further 150–200 persons were executed by drum-head courts martial.

In spite of this, Heydrich was still deeply annoyed by the attitude of the Reich Ministry of Justice and on 1 October he sent a teleprinter message to Bormann, Chief of the Party Chancellery, at Hitler's headquarters: 'In spite of various attempts at obstruction by the Reich Ministry of Justice and Secretary of State Schlegelberger, it was possible, thanks to the excellent support and the political understanding of President Dr Thierack to come to a conclusive and final judgment within three days.'[86] The following day in a speech to the German administration, the Wehrmacht and the NSDAP in the protectorate, Heydrich again stressed that: 'thanks to the loyalty of the president of the VGH and in spite of the Ministry of Justice, it has been possible to deal with the trials against Eliáš and Klapka in the shortest possible time.'[87]

But now Heydrich had mobilized the Reich Ministry of Justice. Feeling his own position threatened, Reich Minister Lammers, the Chief of the Reich Chancellery, who had been informed of Heydrich's wire, wrote a personal letter to Bormann in which he countered Heydrich's insinuations and defended the Ministry of Justice. Schlegelberger had acted correctly and in accordance with his duty. He had acted as he did because he had been left in complete ignorance of Heydrich's independent actions. Lammers then sent Schlegelberger a copy, for which the latter expressed his gratitude. Schlegelberger was, moreover, not slow to detect the sources which had kept Heydrich informed, namely Ministialrat Joel and Thierack himself, and Thierack's attitude Schlegelberger considered as one of gross disloyalty.[87]

A letter was also sent to Heydrich to justify the Ministry's attitude but it seems to have cut very little ice with him. Heydrich insisted on his version and was again full of praise for Joel and Thierack. Schlegelberger again complained of lack of information.[88]

There was still Thierack to deal with. He rejected charges of disloyalty and indiscretion and referred to Stuckart's intervention from the Ministry of the Interior. Quite apart from that, Heydrich had imposed the highest secrecy. Thierack himself had told Heydrich that he would inform Schlegelberger, but Heydrich said he would do this himself by getting in touch with Freisler. In fact, Freisler appears to have been informed, but if so he kept the knowledge to himself.[89] The charge that the VGH in Prague had acted like a drum-head courts martial he tried to disprove by reference to the trial in the Czech press which had praised 'the dignity' of the VGH proceedings.[90] (As though the Czech press could have written anything else!)

But Thierack deliberately ignored the core of the issue. It was not the conduct of the proceedings that was in question but the legislation upon which the VGH and its proceedings were based. The Eliáš case amounted to nothing less than a further step towards delivering the judiciary into the hands of the SS and police, of which, so far, this had been the most blatant. At the end of 1941 the VGH was not yet the revolutionary tribunal which it was to become three years later.

How decisive Thierack's role in the Eliáš case was in promoting him to Minister of Justice a year later is impossible to determine. By that time Heydrich was dead. The only person to make any moves in consequence of Thierack's appointment was Schlegelberger who went into retirement with a 'donation of honour' of 100,000 Marks.[91] Joel, on the other hand, was shunted into a siding within the Ministry of Justice where he remained isolated and powerless.

Another case much discussed, though not publicly, was that of Herschel Grynspan, who on 7 November 1938 had shot and killed the Secretary of the German Embassy in Paris, Ernst vom Rath, the action which triggered off the pogrom in Germany between 9 and 11 November 1938.[92] This is not the place to unravel Grynspan's motivation or to explain and analyse Grynspan's attitude while in the hands of the French police. What may be said, however, is that the hitherto prevailing opinion that Grynspan's action was the result of his parents, of Polish nationality but residing in Germany, having been expelled to Poland together with other Polish Jews, is, to say the least, less than the whole truth.

In July 1940, after the fall of France, Grynspan had been interrogated by the German police for the first time. He was then transferred to Germany, first to Sachsenheusen concentration camp, and from there in the summer of 1941 to the remand prison of Berlin-Moabit. The Reich Ministry of Justice supplied the Supreme Prosecutor of the VGH with two thick files together with an order to draw up an indictment against Grynspan. Allegedly, the idea of mounting a major trial had originated in the brain of Martin Bormann.[93] But after the VGH had studied the files, it raised doubts as to its jurisdiction, although at the time it still seemed that the murder had had solely a political motive.[94] The Ministry of Justice replied that indirectly the murder had aimed at the leadership of the Third Reich and could therefore be the basis of a charge of high treason. Also the Reichspropaganda Ministry tried to make the most of it, its Ministerialdirektor Diewerge having been involved in the affair since 1938.[95]

Initially it was thought that Grynspan could be tried as early as January 1942. Thierack was sick at the time, but nevertheless on 24 January 1942 Goebbels entered into his diary: 'The murder trial of Grynspan is up for debate again.' But then followed a reference on which the entire plan of holding a public trial was ultimately to founder:

Grynspan has used the impertinent argument that he had a homosexual relationship with the *Legationsrat* (First Counsellor) vom

Rath whom he shot. This is naturally an infamous lie; nevertheless it has been clearly thought out and in the event of a public trial would constitute the main theme of enemy propaganda. I shall therefore take the necessary measures to see that while part of trial is public, the rest is closed.[96]

German psychiatrists who examined Grynspan were told that he had made himself sexually available to vom Rath in return for the promise that Rath would assist Grynspan's parents in Germany. It was an embarrassing situation, especially as at the funeral of vom Rath, Hitler himself had given the last salute over the grave. On 11 February 1942 Goebbels wrote in his diary: 'Diewerge returned from Paris and gave me a detailed report from there. He has spoken to Bonnet [the former French Foreign Minister], who is ready to testify in the murder trial of the Jew Grynspan which is to take place soon.'[97]

Nevertheless the German judicial authorities were still uncertain about their jurisdiction and about the fact that Grynspan knew this and could use it effectively if he were to come to trial. But Professor Friedrich Grimm, legal advisor to the German Foreign Office, still believed in April 1942 that the Grynspan trial would take place in Berlin in the middle of the month.[98]

Actually Grynspan's allegation about his homosexual involvement with vom Rath had been circulating in Berlin since December 1941. Diewerge had sent a letter to the Foreign Office asking for a meeting about the propaganda preparations for the trial. It was Diewerge's task to make all the necessary arrangements.[99] The trial was to be conducted by the vice-president of the VGH, Engert, in the Great Hall of the VGH in the Bellevuestrasse.

Dr Lautz and Reich Prosecutor Dr Künze were to lead the prosecution, Dr Weimann appearing for the defence. Loudspeakers were to be built into the courtroom, as well as additional telephone booths for foreign correspondents. Provision was made for an interpreter. The trial was to be as brief as possible. Its extension over several weeks was rejected by Diewerge: no more than seven days.[100]

Then the day-by-day proceedings were discussed. On the first day, if Grynspan should refuse to speak, the French witnesses were to be called immediately. In this connection the first remark was dropped about Grynspan's homosexual claims but the issue was ignored. The second day was to be devoted to discussing the motives of the murderer and the personality of vom Rath while the third day was intended for the discussion of the political background to the crime. The fourth day was also to discuss the political background, and Georges Bonnet was to be heard as a witness. On the sixth day both prosecution and defence would make their pleas while on the seventh day the VGH would give its judgment and pronounce the sentence.[101]

In April 1942 Hitler himself apparently intervened and the date for the trial was now set for 11 May 1942. In a letter to Goebbels, Schlegelberger informed him of this and that the Führer had ordered the trial, and once again drew attention to the fact that Grynspan would insist on his homosexual relationship with vom Rath.[102] Schlegelberger then added the typed summary of a meeting which Freisler had held on 22 January 1942 with all those concerned with the propaganda value of this important trial.[103] In this meeting it had been noted that Grynspan might take exception to the jurisdiction of the VGH in his case, an issue, as already stated, of which the Reich Ministry of Justice was not completely sure. Furthermore he might raise the issue of homosexuality, but Hitler had orderd the trial to proceed regardless.[104] Four days later Grynspan went on a hunger strike, a news item which was communicated by a *Führerinformation* to Hitler's headquarters in Rastenburg.[105] Then nothing happened until a *Führerinformation* was issued with the content: 'The Jew Grynspan in a coded deposition has admitted that the assertions of homosexual relations with vom Rath are incorrect. However, he indicated that the murdered man had entertained homosexual relationships with other men.'[106]

What was meant by 'coded deposition' is unclear, but more important in this connection was the final sentence: 'that the brother of the murdered vom Rath, a first lieutenant and commander of a cavalry squadron has been sentenced by a field court martial of his Division z.b.V. 428 to one year imprisonment and loss of rank for homosexuality with men (sic!)'[107]

With that discovery virtually all interest in staging the trial disappeared. It was not political circumstances, such as the disproportionate showing which the French would have made in such a trial, which saved Grynspan, nor even his alleged homosexuality with vom Rath, but the simple discovery that vom Rath's brother had been similarly inclined and therefore punished. The risk of moral embarrassment was too great and the whole affair was postponed indefinitely. Grynspan was lucky. He survived the ordeal of the concentration camp, returned to Paris, and later emigrated to

Israel, where during the mid-1970s he was still very much alive in Tel Aviv.[108]

In the meantime the German judiciary had come under mounting criticism and by none other than Hitler himself. In his 'table talk' of 1 August 1941 he had expressed doubts at the *idée fixe* of the German judiciary about having unified, centralized legislation. Why could laws not apply to particular territories of the Reich?[109] On 8 February 1942 he expressed the opinion that the German judiciary was not sufficiently elastic.[110] It failed to see the present danger that criminals were providing themselves with an opening into which they could pour once the right moment had come. On 23 April 1942 Hitler complained about a mild sentence handed down to a murderer of a woman, a crime he considered particularly despicable.[111]

He had little time for Dr Gürtner but believed he owed him loyalty because of Gürtner's actions in 1924. On 5 May 1942 he expressed the opinion that the only professional lawyer among his narrow circle of collaborators who was really worth his salt was Reich Minister and Chief of the Reich Chancellery, Lammers, because he knew that his function was to find judicial underpinnings to support and cement the structure of the state and never confused lawyers' abstractions with practical life.[112] On 10 May 1942, referring to the Reichstag fire, Hitler argued that lawyers were as international as criminals but not half as clever, and for this reason the trial had lasted for weeks and ended ludicrously.[113] On 22 May 1942 he addressed himself to espionage, which in his view was committed only by two sections of German society: high society and the proletariat, while the middle class was too 'solid' for this crime. He demanded barbaric punishments for those who committed crimes during black-out, be they thefts, rape, or burglary. If punishments were not meted out brutally two dangers would emerge, first, that criminality would become uncontrollable and, secondly, that a discrepancy would emerge between the decent man who got killed in the front line and the *Schweinehund* (literally, 'pig-dog') who was saving his skin at home by repeatedly violating paragraphs 'xyz'.[114]

On 31 May 1942 Hitler had also touched on the question of the selection of judges. The criteria were in need of fundamental change. Since a judge would require extensive experience in practical life, in future the only people who would be considered for this office would be those who had proven themselves already in other spheres of life and who identified themselves with NS views and were aware of the problems involved in leading them. No one should be able to become judge until he had passed his thirty-fifth birthday.[115] On this point at least Hitler seems to have shared the views which Freisler had put forward for some time.[116]

On 7 June 1942 Hitler referred to the immense espionage organizations which the Allied Control Commissions had left behind in Germany after their departure. That Germany got rid of a very large proportion of those spies was mainly due to the fact that in 1933, without any NS effort, 65,000 citizens had emigrated. Of course there was no certainty that every one of them was guilty, but he was convinced that most of them had been caused to leave by their own bad conscience. What espionage remained had had its neck broken by Heydrich's Security Service. But the judiciary had often made him furious by their treatment of acts of Landesverrat. Hitler cited a case in which clemency was asked for a person who had primarily been engaged in smuggling. He had had great difficulties in convincing Gürtner that the betrayal of bunker buildings amounted to Landesverrat. He had also threatened, in one case of over-lenient punishment of a *Landesverräter*, that he would despatch an SS detachment to collect the criminal and have him shot. Moreover, the VGH had not kept to the strict guidelines he had set. Anyone who excluded himself from the *Volksgemeinschaft* ought to be liquidated.[117]

Hitler did not fail to intervene. When in Poland a Jew was discovered who had hoarded over 30,000 eggs, over half of which had become rotten, and was then sentenced to a mild prison sentence by the military authorities, Hitler converted the prison sentence into the death sentence.[118]

But the incident which caused the thunderstorm that was to affect the entire German judiciary had its roots in the winter campaign in Russia in 1941–2, when Col-General Hoepner withdrew his forces in the face of the Russian assault against Hitler's express orders. For this reason Hitler had him dismissed together with other generals. Hoepner then claimed his pension, which at first he did not receive. Hoepner initiated disciplinary proceedings against himself before an army court and ultimately the Reichkriegsgericht. Everybody denied having jurisdiction to hear the case. Hoepner then went before the civil courts and won his case.[119] Hitler later admitted having acted too hastily in this case and via his Adjudant General, Schmundt, let Hoepner know that he and his family would be looked after adequately.[120]

Nevertheless, Hoepner's victory before the civil court was the straw that broke the camel's back. In addition there was much criticism of the judiciary from other sources. Goebbels, for example, advocated the granting of explicit special powers to the Führer: 'The mere existence of such powers for the Führer, authorizing him not only to dismiss officers who fail to do their duty but discharge them dishonourably, would work wonders. . . . So far the judiciary has always been the barrier to legislation of this kind.'[121]

Nine days later, on 29 March 1942, Hitler stated to his circle that '. . . no reasonable man understood the teachings of the law, which the jurists had prepared for themselves. In the final analysis present teachings of the law amounted to one great systematic denial of responsibility.' He, Hitler, would therefore do everything to make the study of the law despised, that is to say the study of law conceived in this way, because men would not be trained through these studies to be fit for life and suited to guarantee the state the maintenance of its natural legal order. 'All the present studies are an education for irresponsibility.' He would personally see to it that those employed in the administration of justice would be reduced down to 10 per cent of handpicked men. The whole swindle with *Schöffen*, lay judges, would be done away with. He intended, once and for all, to block the opportunity for a judge to avoid assuming responsibility for his decision with the excuse that the *Schöffen* had outvoted him. Today he would therefore declare clearly and openly that for him everyone who is a lawyer is either defective by nature or would become so in the course of time.[122]

The cause for this particular outburst was a case tried on 19 March 1942 before the Landgericht Oldenburg. The accused was a 29-year-old building technician by the name of Schlitt, who had married in 1937 but had been involved in daily marital quarrels with the result that in October 1941 his wife had died in a mental hospital. Schlitt was charged with manslaughter and sentenced to five years' hard labour. When Hitler heard of this, he was absolutely aghast at the short sentence and telephoned Schlegelberger, who knew nothing of the case.[123] Hitler shouted that this was typical for the whole judiciary. A major criminal would be imprisoned for five years at the expense of the state while hundreds of thousands of men put their lives at risk in the front line for their wives and children. He threatened Schlegelberger and the whole judiciary that he would 'chase them to the devil' if this sentence was not revised immediately.

If this did not happen the whole judiciary would come under Himmler's command.[124]

What is interesting about this is not the case as such, but the fact that Hitler personally took note of it, as indeed he did of many other minor details as his 'table talk' amply demonstrates. This contradicts the view held, for instance, by David Irving, that Hitler was far too preoccupied with conducting his war to take much notice of what was taking place behind the front lines.[125] Indeed, Hitler's personal servant, Heinz Linge, has confirmed that Hitler was not only an avid reader of files submitted to him at his headquarters but also eagerly read the secret *Lageberichte*,[126] the reports on public opinion inside Germany which were compiled by the SD at regular monthly intervals. They were compiled within the RSHA by Otto Ohlendorf in order to provide the German leadership with an unvarnished picture of the mood of the German public since shortly before the beginning of the war.[127]

To the exclamation heard very often in Germany during Hitler's rule, 'If only the Führer knew!', one can respond quite unequivocally, 'Yes, he did know!'. Hitler kept himself informed about the German domestic scene down to the smallest detail until his end in his bunker.

This was the immediate background to Hitler's speech before the Reichstag's last session on 26 April 1942. In his speech Hitler stated that he expected certain things:

> That the nation gave me the right, wherever service is rendered less than unconditionally in the task which involves the question of to be or not to be, to intervene immediately and effectively. Fighting forces and home front, transport administration and judiciary must subordinate themselves to one aim only, namely the obtaining of victory. In these times no one can appeal to his well earned rights [Hitler's reference to the Hoepner case] but must know that today only duties exist.
>
> I therefore ask the German Reichstag for its express confirmation that I possess the legal right to force everyone to do his duty, or to punish anyone who in my view does not fulfil his task conscientiously, by demotion or removal from office, without regard to who he is and what well-earned rights he may possess. . . .
>
> Equally, I expect the German judiciary to understand that the nation does not exist for the judiciary but the judiciary for the nation, that is

to say that the whole world, including Germany, is not to be blown to smithereens just in order that a formal law can exist, but that Germany must live on, however much the formalities of the judiciary may be in contradiction with this. I cannot – to quote one example – understand a judgment in which a criminal, who had married in 1937 and ill-treated his wife until she was taken to a mental hospital where she died from the last maltreatment, is sentenced to five years' hard labour when tens of thousands of brave Germans must die to protect their homeland from destruction by Bolshevism. This means that, in order to protect their women and children, from now on I shall intervene in these cases and remove judges who are obviously not aware of the necessity of the hour.[128]

Göring, as president of the Reichstag, naturally moved that these powers be granted, which of course they were with great acclaim. In fact they were powers which Hitler *de facto* already possessed, now draped with the mantle of *de jure* 'legality'. Hitler had finally and formally usurped the supreme judiciary power in Germany. At the same time, so one can assume, he put an end also to the rumours circulating in Germany as a result of the great many dismissals of generals during the winter crisis on the eastern front. No *Führer-befehl*, in whatever area, was any longer open to question. The *Führerprinzip* reigned supreme. As Goebbels put it a day later:

The generals were put in their place, but this only appeared between the lines. He also spoke of individuals who failed at critical moments and lost their nerve. In this connection the Führer demanded absolute plenary powers during wartime for himself to do whatever he considered necessary, even with reference to individuals, without having to take into consideration any so-called well-earned rights. This demand was approved enthusiastically and noisily by the Reichstag. . . .[129]

Yet within the German public, doubts were expressed as to

why the Führer once again demanded special powers, since he had possessed them ever since the office of Führer and Chancellor of the German people were united in his person. . . .[130]

But this episode, on the other hand, also produced calming effects, since it was assumed that the Führer was being informed down to the smallest detail about what was going on in Germany, and that this Reichstag speech served as a last warning to all those who still believed that they need not adjust to the requirements of the time. From this point of view the second part of the Führer's speech found enthusiastic response, especially among the lower levels of German society, and the hope was expressed that from now on all *Volksgenossen* who did not do their duty would be removed irrespective of rank and position.[131]

In some areas of Germany, for example in Leipzig, among workers and intelligentsia alike the word 'dictatorship' was mentioned.[132] The judiciary at large was extremely depressed:

> The Führer's speech has had a shattering effect throughout the ranks of the civil service and left the impression that the goodwill of the majority of civil servants, against which there are only a tiny minority of exceptions to be set, is not being realized. The consequence is a general insecurity, which can be overcome only gradually.[133]

And:

> Insofar as state prosecutors and judges have already been affirming the necessity of a hard line against criminals and other evil-doers during the war and have practiced this policy, they see in the Führer's words a vindication of their attitude. Among those circles of judges to which this hard-line attitude has not yet penetrated, there has been a noticeable change. . . .
>    The emphasis upon the Führer's role as the Supreme Judge . . . corresponds closely in general with most preservers of the law (*Rechtswahrer*), even though they are still unaccustomed to the consequences. Like every spiritual change, this change in the nature of the independence of the judges will naturally also take place slowly and not without reverses. . . .
>    An unvarnished report cannot be silent about the fact that the comment about the judiciary in the last speech of the Führer has caused deep depression among the *Rechtswahrer*.
>    The *Rechtswahrer*, notably the judges, will not understand that they should be political civil servants. . . .[134]

Carl Goerdeler, the former Lord Mayor of Leipzig, described the speech as the lowest form of lawlessness in Germany, to which virtually every German could become the victim without any possibility of recourse to the law.[135] Even Freisler in a private letter a few days later described Hitler's speech as extraordinary, and, as far as the judiciary was concerned, totally unjust.[136] Another judge summarized the effect in the following words:

The effect of the Führer's speech was most depressing to the judges of my area. The full effects of proclaiming the removal of judges and the nature of this proclamation before the world public in the form of an Enabling Act by the Reichstag with its frenetic acclamation cannot even be estimated. . . .[137]

Even Goebbels admitted that. On 12 May 1942 he recorded:

The SD report indicates that the Führer's speech is still the chief topic of discussion among the people. The civil servants and the lawyers simply won't keep quiet about it. Perhaps it would now be timely to give them a pill to soothe their nerves. There is no purpose in humiliating two professions so deeply that they lose all interest in the war and their work. I shall await a favourable moment.[138]

The crisis of confidence became a crisis in the judiciary, and Hitler's manoeuvre had succeeded. While previously there had still been judges and civil servants who opposed any interference in the judicial process by other forces, Hitler's speech had now opened the gates wide. General insecurity spread, the judiciary for a time became the scapegoat for all evils, the death sentence for any independent judiciary had been pronounced. It needed a 'pill'.

Among those least affected by Hitler's speech were the judges of the VGH. Yet, together with the Reich Ministry of Justice, it began to form a defensive front against attacks from without; Schlegelberger wrote a letter of protest to Bormann, Hans Frank wrote to Goebbels.[139] The SS newspaper Das Schwarze Korps, which before the war had commended the VGH on several occasions, on 16 July 1942 published an article 'Unabhängig – wovon?',[140] ('Independent from Whom?'), in which it rejected the objectivity of judges and demanded a political judiciary.

Again, Schlegelberger and Frank protested, as did Freisler. All three referred to the 'dangers for the internal unity of the people' which would arise out of those unwarranted attacks, whereupon Himmler personally directed Das Schwarze Korps to cease attack forthwith, even of the smallest kind, against the judiciary and lawyers. Any violations he, Himmler, would punish personally in the most severe manner.[141]

In his private correspondence, Freisler continued to show himself most violently irritated by Hitler's speech, though his outside attitude betrayed nothing of that.[142] Several months earlier, on 20 January 1942, he had represented the Reich Ministry of Justice at Heydrich's Wannsee Conference, at which the large scale deportation of Jews to the east was discussed.

Freisler's participation in this conference raises questions of course, but so does the protocol and this author fully shares Heinz Höhne's comment: 'It is no accident that most works of historians dealing with the holocaust have only a few paragraphs to spare for the Wannsee Conference. And this with good reason: one knows too little about it.'[143] The sources are thin. The fifteen-page protocol was apparently compiled by Eichmann's Department Four, which was concerned with the 'Jewish Question', of the RSHA but it has no heading and no signature. Moreover the original copy is missing. The National Archives in Washington, Yad Vashem in Jerusalem and the Institut für Zeitgeschichte in Munich hold only photocopies, to mention but three of the major archives. Dr Robert Kempner, the US prosecuting attorney, introduced this document in one of the successor trials to the Nuremberg trials, but ignored the question as to the whereabouts of the original.[144] In the document itself the 'final solution' of the 'Jewish problem', by deportation to the east and destruction through labour as well as direct liquidation, includes the Jewish population of all European countries, those under German control and those outside it, neutrals as well as enemy countries like Great Britain.

Does Freisler's participation in this conference suggest that he was fully aware of the systematic extermination of the Jews in Auschwitz and similar camps? This seems doubtful because at the time of the Wannsee Conference the gas chambers of Auschwitz were not yet in operation. Nevertheless, as the trial of the 20 July 1944 bomb-plotters will show, Freisler was aware then of the general process of the *Judenausrottung*.[145] The Wannsee Conference was not necessarily required to enlighten him on this point.

At this particular point in time the ministry he served was still without a minister.[146] On 20 March 1942 Goebbels had recommended to Hitler that Thierack be appointed Reich Minister of Justice. The discussions took place in the main in Hitler's headquarters, and the person mainly concerned with submitting proposals to Hitler was Lammers, insofar as they concerned personnel changes at the apex of Germany's government administration. Thus a report of 17 August 1942 lists the preparation of the following documents:

a) the appointment of Thierack as Reichsminister of Justice;
b) the appointment of Dr Curt Rothenberger as Secretary of State;
c) the document transferring or retiring Schlegelberger;
d) the document *retiring* Freisler (my emphasis);
e) the document removing the Governor of the General Government in Poland;
f) the document appointing Freisler as President of the Academy for German Law;
g) the protocol for swearing in Thierack; and
h) a decree making financial provision for both Thierack and Rothenberger.[147]

Also discussed was a press release about Schlegelberger's retirement. Furthermore, Thierack was to become *Leiter* (head) and not Reichsführer of the Nationalsozialistischer Rechtswahrerbund (NSRB), formerly the BNSDJ; the Reich Law Office, so far headed by Frank, was to be dissolved and the office of the President of Academy for German Law was to be downgraded to an honorary office.[148] No decision was made as to whether a second Secretary of State should be appointed. The question as to who should become President of the VGH was to be left open, but not for long. Finally, there should be a greater degree of cooperation between the Ministries of Justice and Propaganda.[149]

While it was agreed that Thierack be made Minister of Justice, and Schlegelberger should be retired, Freisler was to leave the Reich Ministry of Justice. Hitler, aware of Freisler's affinities with Frank's ideas about a 'German law' and an NS constitution, considered him unsuitable for the office of the President of the Academy for German Law, but suggested him as successor to Thierack as president of the VGH. If he would not accept, then he should be retired.[150]

At Bormann's suggestion, Thierack was also to head the NSRB. The final decision was made on 20 August 1942 when the proposed appointments and retirements were announced. Schlegelberger's retirement notice crossed with his own letter in which he was submitting his resignation.[151] Thierack and Freisler accepted their new appointments and copies of the documents were sent out. But six days later Hitler issued an additional decree in which he stated:

For the fulfilment of the tasks of the *Grossdeutsches Reich* (the Greater German Empire) a strong judiciary is necessary; I therefore order and empower the Reich Minister for Justice, according to my guidelines and instructions and in agreement with the Reich Minister and Chief of the Reich Chancellery and the Head of the Party Chancellery, to build up a National Socialist judiciary and to take the necessary measures for this purpose. He is empowered to diverge from the existing law.[152]

Thierack was, in effect, made the subordinate not only of Hitler but of Lammers and Bormann.

Hitler's measures, from his usurpation of supreme legal powers as announced in his Reichstag speech to the 1942 decree, did not create legal anarchy; they institutionalized it. What vestiges of independence of the German judiciary still existed – and within the context of the VGH they never had – were now brutally torn away, revealing to all who had so far blinded themselves to this process the callous maked assertion of power which now had replaced the *Rechtsstaat*. Hitler had endeavoured to cover his measures inside Germany with the cloak of legality, although it was an increasingly tattered one. By 1942 he no longer thought it necessary to use what still remained of its shreds. His dictatorship was sufficiently solid to make it unnecessary to invoke Article 2 of the Enabling Act.

Yet when looking at the causal chain, each link being within the overall context a rather peripheral mishandling of justice as Hitler understood it, it is difficult to interpret Hitler's act as part and parcel of a pre-planned programme. Forever suspicious of the legal profession as such, he now reacted with the full venom of his temperament. But Hitler would not have been what he was, if he had not realized the possibilities inherent in this action, and within the course of a few months he exploited them to the full.

Given the unease with which the German legal profession received his measures, it is surprising that not a single judge appears to have resigned in protest. Though anyone who resigned in protest would have brought the full weight of the police state upon himself, resignation for other reasons such as ill health would still have been possible, yet there is no evidence to show that anyone took that step. Why resign at a time when it still appeared that Germany was on the crest of victory? Why resign when the likely alternative was being drafted into the army to serve at the eastern front? The simple truth must be that, irrespective of private misgivings, the German legal profession, above all the judges, had fully succumbed to the power of corruption, not in the material but in the ethical sense. Their politicization in the days of the Weimar Republic had been the first step on a slippery downhill slope and a rapidly accelerating journey into a moral abyss. But the historian should be wary of stringent and sweeping wholesale moral condemnation. Taking everything into consideration he may reflect and conclude, there but for the grace of God (or that of 'late birth') go I.

Yet one prominent voice of protest had endeavoured to make itself heard throughout the first half of 1942 and thus probably precipitated his own downfall. Despite his brutal and tyrannical rule over Poland, Hans Frank had always insisted on the primacy of the law within Germany and in the course of this insistence had come into conflict with many members of the NSDAP hierarchy. In 1933 he had clashed with Himmler because he had initiated enquiries about conditions in the Dachau concentration camp.[153] In November 1941 he had made a private speech in Berlin in which he complained about the increasing legal uncertainty due to insistence on state security and to police interference. He insisted upon the necessity for and the proper scope of an independent judiciary. The NSRB was the combat organization for realizing point 19 of the NSDAP programme, and a legal order was now increasingly necessary for the coming world empire.[154] In reaction to Hitler's Reichstag speech in April, Frank publicly repeated in June 1942 what he had said in Berlin. On 1 July 1942 he delivered a speech which he introduced with the programmatic slogan: 'No Reich without law – not even ours! No law without judges – not even in Germany! No judge without real power – not even the German one!' He spoke out against the police state as being incompatible with National Socialist ideals, and to great applause he pleaded for the renewal of German law and its supremacy within the state.[155] Speaking a few weeks later in Munich to university students, he implicitly criticized Hitler's view of the judiciary as expressed in his speech of 26 April 1942. He opposed the intrusion of the SS into all spheres of life and demanded the formulation of a new legal code for Germany.[156]

His reaction to the changes in the judiciary of 20 August 1942 was to hand in his resignation as governor of the General Government of Poland to Hitler who refused to accept it.[157] In his diary Frank noted that

progressively, and unfortunately even within the ranks of the NS state leadership, the point of view has become dominant, that authority is more secure, the more unlimited the legal insecurity becomes among the citizens subject to it. The extension of the arbitrary use of police executive power has now reached a level at which one can speak of the complete deprivation of the protection of the law to individual *Volksgenossen*. . . . When, as is possible now, any *Volksgenosse* can be taken to a concentration camp, without any means of defending himself, for an indefinite period, when, as is the case, security of life, liberty, honour and the right to property no longer exist, then it is my conviction that the ethical connection between the leadership of the state and the *Volksgenossen* is completely dissolved.[158]

At considerable length he indicted Germany's police state and formulated remedies. But it was already too late,[159] as he realized: 'In the general context of this development of the conflict with the Führer and of controversies about the legal tasks for our time, it is only just that I should bear the whole brunt of hostility to the legal profession. Because I alone am responsible for this development, I take the blame and was bound to be hit if things turned out as they have . . . .'[160]

Frank's campaign did not end with his demotion. Hitler insisted that he retain his post as governor of the *Generalgouvernement* which he did until the arrival of the Russians made his presence in Krakow superfluous. Nevertheless, in 1942 his campaign did receive a strongly worded reply from SS-Brigadeführer Otto Ohlendorf from the RSHA.

Dr Otto Ohlendorf was one of those figures peculiar to the higher administrative and executive level of Himmler's SS empire. A highly qualified young intellectual, he had taken his doctorate in law and gone to work at the Institute of World Economy of the University of Kiel, where he specialized in National Socialism and Italian Fascism and became an expert in the syndicalist elements and the organizational structure of Fascist Italy. He had joined the NSDAP at its re-foundation in 1925 when he had been only eighteen years old, and entered the ranks of the SS a year later. Under the influence of his colleague Professor Dr Reinhard Höhn (who managed to survive the war unscathed and was, until his death, one of the leading influences on the newly established West German army) Ohlendorf worked at the Institute of Applied Economic Science and also entered the SD, in which he became head of the Amt III (Department Three, responsible for domestic intelligence and counter-intelligence) of the RSHA. By no means an uncritical, subservient NSDAP and SS member he insisted that the Reich's leadership be regularly presented with an unvarnished picture of trends of public opinion in Germany. For this purpose he put the SD security service to good use and from late 1938 onwards his situation reports (*Lageberichte*) appeared at monthly intervals and were distributed at the very top of the NS leadership.

As the tide of war turned against Germany, Himmler described Ohlendorf's reports as 'defeatist' and had their circulation proscribed, except to Hitler. A tall, fair-haired northern German, he corresponded physically to Himmler's ideal of what an SS man should look like – very much the opposite to Himmler's own appearance. Like so many other SS leaders, especially the commanders and officers of the Waffen-SS, Ohlendorf never took Himmler quite seriously. There was little Himmler could do about the officer corps of the Waffen-SS, but Ohlendorf was another matter. Himmler, a south German, described him as 'unbearable Prussian, without humour, defeatist and a professional debunker.' Nor had Ohlendorf curried favour with Hitler and Himmler when in January 1939 he had advocated a legally anchored minority status for the German Jews and demanded that no one should be sent to a concentration camp without a previous judicial hearing.

Himmler was determined to 'teach him a lesson' and the opportunity came when the war with Russia began. Twice ordered to take over the command of one of the SD liquidation squads, the Einsatzgruppen, he turned the order down, but a third time he could no longer refuse. Among the Einsatzgruppen commanders he had been the only one who had *not* volunteered for this task. His Einsatzgruppe D was attached to and operated within Army Group South and Ohlendorf later admitted that the death of 90,000 men, women and children had been reported to him.

After this stint in Russia he returned to his desk in Berlin as head of the SD and then to the Economics Ministry. Promoted to Lt-General in October 1944, at the war's end he seriously suggested that the Reichsführer-SS turn himself over to the Allies in order to assume the responsibility for the deeds of his organization and especially exculpate the Waffen-SS which until the end of the war did not know that by two secret orders, both issued in 1940, all uniformed members of Himmler's SS had automatically become members of the Waffen-SS. With his 'liberal' reputation, Ohlendorf continued to serve under Dönitz, Hitler's successor as Chancellor and head of Germany. He was also included on a cabinet list which it was thought would be presentable to the Allies. They, of course, took a different view. Being used at first as a witness for the prosecution in the trial of German war criminals, Ohlendorf was later tried in the

Einsatzgruppen trial and sentenced to death. He belonged to the last batch of German war criminals to be hanged in Landsberg prison in June 1951.[161]

Most of this lay still in the dark when in October 1942 Ohlendorf circulated the text of lecture which he had delivered in reply to Frank's speeches. Though, as seen from the above, there exists evidence that on point of priciple the two men were not too far apart, for reasons which have probably more to do with Ohlendorf's own standing within the SS hierarchy, and with Himmler in particular, he chose to take a stand against Frank. Against his better knowledge he ridiculed Frank's assertions about the police state in Germany, but then stated categorically: 'What now is really happening is that a formal order of law is being shaken in its very foundations and is about to break, an order which those who defend it see as the unchangeable law.'[162]

Not that Ohlendorf negated some form of *Rechtsstaat*; in much in what he advocated he plagiarized Frank's arguments on behalf of the SS. The SS was to become the fountain of all justice, and, as Ohlendorf saw it, 'National Socialism faced the task of directing the view of the individual towards the community. This would also mean a break with liberal conceptions of legal security. By legal security we mean justice in the sense that every single link of the community can be confident that under any circumstances it receives justice.'[163]

Ohlendorf acknowledged the existence of concentration camps, of shootings by the police, of preventive detention, but tried to justify them on the grounds of the necessity of correcting 'unacceptable judicial errors' and compensating for 'the insufficiency of the existing legislation'. In any case, the police acted according to the 'healthy intuitive feeling of the Volk'. Legal uncertainty had not been created by police interventions but by the extraordinarily wide spectrum of judicial sentences for one and the same offence.[164] And beyond the frontiers of the Reich?

> There, too, the German law will have to make its contribution, not as Frank sees it, 'towards the mourning, the tortured, towards the innocent and all those to whom injustice has been done to find justice and redress.' Certainly we have to liberate ourselves from the odium that we impose upon other nations of Europe whom we want to lead together into a new order, the jackboot on their necks; on that we need not waste any more words. But there is no necessity for us to do this by way of penance for injustices allegedly committed. . . . One day

those allegedly tortured peoples will understand the blessing it was for themselves that we have realized our conceptions, because they bring us victory which will be of benefit not only to us but also to all the peoples of Europe.[165]

In its entirety Ohlendorf's paper makes it clear that fundamentally there was very little difference between his views and Hans Frank's. At first glance it could be seen as an attempt to secure the influence of the police and especially the SS on the practice of law, thereby empowering them to correct the decisions of the judiciary. The crisis of the German judiciary had thus come to an end with its complete subjugation to Hitler and the SS state.

Ohlendorf's exposition was a reply to Frank laden with personal motivation. But to leave it at that would obscure a more ulterior motive. The realization of the totalitarian claims of the NS state required the removal of any other monopoly or independent power, such as that represented by a traditional independent judiciary. The instrument for this removal had been, at least since the Röhm purge, the SS. Unlike Röhm, who in 1933–4 had set out to challenge the monopoly of arms of the Reichswehr and had come to grief, Himmler had organized his initially small SS into a tightly knit and well-disciplined order with the aid of which he slowly but steadily infiltrated the existing institutions of the state as well as those important to the state such as industry. Law graduates as a profession were especially overrepresented in the administrative and security branches of the SS.[166] Given the importance in Germany to this day of a completed legal training, qualified lawyers had a versatility that could be deployed in virtually every sector of the state's activity. This author is inclined to attribute to Himmler a much greater degree of detailed, long-term planning than to Hitler. As well as being unscrupulous, he was a careful, meticulous administrator to the point of pedantry.[167] He carefully took one step at a time, each of them calculated to expand and to consolidate the power of his SS 'Black Order' over the long term. Of his intrusion into the apex of the judiciary we have had already occasion to comment. By 1942 his concentration camp state and his control of the police were firmly entrenched and outside any other control. His sphere of influence was such that he was Germany's *de facto* Minister of the Interior a year before he became it *de jure*.

Looked at from this perspective, Ohlendorf's exposition was not simply an answer to Frank, nor a claim to power, but the public declaration that the SS had attained supremacy over the judiciary. The SS could with Hitler's sanction dismiss its claim of judicial independence and demonstrate it to be hollow, devoid of substance. Frank might well complain, but his complaint overlooked one vital point, namely the extent to which the judiciary itself had diligently sawn away at the branch upon which it sat. From April 1942 onwards it was Hitler who, by way of the SS, controlled and administered what he considered justice; and as Ohlendorf implied, this process would not be complete until every judge was also a convinced National Socialist. That this process of selection and careful vetting would be carried out by the SS goes without saying. For the time being it sufficed that the newly appointed Minister of Justice was subordinated to Hitler, Bormann, Lammers, and to Himmler.

# 8

# Freisler as VGH President
# 1942–1944

Freisler was not as enthusiastic about his new appointment as might have been expected, an attitude perhaps explained by the fact that he had not been the first choice. But, as he put it in a private letter shortly after his appointment, quoting Reichswehr Minister Gustav Noske in 1919: 'Well, someone is going to have to be the bloodhound.'[1]

The new president tried to make the best of it, requesting a personal audience with Hitler on the occasion of taking office.[2] Though Thierack promised him to support his request, he did nothing of the sort, ensuring that if anyone should have direct access to Hitler it should be himself as Reich Minister of Justice, not the president of the VGH.[3] Freisler was unaware of this and on 16 October he wrote a letter to Thierack thanking him for his support and stating that he had submitted his report to Hitler in writing:

> In the meantime I have also become accustomed to my office. The work of the VGH I have divided up so that in my own judicial activity I may personally deal with all kinds of High Treason and Landesverrat, committed by Germans or foreigners in the Reich, and combat them in their various forms, extents and degrees of danger, and thus also provide guidance for the court.
>
> Of the high treason committed by Germans, that of the Communists surpasses any other; it flourishes particularly in the Alpine and Danube *Gaue*. Communist high treason during the war the VGH naturally considers an action favouring the enemy.
>
> Among the many trials concluded during the last few weeks, the trial against the former Czech General Homola needs particular emphasis since he was the chief of the second echelon of Obrana Národna, the Czech officers' resistance. He has been sentenced to death.
>
> Of the trials during the next two months, importance must be attached to:
>
> 1. The trial of the former author Dr Klotz who, as an emigrant, has acted very actively as perpetrator of high treason and Landesverrat.

2. Some trials of members of Communist sabotage organizations abroad whose targets were terror attacks on German, Italian and Japanese merchant ships.
According to the order of the Führer the Grynspan case will not be taken up until further notice.[4]

Point 2 referred to the German Communist harbour specialists led by Moscow-trained Ernst Wollweber, who had planted explosives on German ships abroad, notably in Swedish harbours.[5]

Attached to Freisler's letter to Thierack was a copy of another letter to Hitler in which Freisler announced having assumed office to 'the supreme legislator and judge of the German people' and assuring Hitler of his loyalty.[6]

Freisler's letter to Thierack had been preceded by one to him from Thierack. He had wanted to add a few comments, he said.

in this instance it moves me personally to hand over the Volksgerichtshof and its judges, a court which I have built up and led with joy.

In no other court than the VGH does it emerge so clearly that the administration of the law in the highest political court must be in accord with the leadership of the state. It will be your main task to guide the judges in this direction. You will have every indictment submitted to you and will recognize where it is necessary to underline to the judge concerned in confidential and convincing discussion what is essential for the state. I must emphasise again that this must take place in a manner which convinces rather than orders judges. Naturally this direction must only touch the essentials. Superfluous influence only leads the judge into an irresponsible judgement and will be considered by a responsible judge as an unbearable burden. The situation must develop so that judges will come to you in matters which require it, and that in matters in which this is unnecessary, you make them aware of that.

In general, the judge of the VGH must become accustomed to seeing primarily the ideas and intentions of the leadership of the state, *while the human fate which depends on it is only secondary* (my emphasis). The accused before the VGH are only little figures of a much greater circle standing behind them which fights the Reich. Above all this is true in war time.

I shall attempt to clarify this by a few individual examples:

1. If a Jew, and a leading one at that, is accused of Landerverrat or only supporting it, there stands behind him the hatred and the will of Jewry to destroy the German people.

2. If after 22 June 1941 there is still anti-German propaganda in the

Reich for the Communist cause and it attempts to influence the people towards Communism, then this is not only preparation for high treason but also an act favouring the enemy, namely the Soviet Union.

3. When in the area of Bohemia-Moravia the Czechs, always under the influence of London broadcasting, work against the Reich, if only by propaganda, then this too is not only preparation for High Treason but an act favouring the enemy.

Should at any time you feel unclear which line to maintain or what the political necessities are, then turn to me in confidence. I shall always be in a position to provide you with the necessary counsel. . . . I, too, was clear at the time that the treaty with Soviet Russia in 1939 did not change in any way how the state leadership judged Communism, but I did not know whether at the time it was opportune to hand down the heaviest punishments against Communists in the Reich. I had to help myself at that time and today I am available to you at any time in such often not very serious cases.

Dear *Parteigenosse* Freisler, please do not consider this exposition as an attempt to instruct you. I only wrote this letter because I know the significance of your position and I want to assist you.[7]

As events will show, Freisler, despite his inexperience on the judges' bench, needed no guidelines and in fact never sought Thierack's counsel.

At this point of change at the apex of the German judiciary and the VGH it seems important to list the laws, crimes and punishments with which the VGH dealt and to examine the statistics of its activities.[8]

| Law | Decree | Crime | Punishment |
|---|---|---|---|
| StGB | Para 80 | Territorial or constitutional high treason | Death |
| " | Para 81 | High treason by force | Death or hard labour |
| " | Para 82 | Preparing high treason | Death or hard labour |
| " | Para 83 | Incitement to high treason | Death, hard labour or prison |
| " | Para 84 | Lesser cases of high treason | Hard labour or prison |

| Law | Decree | Crime | Punishment |
|---|---|---|---|
| StGB | Para 89 | Landesverrat | Death or hard labour |
| " | Para 90 | Espionage | Death or hard labour |
| " | Para 90a | Fraud by Landesverrat | Hard labour |
| " | Para 90b | Betrayal of former state secrets | Prison |
| " | Para 90c | Complicity with Landesverrat | Prison |
| " | Para 90d | Handing over of state secrets | Prison |
| " | Para 90e | Careless handling of state secrets | Prison |
| " | Para 90f | Treason against the people by propagation of lies | Hard labour |
| " | Para 90g | Disloyalty by Landesverrat | Death or hard labour |
| " | Para 90h | Destruction of evidence of Landesverrat | Hard labour |
| " | Para 90i | Bribery to commit Landesverrat | Hard labour |
| " | Para 91 | Bringing about danger of war | Death or hard labour |
| " | Para 91a | Armed assistance to the enemy | Death or hard labour |
| " | Para 91b | Acts aiding the enemy | Death or hard labour |
| " | Para 92 | Agreement to commit Landesverrat | Hard labour |
| " | Para 94 Sec. 1 | Verbal attacks on the Führer | Prison |
| " | Para 139 Sec. 2 | Serious cases of failure to denounce high treason, Landesverrat or damage to defence *matériel* | Death or hard labour |

*Continued overleaf*

*Continued*

| Law | Decree | Crime | Punishment |
| --- | --- | --- | --- |
| Defence power protection decree (25 November 1939) | Para 1 Sec. 2 | Serious cases of damage to defence *matériel* | Death or hard labour |
| " | Para 5 | Endangering allied forces | Hard labour or prison |
| Decree for protection of prople and state (28 February 1933) | Para 5 Sec. 2 | Attempt to kill president or government member | Death or hard labour |
| Law against economic sabotage | Para 1 | Illegal transfer of economic assets abroad | Death |
| KSSVO | Para 2 | Espionage | Death |
| Decree to protect arms economy | Art. 1 | False evidence on requirements and stocks | Death, hard labour or prison |
| KSSVO supplement (29 January 1943) | Para 5 | Public *Wehrkraftzersetzung* (undermining of national defence) | Death, hard labour or prison |
| " | | Intentional *Wehrkraftzersetzung* | Death, hard labour or prison |

While the laws and decrees represented the legal basis of the VGH judgments it is also interesting to look at the number of denunciations and the number of indictments over the years:

*Number of denunciations:*[9]

| | |
| --- | --- |
| 1939 | 4,918 |
| 1940 | 4,588 |
| 1941 | 5,603 |
| 1942 | 4,727 |
| 1943 | 6,584 |
| 1944 | 13,986 |

| Number of indictments[10] | High Treason[11] | Landesverrat[12] | Other offences[13] |
|---|---|---|---|
| 1939 | 341 | 151 | 189 | 1 |
| 1940 | 598 | 381 | 214 | 3 |
| 1941 | 690 | 376 | 308 | 6 |
| 1942 | 1,044 | 692 | 377 | 15 |
| 1943 | 1,327 | 830 | 494 | 3 |
| 1944 | 2,120 | 1,859 | 256 | 5 |

Whereas the number of denunciations during the period 1939–1944 almost trebled, the number of actual indictments, although their trend too is rising, does not correspond at all with the number of denunciations. What caused this high number of denunciations which in 1944 more than doubled will remain forever in the dark except that 1944 was an 'abnormal' year in view of the bomb plot of 20 July 1944. But behind each denunciation hides a motive or a complex of them which cannot be empirically verified. Was it, among other things, the increased pressure of the war, the desire to avert catastrophe which was now staring Germany in the face? No one will ever know. But this flood of denunciations was by no means a phenomenon restricted to Germany. In occupied France, even in 1944 the wave of denunciations reached a level which made it virtually impossible for SD and Gestapo officers as well as for the authorities of Vichy France to cope with them. Cases of high treason, too, show a rising trend whereas those of Landesverrat show a more fluctuating pattern. This discrepancy is also shown when we look at the figures for new cases and compare it with that of the actual indictments brought:[14]

| Year | New Cases | Dismissal | Handed on to Prosecutor | Completion by other means | Indictments |
|---|---|---|---|---|---|
| 1935 | 5,096 | 1,040 | 2,596 | 1,039 | 317 |
| 1936 | 5,895 | 1,147 | 3,438 | 852 | 268 |
| 1937 | 5,592 | 1,003 | 2,821 | 1,302 | 254 |
| 1938 | 5,171 | 1,095 | 1,556 | 1,707 | 277 |
| 1939 | 4,918 | 989 | 1,573 | 1,740 | 341 |
| 1940 | 4,599 | 951 | 1,218 | 1,367 | 598 |
| 1941 | 5,603 | 1,356 | 1,785 | 1,770 | 690 |
| 1942 | 4,727 | 1,086 | 1,547 | 1,460 | 1,044 |
| 1943 | 6,584 | 693 | 2,872 | 1,287 | 1,327 |

What exactly is meant by 'Completion by other means' is not at all
clear, but there existed a number of offences which the VGH could
hand on to a Oberlandesgericht, and it does not seem too far-fetched
to assume that, in view of the close cooperation between the VGH
and the Gestapo, certain cases never reached the courts at all and
those denounced were incarcerated in concentration camps. Also it is
interesting to note that the number of VGH prisoners on remand
(1,230 in December 1938), had risen in April 1943 to 4,128, and
while in 1934, the year of the foundation of the VGH, the number of
sessions amounted to 57, by 1943 this had risen to 1,258.
Unfortunately, the files for 1944 and early 1945 have been
destroyed.[15]

According to Thierack's and Freisler's own reports between 1937
and 1944 the VGH pronounced the following sentences:[16]

| Year | No. of accused | Death | Life | Hard Labour 10–15 yrs | 5–10 yrs | Under 5 yrs | Prison | Conc. camp | Fine | Acquittal |
|------|------|------|------|------|------|------|------|------|------|------|
| 1937 | 618   | 32    | 31 | 76  | 115 | 101 | 99  | –  | –  | 52  |
| 1938 | 614   | 17    | 29 | 56  | 111 | 91  | 106 | –  | –  | 54  |
| 1939 | 470   | 36    | 22 | 46  | 100 | 89  | 131 | –  | –  | 40  |
| 1940 | 1,096 | 53    | 50 | 69  | 233 | 414 | 188 | –  | –  | 80  |
| 1941 | 1,237 | 102   | 74 | 187 | 388 | 266 | 143 | –  | –  | 70  |
| 1942 | 2,572 | 1,192 | 79 | 363 | 405 | 191 | 183 | 45 | –  | 107 |
| 1943 | 3,338 | 1,662 | 24 | 266 | 586 | 300 | 259 | 42 | –  | 181 |
| 1944 | 4,379 | 2,079 | 15 | 114 | 756 | 504 | 331 | 22 | 2  | 489 |

Between 1934 and 1938 the number of death sentences was still
relatively low, in 1934, with 4 death sentences and 4 executions, in
1935 with 9 death sentences and 8 executions, in 1936 with 10 death
sentences and 10 executions, in 1937 with 32 death sentences and 28
executions, and in 1938 with 17 death sentences and 16 executions.[17]

Within the six senates which existed by 1942, the First Senate led
by the president of the VGH, first Thierack and then Freisler, always
had the highest number of death sentences. This in part was due to
both Thierack and Freisler drawing the most important cases into
their senate. In 1942, before Freisler became president, the First
Senate passed 649 death sentences out of a total of 1,192; in 1943
under Freisler, out of 1,662 death sentences Freisler's senate passed
769; in 1944 out of 2,079, the First Senate passed 866.[18]

Soon after Thierack's letter of 9 September 1942, he began to
introduce the NS-*Richterbriefe*, circulars which periodically went out

to all judges giving the NSDAP guidelines for the administration of justice. All had the same theme, that the judiciary and its jurisdiction were to be reformed in accordance with the Führer's demands, that legal training was in need of reform, that one should go back to old Germanic leadership principle in which the Chief was also the Supreme Judge, and that there was no longer any room for the independent judge. Questions of clemency could only be dealt with by the Führer personally; control of defence lawyers was also required. Furthermore, what was needed were reforms in the law in view of the decline of morality of German women during the war. Judicial procedure was in need of simplification and superannuated lawyers should be retired. Also it was a waste of time and resources to keep convicts locked up in prisons; their labour should be made available to war industry. Of course the treatment of 'inferior peoples' such as Poles and Jews was also mentioned and that they had no right to a proper trial by court since they were by definition 'lawless'.[19]

On 29 January 1943 by decree, all cases of *Wehrkraftzersetzung* (undermining national defence) were transferred to the VGH, though the VGH still had the right to delegate the trial of some cases to a lower court such as a Oberlandesgericht.[20] Insofar as the cases were tried by the VGH the death sentence predominated, especially in the wake of Stalingrad. Between January 1943 and January 1944 alone, 142 death sentences were pronounced and executed for *Wehrkraftzersetzung*. In Berlin alone, the number of actual cases tried in 1943 was 241, while from January 1944 to December 1944 the number of cases tried or pending had risen to 893.[21]

The greater proportion of the accused were so-called 'defeatists', people who in public judged the development of the war pessimistically as far as Germany was concerned and did not trust NS propaganda. Thierack himself divided them into three groups, the remnants of Marxists and Communists, intellectuals who overestimated their own capacities, and those who lacked the feeling and fibre for soldierly virtues. Freisler was more careful and held the view that as defeatism could not be legally defined, one would have to decide from case to case.[22]

Given the absence of complete transcripts of VGH trials other than those associated with the 20 July 1944 bomb plot, we must accept a considerable degree of uncertainty as to the validity of the respective charges levelled against anyone facing the VGH.

One of the first victims of this kind of legislation was a member of the editorial staff of the *Völkischer Beobachter* who had expressed scepticism about how the war would end and made sarcastic remarks about Hitler and Goebbels. He was lucky, receiving only 5 years' imprisonment because he 'was not really an enemy of the state but a weakling.'[23] On the other hand, on 21 May 1943 a 55-year-old retired man was sentenced to death, although he was psychopathic. He had become hostile to the NSDAP because it had not fulfilled one of the points of the programme, the breaking of 'the servitude to interest rates'. During the war he had sent to Hitler and other party dignitaries and NSDAP offices postcards containing gross insults. On one card he stated that Germany needed only one corpse – that of Hitler. He was convicted of *Wehrkraftzersetzung*, especially because he sent his insults on postcards which everyone could read and not by sealed letter. His mental condition was not considered a circumstance calling for a milder sentence, since mentally inferior people needed to be eliminated from the German Volk anyway.[24]

That prominence was no safeguard against the VGH was demonstrated in the case of Karl Robert Kreiten, one of the most gifted concert pianists of this period. Partly of Dutch descent, he had once applied for NSDAP membership but was turned down. After a concert in Berlin in March 1943 he had given expression to his opinion that 'the NS regime ought to be made a head shorter.' Denounced, he appeared before the VGH on 1 September 1943 which sentenced him to death: 'In our present struggle – despite his professional attainments as an artist – he represents a danger to our victory and must therefore be sentenced to death. Because our Volk shall march towards victory strong and united without being disturbed.' The famous conductor Wilhelm Furtwängler intervened in vain on Kreiten's behalf. The judgment acquired its particular note through a commentary in Berlin's *12-Uhr-Blatt*: 'How uncompromisingly one has to deal with an artist who instead of faith sows doubts, instead of confidence injects lies, instead of bravery seeks to produce despair, emerges from a report of the last few days about a well known artist being strictly punished, an artist devoid of honour. Today no one would have any understanding for an artist who has stumbled, if he were treated more leniently than any other *Volksgenosse*. . . .' The commentator was Werner Höfer, until early 1988 the chairman for over thirty years of one of the Federal Republic's most popular political TV-chat shows. He at first denied all knowledge of the commentary but when it could be demonstrated that he had been one of Hitler's Germany's most prolific journalists he had to resign his post.[25]

On 8 September 1943 a medical practitioner called Dr Alois Geiger was sentenced to death because to a patient of his, a woman with child, the wife of a front-line soldier, he had made remarks sceptical about the war. He had violated her confidence in German victory by saying that in the event of Germany's defeat her husband, who was also a member of the NSDAP, would be likely to be killed. The judgment set out in detail the reasons:

In July this year, in his soldier's uniform, the HJ-*Oberbannführer* Will visited Alois Geiger, a Lower Bavarian country doctor, and asked him to look after his wife, who had three children and was expecting a fourth, and who had been evacuated from Berlin to Lower Bavaria. Towards the end of July and early August, Frau Will visited the doctor twice during which he stated the following: 'she must have courage to have yet another child, because if things turned out badly then everything would become rather sad for us.' Upon Frau Will's objection that she was convinced of Germany's victory, he added that particularly in the light of events in Italy, it was possible that Germany would lose the war. It would turn out particularly terrible if the Russians should conquer us because that would mean the physical death of the German people, while a defeat at the hands of the Americans and the British would be the smaller evil. When Frau Will replied that these were seriously troubling us already, he had said she was still too strongly influenced by NS propaganda and to Frau Will's shocked question as to what would happen to her husband, he had replied that if it should come to that, her husband would be one of the first to be done away with.
Geiger admits having said that, and probably he has said much more, because during the trial Frau Will said that he had advised her that her husband should leave the NSDAP, though Geiger himself was also an NSDAP member, although he had now been expelled. People like him had to be expelled and eliminated from the German *Volksgemeinschaft*, so there could only be one sentence: death.[26]

Two days before, on 6 September, merchant Erich Buchin had been sentenced to death by Freisler for defeatist utterances, which did not stop at the person of the Führer. These utterances concerned the devasting series of air raids to which Hamburg was subjected by the RAF and USAAF at the end of July and early August 1943. He had maintained that German fighters could not reach the heights flown by the allied bombers and expressed the opinion that Germany would lose the war. In addition he had said that there would be no peace as long as Adolf Hitler was alive. The accused had confessed fully, but had also tried to excuse himself by saying his nerves were frayed; 'can a soldier in the front line say that he was nervous?' asked Freisler rhetorically in his judgment. The accused represented a serious danger to the German people and would therefore have to be punished by death.[27]

These are just a few cases of *Wehrkraftzersetzung* as tried by Freisler which illustrate that defeatists could not expect mercy or mitigating circumstances from the VGH in general or from Freisler in particular. Though only a small number of the VGH judgments have survived one could still add considerably to the cases already cited.[28]

One of Freisler's early major cases occurred in February 1943, a case which attracted major attention inside as well as outside Germany, for news of it spread over the whole of Europe and the USA. It concerned the youth group centred around Professor Kurt Huber of the University of Munich, Hans and Sophie Scholl and their group of friends. They had engaged in anti-NS activities since 1941–2, largely by distributing leaflets in Germany's major urban centres, and especially in Munich where they studied.

Their story and their public appeals are too well known to require being retold in this study.[29] When they were caught on 18 February 1943 while distributing leaflets in Munich University Himmler appears to have intervened very quickly. Acting probably on the assumption that the students were too young for such widespread activities he correctly assumed that the group, known as 'The White Rose', must have had an older *spiritus rector* to be found most likely among the university's teaching staff. The Gestapo headquarters in Munich's Wittelsbach-Palais issued under Himmler's name a circular to all students and teaching staff of the university. In it he called for the leader to come forward and thus save the lives of the students involved. Although the students could not expect to escape punishment, the male members could atone for their crime within a Bewährungseinheit, a penal unit of the army on the eastern front, a unit of which there existed several within the army and the Waffen-SS, for political as well as criminal delinquents, used in particularly dangerous sectors of the front. Female members of the group could prove their worth to the *Volksgemeinschaft* by engaging themselves in social work for the duration of the war.[30]

Himmler's appeal was in vain: the Scholls, who had initially denied their actions, made a full confession. By the afternoon of 21 February 1943 the indictment had been drawn up and submitted to the accused. The trial was to take place on the following day in Munich. Berlin, north and northwestern Germany were then already subjected to heavy air raids, so that it proved difficult to get the judges, the lay judges and defence counsels to Munich in time, a fact which accounts for the short time which the accused and their counsel had to prepare their case. Nevertheless the action was so clear-cut that any defence, however cleverly constructed, was bound to have feet of clay.

On 22 February 1943, Freisler presided over the trial of the Scholls and their associate Christoph Probst. They were accused of high treason, of acts favouring the enemy with the intent to commit Landesverrat and *Wehrkraftzersetzung*. Freisler conducted the trial coolly and did not allow his temperament to intrude into the proceedings. The accused were given the right at the end of the trial to say some concluding words, a right of which Sophie Scholl did not avail herself. Hans Scholl pleaded only for the life of Probst, but Freisler silenced him because the right was restricted to matters concerning one's own case. Probst asked for his life for the sake of his wife and two children. The sentence was carried out on the same day in Munich-Stadelheim prison by decapitation. But Himmler in Berlin did not wish to create any martyrs: he apparently demanded that the execution be postponed, but his telegram arrived too late.[31]

Whether, within a purely legal context, the trial of the Scholls besmirched German justice is open to debate. The issues involved were clear cut, and that helped considerably to shorten the trial. Naturally the sentences were to serve as a deterrent, but the trial was by no means an instance of Freisler giving full play to his political fanaticism. The defence could not, irrespective of circumstances, have been conducted better that it was.

The execution of the Scholls and Probst caused serious ill-feelings among Munich's student community, but this sentiment was directed against the *spiritus rector* of the group who had failed to come forward to save the lives of his students. A student member consequently denounced him in the presence of witnesses to the *Dekan* of the Faculty of Philosophy of Munich University, who then had no other choice than to inform the Gestapo. This put the police on the trail of Professor Huber who, in his interrogation, implicated a number of other students such as Alexander Schmorell and Otto Graf as well as those who had allegedly given financial support to the group.[32]

On 19 April 1943 Freisler was again in Munich to try another fourteen of the group. Huber, Schmorell and Graf were sentenced to death. A Stuttgart factory owner who had given Schmorell 5,000 Marks was let off with ten years' hard labour. Two others, a young doctor and a student from Freiburg im Breisgau, had had contact with Schmorell. They had had an inkling of his activities, but not being certain had failed to denounce him. Both received sentences of seven years' hard labour. Then there were grammar school pupils who had been influenced by Hans Scholl and were considered his victims and received each five years' imprisonment. The rest received prison sentences ranging from one year to a few months. The last accused was the head of the Weimar National Theatre, Dr Falk Harnack, whose brother Dr Arvid harnack had been sentenced and executed the year before by the Reichskriegsgericht (Reich War Court) for his membership in the Red Orchestra. Freisler, recognizing the cultural services which Harnack had rendered to Germany, considered his situation so unique that he was acquitted.[33]

The action of the White Rose group was in vain: their hopes of bringing Germany to its senses by arousing its conscience were illusory. The cult of remembrance of these young people and their unique sacrifice is resurrected time and again by a guilty elder generation in order to provide themselves with a moral alibi. In recent years members of the younger generation have done the same for more immediate dubious political ends.

Clergymen and nuns did not enjoy an immunity from the prosecution by the VGH. Freisler could rarely refrain from sarcasm when dealing with clergymen, especially with Catholic priests and nuns, but his guiding principle was that everyone in Germany knew the programme of the NSDAP which assured the liberty of all religious confessions and supported what it called 'positive Christianity'. Anti-war or anti-NS sermons preached by the clergy during 'total' war were bound to weaken the powers of resistance of the German people and simply replicated the propaganda of the enemy.[34]

On 4 November 1942, Hitler was sent Führerinformation No. 139 with the following content:

> Three Catholic clergymen in Lübeck, under the pretence of the care of souls, created groups within which, until July 1942, propaganda against the NS state was conducted. Besides leaflets dropped by the English air force, they used the sermons of Bishop Graf Galen [one of several bishops who spoke out against the NS euthanasia programme]

and numerous other hateful propaganda tracts in which it is asserted that heavily wounded German soldiers, war disabled and victims of accidents at work were being killed in field hospitals. The fifty members of the group, half of whom were soldiers, were asked to distribute these leaflets and tracts on the front and at home. The trial will be carried out before the Volksgerichtshof.[35]

The three clergymen, all relatively young, had been arrested. For some time they had individually or together listened to the German service of the BBC and used its news items within the meetings of their groups. One may question the extent to which the propaganda leaflets furthered pastoral care. Naturally the clergymen were concerned by measures taken by the NS regime such as the dissolution of some monasteries and convents to gain further garrison and hospital space. They also discussed the ill-treatment of Poles, and spread reports of alleged mutinies within the German armed forces in addition to the rumours about euthanasia being practised on badly wounded German soldiers. Finally they spread rumours about Hitler and the leading personalities of the Third Reich.

The VGH conducted the trial in Lübeck under Vice-President Engert on 22 June 1943 which ended with the death sentence of the three priests on the following day. They were convicted of Landesverrat, of acts favouring the enemy, as well as of *Wehrkraftzersetzung*. Along with the clergymen two other men were sentenced, one to five years of hard labour, the other to one year's imprisonment.[36]

On 2 July 1943 another Catholic priest, Jakob Gapp, was sentenced to death by the VGH, this time in a court presided over by Freisler. Gapp came from the Tyrol and in 1920 had moved to Belgium where he was ordained. After a spell of parish duty in Austria he was instructed by his order, the Society of Mary, to go to France in January 1939 and from there to Spain. In both France and Spain he had delivered sermons on the global danger posed by National Socialism, especially its danger to religion. Apparently his sermons yielded little or no practical results, so in July 1942 he got in touch with the British Consul in Valencia from whom he received British material directed against Germany. On his way to Germany to distribute it he was arrested. Freisler handed down a detailed judgment. As for the priest's general attitude, he said:

As the German blood in one mighty current united itself from the Alps to the North Sea, he remained apart, even hostile. He regarded National Socialism as the deadly enemy of religion and the Catholic church. . . .

The President has put to the accused that the Führer and the Party Programme, the preferential public-legal position of the church and its financial subvention by the state belie the assertions of the accused about the hostility of National Socialism. Jakob Gapp tried to support his arguments with three points:

a. The closing down of private schools. Quite unjustly. With that measure National Socialism affirms only that the education of the Germans of tomorrow will be carried out today on its responsibility.

b. Rosenberg's *Mythos des 20. Jahrhunderts* (The Myth of the Twentieth Century), as the main trial has shown, he has completely misunderstood, probably because his dogmatism did not allow him to penetrate the book deeply.

c. A broadcast of Radio Vatican in 1938 in which it was asserted that National Socialism was hostile to religion and suppressed Christians, to say the least a rather superficial assertion. He was standing at the crossroads between the loyalty to his Volk and treason to his Volk. He lacks any foundation for his assertions.

Jakob Gapp was clear in himself that his attitude would damage the German people and the German Reich heavily and would also aid the enemy in a war. He declares that for him the order of the Church and her interests stand above the voice of the blood, membership in the Volk and Fatherland. He sees in this war two dangers for Germany; the one danger that England is victorious, for this victory would damage the German people.

The other danger (!!!) (*sic*) is that Germany remains victorious. This victory would be a danger more serious than England's [victory] because then National Socialism would remain. The accused has himself made a statement and added that he knew that National Socialism could not respond like liberalism by accepting any action motivated by one's mental attitude, because like Catholicism its demands were total. Therefore he, Jakob Gapp, would have to combat it as long as he lived. . . .

There can only be one answer: anyone who betrays the voice of the blood, who tries everything to alienate Germany's friends and to aid Germany's enemies, on the grounds that their victory is for our Volk a lesser evil than our victory – such a German has forever, for our generation and the German generations that follow, lost his honour. For treasonable aid of our enemies he must therefore be sentenced to death.[37]

That political jokes could lead to the guillotine we have already seen. A priest told an artisan a joke about a dying soldier who asked to see those for whom he had to die. Thereupon a picture of Hitler was placed on one side of the soldier and of Göring on the other, whereupon the soldier said that now he was dying like Christ. The VGH judgment stated:

> ... with his authority as a priest he has directed the most vulgar and dangerous attacks against our confidence in the Führer, an attack which can reduce the readiness of our people to risk its life for the life of the Volk. And he did not do this only once, because what he has said before us points in the same direction! ... And he did it while we are engaged in the gravest of battles.
>
> Such behaviour is not only an irresponsible misuse of the authority of a priest, it is more than that: it is treason to Volk, Führer and Reich. Such treason causes eternal loss of honour.
>
> To deter others anxious to do the same, such an attack on the morale of our war effort can be punished with nothing other than death.[38]

Again, these were only a few representative examples of many.[39] But there were acquittals, too. A Protestant clergyman accused of *Wehrkraftzersetzung* was acquitted because his defeatism could not be proven.[40] However, by the end of the Second World War at least another 26 clergymen, mainly Catholic, had been sentenced to death and executed,[41] evidence perhaps more of Freisler's virulent anti-Catholicism than of a general anti-Christian attitude.

*Wehrkraftzersetzung* was the charge with which the VGH had had to deal with most frequently. Second to it, however, came the *Nacht-und-Nebel*, 'night-and-fog' trials emanating out of the *Nacht-und-Nebel* decree personally introduced by Hitler in December 1941.

After the Germans had occupied most of northern and western Europe relative calm prevailed until the German invasion of Russia. From then on, guided frequently by Communists, attacks on individual members of the occupying force increased, as did acts of sabotage. Hitler's failure to conclude the war mobilized many who had initially been stunned into immobility, while the invasion of Russia mobilized the Communists. According to Hitler, any participant in a public disturbance or demonstration should, on principle, be either sentenced to death or deported to Germany. The relatives of those shipped to Germany were not to be notified. Keitel, the chief of the OKW, the Supreme Command of the Armed Forces, translated Hitler's instructions into the following order:

> It is the long considered will of the Führer that in occupied territories attacks against the Reich or the occupying power should be met with measures other than those used hitherto. The Führer's view is the following: all prison and hard labour punishments for any such actions will be considered a sign of weakness. An effective and long-lasting deterrence can only be achieved by the death sentence or by measures which keep the dependents of the criminal in uncertainty about his fate. This purpose is served by deporting them to Germany. The guidelines attached for the prosecution of such punishable acts are in accordance with the thinking of the Führer. They have been examined and approved by him.[42]

Following these guidelines, attacks against the Reich or German forces in occupied territories were in principle to be punished by immediate execution. In their six points, Keitel first insisted that he would reserve for himself the decision as to which court was practically able and formally competent to deal with such cases. Secondly, the Public Prosecutor was to base his decision for an indictment on his view of his duty. Thirdly, orders for execution and for release from imprisonment on remand were at the discretion of the Public Prosecutor. Fourthly, the main hearing was to be conducted behind closed doors. Fifthly, the admission of evidence of foreign origin was to be subject to the prior consent of the Public Prosecutor. Sixthly, and lastly, at any time up to the verdict the prosecutor might withdraw his indictment or move for a temporary postponement of the proceedings. The motion of the Public Prosecutor to postpone proceedings temporarily must be granted by the courts. The Public Prosecutor must be given an opportunity to state his attitude, should the court decide to rule against his motion *in re*.[43] In this way all the cards were neatly stacked in favour of the prosecution and against the defence.

The problem still to be resolved was which court was to handle the *Nacht-und-Nebel* cases. The OKW specialist on this matter appended a note in which, in January 1942, he stated that 'nevertheless . . . the question has not been decided whether the OKW within its jurisdiction will give the right to handle the case to the Supreme Military Court (the Reichskriegsgericht) or to lower military courts.'[44]

Advice was sought from the Ministry of the Interior. The question of jurisdiction in *Nacht-und-Nebel* cases was then shifted virtually from Ministry to Ministry – one has the impression that each was glad to hand on such a delicate issue – until it finally found its way to the desk of the president of the VGH. For Freisler the question of delicacy seemed not to exist and in a letter to Thierack on 14 October 1942 he accepted what he considered a challenge. In the letter he referred to a conversation he had had in the Reich Ministry of Justice with Ministerialdirektor Crohne, in which he was informed that it was proposed to give civil courts jurisdiction over criminal acts in occupied territories against the Reich or the occupying power, and that he, Freisler, was to examine the jurisdiction of the VGH in this connection. 'As president of the Volksgerichtshof I have no comment to make on this proposal. It is self-evident that the Volksgerichtshof can and will fulfill such tasks as it may be allotted.'[45]

Freisler went on to refer to previous dealings with the OKW on this matter, but his notes were not put on file because they were *Geheime Reichssache*, strictly secret. Hence we cannot see from the files when the VGH first got involved in the *Nacht-und-Nebel* cases. But what Freisler does not seem to have realized was that everyone else had tried to steer clear of this matter. The Wehrmacht, for example, endeavoured to keep its allegedly 'clean shield' free from blemishes caused by procedures of dubious legality which so strongly assisted the prosecution, and was only too relieved to see the VGH do the dirty work on its behalf.

As far as Freisler was concerned, legal niceties were less important than ensuring that the court would give no other verdict than that demanded by the Public Prosecutor. In order to ensure this technically, Freisler and the OKW agreed first that the Public Prosecutor could withdraw his indictment right up to the pronouncement of the verdict, and secondly, that if the VGH were not to accede to the demands of the prosecution, the latter should be enabled again to make its position on the case unmistakeably clear. In practice this meant that any case that came up in a *Nacht-und-Nebel* trial was predetermined in terms of the verdict and the sentence.[46] Nevertheless, it must be stated that the measure was not so much a product of a policy of terror running wild as it was a reaction to the Allies' policy of terror conducted under Churchill's motto, 'Set Europe ablaze!'

Freisler's attitude in this matter corresponded fully to the guidelines concerning the application of the law in wartime which

Thierack had issued to leading officials of the German judiciary. Thierack had expressed the view that the judiciary must in the first instance serve Germany's victory and support the Führer in his struggle for the liberty of Europe. At the moment this aim could only be served by a gentle direction of the judges, he said, since, owing to Germany's historical development, many preconditions of a united attitude in the exercise of jurisdiction did not yet exist. The judiciary should not push their colleagues but assist them in a comradely, tactful manner. The task of the court was mainly to record the facts. Guidance could only be given as far as the consequences of the facts were concerned. The instruments of guidance should be the superior judges in cooperation with the prosecutors, who in turn were all directly responsible to Thierack.

Then Thierack moved on to examine alternative methods of guidance. Judges needed to be continually informed of the will of the leadership of the state, he argued. In addition, previous judgments on similar or identical charges could be used in the form of precedents to provide guidance for the case in question. The most effective course was for the court to come to an agreement before the case was actually tried. Obviously Thierack was aware that, even in the terms of the Third Reich, he was treading on thin ice on this issue and he therefore explicitly refrained from issuing detailed instructions on this point, instead leaving it to his subordinates to interpret his words in the proper spirit. However, a great many cases would require prior consultation and decisions: those involving matters in which the death sentence would be passed, war crimes, economic war crimes, crimes of violence, violations of decrees restricting contacts between German civilians and prisoners of war, crimes committed by youths, deeds committed out of 'tragic fateful complications', *Nacht-und-Nebel* affairs, and all criminal and civil cases 'in which persons are involved who are officials or leading functionaries of state or party, or persons who otherwise occupy a prominent position in public life, cases in which existing law and the given social and economic realities clash and require solution.' If there should be any difficulties he, Thierack, was the man to whom they should turn for advice.[47]

As far as the *Nacht-und-Nebel* cases were concerned, there is not a single recorded instance in which the VGH or Freisler ever referred back to this fountain of all judicial wisdom. Keitel of the OKW said that anyone sentenced in occupied territory should be executed within 24 hours.[48] Only against women should no death sentence be executed, except for acts of murder and terrorism.[49] The *Nacht-und-*

*Nebel* decree would apply to the western territories and to Norway (Denmark was excepted). Admiral Canaris, the chief of the German Abwehr, agreed with Keitel's measures, adding that recourse should only be had to courts martial if the sentence was one of death; otherwise terrorists should be transported to Germany.[50] However the *Nacht-und-Nebel* decree was not to apply to Germans or racial Germans insofar as they were involved in cases within occupied territories.[51] It did not apply to Jews since they had been excluded from the application of existing judicial procedure and were subject to the SS and police only.[52]

After the Second World War the charge was frequently made that *Nacht-und-Nebel* cases as well as others tried by the VGH involved no more than a preemptory procedure in which indictments were handed to the accused only shortly before the trial or not at all, and that the defence was not briefed in time to prepare the defence of the accused.[53] There is a conflict of evidence here. Some of the post-war affidavits making this claim originated from members of the judiciary who, by inculpating others, notably the dead Freisler, endeavoured to lighten the charges they were likely to face. Other affidavits state that as long as Germany was not exposed to intense Allied aerial bombardment, indictments were received in time and defence counsel were given adequate time for the preparation of their cases; once lines of communication were disrupted for hours and even days all this changed.[54]

Further factors militating against a proper procedure were that the trials had to be held secretly and speedily. For these reasons priests and clergymen were refused admission to the accused. For the *Nacht-und-Nebel*, much the same applied as for those accused of political or serious criminal charges before the VGH and other courts: an acquittal might involve not liberty but the handing over of the acquitted person to the Gestapo and his or her transfer to a concentration camp for the duration of the war. However, here too are exceptions, the criteria for which are not determinable. Instances do exist where persons acquitted were allowed to return to their respective countries on the grounds that it was not their transport to Germany but their fate which was to be secret, particularly from their families.[55]

Those allowed to return home soon dwindled when on 6 November 1943 the OKW ordered the general transfer of all *Nacht-und-Nebel* prisoners, acquitted or not, to the Gestapo.[56] The Gestapo then acquired the further power of deciding who of those transferred to it was to be released home and who was to be interned in a concentration camp, provided, of course, they had not already been sentenced to death. In a circular on 21 January 1944, Thierack emphasised in response to this OKW ruling that the Reichsführer-SS and Chief of the German Police could apply the mildest form of protective custody to prisoners who had been acquitted or whose cases had been stopped by the courts. They were to be informed that for security reasons they were to be detained further. Those sentenced to death were manacled unless the execution was postponed, a decision which applied primarily to women. Ober-reichsanwalt Lautz advocated that the women whose execution was to be postponed should be told of the postponement once they arrived at their respective prisons, but in the face of Bormann's objections this proposal was rejected.

Secrecy even prevailed beyond death. Farewell letters were withheld and destroyed and, although the official registry offices were informed of each case and the names were entered into the death register, any notice or information concerning the death of the person was to be withheld, except in cases where the Reich Minister of Justice had given his personal approval. Another cardinal rule was that the press was not to be informed.[57]

The Wehrmacht judiciary was reluctant to carry out the *Nacht-und-Nebel* jurisdiction and by means of delays and other manoeuvres tried to reduce its own involvement and thus ensure that the VGH would carry the major burden.[58] The Wehrmacht judges were, in any event, already overburdened. In May 1942, the OLG prosecutors' offices in Cologne, Essen and Kiel had to deal with 50 cases, but within less than a year this figure had mounted to over 2,000, while during the same period the number of accused increased from 600 to nearly 6,700, all of whom were imprisoned.[59]

The first VGH trials of *Nacht-und-Nebel* cases began late in August 1942. In addition there were also *Nacht-und-Nebel* trials held before special courts and the Oberlandesgerichte. By late 1942 over 1,000 cases had been submitted to the VGH. Freisler transferred 800 of these to other courts, while the remaining 200 were tried by the VGH itself, mostly by Freisler's own First Senate. Some involved hundreds of accused, probably the largest encompassing 360 accused.[60]

The problem with such numbers was that in Berlin the VGH had to conduct the trials in the prisons themselves. The number of sentences was also such that individual prisons could no longer cope with them and executions had to be carried out in prisons in other areas of the Reich, a procedure which seems not to have been to the liking of other judicial authorities (although they could do very little about it). In Munich, resistance to carrying out Nacht-und-Nebel executions went so far that, of 130 condemned, 30 were actually kept alive from spring 1944 until liberation in late April 1945.[61]

The growing dislocation of German communications produced havoc in such simple matters as the forwarding of the prosecutor's files to the court; correspondence, files and the like did not arrive at their points of destination. Other state prosecutors held on to their files for fear of losing them, so trials could not be held and this in turn meant a rapid upward turn in the prison population, already overcrowded.[62] In an air raid on Berlin on 24 November 1943 all the Nacht-und-Nebel files were destroyed. This meant that the German authorities, Army Field Police and general police in the occupied territories had to start their investigations anew in order to replace the files destroyed, and a day lost to the police was a day gained for the accused.[63]

No reliable figures, not even approximate ones, are available on the total number of Nacht-und-Nebel cases tried by the VGH. We do know, however, that they concerned almost exclusively French, Belgian, Dutch and Norwegian nationals. Offences ranged from acts of terrorism to giving support to RAF members trying to escape back to Great Britain to anti-German word of mouth propaganda. Only after the Allied invasion of France in 1944 did Hitler issue an order which put an end to all Nacht-und-Nebel prosecutions. Investigations and trials were suspended and the prisoners were handed over to the Gestapo for transfer to concentration camps where those considered potentially dangerous were soon liquidated.[64]

Shortly before Hitler issued this order, Thierack wrote to Bormann stating the view of Oberreichsanwalt Lautz that since the execution of women involved in Nacht-und-Nebel cases had been postponed on Hitler's orders and they were now being treated like cases of hard labour, they should also be informed that their death sentences had been suspended. This, however, had yet to happen since the supreme right of granting clemency rested with the Führer.[65] Any answer to Thierack's request was made superfluous by Hitler's cancellation of the Nacht-und-Nebel procedures.

It cannot be said that the VGH sentencing policy in the Nacht-und-Nebel cases was unduly harsh. Similar sentences would have been handed down for the equivalent actions in any of the belligerent countries. What gave the whole matter its specifically inhuman image was, first, the secrecy surrounding the cases, and the fact that none of the dependents ever knew whether the member of their family arrested was alive or dead; and, secondly, the practice, already applied to Germans themselves, of handing over the defendant to the Gestapo and the concentration camp system after an acquittal or a stay of proceedings.

Beside the occupied territories, there were, of course, the territories which had been annexed to the Reich between 1938 and 1940, notably Austria, the Sudetenland, the Protectorate of Bohemia and Moravia, parts of Poland, Luxemburg, the Alsace and the area of Eupen-Malmedy.

In Austria resistance was slow in coming. The Hapsburg legitimists were a tiny insignificant minority, and only Socialists and Communists, though small in numbers, had a semblance of an organization. But the Hapsburg legitimists had one advantage in that they reached across the frontier and were in touch with Bavarian legitimists, whose aim was the restoration of the Wittelsbach monarchy – in itself an act of high treason. Some Bavarians thought in terms of a political union with Austria.[66] Not so much because these Austrian legitimist groups posed a genuine threat to the NS regime as for the deterrent effect, 109 Austrians were accused of high treason as early as 1940, but because of the scant evidence no VGH trial seems to have taken place until 9 July 1942, when the judgment stated that

> the aim of Otto von Hapsburg to restore the Austrian Monarchy with the aid of foreign powers hostile to the Reich and to become the heir of the deceased Emperor Charles are known to the courts. It needs no further mention that this aim cannot be achieved by peaceful and constitutional means. It would require the division of the Reich by force, the tearing apart by force of the former Austrian Federal State through a war against the Reich, or a civil war inside and the overthrow of the NS leadership.[67]

The case in question involved Count Stürgkh, the nephew of the Austrian Prime Minister murdered in 1916, who in the autumn of 1938 had emigrated to Paris where he immediately involved himself in the Austrian League, founded by Otto von Hapsburg. Captured after 1940, he was sentenced to death because he had promoted a

Danubian Federation, including Hungarians, Czechs and Yugoslavs.

> The accused, carrier of an old German and Austrian title of nobility, has put himself at the disposal of a movement whose aim it is to smash the fusion completed by the Führer of all Germans, especially the reunification of the German territory of former Austria with the Reich. . . . The movement for which he has worked was part of the force that was determined to force Germany into the war. It also intended to create for the enemy powers the image that National Socialism and its state leadership enjoyed no backing by the German people and was thus suited potentially to strengthen those forces who opposed the Reich.[68]

Up to and including 1944, four other trials were held by the VGH against legitimist groups.[69] Individuals fared the same as the citizens of the *Altreich*: a political joke at the expense of the NS regime brought the same accusation of *Wehrkraftzersetzung*.[70]

On 17 October 1944, in one of the last cases, Freisler's VGH had tried a schoolboy accused of having listened to enemy broadcasts. The evidence was not clear and the boy was acquitted; and in fact it had been his father who had tuned in to enemy stations while his wife had warned him time and again. Since the father often told political jokes at home, the son naturally repeated them. In a separate trial the father had already been condemned to death. But as far as the son was concerned Freisler was impressed by the fact that he was the region's Hitler Youth Skiing Master, an exemplary member of the Hitler Youth and of its junior branch, the *Jungvolk*. 'No doubt he wants in due course to become a soldier and an officer. Furthermore one could not overlook that the witnesses for the prosecution were unable to describe the incidents in detail and without contradiction. Therefore, in agreement with the counsel for the defence, the accused is to be acquitted.' Thus the 'merciful' Freisler.[71]

As already mentioned, the strongest resistance within Austria came from former Socialists and Communists. Their activities were, in the main, centred in Vienna, though Communist groups existed in all major Austrian cities. During the first seven months of 1941 there were a total of 200 arrests in Vienna and Lower Austria, 154 in Styria and 50 in Linz in Upper Austria. Communist activities continued to increase throughout 1942 when eleven VGH trials were held involving 650 defendants. Another 1,500 suspects could not be arrested because there was no space to confine them. Only in early

February 1944 was the VGH able to register a notable decline in the number of cases involving Communists.[72] Whether this statistic allows any conclusions about a reduction in the scope of Communist activities is more than doubtful. The tide of war had distinctly turned against Germany, the *Anschluss*, welcomed by the majority of Austrians in 1938, had proved a bitter disappointment, and naturally the readiness to denounce activities against the Reich and its organizations declined. Reich Germans visiting Vienna in the summer of 1944 were able to detect a distinctly anti-German attitude.[73] Freisler seems to have come down with a vengeance upon those Socialists and Communists who up to the *Anschluss* had been unemployed but had begun to enjoy considerable material benefits since 1938.[74]

There are many examples of the VGH's activities in the Protectorate of Bohemia and Moravia. Immediately after the establishment of the protectorate, Hitler had announced a wide-ranging amnesty which included treasonable activities by Czechs. A total of 1,219 known cases of Czech espionage against Germany fell under this amnesty, but both Hitler and Himmler decided to draw a line there in the hope of appeasing the Czechs and integrating them into the Reich.[75] Since the Czechs, or at least a large number of them, showed little inclination to favour integration, Hitler ordered renewed prosecution but also warned the VGH off the large-scale trials that were so conducive to martyrdom.[76] Execution squads of German police forces were considered adequate to the task. If cases came to court, they should be withdrawn and trials should not commence until Germany had achieved victory. The judgments then announced would lead to only one sentence, that of death, which would then be commuted into a life sentence of fortress confinement or deportation.[77]

However, the situation in the protectorate continued to deteriorate. Heydrich's appointment marked a watershed after which the Eliáš case was the first prominent VGH case. By March 1942, three months before Heydrich's death, the Chief of the Chancellery of the Presidency, Dr Otto Meissner, informed Schlegelberger that Hitler's decision to treat the Czechs gently had been overtaken by events and that there were no longer any fundamental objections to trials of Czech resistors or to the execution of death sentences.[78] The door was now wide open to the VGH, which could also delegate cases to the Oberlandesgerichte in Breslau, Dresden and Leitmeritz. Czech defence counsel were considered undesirable, though they were not proscribed. As for the language barrier, another problem, the indictment was to be handed to the accused in German while a Czech would provide an oral translation. Trials were also held in German, with a Czech interpreter present.[79]

On 24 May 1941, before Hitler gave the VGH the go-ahead, a total of 3,523 cases in the protectorate were being investigated by the Gestapo, the greatest number belonging to the Obrana Národna.[80] After the Eliáš case, Heydrich felt that the impact of the VGH trial was not the one he had desired and he therefore requested that no more VGH trials should take place in the protectorate.[81] In this he failed. On 8 July 1943 the VGH tried former Czech Staff Captain Zemen because of his activities in a secret military organization. This activity, however, had taken place before the outbreak of war in 1939 and since then had apparently ceased. In view of this, the VGH rejected the plea for the death sentence put forward by the prosecutor and instead sentenced Zemen to ten years' hard labour.[82] On 27 August 1943, however, a Lieutenant Colonel of the Czechoslovak army was sentenced to death for having built around him a military nucleus of former staff officers.[83]

Of all the illegal organizations in the protectorate the Obrana Národna suffered the heaviest; it was the largest and the most vulnerable to infiltration by German counter-intelligence. The VGH was well aware of its potential danger.[84] But despite the German measures and the heavy VGH sentences, resistance could never be fully crushed. From April 1943 on, the opposition published its own weekly paper, V boj ('In the Struggle'), and although the editorial staff were discovered and sentenced to death by the VGH, it continued publication.[85]

Better organized was the Czech Communist Party, the KPC. This emerges clearly from one German report:

> The illegal KPC in the protectorate was built up as follows: the Supreme Party authority was the Central Committee in Prague. Subject to it were the sub-committees for Bohemia in Prague and that for Moravia in Brünn (Brno). Each sub-committee was divided into districts at the head of which there was a leader. In Moravia there were four sub-committees centred on Brünn (Brno), Göding (Hdonin), Olmütz (Olmouc) and Märisch-Ostrau (Ostrava). The districts were again subdivided into sub-districts and those were made up of factory cells and other small local groups. Persons recruited operated usually in groups of three. . . .

Beside the organizational and political apparatus, the control of which lay mostly in one hand, there also existed a technical apparatus. This was responsible for the production and distribution of leaflets and was decentralized down to cell level. To camouflage their work, the illegal officials usually used cover names. For the distribution of their printed material certain centres were established, and for handing on information couriers were used.[86]

Espionage networks continued to prosper in the protectorate throughout the war. In retrospect, therefore, it seems surprising that the Czechs who during the war volunteered to go to Germany to work in her armaments industries continued right up to the end of the war to enjoy the same privileges as German citizens. Unlike members of other eastern nationalities, they were not confined to camps, could live in private lodgings, were not subject to any curfew and received the same wages as their German colleagues. Yet in the protectorate the Germans could never be sure that the Czech authorities who worked under them could be relied upon, and the number of Czech civil servants who were tried between the autumn of 1944 and early 1945 clearly shows that they could not.[87]

Among the many acts of violence and sabotage the most notorious was the murder of Reich Protector SS-Obergruppenführer Heydrich in Prague on 27 May 1942. The assassination had been planned in London, where the Czech government in exile was deeply concerned about the degree of cooperation which Heydrich had managed to establish between the Germans and Czech workers. Heydrich's long-term idea, which he shared with others, was to make the protectorate a member of the Tripartite Pact and to create a Czech force to fight against the Russians alongside the other foreign volunteer units under German command. The Czech government in exile desired to prevent this at all costs, and it devised a means which would drive an irremovable wedge between the Germans and the Czech population.[88]

In their calculation of an excessive German reaction they proved right; upon the death of Heydrich, Lidice was flattened by the bulldozers of German army engineers and the Reich Labour Service, while a police company shot the entire male population in reprisal. The women of Lidice were taken to the concentration camps and those children who were considered capable of integration into the 'nordic' community were distributed over German foster parents. Courts martial, established in Prague and Brünn, condemned a total of 1,351 individuals in the period from 28 May to 3 July 1942.[89]

General Eliáš's execution, postponed because of conclusive evidence showing that he had broken off his contacts with London and Paris about six months before his arrest, was now carried out under Hitler's orders. But the murder of Lidice's male population and the deportation of its women and children had not been ordered by the German government; it was the result of a personal initiative of the commander of the SD and Security Police in Bohemia and Moravia, SS-Standartenführer (Colonel) Böhme, 'the real bloodhound of the Protectorate.'[90] What was supposed to be the beginning of cooperation and collaboration was effectively smothered by the blood and the ruins of Lidice and elsewhere in the protectorate.

What VGH judgments still exist with regard to the Czech Communists concentrate heavily on cases late in 1943 and throughout 1944. Without exception sentences were severe. Hence the case of a Czech civil servant condemned on 28 March 1944: 'From the political development of the accused it can be seen that one is dealing with a convinced Marxist, in whom the military and political events of 1939 cannot be assumed to have caused the slightest change of mind. Indeed the trial has confirmed that P. until his arrest has remained in his mental attitude what he had been for years, for decades: a Marxist.'[91]

Relationships between the KPC and other resistance organizations such as the Obrana Národna seem to have been anything but smooth; hostility between Communist groups and Czech nationalists ensued. Especially in post-war émigré circles, charges and counter-charges of treason reverberate to the present day, of Communists having denounced Nationalists to the Germans, and vice versa.[92] But irrespective of whether the Czechs standing before the VGH were Communists, Socialists, trade unionists or nationalists, they were invariably severely treated, in the main being sentenced to death.[93]

Although in the German-French Armistice of 25 June 1940 France had not formally ceded Alsace-Lorraine to Germany,[94] the territory was, under Gauleiter Bürkel, taken under German control and French inhabitants were expelled into the interior. If not *de jure* it was a *de facto* annexation.[95] To divide Alsacians simply into pro-German and pro-French is an oversimplification. Ardent German patriots originated from the Alsace and so did equally ardent French patriots, like Rober Schuman, the father of the Schuman plan and a French Foreign Minister who in the First World War had served as an officer in a German supply unit. But between these two currents the main current was purely Alsacian, desiring to live in relative autonomy with their Germanic-Alemanic dialect and with as little interference from either Paris or Berlin as possible.

This was the attitude adopted by the Alsacian Youth Front, which protested violently against the introduction of conscription in the Alsace by Germany. They tore down German official proclamations, recruitment posters and the like. Twenty-four members of the group were tried by Friesler on 7 July 1943, who sentenced all members to long hard-labour terms, and reasoned:

> The German Volk in the Alsace received the National Socialist revolutionary armies with enthusiasm. For those with consciousness of and pride in being German which may have lain dormant under French rule, the heart was now to beat faster, they had to put at the disposal of the Reich their strength for the task of reconstruction, and as young Germans put their lives at the disposal of victory. The obligatory legacy of Langemarck existed for German students of all German *Gaue*, including the Alsace, as an example of the fulfillment of duty and surrender. Nevertheless, in the Alsace there gathered a group of German students of Alsacian tribe who betrayed their own blood, our Volk. . . .
>
> First of all: any purely formal legal position would have to take second place to our people's material right to life and therefore the duty of all German young men to make their sacrifice takes precedence. But further: each German in the Alsace was aware, if not on the basis of legal knowledge (which is beside the point anyway), then by feeling and conscience, that France could no longer return to its highly doubtful claims arising out of the diktat of Versailles, because of the hostile policy she had pursued towards Germany by driving Germany into a war, and by her declaration of war, she has annulled the few duties which Germany still had under the Versailles Document.[96]

Freisler adopted an identical attitude to other cases arising in the Alsace, Lorraine, Luxemburg and Eupen Malmedy. The French (and Belgians, for that matter) were dealt with more leniently: at least they were not guilty of betraying their own 'Volk und Blut'.[97]

In the eastern territory, the VGH's jurisdiction was restricted to Poles living within the provinces annexed by Germany from Poland, such as Danzig, West Prussia, the Wartheland and Posen.[98] Within the General Government the VGH had no jurisdiction at all, since the Governor General, Dr Hans Frank, held all power in his own hands and was subject only to Hitler, Bormann and Himmler.[99] But during the early phase of 1939–40 rivalries developed within the annexed provinces between the VGH and the NS Reichsstatthalter residing in Danzig, Posen (Poznan) and Kattowitz (Katowice). Although the VGH could assert itself to some extent, on the whole it was the Reichsstatthalter who managed to keep power concentrated in its hands. They were aided in this by the Penal Code for Poles and Jews, which, as mentioned, introduced summary justice against Poles and Jews, subjecting them to purely authoritarian law of a political character.[100] This allowed investigation, prosecution, trial and sentence to be carried at a pace which even surpassed that of the VGH. Apart from that, Himmler's agencies reigned supreme.[101]

The first major case for the VGH in the east emerged with the discovery of the *Stronnictwo Narodowe*, the 'National Party' in the Wartheland. A total of 568 Poles were arrested. The Oberreichsanwalt stated that by the end of December 1941 the party had extended its activities not only to Posen but also to Warsaw.[102] The VGH held its trial on 17 and 18 December 1941 and sentenced nine of the accused to death. But the more the Germans realized that Polish resistance could not be crushed, the more severe became the sentences.[103]

In south-eastern Europe, strictly speaking, the areas affected were Austria's border provinces of Styria and Carinthia, since they bordered on Slovenia where Yugoslav partisans were no respectors of the German frontier. Their activities caused much disquiet – so much so that on 4 February 1943 the Gauleiter of Carinthia wrote a letter to Thierack in which he demanded a speedy dispatch of the VGH to prosecute cases of treason.[104] An identical demand reached Thierack a month later from the Gauleiter of Styria, who also suggested that the VGH establish a permanent senate in Graz.[105] Though both Thierack and Freisler welcomed positive and quick action by the VGH, the request to establish it in Graz was turned down.[106] Between 7 and 9 April 1943 35 Slovenes, among them fourteen women, faced the VGH in Klagenfurt all charged with high treason and acts favouring the enemy. Nine were sentenced to death for membership in terrorist Communist bands 'which terrorized the German population as well as all others loyal to the Reich', as Freisler put it. The others were sentenced to long terms of hard labour.[107]

Although Hitler's Reichstag speech of 1942 had led to a substantial tightening of the German judiciary and, associated with it, to the further erosion of the principles of the *Rechtsstaat*, the German courts, the VGH among them, were not entirely out of the firing line of NSDAP criticism. Three months after Hitler's speech, Goebbels gave a speech, ostensibly on Thierack's invitation, to the members of the VGH. He introduced himself by stating that the remarks he was about to make had been personally approved by the Führer. Since its very beginning, he said, the judiciary had been the object of public criticism. Even today, judicial decisions were criticized and dismissed as alien to the spirit of the people. The criticism that the judiciary had failed the people could not be rebutted by the objection that every time a criticism was raised an isolated case had been dragged before the public, while the great number of sound judgments were ignored. What was at stake here was something fundamental, that is to say the wrong attitude of some judges who were unable to liberate themselves from old patterns of thought.

The blame for that, Goebbels told his audience, lay to a considerable extent in the wrong conceptual training received by German law students at German universities. It was an essentially one-sided education and later, when they were judges, they lived their enclosed professional lives without any real contact with the outside world. In short, judges possessed too little practical experience of life. However, decisions felt to be alien by the people had a particularly bad effect during wartime, so everything would have to be done to bring about a change before it was too late for the judiciary. No profession other than the judiciary had the privilege of not being able to be removed: even generals could be removed. A powerful state could not forego the right to remove incompetent civil servants and this applied to judges too. The whole idea of their irremovability originated in any case in a world to which National Socialism was fundamentally opposed.

Goebbels insisted that in making a decision a judge had to take as his point of departure not the law, but the basic principle that the lawbreaker must be expelled from the *Volksgemeinschaft*. In wartime it was not important whether a judgment was just or unjust; all that mattered was whether it fulfilled its purpose. The state had to defend itself in the most effective manner possible against its internal enemies and finally exterminate them.

Then Goebbels turned to the problem of the Jews. In his own *Gau* of Berlin, 40,000 Jews were still running about freely; these people were the enemies of the state, and only shortage of means of transport was responsible for them not having been deported to the east. In the treatment of the Jews, the judiciary would have to recognize its political task. Attitudes coloured by emotions were not in place. It was an untenable situation that even today a Jew could raise formal legal objections in court against a demand made to him by the Berlin President of the Police. Jews should be cut off completely from using German legal remedies from the German law and from any right to appeal against any official measure directed against them.[108]

Freisler, still Secretary of State, took his cue from Goebbels' speech and drafted a decree which virtually deprived the Jews of all legal remedies, which was then circulated to Frick, Himmler, Goebbels, Ribbentrop, Bormann, Hans Frank and the OKW. All of them approved. The decree consisted of a single paragraph that Jews in court cases could no longer appeal or use any means to re-open their cases or raise complaints against administrative measures. Finally, on 21 April 1943, it was decided to publish the measure in the form of a decree.[109] Practically speaking, this meant that even the Penal Code for Poles and Jews no longer applied to Jews. They were now beyond the pale of the law; they were *vogelfrei*, a free target for anyone.

Less than a month before, on 31 March 1943, Thierack had issued a decree according to which judges and civil servants of the judiciary could be transferred or retired at will.[110] Goebbels, who had frequently criticized the lack of cooperation between the VGH and his own ministry, had cause to be satisfied not only with the consequences of his speech, but also with the arrangement which from October 1942 onwards made available to him the regular reports of the Oberreichsanwalt to Thierack.[111] They do make interesting reading. Thus on 3 October 1942 Lautz reported:

> On 18 May 1942 Jews placed an explosive and an incendiary device in the exhibition 'The Soviet Paradise', which these devices were intended to burn down. The Jews who participated in this attempt have been dealt with by special courts, sentenced to death and executed.
>
> The investigations carried out by the Gestapo have resulted in the discovery that the Jews involved belonged to two separate Jewish groups in which, especially during 1941 and 1942, membership dues were raised, political instruction with a Communist bias was given, propaganda material was exchanged and preparations made for the production and distribution of other publications hostile to the state. Furthermore, these Jewish groups provided French workers' identification cards to allow their members to stay illegally in Berlin.
>
> At the regular gatherings of these Jewish groups it was concluded

that Bolshevism was the strongest enemy of Germany and that its victory would entail the solution of the Jewish problem in favour of the Jews. Therefore, the Jews had to familiarize themselves with Bolshevik ideas in order to be in a position, if the circumstances required it, to commit themselves to the success of the Bolshevik revolution.

During the preliminary investigations 13 Jews were taken into custody, all aged between 19–23 years. Seven of the accused have escaped. The members of the second group will shortly come before the judge.

In the Alpine and Danube regions the number of accused has not fallen in recent months. New cases amount to 244. But the number of those committing Marxist High Treason known to the Gestapo is much larger. The Gestapo, when the files were submitted, has time and again stated that the arrest of numerous known participants will take place at a 'suitable time'. The reason for the delay lies either in the fact that there exists too little space in the prisons for detainees or in the serious impairment of the efficiency of industries important for the war effort (for example the German railways), which the arrest of the suspects would cause. Because of lack of detention space I have, when visiting Vienna on former occasions, tried to relieve the prisons of the eastern marches. I shall take up this question again.

Also the 244 new cases belong in their overwhelming majority to the organizational framework of the KPO [Austrian Communist Party]. Now, as before, the bulk of its activity lies in factories, among them:

1. the Siemens-Schuckert Works in Leopoldau
2. the firm of Frosa and Büssing in Vienna.

Furthermore, we are to clamp down on factory cell organizations in the great plants of Siemens & Halske A.G., Alexander Friedmann, Simmering-Graz; the Pauker A.G. and Hofherr-Schrantz-Clayton-Shuttleworth A.G. Most of the suspects were active within the Red Aid organization. The following cases should be mentioned specially:

1. In the investigations regarding 17 officials of the factory cell organization in the Siemens-Schuckert Works in Leopoldau, they have all been arrested. The arrest of another 46 known cell members is to take place at a suitable time.
2. The trial of Johann Hornschall, formerly a tramway ticket collector and now an *Oberfeldwebel* in the army, will be expedited by the VGH. Until the end of January 1941 Hornschall had been active as provincial controller and leader of the provisional KPO in Vienna. The case against the accused had been formerly in the hands of the Reichskriegsgericht.
3. The tramway engineer, Friedrich Fass, was at first *Kreisleiter* and then until March 1941 Territorial Leader in District III of the KPO

in Vienna. He cooperated closely with the leadership in Vienna and was an active liaison man between the leadership and the illegal Communist youth organization. He also maintained connections with provincial officials of the KPO and was active in disseminating Communist propaganda material.

4. Leopold Morawetz, a mechanic's mate, served until the summer of 1940 as District Leader in the XIIth Vienna District for the KPO. He engaged in the distribution of Communist propaganda and had connections with Communist officials in the Burgenland.

5. The case against Mastny (born 1921) and Fischer (born 1916), both members of the Wehrmacht, has been transferred to me by the Reichskriegsgericht. Both accused, until their arrest in May 1942, that is to say after the war with Russia had begun, had been active in carrying out Communist word-of-mouth propaganda and distributing Communist propaganda material to army personnel and civilians alike.[112]

Reports such as this were then edited and made available to Goebbels, though he would have preferred to have done the editing himself. However, these reports show a considerable degree of anti-NS activity within Greater Germany. This is also borne out by the statistics quoted earlier in this chapter on high treason and Landesverrat. Then, of course, there is the unknown number of those German opposition elements never discovered or those who never faced a court, but instead perished in concentration camps.

Thierack's aim was to set the entire German judiciary on a rigid NS course. In this he enjoyed the close cooperation of Himmler and Heydrich's successor, Ernst Kaltenbrunner. Rumour has it that he recommended himself especially to Himmler by visiting the various Berlin prisons during air raids and ordering the immediate execution of political prisoners there.[113] He did not bother about the jungle of clauses of the law and therefore represented a guarantee that the judiciary and NSDAP would 'cooperate' in the spirit of mutual confidence. In particular, the cooperation between judiciary and police provided an outward appearance of calm. Since they had legal backing, police actions were no longer found as arbitrary as before by the public at large. At the same time, however, the new laws meant the extension of police powers. The broadening of the functions of the police made the 'corrective' role to which Ohlendorf had referred superfluous. To upgrade the role of the judiciary, Thierack issued a circular on 12 October 1942 in which he stated that judges occupied a special position among the servants of the state. Expressing himself in feudal terms, he described the judge as the liegeman of the Führer, holding his fee of the Führer himself by his direct order. As a result there was a fundamental difference between judges and other civil servants and in future this difference should be expressed constitutionally by judges being lifted out of the civil service. Judges should no longer be described as civil servants but as what they were, judges.[114]

If further coordination were needed Freisler certainly aimed to contribute his part. During the last week of October 1942 he visited the Protectorate and conferred with his longstanding friend Kurt Daluege, the Deputy Reich Protector.[115] The main topic of their conversation was the role of the investigating judge. Apparently Daluege expressed his complete satisfaction with the work of the VGH investigating judges in the Protectorate and it was agreed that in future, and in all cases, the investigating judge of the VGH, the Oberreichsanwalt and the police should work closely from beginning to end, that is to say until the indictment was drawn up. The persons referred to were Oberreichsanwalt Lautz, the chief of the VGH investigating judges, and Daluege.[116]

Another measure introduced during the later part of 1942 was the withdrawal of spiritual assistance to those sentenced to death. When the Evangelical Lutheran Church of 28 December 1942 raised objections to this measure, they were curtly dismissed by the Ministry of Justice on 13 January 1943.[117]

In February 1943 the ruling was made that in VGH cases involving citizens of occupied states it was a matter for the judge's discretion as to whether the defendant would be represented by defence counsel.[118] Cases also arose in which Himmler apparently did not consider it in the public interest that the case should be tried before the VGH or any other court and consequently had the persons concerned shot. On 19 January 1943 the SS judge in the office of the Reichsführer-SS, SS-Obersturmbannführer Munder, wrote to the new Secretary of State in the Reich Ministry of Justice, Dr Rothenberger. Rothenberger had requested that the news of such executions should not be made public in order to avoid diminishing the reputation of the courts. Although Hitler had originally ordered such publication, Himmler now decided that any publication would first require his own personal approval.[119]

From early 1943 the Allied bombing offensive began to take effect, a development which had a dramatic impact on the character and duration of the trials and of the procedures of the VGH. The lay judges could not attend punctually since they travelled to court from all parts of Germany; the required number of defence lawyers was not always available; and trials were obstructed because the defence lawyer had not arrived – often he arrived so late that he had not more than an hour to discuss the case with his client, a quite insufficient time for the preparation of a case. Hence in a letter marked 'Secret' to Freisler, dated 9 February 1943, the Oberreichsanwalt Lautz suggested that the ultimate decision about whether a defence counsel should appear at a VGH trial or a special court trial should lie with the judge himself. Freisler did not express himself in favour of such a ruling but preferred flexibility; in principle he preferred the restriction of the judge's power in this matter rather than its extension.[120]

The rumour, if indeed it was simply a rumour, that Thierack's visits to prisons and subsequent ordering of prisoners' executions gained substance on 17 August 1943 when Lammers wrote to him from Hitler's headquarters expressing Hitler's concern that about 900 prisoners sentenced to death were still in prison, some of them prisoners for two months or longer. According to Hitler these prisoners represented a major danger, particularly in big cities, and therefore it was necessary to come to a quick decision about their execution. For the duration, he said, requests for clemency should no longer be raised and a prisoner once sentenced should be executed immediately, preferrably by an SS or police commando. But this order should be restricted to those cases in which the death sentence was arrived at without the slightest doubt. In all VGH cases this was the case. Hitler's restriction, if it can be called that, benefited only common criminals. Ten days later Thierack issued an implementing circular and the formal decree was issued on 8 September 1943.[121]

Among the auxilliary judges of the VGH quite a number had been called to the colours and their shortage was, by 1942, making itself acutely felt. But not until 1943 were new criteria issued for the selection of judges. First, they had to be members of the NSDAP and actively involved in the work of the party. Secondly, they had to be suitable in terms of their personality and their attainments and, if possible, should have some experience in the penal law. Potential VGH judges should already be on the list for promotion to either *Landesgerichtsdirektor* or *Oberlandesgerichtsrat*, and, most important, they should belong to an age group which was no longer liable to be called up into the armed forces.[122]

By 1944, Germany's control over the annexed territories had

become increasingly uncertain. Lautz's report of 19 February 1944 gives us a sense of the issues facing the VGH. The report is divided into sections A to E: Section A deals with high treason and *Wehrkraftzersetzung* within the *Altreich*, including Austria. In his general remarks, Lautz stated that investigations of preparations for high treason had not increased. No doubt groups with attitudes hostile to the state still existed, they still exchanged ideas and propaganda material, but they had not increased in number or in the scope of their activities. The greatest danger was still the KPD, whose former members would be most vulnerable to recruitment to new Communist groups should they emerge. On the other hand, Communist-inspired cases of high treason in the Alpine and Danube districts were definitely on the decline. Nonetheless, resistance seemed to be spreading: the number of cases of *Wehrkraftzersetzung* had increased to the alarming rate of 25 per day. These he grouped into five categories: (1) acts designed to undermine the morale of the members of the armed forces; (2) cases of utterances by people prominent in public life or in the economy whose statements had great impact upon the public; (3) systematic agitators; (4) those requiring 'special treatment' because of their personality, the nature of their offence and its objective; and (5) clergymen.

But Lautz also emphasised that no increase of political offences had been noted from areas which had suffered heavily from Allied attacks. Indeed it was an encouraging sign that people behaved in as disciplined a way as they did. Where individual cases had come before the court – such as that of Dr Robert Havemann and the *Edelweisspiraten*, discussed earlier – they had been severely sentenced.

Section B deals with the protectorate, the Sudetenland, and Alsace-Lorraine, in none of which the situation had deteriorated. Section C discusses Landesverrat and espionage in the eastern territories annexed by Germany.

Section C also deals with acts favouring the enemy and here the majority of cases concerned aid given to escaping prisoners of war. Between the end of September 1943 and the end of January 1944, 37 trials involving a total of 75 accused had been held. The French POWs benefited most from escape assistance from Germans, British POWs virtually not at all. Another cause for concern were the leaflets being dropped by Allied aircraft. They had given rise to fifteen trials in which the accused were charged with having taken possession of the leaflets, instead of handing them in to the nearest police station as ordered, and with circulating their contents. It was also noted that requests to foreign workers by their German colleagues to translate the contents of leaflets which had been dropped in a language other than German had been met with outright refusal. Finally, the war effort was being undermined. Foreign workers in Germany, especially the French, had allowed themselves to be tempted into carrying out acts of sabotage, and the number of cases had soared. Offences range from direct sabotage to excessive sickness leave and self-mutilation.

Section E concerns Landesverrat by negligence. No details are given except for the remark that in view of the wartime situation, paragraphs 90c and 90d of the StGB no longer sufficed to deal with this problem.

In conclusion Lautz noted the satisfactory state of affairs in the work of the VGH. Even files that had been destroyed in air raids had been restored and recopied to a very large extent. But, in his view, the clergy still played a major role in the cases before the VGH. To subdue any rumours among the population at large, Thierack wrote to Freisler on 15 March 1944 pointing out that in his Plan for the Distribution of Business of the VGH, the description of 'offences committed by Catholic Church tendencies hostile to the state' should be replaced by 'confessionally-conditioned acts hostile to the state'.[123]

In order to gain an insight into the organizational workings of the VGH under Roland Freisler, it is useful to summarize Freisler's submission to Thierack of his Distribution of Business Plan for 1944, a proposal engendered by the upsurge in cases. It is alphabetically grouped into ten sections.

Section A concerned Freisler's own First Senate, the jurisdiction of which was to include treasonable activities such as attacks on the Führer, the state, the NSDAP, the armed forces and prominent Germans abroad, and offences committed by the German intelligentsia or heads of industry. Confessionally-conditioned acts hostile to the state, Marxist and non-Marxist high treason and defeatism were split up according to *Gaue*, or territories, annexed by Germany, with the First Senate having the major share.

The latter also applied to Section B, the Second Senate, and for that matter to the other remaining four Senates. Section C stated that the Third Senate was to try all cases of Landesverrat committed in favour of the Soviet Union and Poland, as well as defeatism,

*Wehrkraftzersetzung* and wilful evasion of war service. Section D had the Fourth Senate oversee all cases of Landesverrat excepting those in favour of Soviet Russia and Poland. Furthermore, it was to try cases of damage to war *matériel* and offences committed by Germans from Lorraine, as well as offences by foreigners from Moravia. Section E confined the Fifth Senate to all cases arising in Austria, while under Section F the Sixth Senate had much the same business as the Fifth Senate, though in addition it was to deal with separatism in Bavaria and the Alpine *Gaue* of Austria.

Section G covered indictments arising out of the failure to denounce a crime. Trial of this offence would be dealt with by the Senate with the appropriate regional jurisdiction. Section H addressed itself to special cases of high treason and Landesverrat and left it to Freisler to decide which Senate would be responsible. Section J simply stated that this Distribution of Business would apply to any indictments which had arrived before 1 April 1944.[124]

Apart from the structure of Freisler's VGH which this summary reveals, another aspect is important, namely that Freisler, like his predecessor, quite intentionally reserved all potentially important business for himself. He implicitly retained for himself, for instance, the discretion to decide which cases of high treason and Landesverrat should be tried by the First Senate. Thierack had previously sent him a friendly warning that he should not concentrate everything in his own hands but give leeway to the other senates well, a warning which Freisler chose to ignore.[125]

However centralized and efficient the structure of the VGH, it was not without its critics. The legal expert of the NSDAP in Carinthia wrote to the Reich Ministry of Justice on 3 June 1943 maintaining that the VGH was entirely unsuited to deal with the internal and external enemies of the Reich. Punishment should follow immediately on arrest and for this task the over-centralized structure of the VGH was inappropriate. In Carinthia there was only one known case in which a person was arrested and sentenced within three weeks – a speed explained by the personal intervention of the Gauleiter. Generally, prisoners remained in custody for years; when the judgments were made years later, their deterrent power was lost. The NSDAP legal expert therefore advocated nothing less than the introduction of drum-head courts martial by the police to circumvent the judiciary.[126]

Nevertheless, the jurisdiction of the VGH was further extended as a result of the bomb plot of 20 July 1944 (see next chapter). Hitler personally rescinded his order of 21 June 1943 and replaced it with one by which all political crimes of all Germans, including members of the Wehrmacht, SS and police, tending to damage confidence in the political and military leadership of the Reich were to be tried by the VGH or, if necessary, by special courts. Investigations were to be taken up immediately; if absolutely necessary, the Commander was to act on his own initiative and have the accused executed. Notice of any investigation was to be given within six days of its inception to the OKW and the Reich Minister of Justice. The result of the investigation was then to be forwarded immediately to the chief of the respective service, the OKW and the Ministry of Justice. As far as the SS and police were concerned, the Reichsführer-SS took the place of the OKW; it was then up to the Ministry of Justice to decide whether the case should be dealt with by the VGH or by Special Court, the Sondergericht. Once this decision was made, the Führer would determine whether the accused would be 'released' from the Wehrmacht, SS or police, or expelled from the party and its formations, and transferred to the civil judiciary. If the Ministry of Justice decided that a trial would not be necessary or that, despite the acquittal of the accused, the accused's action nevertheless represented a violation of the 'Duty of Loyalty' towards *Führer, Volk und Reich*, then the respective file was to be submitted personally to the Führer by the OKW or the Reichsführer-SS.[127]

In the final phase of the war, Thierack tried to infuse new optimism into the legal profession by distributing, in addition to his *Richterbriefe* ('Letters to Judges'), *Rechtsanwaltbriefe* ('Letters to Lawyers'). In the first *Rechtsanwaltbrief* he pointed to the necessary cuts and simplifications in the legal system, but at the same time extolled the extreme concentration of the forces of the judiciary. Such concentration, he said, was essential if the law was to be able to cope with the tasks imposed on Germany by total war. It was the duty of every lawyer to focus on the struggle for liberty. Anything not concerned with this effort was of a subsidiary nature. The aim was to deal with all cases in the quickest and most rational manner. This implied a position of special responsibility for the lawyer who, in his work, had to have regard only to the goal of a National Socialist victory.[128]

Freisler himself had recently provided an undated summary of the German judiciary's work in the fifth year of the war. The judiciary had to be particularly careful, he wrote. In the light of the wartime situation different yardsticks were necessary from those of peacetime.

A person who tried to enrich himself from the consequences of air raids on Germany, for instance, was not simply violating property rights – he was breaching the loyalty to the *Volksgemeinschaft*, which during the war must protect its property as in times of peace. Such actions undermined public morale and thus the German war effort as a whole. The criminal therefore helped the enemy. The Volk demanded his elimination. Moreover, war produced, in biological terms, a counter-selection. While the best fell at the front, criminals could not be allowed to emerge behind the front; they must be eliminated as well. Up to 1940 criminal cases had declined, but since 1940 they had been on the rise again. In 1937 there had been 17,931, in 1940 there were 243,351 and in 1942, 288,688 cases. (The figures for 1943 and 1944 were as yet not complete.) Female crime was also on the increase.

Unsatisfactory also was the situation with Germany's youth, which in 1940 was involved in 21,274 cases, a figure which by 1942 more than doubled to 52,426. Youth crime fell into three groups: crimes committed by the political opposition; those of liberal-individualist groups; and those of criminal, anti-social gangs. The first group derived from the former Youth Leagues, the *Bündische Jugend*, and were opposed to the Hitler Youth, although many of them, ironically, were members of the Hitler Youth. Their criminality arose from ambushes on Hitler Youth leaders and patrols.

As far as the liberal-individualist groups were concerned, the so-called 'swing-youth' was characterized by its English fashions and manners, its hostile attitude to military affairs and its sexual excesses.

The criminal gangs consisted in the main of congenitally biological inferior youths and held no ideological aims.

The doors were wide open to a whole host of dangers from youth criminality, while education at home, and in the Hitler Youth, schools and factories had been weakened through the call-up and the separation of families by bombing raids.

Death sentences were on the rise, Freisler reported. This was due largely to the growing number of cases of high treason and Landesverrat. In 1943, 1,745 people were sentenced under these laws, followed only by 894 death sentences in the territories recently incorporated into the Reich. For 1943 as a whole the number of death sentences was 5,336. Freisler then went on to detail the various crimes individually, noting particularly the incidence of women convicted in 1943 for forbidden liaisons with POWs, a total of 6,500 convictions in 1943. He also noted that the major proportion of crime was committed not by a core of hardened criminals but by unstable characters. Therefore, it was important to keep the country clean and to consolidate public opinion behind the forces of law and order, a precondition for the stability of Germany's defensive power. New punishments for minor offenders should be introduced: farmers should be forced to increase their supplies, workers to increase output and other offenders to perform unpaid services for the commonweal.

It was difficult to prosecute economic crimes because the accused were often the same people who were indispensable to the factories in which they worked. This posed a danger which needed to be combatted. Also, many criminals had good connections with members or leading functionaries of the NSDAP, who wrote the most splendid references for them. All NSDAP members had now been forbidden to issue such references to anyone.[129]

Freisler himself was the object of various attacks, including some from the NSDAP. Hence Thierack wrote to Freisler on 18 October 1944, stressing that the role of the VGH in maintaining the home front had recently increased manifold. The task of the VGH was not to be confined to imposing well deserved punishment upon the guilty but to extend to the exercise of political leadership. The people must not only recognize the VGH's judgments as correct; they must also be informed of the reasons for the punishment.[130]

The conduct of trials by many heads of the Senates often suffered from their failure to highlight the political importance and gravity of the deed against the backcloth of the situation of *Volk und Reich*. What was important was to stress the political content of a crime, and the presiding judge must be able to make clear the grounds on which he found this particular act dangerous to Volk and Reich. The myriad 'defeatism' cases, for example, had to be dealt with by an 'ice-cold' conduct of the trial. Freisler would select the judges who were capable of dealing with the matter before them in a political context.[131]

Certainly Freisler himself never failed to point out the political implications of an offence. But the sample of surviving judgments handed down by the VGH is too small to allow any sweeping generalizations about his colleagues. It is quite possible that, from mid-1943 onwards, when the war decisively turned against Germany, Freisler's fellow judges were rather more anxious to stress the formalities of the law than to deliver sermons of political instruction, a procedure, so they may have thought, which would make them less vulnerable after Hitler's defeat.

It was clear that the tide was turning. In the wake of Stalingrad the Russians, together with German Communist émigrés such as Wilhelm Pieck, Walter Ulbricht and Erich Weinert, and relatively junior officers like Lieutenant Count von Einsiedel (a great-grandson of Bismarck) founded the National Committee for a Free Germany (NKFD), which was followed shortly in September 1943 by the founding of a 'League of the German Officers' (BDO). Its head was the former Field Commander General von Seydlitz-Kurzbach.[132] The NKFD marked the creation of a 'Popular Front' of all 'anti-Fascists' in the Soviet Union. Small individual groups were selected by the Russians for special training, after the completion of which they were dropped behind German lines to make their way into Germany. The largest group of the NKFD was founded in Berlin by the former Communist official Anton Saefkow who, together with his associates, managed to establish contact with former Social Democrats, the conservative opposition under Carl Goerdeler and two trade union leaders, Dr Julius Leber and Anton Reichwein. They were quickly discovered and arrested, tried and executed, but their partial success showed a chink in the German armour.[133]

Two other NKFD groups operated in Leipzig and in Thuringia. Both groups, like that of Saefkow, were quickly arrested early in July 1944, their members tried and sentenced to death by Freisler.[134]

Large numbers of Communists were arrested at about the same time, although it is impossible to verify to what extent, if at all, they had cooperated with the NKFD. But that the NKFD preoccupied the German leadership until the last months of the war is shown by *Führerinformation* No. 190, 1945, in which Thierack informed Hitler that the OKW had, in December 1944, handed over files to him concerning 32 members of the Wehrmacht who were alleged to have been active in the NKFD and BDO in the Soviet Union. These files had been handed on to the Oberreichsanwalt.

On close examination of the material, however, it appeared that in quite a number of cases difficulties existed. The existing Russian evidence, such as leaflets, brochures and pictures, were suspected of having been extensively faked; a number of pictures were in fact photographic montages. The evidence of some of the written matter had evaporated as well, since the graphological experts of the Gestapo had shown that most of these were faked as well. They had even gone as far as to employ their own forger, who produced a letter which the Gestapo expert acknowledged as authentic. What remained was the evidence of the so-called 'returnees'. Precisely what was meant by this term is not entirely clear, but there were cases of repatriation of both Russian and German soldiers via Sweden. At the same time it was not at all certain to what extent these could be used in order to provide testimony against NKFD and BDO members. One group of them had been returned to their army contingents, another had been accommodated in a camp near Graudenz, but precisely where the VGH did not know. A third group had been held in a camp near Lissa but the RSHA later indicated that inmates of this camp had been shot to prevent them from falling into Russian hands.[135]

By late 1943, if not before, and in spite of his rigorous conduct of the trials before his Senate, Freisler had begun in private to express doubts. In a letter dated 2 October 1943 he commented:

We have indeed proclaimed Total War, but are we actually conducting it? I am well aware of the special restaurants in all the major cities of the Reich which are frequented by the prominent, NSDAP and armed services as well, in which one can eat as though the war did not exist. But the worker knows them too, and he is the man who carries, alongside our front-line soldiers, the burden, irrespective of air-raids. It makes one feel bitter sometimes to have to condemn a simple man because of an utterance directed against prominent party and state leaders which arises out of such a background. I can do no more than to draw the attention of those with whom I am closely connected to these problems, what I cannot do from my judge's bench is to indict this corruption publicly, for then not only would I be the first victim, but on top of that I would provide the other side with excellent propaganda material. Thus I am aware of the one-sided justice I have to deal out on occasions but carry on doing it in order to pursue a purely political purpose: to prevent a repetition of 1918![136]

In a letter dated 4 February 1944 he mentions

that actually the whole legislation on listening to foreign radio stations seems ludicrous and not only on the surface. I doubt whether it would ever have been enacted if we Germans were a united consolidated Volk, with a national consciousness and a national pride which was taken for granted and was self-evident, which needed no great emotional appeals to raise it, the kind of nationalism which the French and the English have. But they have had centuries of uninterrupted national consolidation while at the same time our Reich was fragmented and led into the *Kleinstaaterei*. How shaky internally our morale was has best been demonstrated in 1917/1918. I still feel sure that we could not have won that war, but by our internal collapse we virtually invited the victors to impose upon us conditions which under normal circumstances they would have never dared to demand. But with the home front in dissolution who was there to look after Germany's interests? That must never happen again. But again the life of some people at the top provides no encouragement; many of them seem to have nothing else to do but trip their colleagues so that they can put another star on their shoulder boards, another title to their name, and another medal to their chest. In retrospect, I often marvel how in fact we managed to get as far as we did between 1933 and 1939, and it seems almost a miracle to me what we achieved militarily between 1939 and last year – what we achieved, we achieved almost in spite of ourselves. Hence rigorous watchfulness is the order of the day so that 1918 never re-occurs, even if we all have to fight to the last until our own ruins bury us. This is the last attempt to forge under German leadership a United Europe that can face America, the British Empire and others on equal terms. If it fails, and the future seems to hold little promise – the European nations will either be gobbled up by Stalin or they become mere satraps of the Great Powers. And what is left of Germany and the Germans will eat humble pie and indulge in a litany of self-accusation. But the German nation and the growing healthy German nationalism will have disappeared forever.[137]

Even before the bomb plot trials began, Freisler's VGH came under fire. On 29 July 1944, Lammers wrote to Thierack enclosing a copy of a letter from a person 'known to be trustworthy' who objected to VGH trials being open to the public.

The trials before the VGH take place before many listeners, before the bombing of the court, before 500 [people], now in the small hall before 150, roughly a *Sportspalast* composition, a section of the people, invited and uninvited. [The trials] are an attraction like the cinema.

The President, Secretary of State (*sic*) Dr Freisler, wants the public. His reasons are not difficult to discern, but his attention must be drawn to fact that earlier 500, now 150 people, hear day after day information which they afterwards spread, such as for example: The Führer was in a violent emotional state after Stalingrad in the Reich Chancellery, etc., etc., followed by the carpet story [a reference to the discredited story of Hitler the carpet biter] which the accused has heard from a General, and how the Führer is known within the Wehrmacht by a certain name (*Gröfaz*, the popular corruption of *grösster Feldherr aller Zeiten*, "the greatest warlord of all time"].

Everything comes out thick and fast, all the hateful names and allegations about the Führer in front of these 150 people, mostly humble people.

Even though Dr Freisler conducts his trials grandly, in masterly form, almost with genius, and produces evidence that all that has been said has been invented, nevertheless 150 people have heard of the alleged scenes in the Reich Chancellery and that the Führer has a certain nickname in the Wehrmacht. They are bound to tell their tale outside. No one is instructed to keep silent about the proceedings. And in that way via the VGH the most evil rumours are spread.

Or in the trial against *Botschaftsrat* Kiep, Frau Solf [widow of the former German Secretary for Colonies, Foreign Minister and Ambassador] and others, 150 listeners, hear among other things, that well-known German public figures and their social circle, who, so it is assumed, are especially well-informed and good judges of the situation, now say that Germany's victory is impossible and find it necessary to get in touch with Wirth, Hierstiefer and other fellows. These 150 listeners may all, though this is subject to doubt, consider the judgment just. But everyone of them will tell one or more others the details of the trials of defeatists, and thus contribute to more and more *Volksgenossen* saying to one another: if these much better informed diplomatic circles (Kiep was a Major in the OKW, Frau Solf the wife of our Ambassador in Japan) are already despairing of the outcome of the war, from where should we take our hope for a good ending?

This worry moves me to bring to your attention this undoubtedly important question.[138]

Thierack discussed the matter with Goebbels and Freisler and wrote to Lammers that he, Goebbels and Freisler had considered the matter and that Freisler had been told to be more careful in public trials.[139]

The year before, on 11 September 1943, Freisler had received a mild rebuke from Thierack. He wrote that Freisler interpreted the term 'public' too widely: 'If everything that is being talked about politically is fundamentally assumed to have been said publicly then the term "public" as used in paragraph 5 of the KSSVO would no longer make sense.'

In his reply on 28 September 1943, Freisler stated that on the basis of Thierack's letter he had reviewed a number of cases and had come to the conclusion that in some instances the ideas expressed by the judgment did not coincide with the National Socialist conception of the Reich. A judgment should reflect the security requirements of the Reich without at the same time making every conversation a public one. The court could interpret the law on *Wehrkraftzersetzung*, for example, according to 'the healthy feeling of the Volk'. As he, Freisler, understood the law, this pointed to the fact that this conception did not conflict with the existing law.[140]

On 16 November 1943, Melitta Wiedemann, the editor of *Die Aktion. Kampfblatt für das neue Europa*, addressed a letter to Thierack in which she strongly criticized Freisler. She referred to former talks they had had and then went on to say:

> Our former talk has remained in my memory, and not only the part about which I had actually to report, because you provided logical and psychologically effective reasons which are suited to make the harshness of our laws understandable to the broadest circles of the population, and even abroad.
>
> Unfortunately, by accident I have heard from a number of very superior witnesses comments which expressed great concern about the law and that at the VGH (First Senate) a series of trials is being conducted which shows no evidence of awareness of the necessity for psychological and propagandistic understanding.
>
> Thus, a short time ago, a Koblenz doctor was sentenced to death who, angered by a fine for insufficient blacking-out, had made absurd utterances to his barber about the influence of Italy's treason upon our domestic situation. Present at the trial were numerous members of Berlin's medical society, partly invited, partly summoned. In any case the hall was full.
>
> The accused, a higher civil servant and party member, had behaved incredibly. Before the court he made a nervous, unrefined, in any case an unsympathetic impression. It would have been a child's play to conduct the trial in a way that all present might have accepted the death sentence as hard but necessary.
>
> Instead, the presiding judge was so hard, unjust and unfriendly towards the accused, that he was obviously endeavouring to obstruct the man in his defence, although he was as good as sentenced to death already, while he openly courted the witnesses.
>
> As the propaganda campaign just started proves, the mood of the German people is considered particularly important. Therefore it is important to reshape VGH trials . . . [so] that the public is confronted by matter-of-factness, a humane treatment of the accused, so the conviction reigns supreme [and people will understand that] the subsequent harsh judgment has been necessary in the interest of the state and therefore deserves affirmation. . . .[141]

Wiedemann then touched on another point, namely that every person in Germany knew a black marketeer who sold part of his goods at excessive prices. This was illegal, but people refused to denounce the black marketeers, she said, because the punishment exceeded 'the healthy intuition of the Volk.' The more death sentences are announced, she concluded, the less people will denounce others except as an act of personal revenge.[142]

One may object that this evidence about Freisler's conduct during the trial of the Koblenz doctor is not that of an eye-witness but was hearsay. Nevertheless, it has been substantiated by other direct witnesses, though most of them testified after the Second World War. More importantly, Freisler's temperamental outbursts have been recorded on film.

As we have seen, Freisler was already showing the first signs of inner doubts on the condition of NS Germany and its future. At the same time, Freisler appeared to take little notice of his critics, nor does it seem that their letters were actually forwarded to him. All that was done was to close VGH trials to the general public. His attitude to those before him in the dock seemed to depend largely on their own attitude. Blatant attempts to belittle or deny what Freisler considered to be obvious crimes were met with the full force of Freisler's considerable venom. Those who stood by their actions appear to have met with a more even temper, though this may have changed nothing in the final outcome.

Freisler, perhaps intent upon putting his own personality to the fore, suggested in April 1944 that the tenth anniversary of the founding of the VGH should be duly celebrated. But for this he needed the sanction of his Minister.[143] Less anxious than Freisler to be exposed to the limelight, Thierack wrote to Bormann on 18 April 1944 broaching the matter, but expressed his doubts as to whether in the fifth year of the war such a celebration would be suitable. The letter, sent by teleprinter, received a reply the next day. Bormann wrote that because of the war the Führer did not wish such a celebration to take place; perhaps later there would be a more suitable occasion.[144]

Among the higher civil servants in the Reich Ministry of Justice, Freisler's reputation during the early summer of 1944 also seems to have begun to suffer. For one thing there was the problem, still unresolved, of the lay judges who, in increasing numbers, produced medical certificates excusing them from attending VGH sessions. At that stage of the war perhaps one was no longer anxious to be associated with this tribunal, especially under Freisler. But his views on the law, too, received internal criticism. It was suggested that the

VGH would only gain if its judgments were printed more extensively in the press rather than in stereotyped formulae.[145] Freisler was ridiculed on two points: his admitted inability to define 'defeatism' adequately (he could explain it only by reference to several practical examples), and his view that the statement of the StGB in paragraph 51, section III, that the defendant *can* be punished mildly, means that he should *not* be punished mildly.[146] Hardly any of his critics expected that Freisler's great personal hour was yet to come.

# 9

# Conspiracies Against Hitler

There had been numerous attempts at Hitler's life, most of them by individuals. One such attempt dated back to 1938 when Marcel Gerbohay, a Frenchman who intended to become a Roman Catholic priest, together with ten other students destined for the priesthood, founded the 'Compagnie du Mystère' whose sole aim was allegedly combatting Communism. As leader of this organization, Gerbohay had sent fellow member Maurice Bavaud to Germany with orders to persuade the Führer to declare war on Russia and to kill him if he did not. Bavaud, of Swiss nationality, travelled to Germany in October 1938 and in November tried to kill Hitler in Munich. Captured, he was tried by the VGH on 18 December 1939 and was sentenced to death, although the execution did not take place until 14 May 1941.[1]

Gerbohay's plot was bizarre, but the attempt in Munich's Bürgerbräukeller on 8 November 1939 surpassed it in drama. Moments after Hitler had left the speaker's platform, the column behind it blew up, causing eight deaths and numerous injured. Hitler himself had left earlier than planned and thus was not among the victims.[2]

On the same evening at about 8.45 pm a man was picked up near Lake Constance trying to cross into Switzerland under the cover of darkness. Apparently the border police officials were inside a house with the window open from which they could cover a large area of their district. At the same time they were listening to Hitler's speech in the Bürgerbräukeller. The arrested man identified himself as Johann Georg Elser and maintained that he wanted to visit an acquaintance but had lost his way. But within a matter of days he admitted having carried out the attempt on Hitler's life on his own initiative, without aid from anyone else.[3]

Hitler, Himmler and others did not believe the confession so the matter was put under the sole charge of the Gestapo, which was to seek out the foreign agents presumed to be behind Elser. Otto

Strasser was suspected of being backed by the British intelligence service, and when on 9 November 1939 Captain Best and Major Stevens were caught by the SD at the Dutch-German border, where they were contacting an alleged group of the German resistance movement, they were instantly portrayed by the German media as the instigators of the plot. However, Elser insisted that he had acted on his own. He stated that he had made the decision to kill Hitler in the autumn of 1938, and from memory he drew up the plans of the time bomb. As motivation he claimed the deterioration of workers' living conditions, the lowering of wages, the violence applied in all sectors of German life and religion, Hitler's expansionist foreign policy and his responsibility for the outbreak of war. Elser also successfully tried to avoid implicating anyone who could have assisted him either by negligence or thoughtlessness.

Soon the state and the NSDAP had to counter rumours that the bomb plot had been ordered from above. These rumours are extremely unlikely to have been true. Even if the SS had manufactured such a device it is unlikely that Himmler and Heydrich would have allowed Hitler to speak in front of a time bomb, since fuses at that date were still highly unreliable. Nor is it likely that Elser would have been a free man, able to roam about until he was picked up by the border police.

After his interrogation, Elser was transferred to Sachsenhausen concentration camp, some twenty miles north of Berlin. He received privileged treatment, a specially spacious cell and all the tools necessary for a carpenter. Under the orders of the Gestapo he reconstructed his time bomb. He was a talented wood carver and widely popular with the guards. He was allowed to play billiards and could play the zither at will. The reason for Elser's preferential treatment are obscure. Perhaps because it was thought that one could deploy such an extraordinary 'talent' some time in the future; perhaps because he was to be 'conserved' for some spectacular show trial before the VGH. Hitler himself was not to be moved from his belief that Elser had not worked without 'wire pullers' in the background. Himmler had to keep at it; there was always the chance, after 'final victory' had been achieved and London's archives searched, that they would find the necessary evidence and try Elser, Best and Stevens together.[4]

Early in 1945 Elser was transferred from Sachsenhausen to Dachau and there imprisoned in the compound for prominent prisoners who received favoured treatment. The group included

Stevens, Best, Léon Blum, Hjalmar Schacht, Pastor Niemöller and a number of prominent army personnel, including Generals von Falkenhausen and Halder. On 5 April 1945 the Gestapo sent orders to Dachau that on the next suitable occasion, such as an air raid on Munich, Elser was to be liquidated unobstrusively. On 9 April 1945 the order was carried out.[5]

Elser had been a typical loner, an almost fanatical amateur mechanic, a perfectionist who would not part with a single piece of his work until it could withstand any criticism. What really motivated his deed? According to his evidence, he hardly read any books or newspapers. He possessed no ideological education and showed little interest in participating in political discussions. Though a former member of the Red Front, he had never participated actively in trade union discussions and rarely attended rallies. By social origin he considered himself a worker; in pre-1933 elections he had voted KPD not because he approved of its ideological programme, but simply because he wanted to improve the working conditions of the German people. That this silent man rejected Hitler and the NS regime was noticeable even to his close circle only on the basis of rare remarks and of his refusal at public rallies to salute the swastika.

He was, however, a regular listener to foreign radio stations. The decisive point for Elser came with the Sudeten crisis and the danger of war; this political development could only be stopped if the man at the centre of these events, Adolf Hitler, were removed. For a whole year he worked at turning his idea into reality and in this process the idea became an *idée fixe*. That he was not a common criminal even the *Völkischer Beobachter* acknowledged in its issue of 22 November 1939: 'This man has no obvious criminal physiognomy but intelligent eyes, quiet carefully chosen words; the interrogations become endless, since he thinks over each and every word until he replies, and as one observes him one can easily forget the sort of satanic animal one is facing and the cruel burden his conscience has to carry with such apparent ease.'[6]

But Elser was not without a conscience. While planning Hitler's death he visited several churches seeking strength for his undertaking, which he considered his own personal task and responsibility. Protestant that he was, he convinced himself that his deed was not criminal, that it was not a sin because his aim was that of preventing further bloodshed, a conclusion which a minority within the German officer corps did not reach until 1943. He had to take into account the fact that other people would be killed by this bomb; this was a burden on his conscience, but one he had to carry. When confronted with photographs of those killed he broke out in tears. 'I didn't want that!' he cried out.[7]

In the end, during his imprisonment, his belief in predestination convinced him that his deed was not meant to succeed and that therefore he had done wrong. But what if he had succeeded? As a carpenter it would have been highly unlikely for him to have headed a conspiracy. Only men in the key positions could have brought about a change, and if Hitler had been dead, only they could have saved Germany. But the leaders of the military and the conservative opposition, of whose existence Elser knew as little as they did of Elser, had already capitulated. It is far fetched to think that they would have incited a *coup d'état*. But as events developed, their influence among the leaders of Germany would have been much stronger if the charismatic character of the Führer had been removed, and perhaps then a more moderate government would have come to power.

Elser's deed was that of a pronounced individualist. It came to nothing, but how did German public opinion react to it?

The entire German people was yesterday affected by the assassination attempt carried out against the Führer. In all parts of the Reich the population discussed this topic with passionate emotion. In many churches the hymn 'Now thank we all our God' was sung. Many factory leaders informed their factory personnel of the event. The general public was very uneasy throughout yesterday morning before the details of the assassination attempt were known. Rumours sprang up, for example that the Führer was seriously wounded and many leading men of state and party had been killed. As in the course of the day more detailed news was received, attention turned to general problems arising out of this deed. The Jews and the English were talked about with bitterness and are considered to be the men behind the scenes. At some places demonstrations against the Jews took place. It is widely hoped that in future the Führer will no longer expose himself to dangers of this kind, as he has often done recently. Furthermore, measures of retaliation are expected imminently against enemies of the state and externally against Great Britain. Often – frequently among workers – the talk is that that one 'should not leave one stone on another in England' or that Göring should have his fliers leave 'London in rubble and ashes'. With the joy which has been expressed over the failure of the assassination, there arose an obvious unequivocal feeling embracing the whole community, filled with gratitude to providence and with the strength of the trust which the

Führer now possesses all over, even in circles of former Marxist workers.[8]

The tenor of other reports of public opinion is virtually identical. The German public believed that it had been carried out by the British Secret Service, a reaction, as we shall see which, at least initially, dominated the response of the German people to the bomb plot of 20 July 1944. Only one dissenting action was recorded. On the night of 9–10 November 1939 in Berlin, a shop window displaying pictures of the Führer was smashed.[9]

Another individual attempt at Hitler's life was planned by one of his close associates during the early period of the NSDAP. The man in question was Captain Josef (Beppo) Römer, who in 1921 had led the Freikorps Oberland against Polish insurgents in Upper Silesia. He had been highly decorated during the First World War. An initial NSDAP sympathizer, he joined the KPD towards the end of the 1920s. He established connections with Ernst Niekisch and Otto Strasser. Arrested several times after 1933, his war record got him released every time. But still he remained active, ultimately coming to the conclusion that only Hitler's death would solve Germany's problem. With the financial support of the industrialist Nikolaus von Halem he set out to assassinate Hitler, but before coming anywhere near his target, he and several of his associates were arrested by the Gestapo in late 1943. It was 25 September 1944 before Römer was arraigned before the VGH, sentenced to death and hanged immediately afterwards. Subsequently a number of trials took place, all of which ended with the same severity.[10]

When speaking of the German resistance movement as a whole, one has to differentiate between the military opposition and the civilian opposition, and within the latter between the so-called Goerdeler circle, the Kreisau and the other groups. In essence all were conservative by nature and in outlook.[11]

The military opposition began to form around 1937–8. It was directed against Hitler's foreign policy methods, not his aims. In principle there had been plenty of issues to divide the army leadership and the officer corps from Hitler. Yet the introduction of the so-called 'Aryan paragraph' in the armed forces met with no opposition with the exception of that of Colonel von Manstein, later Field Marshal, who addressed a memorandum against it to von Blomberg. Even he did not argue against anti-semitism as such but stated that the application of such a rule would undermine the spirit of comradeship within the armed forces. Blomberg had it filed away.[12]

This lack of protest raises the question of the attitude to the 'Jewish problem' among the military and civilian resistance – an issue which until recently has been skirted by historians of the German resistance to Hitler. Hans Mommsen characterizes it with these words: 'among the members of the resistance movement the Jewish question became a source of vexation only when the methods of persecution began to affect the assimilated Jewish groups in Germany as well as the half-Jews and *Mischlinge* (half-breeds), while on the other hand the fiction was readily embraced that it would be necessary to eliminate the influence of eastern Jewry in German society.'[13] Mommsen's remark finds extensive support in the findings of a recent more detailed study which provides convincing and irrefutable evidence that, for instance, while the Goerdeler group disapproved of the extermination of the Jews, they affirmed the existence of a 'Jewish problem' in Germany, which they hoped to counter in the short term through legislation which differed only in nuance and not in substance from the Nuremberg laws, while in the long term the problem was to be solved by deportation (*Abschiebung*) to Canada or South America.[14]

The racial ideas of National Socialism were to be adhered to, although Hitler's methods of dealing with the Jews were rejected. He was accused of betraying his own racial principles by, on the one hand, sacrificing valuable German blood, and, on the other, drafting 'racially inferior' foreign labour into Germany.[15]

The attitude of the 'conservative opposition' to Hitler adopted in the 'Jewish question' is made quite clear in a memorandum drafted by the historian Gerhard Ritter at the turn of 1942–3. Its final section, divided into three parts, deals with the solution of the Jewish problem.

In the part on 'religious foundations', we read: 'It is Christendom's task to spread the gospel to all peoples. This task exists also *vis-à-vis* the Jewish people *whose decisive guilt it is to have opposed to the present day the revelation by God in Jesus Christ* (my emphasis throughout). To accept Jews into the Christian community, solely for superficial reasons, without having awakened the Christian faith in their hearts, would be a sin against the church.'

In the second part, on 'historical development', Jews are broadly indicted. Although legally emancipated, only the smallest part of them had allowed itself to be absorbed by the peoples among whom they lived. Moreover, 'they did not distribute themselves in balanced proportions across the professions . . . instead they are concentrated in certain branches of commerce, in the press, as medical doctors and lawyers, as well as in party politics. In these professions they achieved in many instances a strong, even dominating position. . . . The strong influence of the Jews, especially in these vital areas provided . . . the foundation for the emergence of anti-semitic currents.' After 1918 these gained further strength, because 'political parties which formerly had been in opposition *and in which numerous Jews occupied leading positions*, now came to power and *allowed not a few Jews to take over influential offices. Thus to many the Jews as such appeared to be the beneficiaries of the national misfortune*. . . . The mass support attained by the National Socialists in Germany was due not least because of the exploitation and the further spreading of anti-semitic feelings.' However, Ritter condemned the NS Jewish policy because it cast the Jews in the role of a bad, dangerous and despicable people and suppressed it by means of uncontrollable police measures, 'which during the war since 1939 within the Reich and the occupied territories are practiced to a much wider extent and have taken on much more terrible forms.'

In the third part the demand is raised that injustices must be atoned for and made good again 'and that living conditions are created acceptable to the Jews.' Illegally appropriated goods must be returned, but restitution is impossible in cases '*in which human life has been destroyed or human health broken*.' In so far as material goods are not concerned,

*financial compensation cannot be so high that those concerned are put back into the same economic position they once occupied before they had suffered the damages. After all, all parts of the German Volk as a result of National Socialist policy, the war and its consequences, have sustained serious inroads into their previous standard of living. The wronged Jews cannot be excepted from the general impoverishment*. . . . This, however does not solve the Jewish problem. There exists also unanimity *that every state must have the right to close its frontiers against any Jewish re-immigration, if it considers this as necessary in the interest of the whole of the people*.

This demand mirrors that already raised in part one: Every Christian '*for the sake of the love of his own Volk must . . . keep his eyes open and watch whether not too close contact or even mixing with other races will not produce damaging effects on body and soul.'*

This is followed by proposals of an institutional nature to solve the Jewish problem, but great insistence is placed on the statement that 'Jews in all states in which they are at home occupy the position of foreigners.' Jews who convert to Christianity remains Jews 'as long as they have not been naturalized by the state in which they have their home.' And lastly: 'Jews are to be naturalized if they apply for it *and can produce sound justification*, especially in cases when they can refer to a corresponding tradition within their family *or can point to extraordinary achievements for the Volk within which they reside.* The decision then is made from case to case. . . .'[16]

Parts of this exposition, perhaps even all of it could, if one did not know the author and his collaborators, could have originated from the official party programme of the NSDAP. At the least it corresponds to the mind-set of moderate anti-semites.

Anti-semitism apart, there was the effect of the murders of von Schleicher, his wife and von Bredow in the course of the Röhm purge. Though within the officer corps voices of disquiet came to be heard, demanding an enquiry, Blomberg ignored them and in time they vanished.[17] More crucial but less divisive was Blomberg's own *mésalliance* with a lady of doubtful virtue.[18] It meant the end of his career. The same applies to the more infamous Fritsch, who had to retire because of his alleged homosexuality.[19] The Reichskriegs-ministerium disappeared to all intents and purposes, and into its place stepped the Wehrmacht's OKW. Keitel was its nominal head, but in practice Hitler assumed more and more control until he controlled it fully.

Several army generals had already distanced themselves emotionally from the political leadership of the Reich before the war, among them General von Witzleben and General von Stülpnagel.[20] The crisis came only with Hitler's sudden expansions into Austria and Czechoslovakia. In both cases it was feared that the invasions would lead to a world-wide conflagration for which the German army then was neither trained nor equipped.[21] Parts of the military opposition largely overlapped with the civilian opposition under Carl Goerdeler, the former Lord Mayor of Leipzig, and Reich Price Commissioner. Both established contact with official circles in London, notably the Foreign Office, which Goerdeler fed with a flood of memoranda, sometimes with contents too extravagant to be credible.[22] The civilian opposition eventually realized that it could do nothing without the support of the army. But its hopes evaporated with the departure of Fritsch and the installation of General von Brauchitsch as chief of the army – a man with neither the strength nor the inclination to put up a bold front against Hitler and his plans. Similarly, when Chief of the General Staff General Beck left in protest against Hitler's Czech policy, he was replaced by General Halder, a competent man who was aware of the disastrous course on which Hitler was taking Germany, but who confined his opposition to mere grumbling. The plot seemed to come to fruition during the events leading up to the Munich crisis, when an assault company led by a former Freikorps member, Lt-Colonel Friedrich Wilhelm Heinz, is alleged to have been stationed near the Reich Chancellery, ready to take it over and arrest and, if necessary, kill Hitler. When Chamberlain offered to meet Hitler at Berchtesgaden, then again in Bad Godesberg and finally in Munich, the wind had been taken out of the opposition's sails and they had to cancel their venture.[23]

There is little sign that the German military opposition took action during the build-up to the outbreak of war with Poland. The reason was simple: the territories which Poland had gained from Germany after 1919 were a festering sore in the heart of every German patriot. True, Goerdeler kept up his contacts with London. What effect they had is not as yet fully assessed. But certainly among British, French and Polish government circles it was believed that the day war broke out the NS regime would be swept away by the German army.[24] Even between October 1939 and April 1940 the German opposition let it be known that something would soon happen inside Germany.[25]

This bravado may in part explain the 'phoney war', the inactivity of the Western Allies and their vain hopes that Hitler would be swept away. Apart from a futile plan to arrest Hitler which allegedly could not be realized because Hitler had changed his time table, nothing happened and on 10 May 1940 when Hitler launched his campaign in the west, the very generals who had belonged to the opposition led their forces, and did so not only faithfully but successfully. And when, finally, on 19 July 1940, Hitler created Field Marshals by the dozen and handed out Knight's Crosses, batons, and other promotions, the opposition generals accepted them as thankfully as did those who loyally supported Hitler. Thus both civilian and military opposition came to a halt until the war with Russia began. Yet even here, the generals opposing Hitler did their duty. No objections were raised by Hitler's opponent, General Hoepner, Chief of Panzer Group 4, to the addition to his group of police forces of the Einsatzgruppen, which usually made short work of the Jews and any potential partisans in the rear of the front-line troops.[26] The chief of Einsatzgruppe A, SS-Brigadeführer Dr Franz Stahlecker, reported; 'Right from the start it can be stated that the co-operation with the Wehrmacht was in general good, in individual cases, as for example with Panzer Group 4 under General Hoepner, very good, even hearty. Misunderstandings which had occurred during the first few days were quickly removed by personal contact.'[27]

It was Hoepner, too, who, in a report of 6 July 1941, emphasised that acts of sabotage were mainly the work of Jews.[28] Shortly before the invasion of Russia, Hoepner had issued an order of the day to all his forces: 'The fight against Russia is the inevitable result of the struggle for survival forced upon us. . . . It is the ancient struggle of the Germanic race against the Slavs, the defence of European culture against the Muscovite-Asiatic flood, the throwing back of Jewish Bolshevism. The struggle must be conducted with utter ruthlessness. Especially to the present supporters of the Russian-Bolshevik system no mercy must be shown.'[29]

At about the same time another member of the opposition to Hitler, the Chief of Office V of the RSHA, SS-Brigadeführer Arthur Nebe liquidated more than 40,000 Jews.[30] He had volunteered for the job, in contrast to Ohlendorf.

The opposition came to life again only after the Russians had checked the German advance before Moscow. Many generals like General Hoepner withdrew their forces in the face of the winter hardships and the Russian offensive in direct contradiction to Hitler's explicit order to stay and fight.[31] Hitler came to the front in person, sacked a host of generals (among them Hoepner) and personally took command.[32] Hitler's very drastic action stabilized the eastern front under conditions that were almost indescribable, but if anything represented a starting point for the resurgence of the military opposition, then it was Stalingrad a year later. From then on relatively junior officers at home and in the field tried to bring their superiors over to their side, pointing out the need for Hitler's removal. But what had they got to offer? Goerdeler then was still optimistic: Germany within the frontiers of October 1939! But when the question was raised as to who would guarantee that, the silence was unequivocal.[33] Roosevelt's and Churchill's Casablanca Directives,[34] with the demand for unconditional surrender, pulled the rug out from under the feet of the conspirators. Nevertheless, during 1943, several attempts on Hitler's life took place. All proved failures, either because detonators failed to go off or because Hitler was surrounded by too great a number of his entourage.[35] Personal courage was also conspicuously absent among the conspirators. Admiral Canaris, who had unlimited access to Hitler until late 1943, never thought of pulling a pistol on him, nor did General Fellgiebel, Head of Signals and Communications in Hitler's headquarters.

A belief in the need to kill Hitler and the courage to do it was possessed only by the relatively junior Colonel Claus Schenck Graf von Stauffenberg, an officer who had seen service on all fronts, most recently in Tunisia where his car was blown up by a mine which deprived him of his right eye, left arm and two fingers on his right hand. After recovery, he was made Chief of Staff of the Home Replacement Army, headed by General Fromm. It is no exaggeration that, from the moment of Stauffenberg joining the resistance movement, both civilian and military components were infused with new life and energy; without him, it would have remained a drawing-room conspiracy with little or no practical effect, indeed an effect no greater than the Kreisau circle.[36]

Having Stauffenberg as the driving force of the conspiracy did not, of course, solve the problem of whether even a successful attempt at Hitler's life would enjoy the backing of the German armed forces. Bundeswehr General Graf Kielmannsegg recounts a meeting in the autumn of 1943 with one of the leading conspirators, General Henning von Tresckow, in which Kielmannsegg, according to his own account, expressed his scepticism about killing only Hitler but advocated instead having the entire headquarters, Hitler included, arrested by troops with front-line experience. Tresckow replied: 'I may well find a divisional commander who will undertake this, but not a division', simply because the majority of the German soldiers felt themselves still as 'soldiers of the Führer.'[37] This was still the situation in 1944.

The Kreisau circle, by contrast, had no real leader. It was a group of leading conservatives who met from time to time at the estates or urban residences of its members. They, like Helmuth James Graf von Moltke, did not think in terms of overthrowing Hitler themselves. They confined their endeavours to drawing up plans for the future of Germany after Hitler, plans which the Casablanca directives had made irrelevant anyhow. The circle was a collection of individualists with their own convictions and consequently one cannot even say that a consensus existed among them over major issues, whether these were the nationalization of heavy industry, the problem of denominational schools or the creation of a centralized or federal government structure. There was one point of agreement: Christianity was to be the basis upon which Germany would be built, a point especially advocated by Dr Dietrich Bonhoeffer,[38] the Protestant clergyman. Elements of an utopian Socialism were also present.[39]

On other issues, the Kreisau circle's approach came closer to that of the military opposition, as in the principles concerning work and the political activities of the citizens. 'Work must be shaped in such a way that it furthers readiness to accept individual responsibility. . . .'[40] Part of this was the support of the state for vocational further education, co-responsibility in the factory and in the entire economic context, with the overall purpose that of returning to the individual his 'organic function' and a sense of purpose in life. Great emphasis was placed on local self-administration, a point represented particularly by Fritz-Dietlof Graf von der Schulenberg.[41]

Considered as a whole, however, the ideas of the Kreisau circle were much less authoritarian than those espoused by Goerdeler and his group or for that matter by the military opposition.[42] At the same time, all of them rejected a return to the Weimar Republic; the question of political parties was left open. Weimar signified the division of the nation, the selfish and unscrupulous struggle between the parties which had only brought harm to Germany.[43]

The Kreisau circle took its name from the Moltke family estate, a frequent meeting place for the group. Moltke was a trained lawyer who practised law in Berlin and had been a barrister in London.[44] His mother was English and when, as an expert in international law, he was called up for the OKW he soon turned his mind to envisaging a new order in Germany – a picture of the future which completely rejected National Socialism. His views were shared by both Peter Graf Yorck von Wartenburg[45] and by von der Schulenberg. Around Moltke and Schulenberg there crystallized a circle of intellectuals including the Legation Counsellors in the German Foreign Office, Adam von Trott zu Solz,[46] and Hans Bernd von Haeften,[47] the former Social Democrats Carlo Mierendorf[48] and Dr Adolf Reichwein, the Protestant clergyman Dr Eugen Gerstenmaier[49] and the Jesuits Augustin Rösch and Dr Alfred Delp.[50] Delp in particular tried to establish links with a group in Bavaria led by the former Reichswehr Minister Dr Otto Gessler, Prince Fugger zu Glött and Dr

Franz Reisert. While this connection proved successful, that with the Goerdeler group was more tenuous, often breaking out into open hostility. Still, members of the Goerdeler group, among them the former trade unionist Dr Julius Leber and Hermann Maass, one of the leaders of the former German youth movement, participated in several meetings of the Kreisau circle.[51]

There was also the Solf group, already mentioned, which centred around the widow of Germany's former Secretary for the Colonies Foreign Minister and later Ambassador Solf who had died in 1936. It was a loose group of friends.[52] They were discovered by the Gestapo and among those arrested were Frau Solf, Elisabeth von Thadden (the step-sister of West Germany's right-wing politician Adolf von Thadden) and the former envoy Dr Otto Kiep. In January 1944 Moltke was arrested on the grounds that he had warned Kiep of his imminent arrest.[53] Only after the failure of 20 July 1944 did the Gestapo discover masses of evidence which put Moltke's detention on an entirely new basis and led to the arrest of virtually all members of the Kreisau circle. But Moltke's arrest, plus the arrest of some of the members of the Goerdeler group, did show that what was required was rapid action in order to remove the impending threat.[54]

In the meantime the Allies had invaded northern France, although they had not yet succeeded in breaking out of their large bridgehead. In Italy German troops had withdrawn from Rome and Allied troops had entered. More important, the Russians had launched a massive offensive on 22 June 1944 which had almost annihilated the German Army Group Centre.

Stauffenberg had to act. His plan was based on that of Operation Valkyrie, a plan designed to quell any nation-wide rising staged by foreign workers in Germany. Those under his command were in no doubt as to what actual purpose this operation was to serve. Unable to win the support of major military figures except Rommel – and his support was conditional on the promise that Hitler would not be assassinated but arrested and put before a properly constituted court[55] – Stauffenberg had recruited his supporters from the junior ranks and his persuasiveness drew many a young and politically inexperienced subaltern officer into the plot. But so strong was the sense of loyalty within the officer corps that no one who knew of the plot, from Field Marshals down to lieutenants, ever denounced the plotters to the Gestapo.[56]

Himmler himself had his finger in the plot via Hartmut Plaas, a former member of the Ehrhardt Brigade and right-wing terrorist in the early days of the Weimar Republic. After Hitler came to power, Ehrhardt ordered Plaas to join the SS so that he would have an ear inside. In his military capacity Plaas joined the Luftwaffe as Captain and was employed at its spy centre, the Luftwaffenforschungsamt.[57] Through Plaas, by character and conviction far more inclined towards the plotters than to Himmler, Himmler had a fair idea of what was going on for a number of years and did exactly nothing. He was also in touch with them via the former Prussian Minister of Finance Popitz. Probably he wanted to play it both ways and when the point of crisis drew near he suddenly removed the only one who knew about this link, namely the link himself. On 19 July 1944 Hartmut Plaas was arrested at his workplace and executed on the same day at Sachsenhausen concentration camp.[58]

In July 1944 several assassination attempts were mounted, all of which were called off. The aim was to kill all three top leaders – Hitler, Göring and Himmler – but the latter two rarely accompanied their chief. Finally Stauffenberg decided to act despite their absence and on 20 July 1944 he placed a briefcase with explosives against the table from which Hitler was holding a situation conference. Stauffenberg departed unmolested, on his way to the aircraft seeing a vast explosion from which it seemed no one could have emerged alive. However, Hitler received only superficial injuries. Meanwhile, Stauffenberg flew back to Berlin while his co-conspirators in Berlin did nothing. Only upon Stauffenberg's arrival was the codeword 'Valkyrie' issued, but it was issued by Stauffenberg with Witzleben's signature, not by Fromm, who, unconvinced that Hitler was dead, wanted nothing to do with the plot. Every soldier knew that Witzleben had been retired; after the French campaign he had fallen ill and had since then been in the army's 'leadership reserve'. Even the presence of the former Chief of the General Staff, General Ludwig Beck, made no difference. The plot failed ignominiously.

The plan had been based on one gigantic bluff, namely the assumption that every German soldier and officer would unquestioningly do as ordered.[59] Then chance, too, played a major role. For one thing, the conference should have been held in a bunker, in which case everyone in it would have been killed. As it was, construction work caused the meeting to transfer to a barracks where the blast could not effect maximum damage. For another, in Berlin on that day Hans Hagen, a young lieutenant of the reserve and a political instructor, an NS-Führungsoffizer (NSFO), thought he saw Field Marshal von Brauchitsch in full uniform driving down one of the main avenues in Berlin. Hagen knew, of course, that Brauchitsch had been retired during the winter crisis of 1941–2[60] and became suspicious. Shortly after he arrived at his regiment, part of the Grossdeutschland division stationed in Berlin-Moabit, the regiment's commander, Major Remer, received the codeword 'Valkyrie' and orders to occupy the government district and to arrest Dr Goebbels. Hagen's suspicions were now firmly aroused and he aired them tête-a-tête with Remer. Remer allowed himself to be talked into visiting Goebbels. While his regiment took positions as ordered, Remer and Hagen went to see Goebbels, who in his most charming manner put Remer at ease and then suggested that he should personally speak with the Führer at his Rastenburg headquarters. The connection was established. Hitler promoted Remer to full colonel and then gave him extensive powers to put down the rebellion.[61]

This Remer did speedily. The officers in the Bendlerstrasse supporting the regime, including Fromm, were liberated and Stauffenberg and his associates arrested. Possibly in order to eliminate evidence against him, Fromm had Stauffenberg and three of his comrades shot by the light of the headlamps of two lorries.[62] The bomb plot had miscarried, the aftermath was yet to come.

But what if it had succeeded? What if Hitler had been dead? After all, the bomb did cause fatal injuries. Would it have made any difference? Assuming that Hitler had died, a decree of 1 September 1939, reaffirmed in 1943, had pronounced Göring successor. True, there was a good deal of rivalry among Hitler's satraps. But considering to what danger they were all exposed, the strong likelihood was that they would stand together to overcome the imminent danger, however much they might have fallen apart later. They possessed a monopoly of power, press and radio and knew how to handle them like no one else in Germany. Another hypothesis is that for whatever reasons they might have handed over power to the army and the resistance much in the same way as Mussolini had a year earlier. The Allies had stated their war aims – unconditional surrender. Beck could only have played the role of another Badoglio and sooner or later that government would have faced the same fate as that of the Dönitz government on 23 May 1945 – an ignominious end.

In terms of German public opinion, the immediate effect of the attempt on Hitler's life was a temporary consolidation of support for the regime, a fact in itself sufficient evidence of the degree to which the conspirators operated in isolation. All the reports show that the majority of Germans, not only National Socialists and the undecided, but also opponents and critics, reacted against tyrannicide at a time when the fate of the nation appeared to balance between life and death. The action was condemned most strongly in the lower and middle strata of German society; even among the circles of the former elite, the very circles from which the opponents came, there was no unanimous support for the assassination attempt. In the short term, the NSDAP leadership even managed to radicalize the lower strata against the upper strata.[63]

The first studies of public reaction came as early as 21 July 1944. They originate from two sources, from the RSHA where they were compiled by SS-Obersturmbannführer von Kielpinski and from the Reich Propaganda Office of the NSDAP. Their findings are confirmed by the reports submitted by other high NSDAP functionaries, high civil servants and members of the judiciary and by a flow of letters from the population:

> In all reports there is agreement that the news of the *Attentat* (assassination) has elicited among the people shock, disturbance, deep disgust and rage. From several cities (for instance Königsberg and Berlin) it is reported that women in the shops broke out in tears and were unable fully to comprehend what had happened. The joy over the relatively harmless outcome was exceedingly great. With a sigh of relief everywhere it was noted 'Thank God, the Führer lives!'
>
> To some degree one also noted a certain depression which clouded the joy that the Führer's life had been spared. The *Volksgenossen* suddenly realized the dangerous and serious situation. Everywhere one could encounter after the first shock, and the first consolation that little had happened to the Führer, a reflective mood.
>
> So far no utterance has been recorded which would indicate that even one *Volksgenosse* was in agreement with the action. On the contrary, it was observed throughout that even parts of the population, which did not stand 100 per cent behind National Socialism, rejected the attempt at assassination. For instance, a whole series of voices from north Berlin had been recorded to that effect, from people who formerly stood firmly in the opposing camp. Workers from the northern parts of the Reich declared that it was a *Mordschweinerei* to commit treachery against the Führer. 'There is no point in stopping the war now. We must win it. Only no civil war!' Or, 'However did the assassins think the war was to be continued if the Führer were no longer with us?'
>
> Everywhere the consequences of a successful assassination were considered unthinkable. The *Volksgenossen* sometimes entertained

dark prognostications of the unthinkable harm that would have come over our entire people. In the opinion of many *Volksgenossen* at the present moment the death of the Führer would have meant the loss of the Reich. 'That's all that was needed; that would have been the end' is a view uttered time and again. Questions are asked how such a thing could happen and the intervention of providence was cited time and again.[64]

A second report of the same day from the Office of the Chief of the Security Police and the SD confirms the first observations. Again, the feeling was that of shock and disgust, and the central question was what would have happened if Hitler had been killed. The attempt was a plot by the forces of reaction; now people understood, the report said, Hitler's words on the occasion of the state funeral of General Dietl when he had indicated that in the German Officer Corps everything was not as it should be.[65] From all parts of Germany reports of a similar nature were received. Hitler's speech to the German population the same night elicited less response:

While no further comments are available on the Führer's speech, reports on the reactions to the speech of the Reichsmarschall [Göring] show that it was thought to have thrown the seriousness of the present situation into starker relief than had the speech of the Führer himself. From the words of Göring, one could understand that a kind of treason had been in the making comparable to events in Italy at that time. All the greater is the joy of the population that the attempt misfired in every way. . . .

It is generally expected that ruthless action will now be set in train against the enemies of the people, irrespective of person, position or family. Therefore, the appointment of the Reichsführer-SS [as Commander of the Home Replacement Army] produced great hopes that he would use a strong hand to establish order and with an iron broom remove from the Wehrmacht all elements which are opposed to the state [Königsberg, Berlin]. The appointment of Guderian as Chief of the General Staff was seen as a further concentration of all active forces to iron out the defeats in the east, which are blamed on the generals' clique.[66]

Even if one considers that the failure of the bomb plot and the fear of further repressive measures and new terror may have masked the true popular response, one must still admit that the plot was not popular either with the German population or with the mass of front-line soldiers.[67] The picture is more differentiated in the officer corps, where many an officer had to suffer a conflict of conscience.[68] Von Kielpinski's assertion of 22 July 1944 seems to come closest to the truth, if one considers the broad mass of the people as consisting of 60–70 per cent of the population: 'No event of the war has touched the broad masses deep down like this attempt at murder. Never has it been so clear with what loyalty the people stand behind the Führer.'[69] The churches, too, opposed the attempt. They condemned tyrannicide both in 1944 and after the war.[70] So strong was the people's connection to the Führer that it was noted by American psychological warfare officers who interrogated German prisoners. In the period of 1–17 July 1944, 57 per cent of all prisoners expressed their confidence in Hitler, while in August 1944 this figure increased to 68 per cent.[71]

According to the SD, only in markedly particular cases was the attempt not condemned. One *Kreisleiter* reported that 'only intellectual circles which are always disagreeable would have accepted it with satisfaction if an overthrow had succeeded. These people cannot be observed too much and their influence and position of power needs to be reduced.'[72] Much agitation was carried out against Germany's blue-bloods; at the highest level, Dr Ley, the leader of the German Labour Front, publicly criticized the German nobility.[73]

The attitude of the nobility is difficult to assess for lack of evidence. Now under fire, they were unlikely to identify themselves with the bomb plot, while many other aristocrats had originally strongly sympathized with the NS regime. Among the higher leaders of the SS the aristocracy was prominently represented. But as the true nature of the NS regime had revealed itself more and more clearly many may in private have distanced themselves from the regime. Much the same can be said of Germany's industrialists, one of whom, Robert August Bosch, had before the war financed Goerdeler's extensive travels abroad.[74] The diminishing of industrialists' status to that of mere state managers with the onset of war was greatly resented and while in the early years of the Third Reich they had obviously made their profits, by 1944 it was clear which road Germany was taking. Some had already began to plan for peace-time production, and that, of course, implied a Germany without Hitler.[75] The bomb plot had suddenly highlighted this situation and the bulk of industrialists as well as some aristocrats began to carefully distance themselves from the Third Reich.

In Vienna, Berlin and especially the Catholic regions of Germany, mass rallies were held in support of the Führer. At the same time, a wave of denunciations swept the country – denunciations of public utterances against the state, of Marxist high treason and of 'actions favouring the enemy' (Feindbegünstigung).[76]

The 'stab in the back' legend assumed new life, and the demand was widespread that those wielding the dagger should be mercilessly weeded out. Treason began to be seen as responsible for Germany's military reverses, in particular the mass breakthrough of Soviet armies through the Army Group Centre at Minsk.[77] Suddenly the population turned its attention to prominent leaders who had been killed in 'accidents' – Udet, Mölders, Dr Todt and General Dietl. Here too a conspiracy was suspected, with implications directed against the entire officer corps.[78] The question was asked whether Germany throughout its history since Armin the Cheruscan had not always suffered defeat because of treason.[79]

The consequence for the National Socialists was to make the war even more total. Goebbels decreed a Spartan life-style to which allegedly even he adhered.[80] Pleasure, luxury, large parties became a thing of the past.

But in order to ward off the population's dangerous hostility to the officer corps, Martin Bormann issued the following guidelines on 24 July 1944: 'The Führer desires that no one in dealing with the events of 20 July 1944 should lose his temper and attack or insult the officer corps, the generals, the aristocracy or any other branch of the Wehrmacht as a body. Instead it must be emphasised that as far as the participants of the putsch are concerned, they were only a relatively small clique of officers.'[81]

Hitler may well have believed that at the time. But the following weeks showed him, as well as the German people, the true dimension of the conspiracy. Even at the apex of the German leadership not everyone had agreed with Hitler's initial assessment. Himmler, for instance, stated: 'I am convinced that the greater part of the difficulties on the eastern front, the failure to hold the line and the dissolution of entire divisions is to be explained by the immensely clever infiltration of soldiers of the Seydlitz army and German prisoners of war who were converted to Communism by the Russians.'[82] The collapse of Army Group Centre and, by early August, the American breakout from the Normandy beachhead at Avranches, helped to convince the German people that every reverse, past and present, was caused by treason.[83] In a letter of 1 August 1944 Freisler remarked: 'It is a sad fact that suddenly we have to realize that our *Volksgemeinschaft* is infested with traitors. If they succeed, 1918–19 will be a child's play by comparison. They will have to be weeded out now without any thought of mercy.'[84]

In Germany stories of fleeing German soldiers in the east, of the failure of officers who had left their troops in the lurch, of the bad morale of the soldiers who sometimes sold their weapons had never been believed; the fighting German officer and soldier seemed to be above criticism. For too long Germans had been convinced of the superiority of their own armed forces. The successes of the blitzkrieg had been too easy for them to be able overnight to admit that the efficiency, bravery and courage of the armed forces had their limitations, that the entire effort was bound to fail in the face of the overwhelming superiority of men and *matériel* of Germany's enemies. Therefore it was easier to believe in treason, and the day by day revelation that the circle of conspirators was much larger than had originally been assumed intensified this conviction:

> If at first it had been believed that one was dealing with a small clique of officers which attempted something that was hopeless from the very start, it is now thought that the traitors had been sabotaging the intentions and orders of the Führer for a long time. This view is arrived at on the basis of mounting evidence contained in the letters or conversations of soldiers of the eastern front, which now express the reasons why they did not get any replacements, why more than often units were moved to and fro in the front line with no apparent purpose behind it and why in parts the front was denuded altogether.[85]
>
> The great majority of the population is coming more and more to the conclusion that the clique of officers and traitors who prepared the bomb plot against the Führer must for a long time have been actively and systematically pursuing sabotage in the field of defence, so that the eastern front received neither the necessary supplies nor the necessary weapons and ammunition.[86]

But the thesis of treason also had its dangers. Either, so the argument went, the Führer could not know about these things and had been kept, like the late Kaiser, ill-informed about the real circumstances, or the Führer was not after all the *grösster Feldherr aller Zeiten*, the greatest warlord of all time. Over the weeks and months, the reports of the SD indicated that after the initial repugnance to the bomb plot only the activists of the NSDAP and a small minority still believed in victory, short of a miracle.

The putsch had made it clear that the German people were being lied to by its leading statesmen in the most vulgar manner. All publicists and statesmen, among them the Führer, Dr Goebbels, Ley and so on, had over the years asserted that time was working for Germany, that Germany's war production was mounting from day to day, that the day on which the Germans could return to the offensive was firmly set, and that it was equally a fact that Germany held decisive new weapons in reserve. Yet from the mouth of none other than the Führer himself, Germans were being told that his measures had been sabotaged for years, and that only now after the last obstructions had been removed could full war production be resumed. In other words, the Führer admits that, until now, time had not worked for the Germans but against them. When as exalted a person as the Führer allowed himself to be deluded – one could only laugh at Goebbels' assertion that the Führer had known everything – then either he was not the genius he believed himself to be, or else, in the knowledge that saboteurs were at work, he lied to the German people deliberately. One thing was as bad as the other, because with enemies in his own house war production could never have been increased and therefore Germany could never win the war. In all those years therefore time has not worked for but against Germany, especially as in those years American and Russian war production came fully into their own. . . . Of most cause for concern in the whole affair is that most *Volksgenossen*, even those who so far had believed unshakeably in the Führer have now lost faith . . . this must be stated firmly.[87]

Hence what we register in terms of public opinion is a short-lived and sudden consolidation of public opinion behind Hitler and his government, followed by a period of reflection which gave rise to a far greater inclination to pessimism than had been the case at the beginning of 1944. The series of trials before the VGH at which the conspirators were arraigned hardly counteracted this trend; on the contrary, they were bound to accelerate it.

# 10

# The Trial of the Conspirators

It is against this background that one must look at the series of trials held before the VGH and presided over by Freisler until his death.[1] Freisler's objective in dealing with those implicated in the plot against Hitler was to keep strictly to the crime itself, allowing defendants and their defence counsels to speak only about the crime, and preventing them from making public statements in court about the general nature of their aims and their moral motivation. It must be said from the outset that with few exceptions the defendants did not make a very favourable impression on the court, either with their general demeanour or with their vain attempts to extricate themselves from the accusation of this heinous crime.

Hitler's original intention was to hold a great public trial which would be covered by press, radio and film so that every German would be exposed to the maximum impact. Himmler saw potential psychological dangers in this course of action and under his influence Hitler changed his mind and ordered a trial which excluded the general public, admitting instead a highly selective but large group of listeners. The trial was to be conducted by the VGH, a decision made mainly as a result of Thierack's immediate approach to Bormann and Himmler.[2] Hitler's suspicion of the military judiciary, whom he suspected of sympathies with the would-be assassins, decided the issue in favour of the VGH. But since most of the accused in the first trials were members of the armed forces, they would by law be subject to the military judiciary. To circumvent this technicality, Hitler created a Military Court of Honour under the presidency of the frail Field Marshal von Rundstedt. The court expelled all the accused members of the armed forces from the Wehrmacht and then handed them over to the civil powers.[3] Later, on 20 September 1944, Hitler extended this measure by handing over all political trials of members of the armed forces to the VGH.

Hitler's original decree of 4 August 1944 established the Court of Honour, the most prominent members of which (beside von

Rundstedt) were Field Marshal Keitel and Colonel-General Guderian. It then listed all those who had been expelled from the Wehrmacht so far, those who were to be arraigned before the VGH, those who had committed suicide after the abortive putsch like General Beck and those who had deserted to the enemy.[4]

With this measure Hitler had created a precedent which the Allies a year later were also to put to good use. In 1945, when Göring, Dönitz, Keitel, Jodl and other German military leaders were arrested, they were formally prisoners of war. The Allies then deprived them of military rank and POW status in order to be able to prosecute them as war criminals. This exercise was also carried out on a mass basis, as with the prisoners of the Waffen-SS whose military status was simply denied.

Throughout 1944 Freisler had been busy with a host of minor trials. One such trial was that of the Solf circle, which included Frau Solf, Elisabeth von Thadden, Dr Kiep, the former Secretary of State Dr Zarden and Legation Counsellor Dr Hilger van Scherpenberg, and a son-in-law of the former President of the Reichsbank, Dr Hjalmar Schacht.[5] In 1943, in the midst of Italy's capitulation, the group had discussed Germany's prospects and the possibility of a *coup d'état* had been mentioned. Persons were named who might win the confidence of the western powers and the measures to be taken in Germany at the end of the war were also discussed. Elisabeth von Thadden was persuaded by a traitor within the group to make contact with an acquaintance in Switzerland. A letter to him was entrusted to the spy for delivery. However, the Gestapo was aware that the Swiss acquaintance had tried on Goerdeler's request to establish contacts with the Church of England and the British government; it also knew that he was in touch with the former Reich Chancellor Wirth, now living in Switzerland, and that he had a hand in the work of the Red Orchestra. The whole Solf circle was arrested on 12 January 1944.[6]

The assertion is made that at the trial Freisler obstructed the defence so that it could not really become operative. This is said especially in the context of Elisabeth von Thadden.[7] Her associate Kiep had given up altogether and did not defend himself. Both were sentenced to death. Yet if Freisler had obstructed the defence, how can that same historian argue that the defence of Hilger van Scherpenberg was conducted so cleverly that finally he was sentenced only to two years' prison for not denouncing the Solf circle?[8] Frau Solf and the other accused of the circle were not tried, but remained in prison and concentration camps until they were liberated. Regardless of the nature of Freisler's behaviour, the true effect of the VGH trial of the Solf circle was to hurry the conspirators of 20 July 1944 into carrying out their attempt.

On 7 and 8 August 1944 the first of a series of trials commenced before the First Senate of the VGH. All major VGH trials were recorded on Goebbels' orders, presumably for posterity. To improve the quality of the recording, Goebbels had three microphones installed in front of Freisler, who, being unused to microphones, tended to speak as loudly as he would have in their absence. This habit distorted his voice on record and on film just as the early speeches of Hitler were distorted by his unfamiliarity with the microphone.[9]

Freisler opened the trial by stating that the VGH of greater Germany was now meeting in the form of the First Senate, with the President of the VGH as presiding judge, the senate president Günther Nebelung as Deputy President, with General Reinecke, Hans Kaiser, landscape gardener of Berlin, and Georg Seuberth, merchant of Fürth, as honorary lay judges, and with Emil Winter, baker, and the engineer Kurt Wernicke, as honorary deputy lay judges. A VGH counsellor was responsible for drawing up the minutes and Oberlandesgerichtsrat Dr Köhler was deputy judge. The prosecution was in the hands of Oberreichsanwalt Lautz. The officially appointed defence counsels were Dr Weismann, Dr L. Schwarz, Dr Neubert, Dr G. Schwarz, Dr Kunz, Dr Falck, Dr H. Bergmann and Dr Boden.[10]

Then the first explosion happened. Freisler asked Lautz to introduce the indictment against Erwin von Witzleben. Witzleben stood up and approached the bench with his right arm stretched out in the Hitler salute. It is significant that this incident has been completely ignored in writing on contemporary German history. Although the scene exists on film and recordings, for German and foreign public consumption it has been cut.

Little wonder therefore that Freisler burst out: 'You are Erwin von Witzleben. In your place I should no longer use the German salute! The German salute is used by people who possess honour. That does not mean that the final judgment has already been determined. But in your place I would feel ashamed still to use the German salute!'

Witzleben was then asked for his date and place of birth. He was followed by Erich Hoepner, Hellmuth Stieff, Albrecht von Hagen, the former Berlin City Commander Paul von Hase, Robert Bernardis,

Karl Klausning and Peter Graf Yorck von Wartenburg. Freisler then read out in its entirety Hitler's decree of 4 August 1944. After that the Oberreichsanwalt was called on to speak: 'Defendants von Witzleben, Hoepner, Stieff, von Hagen, von Hase, Bernardis, Klausning and von Wartenburg, I indict you on the charge that you have, within Germany and as participants in a numerically insignificant clique of leaders of discouraged officers, undertaken a cowardly attempt to murder the Führer in order, after the removal of the National Socialist regime, to usurp power over army and state and to end the war through undignified negotiations with the enemy. As *Hoch- und Landesverräter* you have violated the [the law].' This was followed by the list of laws and decrees violated.

Then Freisler took up the cudgel:

This charge, defendants, is the most terrible which has ever been made in the history of the German people. The Herr Oberreichsanwalt asserts that he has evidence that you have committed the most horrible act of treason which is known in our German history. Today our task is to determine what you have done and then, according to our German feeling for the law, to arrive at a judgment.

I shall proceed as follows. With each of you I shall discuss what he is accused of. I shall take as my point of departure a brief sketch of your career. Insofar as a more detailed description of your career may be of interest to us, it will emerge once we know what you have done. Because there exist deeds of cruel treason so extreme as to eliminate everything you may have done before. In the event that you turn out to have committed such deeds then further details of your career will be of no interest to us. Therefore in the initial sketch of your life I shall be brief.

Freisler then asked Stieff to stand up and approach the bench.

In the first instance I shall tell you something which applies to all other accused. Although the indictment which is in your possession is one of the most important foundations in our present search for the truth, it has a special purpose, the purpose of enabling us to be prepared for today's main trial.

Insofar as the indictment sketches out the deed, the function of the indictment is fulfilled. I say that because, as I can see, you all have a copy of the indictment in your hands. What is of validity now is what is being tried here and if I omit anything which is contained in the indictment, then you may be sure that it will not operate to your disadvantage when we come to a judgment. Therefore it cannot be of

disadvantage to you when I now ask you, insofar as you are able to do
so, to discuss the matter face to face.

The proceedings were then interrupted by an appeal by Lautz for
the public to be excluded. After it had turned out that those present
were functionaries of the NSDAP and its formations and officers of
the armed forces, each of whom had been individually vetted, Freisler
formally excluded the public because secrets of the Reich might have
to be discussed, but then allowed those present to stay. In other
words, the 'general public' which was not there in the first place was
excluded; those who were present could stay.

Freisler then went on to question Stieff on the basis of the record
of Stieff's police interrogation. The questioning began with the
details of the accused's career and service record and Stieff affirmed
that after Hitler's assumption of power he adhered to National
Socialism unreservedly, a point at which Freisler interrupted to
emphasise that an affirmation of National Socialism 'involves the
whole man, he can never again leave this creed any more than this
creed would leave him. An affirmation of National Socialism is an
affirmation of our Führer, as an affirmation of our Führer is also the
affirmation of National Socialism. The two are inseparable and
indissoluble for all time and eternity.'[11] It would now be up to the
court to find out whether Stieff had just told the truth or a lie. Stieff
asked leave to talk about his inner motivation, a response which
Freisler rejected outright. The basis of the indictment was the record
of the police interrogation and by implication any admissions which
evidenced the violations of the laws listed in the indictment.[12]

Of course, prohibiting the accused from discussing their motivations was of primary concern to the NS regime, because such a
discussion would have opened up precisely those issues which would
have provided food for thought to all present in the court room, as
well as to the German public at large and certainly to Germany's
enemies. This would hardly have been in the interests of the
regime.[13]

Freisler then led Stieff through a number of discrepancies in the
evidence, that is to say between what Stieff had said to the police and
what he had said to the prosecution's investigating judge. Confronted
with the discrepancies Stieff found himself compelled to admit that
he had not told the full truth during his first interrogation, which
earned him from Freisler the venomous charge of being a
hypocrite.[14]

He then took Stieff through the course of the events from the summer of 1943 onwards, notably Stieff's conversation with a Colonel von Tresckow, who had stated that the precondition for a negotiated peace was the removal of the Führer. When asked by Freisler whether he had reported this conversation to his immediate superior, Stieff said he had reported it to General Heusinger, Deputy Chief of the General Staff, but that he did not report it to Hitler directly.[15] This again raised the issue of 'inner motives' which Freisler cut short by declaiming: 'For me, comrade judges, it is quite enough that somebody, irrespective of what he may believe, dares to declare that it is the historic duty of a General Staff officer to participate in the assassination of our Supreme Commander . . . our Führer. There is only one thing: obedience, conquer or die, no right, no left. We don't want to hear anything from you about that.'[16]

Freisler then continued to interrogate Stieff on similar conversations with Generals Olbricht and Beck and Field Marshals whom Freisler would 'not name because it would be shabby slander.'[17] The intention, of course, was to suppress such names as von Kluge, von Manstein and Rommel. Instead he led Stieff directly to his first contact with Stauffenberg and brought him to admit that he had not rejected Stauffenberg's appeal for assistance because he wanted to have, as Freisler put it, and Stieff agreed, 'his finger in it'.[18]

When Freisler invoked 'National Socialist manly loyalty' Stieff interjected 'towards the German people'[19] which gave Freisler once again occasion to hold forth on his concept of loyalty: 'National Socialist manly loyalty! Führer and Volk are one. What kind of jesuitical-reactionary reservations are you making here? What do you believe would have happened if one of the last Goths at Mount Vesuvius had made the same reservations? . . . He would have been submerged in the nearest bog, because slime belongs to slime. . . . Politically schizophrenic people we cannot use, those who think they can separate loyalty to the Führer from loyalty to the Volk.'[20]

While Stieff could claim to have rejected Stauffenberg's offer to involve him in the assassination plot, he could not deny having known that Stauffenberg planned to carry it out himself, or that he, Stieff, had actually harboured the explosives for a time. Particularly incriminating also was Stieff's knowledge that Stauffenberg initially planned to plant the explosives in the ranks of highly decorated soldiers who had been selected to model newly designed combat uniforms for Hitler at Berchtesgaden, an admission which once again caused Freisler to shower Stieff with abuse.[21] Nor did it help Stieff to point out that he himself had been instrumental in this particular plan coming to nothing. In his interrogation Stieff had also managed to involve other generals, notably Wagner, Lindemann and Fellgiebel, who was responsible for the communications centre of Hitler's headquarters. Finally, in the light of the evidence, he was forced to admit having had foreknowledge of the plan for 20 July 1944 and having failed to report it. Stieff's claim to have acted 'for Germany' Freisler dismissed with derision: 'For Germany? It is reprehensible that you are not ashamed to be still saying that, because I already told you what Germany is. Our Führer is Germany and we are his followers, they who ought to feel that he is the military and political soldier. *You* cannot speak for Germany. . . .'[22] No doubt on this point, as on many others, Freisler spoke for himself.

The next important interrogation was that of the most prominent member of the conspiracy, Field Marshal von Witzleben, who had been transferred by Hitler to the leadership reserve, and whose name had appeared on the orders to take control of the government.

Witzleben was an easy target for Freisler. He had received his honours as Field Marshal, Freisler remarked, at the Reichstag session of 19 July 1940 when Hitler had handed out military decorations and Field Marshals' batons in a number unparalleled in the annals of German military history.[23] Considering that he had been one of the first participants in the military conspiracy (since at least 1937), it did not reflect credit on Witzleben that he had accepted the honour. Resigning from the army before 1939, or refusing the honour in 1940 would have been a sign of personal integrity. No doubt it would have made him politically suspect, but neither in 1939 nor in 1940 would it have entailed the consequences which any similar action would have had four years later. Witzleben accepted honours and promotion and continued in military command until Hitler replaced him. Freisler pointed with acid sarcasm to the discrepancy between accepting military honours from Hitler on the one hand, and opposing him on the other.

As Freisler pursued his line of questioning, Witzleben began to appear to be a conspirator motivated only by a personal military pride wounded by the loss of his position when Hitler had transferred him. His connections with Generals Beck, Olbricht and Fromm, the Chief of the Replacement Army, and others were quickly established. Freisler noted that in his police interrogation Witzleben had denied having had anything to do with the bomb plot, to which Witzleben

replied 'Yes unfortunately' – a statement which immediately prompt-
ed Freisler's riposte 'You are right to say "unfortunately", because
somebody who was then a Field Marshal must stand by what he
has done . . . and not give such a deplorable – I don't say female,
because women do nto behave like that – to give such a deplorable
show.'[24]

From there it took Freisler little effort to demonstrate that
Witzleben had not opposed the assassination attempt in principle,
but had simply been enraged by its amateurish, dilettante character.
He had arrived at the headquarters of the conspirators in Berlin's
Bendlerstrasse on 20 July 1944 to find a disorganized, shabby level of
planning and a series of orders and decrees had been issued with his
name but without his authorization.[25]

Witzleben had also to retract his earlier statement that he had not
made any agreement with anyone concerning an insurrection, which
in Freisler's view branded him as a liar.[26] Freisler then traced the
steps of the conspiracy's evolution back to 1943 and manoeuvred
Witzleben into the implicit admission that he believed that Hitler
would have to be removed in order to turn the war again in Germany's
favour by better generalship, or if the worst should come to the
worst, to arrive at a negotiated settlement with Germany's enemies.[27]

When Witzleben tried to reject the charge that he and his
associates wanted to govern 'against the will of the people', Freisler
read out to him the decrees which the conspirators had drawn up,
such as the transfer of all law-breakers to courts martial, prohibition
of public assemblies, introduction of curfew hours and travel
restrictions. 'These things demonstrate that next to you the unjustly
defamed Metternich was a progressive. You represented ultra-
reaction, because what you did was as follows: a small clique of
shameless traitors takes away from the people its own way of life,
our National Socialism. With these quotations we have provided
some gems of the decrees issued by you or under your responsibility.
Is that right?' To which Witzleben replied: 'Certainly.'[28]

Freisler's final question to Witzleben was 'one thing is still unclear
to me. Field Marshal of the German Reich, may I ask you the
following? What do you believe the other Field Marshals would have
said?' And then answering his own sarcastically phrased question:
'They would condemn you as is their duty. You said once: "As truly
as I sit here, none of them participated." Say that aloud here!' 'That
is correct!' replied Witzleben.[29] This was a clever move on Freisler's
part, and one obviously designed to put an end to rumours among

the German population before they even had a chance to start about a Field Marshals' conspiracy.

We can also assume that this was what Freisler actually believed himself. As we shall see in the next chapter, he went on record expressing his surprise about the scope of the conspiracy. From this it seems fairly reasonable to infer that the VGH was informed of the police investigations only to the extent of actual cases submitted to it for trial. Of the wider investigations it seems to have known very little, if anything.

Next to be questioned was Hoepner, whom Freisler accused of cowardice and disobedience, qualities, Freisler said, which had led to his dismissal from command.[30] He then charged him with having lied, like everyone before him. 'Only one has not lied. He has told the truth from the beginning. That is the defendant Yorck von Wartenburg. All others have told cowardly lies from the beginning to the end. That is correct?' asked Freisler. '*Jawohl*,' replied Hoepner.[31] Freisler at first concentrated his questioning on Hoepner's relationship with General Olbricht, who, according to Freisler, should also have stood in the dock, but whom General Fromm had executed with Stauffenberg and two others late on 20 July 1944.

Hoepner adopted a line of defence similar to that of Witzleben. He argued that from 1943 onwards both he and Olbricht had become increasingly concerned about the progress of the war and had finally come to the conclusion that Hitler and his advisors, notably his Foreign Minister von Ribbentrop, would have to be removed. Hitler and Ribbentrop stood in the way of a negotiated settlement.[32] Of particular concern was the eastern front where Field Marshal von Manstein had been relieved of his command by Hitler, though they had parted on the best of terms.[33]

Hoepner tried to defend himself on the grounds that all he supported originally had been 'an orderly, legitimate change', one which would also enable him again 'to become a soldier again'.[34] But he also said that agreement to his participation in a putsch was given '*ad interim* and contingently', which Freisler interpreted as meaning 'I come in later, when the matter is a sure thing.' To this charge Hoepner replied in the affirmative.[35]

Once again Freisler was provided with the opportunity to interject his historical analogies:

If Frederick the Great had had subordinate generals of your type like a few – fortunately few – of those we have been blessed with today, no

longer generals, but now appearing before us, they would have been a
sorry burden to him, running low on courage every time things got
sticky. But after Kunersdorf [Frederick's most disastrous defeat on 12
August 1759], after the army had been reduced to nothing, when the
enemy had entered Prussia's capital, still victory came, because, like
our Führer today, there was a man at the top then, who was imbued
with honour like our Führer and who had men around him like our
Führer. . . .[36]

While Hoepner tried to take refuge in euphemisms like 'changes at
the top', Freisler tied him down to his previous phrase of '*ad interim*
and contingently', while at the same time pointing to discrepancies
between the testimony given to the police and that given in court and
confronting him with the verbatim transcript of the police interrogation, the veracity of which Hoepner, time and again, confirmed.[37]
Freisler then questioned him in great detail about the events
leading up to 20 July. The exchange was not without difficulty
because of Hoepner's evasive tactics.[38] On one point Hoepner
remained adamant: it had not been his intention that Hitler be
removed with the aid of explosives. But this lack of intention could
hardly change the ultimate outcome of his case.[39] On two occasions
Freisler severely reprimanded Hoepner for laughing; under the
circumstances it seems doubtful whether Hoepner was in a frame of
mind to laugh and he denied it accordingly.[40]
One point which attracted Freisler's particular attention was the
premature launch of Operation Valkyrie on 13 July 1944. In
anticipation of Hitler being removed on that day, Olbricht, Fromm's
Chief of Staff, had issued the code-word but had it withdrawn within
an hour or two. Nevertheless, he could not prevent the Panzer
training establishment in Kramnitz near Berlin from being placed on
the alert. Olbricht had apparently expressed concern that General
Guderian (then Inspector of the Panzer Forces) would immediately
take over the Kramnitz Panzers and deploy them on the borders of
East Prussia, then threatened by the Russian onslaught.[41] Freisler
promptly fastened on to this:

So, the danger existed that Guderian, having seen the Panzers on the
move, would take them away and use them for the front. What are
Panzers there for, once they are finished and the crews are ready? They
are there for the front. Thus one important detail emerges for the first
time. . . . Well, this is something our soldiers, our grenadiers ought to
know: that among such crooks there was talk of the danger that a

general in this or that position taking care that Panzers should arrive at the front.[42]

Freisler dismissed Hoepner's objections that only Panzers in training were involved.

Moving on directly to the events of 20 July Freisler concentrated on Hoepner's luncheon with Olbricht in Berlin.

> You had half a bottle of wine between you for lunch. Now with half a bottle you can't exchange many toasts; but the one time you did toast to one another the following happened: 'During the meal he [Olbricht] toasted me with the words: "Now we shall see what happens today" ' – the forces of reaction lifted their glass of wine. One can practically see their pleasure in putting an end to this damned National Socialism ... in oppressing the Volk by emergency decree, 9 pm curfew – oppressing it with drum-head courts martial, prohibiting any form of community life, liquidating anything in the way of community life, all without any idea behind it. A sip of wine to that! ...[43]

Then followed detailed questioning on the events in the Bendlerstrasse itself, the degree of confusion and uncertainty among the conspirators as well as among those who did not believe that Hitler was dead. Cuttingly Freisler asked Hoepner 'who gave you the *right* [author's emphasis] to know that the Führer was dead?'[44] – a question more revealing, as we shall see in our conclusions, of Freisler's personality than of Hoepner's attitude.

Hoepner then recounted in great detail the events of that afternoon and evening which culminated in the collapse of the conspiracy. Unlike Beck, Hoepner did not consider himself such a '*Schweine-hund*' ('pig-dog') as to have to commit suicide. Freisler asked: 'Tell me: which zoological characterization do you consider appropriate for what you have done, if you reject the other?' Hoepner replied: 'An ass!' But Freisler objected: 'No, an ass applies to a question of the intellect, a *Schweinehund* is a matter of the character in our use of the language. ...'[45]

The next defendant was Peter Graf Yorck von Wartenburg. As with the other defendants Freisler went over his career and political attitudes, and in the course of this Yorck said he had not been a member of the NSDAP although he had voted for it. As his reason for not joining the NSDAP he stated: 'Because, taken as a whole, I am not a National Socialist.' '[T]hat clarified that point,' noted Freisler.[46] The trial touched upon his service as an officer of the

Reserve, his transfer to the Economics Staff East, and his decoration with the Iron Cross Second Class. As a cousin of Stauffenberg he had been in the picture since 1943 as far as the planning of the conspirators was concerned, and he readily admitted his approval of plans and his readiness to be at the disposal of the conspirators in a future administration. He was at odds with the development National Socialist ideology had taken, a point at which Freisler interrupted him: 'you were not in agreement! To put it in plain terms, you told him [Stauffenberg] that as far as the Jewish question was concerned you did not like the *Judenausrottung*. . . .'[47]

In his study of the July conspiracy, the historian Peter Hoffman argues that the official VGH protocol did not allow utterances of this provocative nature.[48] His argument is purely speculative and in view of this author indeed unsupportable. It raises the question of how it came about that one of the later defendant's description of Hitler 'as the executor of evil' found its way into the record,[49] or, for that matter, of how Freisler's reference to the *Judenausrottung* was retained in the trial transcript when it could easily have been suppressed. W. Wagner argues unconvincingly that this particular reference to a crime which was then 'kept highly secret' slipped accidentally from Freisler's lips.[50]

In fact, Freisler's reference provides a clear indication that he was aware of what was happening to the Jews, though whether he was aware of the full extent of genocide and of the means deployed to achieve it must remain an open question.

Under interrogation from Freisler, Yorck also raised his objection to 'the totalitarian demand of the state *vis-à-vis* the citizen' which eliminated 'his religious and ethical obligations towards God.'[51] Freisler protested:

> Tell me: precisely where has National Socialism eliminated the ethical obligations of a German? National Socialism has led to an infinite recovery and deepening of the ethical obligations of every German, man or woman. I have never heard that it eliminated ethical obligations. As far as religion is concerned, basically National Socialism has been rather modest. It says to the church: please do as you like, only keep your demands to the hereafter, because the souls should flutter about in the hereafter, but here on earth our present life is of value. . . . What you are saying is, to say the least, seen from the wrong perspective, it makes no sense.

To this Yorck simply responded: 'I only wanted to supply an

explanation.'[52] Thus, within the span of a few minutes, Freisler publicly divulged his knowledge of the extermination of the Jews and then tried to counter the charge that National Socialism was eliminating ethical obligations, so presenting a contradiction of which he was probably unaware.

In the course of further questioning Freisler took objection to the act of giving one's word, or, more specifically, to putting one's word above the loyalty every German owed to the Führer.[53] In Yorck's case Freisler displayed marked sarcasm only in two instances. One concerned the appointments in the future administration (which Freisler described as 'dividing up the bear's skin beforehand');[54] the other concerned Yorck's competence to nominate persons suitable for high administrative office: 'This is terrific! You are a middle-ranking civil servant (*Oberregierungsrat*) in a central administrative office, not in a Ministry, but just another central administrative office, and you had insight into the professional qualifications of the many men, who were actively engaged and working for years, loyal to the Führer, in most important areas, areas of which you do not understand anything! Modesty, you think, may well be a good quality, but one gets further without it. . . .'[55] The rest of the questioning concerned Yorck's activities on the day of the assassination attempt.

This was the first of a whole series of trials concerning the events of 20 July 1944 which were to last into March 1945. Apart from Stieff, Witzleben, Hoepner and Yorck the other defendants were the Berlin City Commander General von Hase, Lt-Colonel Robert Bernardis, Captain Friedrich Karl Klausning, and First Lieutenant Albrecht von Hagen. Many others were to follow.

Since then, the date of 20 July 1944 has not only become a symbol of the German resistance to Hitler, but also a legend. Undoubtedly the demonstration of judicial power of the VGH was almost overwhelming, the scene intimidating. Because the original building of the VGH in the Bellevuestrasse had been damaged by bombs, the trials took place in the great hall of the Berlin Chamber Court in the Elseholzstrasse. Behind the bench of the professional and lay judges presided over by Freisler, the walls were draped with swastika flags; a bust of Hitler decorated the room. The public gallery was always filled to capacity, the audience consisting of officers of the armed forces, party functionaries and civil servants, all carefully selected. In addition there were great numbers of journalists and broadcasting and film crews. Though closed to the general public, the public nevertheless participated indirectly through press reports and word of mouth. The trial itself was phonographically recorded on records and taken down by shorthand experts who had been recruited from the Reichstag.

One part of the legend surrounding the 20 July 1944 trial is the assertion that the defendants were no match for Freisler. The full transcript of the trial shows that Yorck's performance certainly contradicts this assertion, as do some others. These men managed to present their deeply held, genuine motivation, while in contrast Stieff, Hoepner and Witzleben – with his embarrassing attempt at the Hitler salute – cravenly tried to minimize their role in the events. It was not as if the VGH was anything new to them; by this time its reputation permeated all layers of German society. Only wishful thinking could delude them into believing that they could escape death. Hence more than forty years after the event one cannot escape the conclusion that they would have served their cause better had they stood by it and not tried to evade responsibility in the most unheroic manner. Yorck gave an example of how others should have behaved. Precisely their cowardice made them an easy prey to Freisler's ridicule, while, taking Yorck again as an example, the record shows that Freisler showed him far less contempt than he did the senior generals.

In a letter dated 11 August 1944, Freisler wrote:

> Once I was lieutenant myself and anything beyond the rank of a major was a demi-God to me, let alone a Field Marshal. Apart from their attempt to sabotage the great cause for which our nation is fighting, apart from the attempt to murder the man who has led our fatherland to unforeseen heights and to a degree of national consolidation Germany had not experienced since the High Middle Ages, apart from all that, nothing shook me more to my very foundations than the cowardly behaviour of men who occupied positions which, until they appeared before me, I considered almost sacrosanct. In this first trial there were two exceptions, [Yorck and von Hagen] but in terms of military rank they were insignificant. If Witzleben or Hoepner, for instance, had stood up for what they had done, I think we should have been compelled to exclude even the selected audience, but at least they would have died as upright men. As it turned out, they behaved and perished like worms.[56]

To Witzleben is attributed this exclamation to Freisler: 'You may hand us over to the hangman; in three months the disgusted and tortured people will call you to account and drag you alive through the mud of the streets.'[57] No source has been supplied for this quotation: it is contained neither on the shorthand transcript, on record, nor on film, although the entire trial was recorded and filmed. It is one of many exclamations and noble motivations alleged to have been expressed by the conspirators for which a source is lacking or, if it exists, comes from the survivors of the July plot themselves.[58] Moltke himself, for instance, wrote from prison to his wife and children that their task would now have to be to 'fabricate their own legend'.[59] In this the conspirators, dead and alive, were successful. *Der 20 Juli 1944* has become the alibi of a nation.

The special commission of the SD appointed to investigate the plot and composed of 400 men of the Gestapo and the criminal police, came to its own conclusions. Heydrich's successor, Dr Ernst Kaltenbrunner, sent its reports directly to Hitler's headquarters from August until December 1944. In one report the defendants in the first trial were characterized as follows:

> During the first trial before the Volksgerichtshof, the investigations of the special commission were supplemented by the following impressions. Von Witzleben appeared as a completely used-up old man who had lost all his carriage and dignity. It emerged clearly that he was very angry about having been transferred to the Army Leadership Reserve and that this largely determined his attitude and his participation in the assassination attempt. In his time of inactivity he continuously expressed criticism of the conduct of the war and increasingly believed that he could do better. Witzleben admits to being completely alienated from all political life and that he received his knowledge and views only from the small circle of like-minded people. To the question how he envisaged political developments after a successful attempt he replied: 'I don't understand anything of all these political and civilian things. . . .'
>
> Hoepner offered a very pitiful picture. In his case, too, expulsion from the Wehrmacht and the form of his demotion . . . led to the ambitious wish that through a change of the regime he could become a soldier again. Significant in Hoepner's case is that he wanted to take no risk. Rather he intended to appear *ad interim* and contingently, that is to say, to participate only when the enterprise had succeeded.
>
> Since in the Bendlerstrasse on 20 July, Hoepner pretty soon noticed that the enterprise was not going as smoothly as he had envisaged, his vacillating and indecisive attitude *vis-à-vis* the Commanders of the Defence Districts in the Reich resulted in the putsch attempt in the

Reich having no very great consequences and collapsing within hours. . . .

Stieff, in the trial of 7 and 8 August, came across as a nasty little piece of work, sly, personally cowardly and cocky. Like all others, he had no idea of the political consequences of a successful attempt. His horizon ends with military specialization. . . .

Yorck gave the impression of being a degenerate intellectual. During the trial he readily admitted that even after 1933 he did not join the Party or any of its formations because he had never been a National Socialist. Yorck, too, apart from his mental attitude towards National Socialism, felt more firmly bound by his word of honour to Stauffenberg than by the oath which he had sworn as a civil servant . . . and as an officer . . . .[60]

The belief in the significance of one's word, the report went on, also played a decisive role in shaping the behaviour of the other accused young officers. Klausning is quoted as having said that if he had known what men headed the conspiracy and were to be entrusted with responsible positions, he would have been convinced that nothing would ever come of a coup.[61]

It is easy, especially with the tyranny of hindsight, to take exception to these comments, considering the source from which they come. To be repelled by them comes almost instinctively, yet revulsion alone is hardly an instrument suitable for critical analysis. They do serious injustice to Yorck, especially in the light of Freisler's privately expressed views. To argue that the defendants were fighting for their lives is stating the obvious, but it can be countered by the equally obvious argument that they knew, or should have known, that their lives were lost before they ever set foot in the courtroom.

Yorck certainly seems to have cherished no illusions. But the majority took cover under pro-Hitler statements. Was this volte-face, so apparently at odds with their behaviour, the results of split personalities, of people who had opposed Hitler, yet who were at the same time prepared to accept the honours bestowed upon them by the Führer? Was it, to take Witzleben as an example, perhaps a glimmer of hope that a Field Marshal of the Reich would not be dealt with in the same way as a common criminal? If this glimmer existed for Witzleben, it was a sheer delusion of which he should finally have been cured when the 'Court of Honour' expelled him from the Wehrmacht. Such honour as was saved in this first trial was not saved by a Field Marshal but by a mere Lieutenant of the Reserve, Graf Yorck von Wartenburg. He, and a few others like him, represent the beacon of morality for present and future generations. Without them the conspiracy of 20 July 1944 could be summed up as one which contained idealists unrealistic in the assessment of their chances of success, and opportunists for whom the wish to restore their past careers played a vital supplementary role in determining their motivations.

The SD reports on the interrogations make interesting reading, not least because they reveal the astonishing readiness and expansiveness with which most of the conspirators talked to their interrogators. Allegations have been raised about torture, but they remain unsubstantiated.[62] In post-war Germany not a single charge has ever been brought against a former member of the SD or the police for applying torture to members of the 20 July 1944 circle. One Gestapo official openly admitted to his prisoner: 'There is no doubt that you and your friends are good Germans. But you are enemies of the system, and therefore you will have to be destroyed.'[63]

Freisler acted not only as a judge whose task in terms of German judicial procedure was to get at the truth, but as the Grand Inquisitioner himself, determined to destroy root and branch of what he considered evil. Oberreichsanwalt Lautz kept surprisingly silent. According to one post-war affidavit he had known of the conspiracy. But that did not stop him from becoming more vociferous in his final speech, in which he demanded the death sentence for all defendants.[64] Both he and the Gestapo had an easy task: those caught talked freely; according to Lautz, Goerdeler made extensive written affidavits for the Gestapo in which he implicated numerous persons, accusing them of knowing of the plot and participating in it as far back as 1942.[65]

The defence played an extremely passive role. In the light of the evidence given by the defendants this comes as no surprise. Only on Stieff's behalf was the objection raised that he had not committed Landesverrat, but Freisler dismissed the plea, arguing that for anyone not to have denounced the affair the moment he understood its murderous purpose was tantamount to detonating the explosives himself.[66]

Neither in Hoepner's nor in Witzleben's case could the defence make any effective plea: 'The action of the defendant stands and the guilty man falls with it.'[67] Ultimately all defendants asked to be shot, a request denied to them by Freisler:

At the time our Reich created the law which allows hanging in cases of particularly shameful crimes, it passed it in view of the terror action of

1933 [the Reichstag fire of 28 February 1933], a very dangerous act of terror as we well remember. Today we are surer of ourselves. The action under the impact of which this law was decreed then is only a pale shadow of the deed which these defendants . . . have committed.

That is all there is to say. We have noted that they, devoid of honour, have committed treason against everything we live and fight for. Thus we state here: there is nothing for it but death. We state: it is the most shameful deed ever committed in our history.[68]

In fact, in the case of Stieff, who had supplied the unused explosives, Freisler could have invoked a precedent established during the Weimar Republic. When Rathenau was assassinated in 1922, Ernst von Salomon, not quite twenty years of age, had managed to organize the car with which the assassination was to be carried out. But the two assassins changed their mind and used another car. Nevertheless, the Reichsgericht sentenced Salomon to five years' hard labour,[69] a sentence based on retroactive legislation. As noted earlier, the Weimar Republic was the first to break with the established German legal maxim *Nulla poene sine lege* ('no punishment without law'). True, this was not the death sentence, but the abrogation of this principle laid the groundwork for a system of punishment without full legal protection in its most extreme form. Indeed, what else could one expect when total war reached dimensions hitherto unknown and, of course, when the sentences had the backing of the German public?

Of course, the trials were not completely without adherence to legal procedure. Any reading of the transcripts shows that no comparison can be made between that trial and the show trials in the Soviet Union under Stalin. Undoubtedly, an element of show was present, for otherwise there would have been no need for an invited audience, but the overriding – and chilling – feature of Hitler's judiciary was its concern that the law be followed. Equally, Freisler's comments as judge were often cutting and insulting, but they were so primarily in those cases where, for him, and for that matter any other jurist, the case was open and shut. Freisler's rage was in the main caused by vain endeavours to minimize or to deny the role played in the plot by any of the accused. Whether the same action at that time in any other country involved in the Second World War would have yielded different results one may only guess. One need only look at what happened to the judicial process in France after liberation to see what uncontrolled passions may be aroused.[70]

The assertion that the film made about the trial met such public repugnance that it was soon withdrawn is based on an extremely doubtful source.[71] First of all, although a film was made about the proceedings, this film was shown only in Hitler's headquarters, while the German public was only shown excerpts within the context of the weekly newsreel.[72] The relevant SD report records general agreement and support for the way in which the trial was conducted and the sentences handed out. Only very few dissenting voices were heard, although amazement was expressed that men who by Hitler's action had risen to high ranks could offer such a poor showing before the court; one would have expected of them much greater uprightness. Equally, surprise was expressed that it had actually been possible for the conspirators to make such preparations over a long period undetected.[73] It would not have been such a surprise had the general public been aware that Himmler had also been in the know not only via Harmut Plaas but also via the former Prussian Minister of Finance, Johannes Popitz, who was also to become one of the victims of trials yet to come.[74] Admittedly, the evidence as to Himmler's involvement in the plot is scanty and inconclusive, but several facts stand out. The trials reached their climax just at the time when Himmler, on his own initiative, without Hitler's express sanction, ordered the termination of the mass killings of the Jews.[75] And one further point should provide food for thought: on none of the dates planned by the plotters was Himmler present; he had previously announced his arrival, but had then deferred it.[76] After the abortive putsch, Himmler arrived at Hitler's headquarters within a suspiciously short period of time – ready, perhaps, to seize the reins of power?

The defendants were executed on the very afternoon of their sentencing. Again, legend has it that they were strangled by a 'thin cord' or a piano wire[77] hung from butchers' hooks and that their slow deaths were filmed on Hitler's personal wish. In spite of extensive searches, no copy of the film has ever been found, though two eye-witness accounts, from camera men who in spite of an extensive search could not be traced, state in a German government publication that the sentence was carried out by hanging: hemp rope nooses were placed around the condemneds' neck and fastened to hooks and the stools upon which the convicted men stood were kicked away so that the bodies slumped down just above foot-level. Death occurred within seven to twenty seconds.[78]

It is not, and cannot be, the task of this study to recount in any great detail how the events affected the dependants of those convicted. A short summary must suffice. However, one point should be stressed, that in spite of the gravity of the offence, and although it was officially stipulated, the property of those convicted were rarely confiscated. In the case of Graf Helmuth James von Moltke, Freisler let the family know even before Moltke's trial that they would retain their Kreisau estate and that their property would not be confiscated by the state.[79] There is also a curious correspondence in which an official of the Reichskommissar für die Festigung deutschen Volkstums (the Reich Commissioner for the Consolidation of the Volkdom), the Reichskommissar being none other than Himmler, wrote to Thierack on 22 October 1944 forwarding a draft decree for the confiscation of the property of those convicted to death in relation to the events of 20 July 1944.[80] A similar letter was sent to the Ministry of Finance.[81] Unfortunately the draft decree is missing in the documents.

Whatever its contents, however, two days later Thierack wrote directly to Himmler in which he stated that he assumed the property concerned to be the considerable estates in East Prussia and Silesia. But against the executive measures as detailed in the draft decree, Thierack raised substantial objections. First of all, the property consisted not only of landed estates but also of other valuables like shares, household property, urban property, which was in many cases subject to claims by third parties. Thierack also assumed that Himmler would place most value on landed property for the purposes of settlement. This Thierack was prepared to support. But then follow the important sentences: 'Apart from that, I am informed that the Führer desires a generous provision for the dependants of those judged and sentenced which Obergruppenführer Breithaupt is carrying out. It is desirable that part of the confiscated property be used for that purpose and it is in fact being used so already. That applies above all to household goods, linen and the like, and other moveable property. . . .'[82]

With the contents of this letter Himmler agreed.[83] It appears, then, that the accounts of the terrible hardships suffered by the dependants of the conspirators are yet another story that belongs in the realm of legends, legends which partly include that of *Sippenhaft*, i.e. the arrest and transfer to concentration camps of all the immediate relatives of any of the conspirators. Arrest of their families was threatened by police interrogators to members of the conspiracy. Arrests also took place, but they were carried out rather arbitrarily;

the great bulk of those arrested were released once it was established that they had had no part in the conspiracy in spite of Himmler's blood-curdling oratory. Only a small group was detained, first in Dachau and then in the Tyrol where in 1945 they were liberated not by the approaching Americans but by units of the German army who had disarmed the SS guards.[84]

The second phase of the trials was to last until the early spring of 1945. In that series Regierungspräsident Fritz-Dietlof Graf von Schulenburg stood out for adopting much the same attitude as Yorck's. He stood by what he had done without reservation, giving as his motive his wish to save Germany from utter misery. He blandly told Freisler that he expected to be hanged but that this would cause him no regret.[85] Unfortunately, the more aggressive remarks he is alleged to have made to Freisler are not contained in the recorded proceedings. We find them only in post-1945 publications. Nor, in strong contrast to most of the other trialists, did he display any regrets in his final letter to his family.

Thus Stieff had written: 'My life is destroyed. Yesterday and today the main trial has been held. The death sentence has been demanded and it cannot be otherwise. It is *just*. What suffering and shame I have brought you! This is the thought which gives me most pain. I am going quietly into death which I have brought on myself.'[86] Others, yet to be tried, wrote in the same vein. Major von Leonrod wrote: 'I am not worthy to have been a Leonrod. I hope that I will not be included in the family history; I brought too much shame for that. My dear brother may have more regard for his name and also be more clever.'[87] Major Knaak wrote before his execution: 'Forget me, I who am unworthy',[88] while Colonel Jäger wrote: 'An accident brought me to Berlin, which caused me to be guilty as well. But there is nothing that can now be changed.'[89] Berlin's police president Graf von Helldorf, who as an SS leader had played a prominent part in the Röhm purge of 1934, wrote: 'During my interrogation I admitted my guilt which consisted of disloyalty towards the Führer and the Movement. The consequences of my actions are clear to me and I shall have to bear them.'[90] Lieutenant von Hagen's last lines were: 'About me there is not much to say. I cannot argue with my fate because I have caused it myself. So all that remains is to keep one's countenance during the last hours, which all my life I have considered the basic precondition of nobility.'[91] Even Goerdeler stated:

I opposed the assassination and demanded an open discussion with the Führer. The failure of the assassination has, as an answer of providence to the violation of a divine commandment, not surprised me. . . . When we put the fatherland above everything else, which is the faith of us all, then we have to respect 20 July as a final judgment of God. The Führer has been preserved from almost certain death. God did not want Germany's existence, for the sake of which I wanted to participate, bought by an act of blood. He has entrusted this task anew to the Führer. This is an old German concept. Every German in the ranks of the Movement who supported the coup is now compelled to fall in behind the Führer, saved by God, and also offer him, as the new government, support without stinting; whether he wants to use them, or considers them suitable, is his own decision.[92]

No doubt these letters reflect the immense psychological pressure operating on their authors, writing, as they did, under the shadow of the hangman's noose. Certainly they show their concern about the fate of their families, but all the same there is no reason not to assume that they, like the majority of the German people, saw in the failure of the assassination attempt the 'Lord's judgement'. However, neither Yorck, Schulenburg nor several others, including Graf Moltke, left farewell letters of similar content.

As in the account of the first trial, so from the successor trials we shall touch upon only the most important cases. The first prominent case concerned Wolf Graf von Helldorf, an officer in the First World War and subsequently a member of the Freikorps who had joined the NSDAP in 1926. Not long after Hitler had been appointed Chancellor he became chief of police of Berlin but soon seems to have become disillusioned with Hitler and his policy. As early as 1938 he had expressed his agreement with the army's putsch plan. His *spiritus rector* was the somewhat dubious personality of Hans Bernd Gisevius, a former Gestapo official and later agent of the Abwehr in Bern who after 1945 published his memoirs and several other works, all of them highly unreliable. On 20 July 1944, Helldorf had made several police officials available to Stauffenberg.[93] Among those accused with him was Legation Counsellor Adam von Trott zu Solz, who had also belonged to the opposition to Hitler from an early date. A former Rhodes Scholar, he had made his way in the German Foreign Office. Prior to the entry of the USA into the war, he hoped to get US support for the German resistance. He failed for two main reasons, namely that the political and territorial aims of the German opposition were still considered excessive in the USA and Great Britain, and secondly because he was suspected of being a German government agent.[94]

During the trial Freisler's main target was Helldorf, who in the end publicly admitted that he was a traitor.[95] Another accused, Legation Counsellor Bernd von Haeften, asked by Freisler why he had broken his oath of loyalty to the Führer, replied: 'Because I consider the Führer the executor of evil in history', to which Oberreichsanwalt Lautz retorted that this remark put in the shade anything that had been said so far during that or any previous trials.[96] This may well be the case, but in any event all the accused were sentenced to death. In Helldorf's case it has been asserted that upon Hitler's order he was to be held back so that he might watch the death of his comrades before being executed himself. However, the source of this assertion is a person who was not present at the execution and the claim has been strongly denied by one of the executioners.[97]

One of Helldorf's close friends, Gottfried Graf von Bismarck-Schönhausen, a direct descendant of Bismarck, was acquitted for lack of evidence. But Freisler did not refrain from remarking that he had had social relationships with highly dubious persons, 'persons who played highly significant parts in the course of 20 July.' He, Freisler, did not share the conviction that Bismarck had shown himself to be a loyal National Socialist, but in order to demonstrate his impartiality, as he put it, he would let lack of evidence preserve him from being convicted.[98]

General Fellgiebel, Chief of Signals and Communications in Hitler's headquarters, and his subordinate officers were also sentenced to death.[99] Major von Leonrod, a member of Bavaria's old nobility and a fellow conspirator, used in his defence the excuse that he had visited his father confessor in Munich in order to obtain advice. The Munich priest, Chaplain Hermann Wehrle, did not enquire into any details, nor did he take Leonrod into the confessional, in which case he could have pleaded the sanctity and secrecy of confession, but instead consulted some theological works and then declared there was no need for confession but advised him to keep out of any treasonable enterprise. Leonrod had given away Wehrle. Freisler gave full vent to his anti-Catholic sentiments and Leonrod as well as Wehrle were sentenced to death, the latter for not denouncing the impending coup.[100]

One of the generals involved in the plot, General Fritz Lindemann, had gone underground after the failure of the putsch, but was caught on 3 September 1944. Shortly afterwards he committed suicide.[101] This act brought to Freisler a number of people who had given shelter to Lindemann, one of whom, Lt-Colonel von Petersdorf, though expelled from the Wehrmacht and the NSDAP, was acquitted for lack of evidence.[102] Others were sentenced to death or to terms of imprisonment.[103] Lindemann's eldest son, a lieutenant, was sentenced to seven years' hard labour because after the failure of the coup he had asked whether it might not have been better if it had succeeded.[104] Lindemann's youngest son, an Oberfähnrich (one rank before second lieutenant) received five years' hard labour because he had known of his father's plans and failed to report them. His youth and the influence to which he had been subjected at home were accepted as mitigating factors.[105]

Captain Dr Gotthard von Falkenhausen, a member of the conspiratorial group in Paris, faced up to Freisler firmly in court and gave as good as he got, an attitude that made such a profound impression on Freisler that he gave him the benefit of the doubt and acquitted him.[106] Others did not fare as well. The last of the military to face the VGH did so after Freisler's death.

One was First Lieutenant Fabian von Schlabrendorf, a conspirator from the first. Just before the outbreak of war he was sent to Great Britain to establish contact with Winston Churchill. He introduced himself with the words: 'I am no Nazi, I am a patriot' to which Churchill replied 'So am I.'[107] Churchill's subtle ironic contempt seems to have eluded Schlabrendorf. A lawyer by profession, he knew how to deal with the prosecution and the judges, especially since by the time his trial ended Freisler was already dead. Schlabrendorf was acquitted.[108] The other case concerned General Fromm, former Commander of the Replacement Army, who had known of the plans but, unwilling to commit himself, had waited for the outcome. His prior knowledge and failure to inform the authorities sufficed to condemn him. Apparently he was the only one not to be hanged but shot. His last words are said – though by a curious source – to have been 'Heil Hitler!'[109]

The most prominent member of the civilian conspirators was, of course, Dr Carl Goerdeler, who was tried on 7 and 8 September 1944. Freisler described him as 'the head and motor' of the conspiracy; what he did not say that he was a rather noisy motor who, like many of the resistors, frequently talked and wrote too much for their own good and that of their associates.[110] Up to 1937

Goerdeler had shown considerable sympathy for Hitler and his movement, though, as a conservative, he did not join it. He resigned his post as Reich Price Commissar because of differences over economic questions. Backed financially by the industrialist Robert Bosch he took on the task of removing the NS dictatorship. He urged the generals not to allow themselves to be emasculated, and began to travel abroad widely, notably to Great Britain, France and the USA.

In France he appeared to have obtained little hearing. The Foreign Office in London was polite enough to listen to him and read his memoranda, which in fact were a mixture of fact, fiction and pious hopes, especially on the subject of what would happen to London once the war broke out.[111] None of his predictions came true, and as far as Germany's territorial ambitions up to and including the war with Poland were concerned, they differed little from Hitler's. A prolific writer of memoranda, emergency decrees, proclamations and so forth, he could not prevent most of it from falling into the hands of the Gestapo. On 18 July 1944 he was warned that the Gestapo was about to arrest him, and until 8 August, when he was captured, he lived underground.[112]

After his arrest, he not only gave away those who had given him shelter[113] but also talked so extensively that there was really no case for the defence, and he was sentenced to death.[114] That Goerdeler and his fellow accused were intimidated is contradicted by the firm and forthright defence of his fellow accused, the lawyer Josef Wirmer.[115] This, however, did not save any of the accused from the gallows, including Germany's former Ambassador to the Vatican, Ulrich von Hassell.[116] However, Goerdeler was kept alive until 2 February 1945 and the question arises why. It may have been, because as Freisler's letter of 26 October 1944 (see p. 239) and Lautz's testimony[117] would indicate, Goerdeler's phenomenal memory began to work for the benefit of the Gestapo, or because Himmler was trying to use him to make contact with the Allies behind Hitler's back.[118] A third explanation is that he was spared to work out detailed plans for Germany's reconstruction, particularly in regards to price supervision and local administration, two topics on which he was an expert.

In view of Hitler's scorched-earth policy, once the Allies had crossed the German frontiers – and by the end of September they had done just that – it is unlikely that Hitler would have sanctioned Goerdeler's retention to work for a Germany from which he, Hitler, would have disappeared. Moreover, as events in 1945 were to prove,

Himmler had sufficiently good contacts in Sweden not to need Goerdeler's assistance.[119] Hence this author is inclined to give credence to the first explanation rather than to either of the others.

Be that as it may, on 2 February 1945 Goerdeler was executed – at just the time when Himmler was about to establish contacts with the Allies via Stockholm.[120]

Associated with Goerdeler were a number of former prominent German trade unionists, among them Dr Julius Leber, Hermann Maass and Gustav Dahrendorf.[121] Only the latter escaped the gallows with a sentence of ten years' hard labour. In a later trial the trade unionist Hermann Lüdemann was acquitted, although he was later arrested and transferred to a concentration camp, from which he emerged in May 1945.[122]

Former prominent politicians of the Weimar Republic, its first Reichswehr Ministers Gustav Noske and Dr Otto Gessler, were also accused. Noske, however, fell ill and was transferred to prison hospital where he survived.[123] Though an indictment had been drawn up against him, Gessler was taken to a concentration camp, which he also survived.[124]

Dr Andreas Hermes, a member of various cabinets from 1920 to 1923, faced Freisler on 11 January 1945. His cooperation with Goerdeler had been close. His trial appears to modify the usual cliché of the 'raving Roland'. The trial report stated: 'Impressive appearance, correct attitude. Language matter-of-fact and open. Refused to put a gloss on any action and was therefore treated by Dr Freisler in a gentle manner. . . .'[125] But Freisler's self-restraint did not save Hermes from the death sentence, although it was not carried out. Albrecht Fischer, another of Goerdeler's and Robert Bosch's associates, was saved by his defence counsel, who argued that Fischer's name had been put on one of the many lists for a future government drawn up by Goerderler without his knowing. Freisler seems to have been at great pains to phrase his questions in a manner that would allow Fischer's defence plenty of room for manoeuvre. Depsite some reservations, the prosectution asked for an acquittal and Freisler agreed.[126]

Another former Socialist destined for a government post was Matthäus Herrmann. A member of the SPD from an early age, he had been a deputy in the Bavarian Diet and had been recruited by the opposition in March 1944. This was just after he had undergone a serious operation and his defence counsel argued that at the time he was quite incapable of absorbing what was proposed to him. Freisler acquitted him. Giving his reasons, he said: 'We cannot charge someone with having formerly been a Social Democrat. Of the masses of the people who now pledge themselves to National Socialism, there were only a few who at the very beginning heard the call of destiny. A traitor must be eliminated. But he who has not crossed the boundary of treason must be maintained within the community of the Volk.'[127] The trial report sent to Bormann stated that Herrmann was a 'decent old man, hard of hearing, remote from political life. He honestly admitted not having shed his Social Democratic skin entirely, but said equally honestly that under the influence of his children he was gradually understanding what National Socialism was.'[128] One of the accused in another trial escaped conviction by claiming that his statement to the police had been made under threat: either he made the proposed statement, or the police would arrest his family. Freisler accepted that submission and the accused, Bartholomäus Kossmann, another former Socialist, was acquitted by Freisler, although the prosecution had demanded a two years' prison sentence.[129]

The former Prussian Minister of Finance, Johannes Popitz, was tried on 3 October 1944. Popitz, at a civilian level, was Himmler's link with the civilians, as at another level Hartmut Plaas had been with the military opposition. On 26 October 1943, he had met Himmler and pointed out to him that Hitler had failed and that it would be advisable to remove him and bring the war to an end. Instead of arresting him, Himmler was apparently convinced and Popitz was able to continue with his activities while the Berlin lawyer Dr Carl Langbehn, who had brought about the meeting, was detained but brought to trial over a year later together with Popitz. At the trial Freisler seems to have used all his skill to prevent Popitz from making his relations with Himmler the focus of his defence. Popitz and Langbehn were sentenced to death, though Popitz's execution was not carried out until 2 February 1945, when he was hanged together with Goerdeler.[130]

Next to Goerdeler, the most prominent accused among the civilian opposition was Germany's former ambassador to the USSR, Friedrich Werner Graf von der Schulenburg. He had played a vital part in bringing about the Russo-German Non-Aggression Pact of 23 August 1939, and had opposed the war against Russia. When in 1943 he heard that Ribbentrop was receiving peace feelers from the Russians via Dr Peter Kleist, a foreign office official in Stockholm, he immediately urged that the German opposition use this opportunity to establish contact with Moscow.[131] Nothing came of it. Since 1941 he had been involved in the conspirators' plans, an accusation he could not deny and which caused him to be sentenced to death. Another prominent member was Helmuth James Graf von Moltke, who had been in close contact with both Goerdeler and Stauffenberg. He exposed himself to a litany of abuse by Freisler when he used the rather naive excuse that all he had done was to organize resistance movements to be mobilized in the eventuality of enemy occupation.[132]

Accused with Moltke was Father Josef Delp SJ, a Catholic convert who had become a Jesuit priest in 1937. Within the Kreisau circle he represented the Catholic point of view and his Munich flat became a meeting place of members of the circle. Delp opposed the 'reactionary' and conservative course of the Goerdeler group and advised Stauffenberg against any association with it.[133] As in Wehrle's case Freisler gave full play to his anti-Catholic prejudices, but Delp stood his ground – which made Freisler all the more furious. His death sentence, like Moltke's, was a foregone conclusion.[134]

During the course of the VGH hearing of 3 February 1945 on the Sohlabrendorff case, the proceedings were interrupted by an Allied air raid in the course of which Freisler was killed.[135] Freisler was buried in a simple ceremony; Hitler himself had objected to a state funeral.[136] His obituary appeared in the last issue of *Deutsche Justiz* on 16 February 1945.[137]

There was then an interval of about three weeks until the trials of the members of the German resistance were resumed. The next trial was that of Goerdeler's brother, who had given him shelter while he was on the run. Since he was also implicated in the conspiracy he was sentenced to death.[138] On 25 February 1945 a former prominent National Socialist, the head of the Reich Criminal Police Office within the RSHA, Arthur Nebe, faced his judges. Nebe had joined the NSDAP in 1931 and became an SS-Gruppenführer and Lt-General of the police. Initially he had supported the NS regime, but probably in the light of the adverse development of the war for Germany had changed his mind. A fact frequently omitted is that in 1941 Nebe had volunteered to head Einsatzgruppe B in Russia.[139] This makes the assertion that Nebe was an early member of the resistance highly unlikely since it is unsupported by original sources and based only on the dubious memoirs of Gisevius.[140] In any event, Nebe did not appear among the conspirators until early in 1944, when presumably he was recruited by Helldorf. Nebe's task was to select officers of the criminal police to assist the military action in

Berlin.[141] After 20 July 1944 he stayed put, pretending to pursue the conspirators. Only when Helldorf was arrested did he go into hiding; he was caught on 16 January 1945. At his trial Nebe admitted everything so that it was unnecessary to produce any evidence. He was sentenced to death and hanged.[142]

The last prominent case of the civilian conspirators was that of Ewald von Kleist-Schmenzin. This was the trial begun by Freisler but interrupted by the air raid in which Freisler was killed. A large landowner, he was a member of the German National People's Party (DNVP) during the Weimar Republic and an arch-monarchist who had spoken out against Hitler at least since 1923. When General von Schleicher became Chancellor, Kleist recommended a *coup d'état* and urged Hindenburg to desist from making Hitler Chancellor (although at the time Hindenburg had no such intention). The National Socialists could do nothing about him other than to put obstacles in his way wherever there was an opportunity. Kleist replied in kind. However, they could not stop him from travelling abroad, especially to Great Britain, where he warned the Foreign Office of Hitler's imperialist plans, without, however, having any detailed knowledge of them, a case rather like Goerdeler's.[143] He was reluctant to join any of the groups – Goerdeler's because he did not trust his ability, Beck's because of his indecisiveness, the Kreisau circle because he considered it too introspective. Still his name was on Goerdeler's list since he had declared himself prepared to accept office. He also knew in detail of Stauffenberg's plans. Once arrested he was sure that he would not survive. At the beginning of his trial on 3 February 1945 he proclaimed that he had committed high treason and fought against Hitler and National Socialism. He considered this a duty to God.[144]

Twenty days later, on 23 February, the trial against Kleist was resumed. Without Freisler he seems to have thought that he had a chance. He pointed out that he had left the church, that two of his sons served in the Wehrmacht and that he was an enemy of parliamentarianism. The vice-president of the VGH, Dr Crohne, who presided over the case, allowed it to drag on until 15 March 1945. On that day Kleist-Schmenzin was sentenced to death for high treason. With barrages of Russian artillery already thundering and exploding in the heart of Berlin, he was decapitated on 9 April 1945.[145]

This was the end of the German conservative and military resistance. To argue that it did not exist would be contradicted by the plain facts.[146] But to cast them in the mould of '*Ritter ohne Furcht und Tadel*' (Knight without Fear and Reproach) would be going to extremes. Understandable though the resistance mythology may have been in the context of Germany's immediate post-war development, more than forty years after the event it is high time to assess the true proportions, effectiveness and the weaknesses of this variety of resistance. Democracy in the Federal Republic of Germany is strong enough to cast overboard the kind of mythology which, while possibly necessary for its early development, can only do it damage today.

# 11

# The Final Days of the VGH

Freisler was now dead and buried in the cemetery in Berlin-Dahlem. The funeral had been attended only by his wife, a few colleagues of the VGH, a representative of the Ministry of Justice and a few NS functionaries. But he had left behind his 'Distribution of Business of the VGH' for 1945, which in general differed little from previous business distribution plans, except that it proposed the even further concentration of all major matters in the hands of the First Senate and the establishment of options to draw to this senate any case of high treason and Landesverrat normally dealt with by another senate as well as 'offences committed by circles of the intelligentsia'.[1]

The question of a successor arose. Goebbels, more than a month later, recorded in his diary:

> The Fromm case has been submitted to me by the Führer. Without doubt Fromm behaved in the face of the enemy, that is to say the putschists, like a coward, but in view of the present composition of the Volksgerichtshof no death sentence can be expected. The Führer is turning back to the thought of appointing Frank President of the Volksgerichtshof. Though not an ideal figure, he is nevertheless a political judge. Otherwise there is nobody available and I cannot suggest another suitable candidate.[2]

Thus it seems that even during this final phase there still existed doubts about the absolute political reliability of VGH judges. But Goebbels' fears proved unfounded, for the VGH did sentence Fromm to death, and Dr Harry Haffner was appointed last president of the VGH.

Haffner was born on 28 May 1900 at Uslar, Lower Saxony, and completed his law studies in 1926 with average-to-low grades and worked within the local and regional judiciary as prosecutor. He joined the NSDAP on 1 May 1933, and then joined the SA and other NS organizations. In January 1944 he was appointed General State

Prosecutor in Kattowitz in Upper Silesia, annexed by Germany in 1939.[3]

Little is known about his activities there, except that on 28 June 1944, he, together with other judges and civil servants, visited Auschwitz. In his subsequent report on the concentration camp, he noted the very favourable impression the prisoners, men and women alike, had made on him. Their standard of nourishment and physical fitness 'surpassed the standards of penal institutions within the Reich', he said. 'On our way back into the camp we passed a crematorium, where corpses are apparently also burnt on piles of wood.'[4]

Precisely what criteria caused Haffner to be appointed as Freisler's successor is unknown. Only two cases were dealt with by the VGH under his presidency, both concerning higher civil servants who had left their post prematurely in the face of the advancing Russians.[5]

In 1945 he turned up with his wife in Sontra, Hesse, in the American zone of occupation under the name of Heinrich Hartmann. He seems to have had ample funds and in April 1948 he started producing buttons and clothing accessories, eventually employing four people. By 1952, however, he had returned to his native Lower Saxony and made an attempt to surface. In September of that year he had a personal interview with the SPD Minister of the Interior as well as with the representative of the Lower Saxon branch of the Office for the Protection of the Constitution. He argued that he had gone under cover only because he feared that he might be extradicted to Poland. Ultimately he was advised to stay under cover because his name was on the US Central Registry of War Criminals and Suspects. He decided to stay in Uslar, near Hanover, in the British zone of occupation; apparently the British were no longer interested in hunting down war criminals. A year later he was informed that the entry of his name on the US watch list had become irrelevant. He could assume his proper name again and from 1954 onwards received his full pension. Although three investigations were mounted against him, one in connection with his role in providing false death certificates for the euthanasia programme, all three were stopped. The relevant files were destroyed by Lower Saxony's Ministry of the Interior, and when Haffner died on 14 October 1969[6] the full story of his wartime activities had still not been revealed.

By the time Haffner took over his office, the VGH had moved to Potsdam. In his diary entry of 14 March 1945, Goebbels recorded: 'For the time being we are not establishing drum-head courts martial in Berlin, although we have become a city close to the front. As long as the Volksgerichtshof remains in Berlin, this will, I believe, suffice.'[7]

The trials following the plot against Hitler constituted the apex of the VGH's development. Of course the other senates continued their relentless prosecutions of 'crimes' such as defeatism and related offences. There was no letting up in their vigour. From the second half of 1944 onwards, there was hardly, if ever, a week on which the billboards throughout Germany did not show a new poster, pink in colour, headed 'Im Namen des Volkes' and announcing the death sentences for defeatism, for listening to foreign broadcasting stations, for plundering after air raids, for thefts of postal packages destined for soldiers on the front. But the bomb plot trials represented the VGH's culmination.

When it was first established in 1934, the VGH had nineteen judges; by 1935 it had 43. These lay judges were comprised of thirteen SA and SS leaders, ten NSDAP functionaries, civil servants and others, as well as seventeen officers of the armed forces and three senior police officers. What was noticeable was the high proportion of officers among the lay judges; they were required since they possessed the expertise necessary for trials concerning espionage, high treason and Landesverrat. By 1939 the number of lay judges had risen to 95: 48 SA, SS and NSKK leaders, four senior police officers, thirteen NSDAP functionaries and civil servants, and thirty officers of the armed forces. By the time the bomb plot trials took place, the number had risen to 173 lay judges, including 82 SA, SS, NSKK and Hitler Youth leaders, thirteen senior police officers, ten leaders of the Labour Service (RAD), 38 NSDAP functionaries and civil servants and thirty officers of the armed forces.[8]

This rapid expansion of the number of lay judges is not simply explicable in terms of the increased business with which the VGH was occupied, but arose also from the impact of the Allied bombing offensive, which, as previously indicated, severely disrupted communications, making it frequently impossible for lay judges to attend the court's sessions. Hence additional substitutes had to be appointed. The criteria of selection had already been laid down by Freisler in 1936:

> Until the National Socialist seizure of power the so-called lay judges were chosen by lot, risking the possibly very strong element of chance and the misuse of the choice by lot; the fear of the power of the state led to the proclamation of the most nonsensical choice of judges as the

guardians of the liberty of the citizen. National Socialism, however, selects its own People's Judges according to their personal suitability and special expertise. Upon the suggestion of the Reich Minister of Justice the Führer appoints the People's Judges who come from the Wehrmacht and the police, the NSDAP and its formations, and who are uniquely suited to make the people itself the bearer of justice.[9]

In contrast to previous practice, lay judges, once instructed as to their functions, were given access to the indictments, thus opening the possibility of prejudging the case before they had actually heard it.[10]

Originally the VGH had begun with three senates, the first two dealing with high treason and the third with Landesverrat. From November 1935 a further, fourth senate had been added, also dealing with Landesverrat.[11] On 1 November 1941 came a fifth, and in December 1942 the sixth and last senate was added.[12] The division of jurisdiction between the various senates was not always clearly defined, and especially under Thierack and Freisler the distinctions were blurred. Thus the distribution of business for 1939 shows that the First Senate also dealt with Landesverrat, indeed with all Landesverrat and high treason cases from Austria; in addition it dealt with economic sabotage, while the Second Senate dealt with wilful damage to the war effort. Two years later these distinctions had disappeared and from the time Freisler took over only the Third and Fourth Senate were concerned only with Landesverrat, although they operated with the reservation established by Thierack that the First Senate could try any treason case it thought important for the president of the VGH to deal with.[13] Freisler readily followed the precedents established by Thierack and further expanded them.

Any assessment of Freisler is a difficult task. The dead no longer have a voice. Those alive shifted their own guilt onto the backs of those who could no longer defend themselves. Freisler cannot be rehabilitated because he condemned himself, in the same way as the Third Reich can never be rehabilitated. Yet in both cases there is room for correction and de-mystification.

Between 1937 and 1941, the VGH handed out 240 death sentences, one-sixth of the death sentences pronounced by the German judiciary during this period. The trend towards the increasing application of the death sentence had been introduced by Thierack. Freisler took over his office – a court whose existence and further development had been one of his major preoccupations as Secretary of State – at a time when the tide of war was turning

against Germany, not slowly and almost imperceptibly, but drastically. The radicalization of the judiciary kept pace with the
radicalization of the war, with the latter being the driving power not
only of the VGH but, as will be demonstrated below, of the military
judiciary as well. Thierack had begun the policy of concentrating all
the important cases in his First Senate; Freisler merely continued it,
although now Thierack raised mild and ineffective protests against
what he himself had initiated.

Freisler was a fanatical National Socialist to the core; nothing
would be further from the mark than to accuse him of opportunism.
He stood for a 'new law', however perverted it may have been in the
light of liberal judiciary practice. The judge was the Führer: he led
his professional and lay judges, and he discussed the cases with them
beforehand, which in many instances may have been tantamount to
pronouncing sentence. Whether this took place in all, in the majority
or only in some cases, cannot be ascertained.

Yet in principle Freisler saw nothing wrong in this practice because
he only saw two colours, black or white. He who is not for me, is
against me, seems to have been one of his guiding maxims. He was
an able dialectician who used his dialectics with devastating
destructive effect. He had his ingrained prejudices, especially against
the Roman Catholic clergy. His other main target was the Jews. But
the assertion that anyone who came before Freisler was automatically
lost cannot be substantiated. He handed down a substantial number
of acquittals – irrespective of what happened to the acquitted
afterwards.[14]

Freisler became the scapegoat of the German judiciary of the Third
Reich, as well as its alibi, after 1945. The Nuremberg affidavits make
remarkable reading inasmuch as all the guilt is loaded on Freisler's
back, but they also produce contradictions. There are affidavits
sworn on oath that Freisler impeded the defence, and there are
affidavits which assert the contrary.[15] Which assertion is to be
believed?

There are quotations taken from second- or third-hand sources
that Hitler stated that Freisler 'is our Vhishinsky'. Yet if one checks
the sources they are of doubtful value.[16] Freisler was called upon to
deliver judgments which did not deal with legal abstractions and
infinite lists of paragraphs of the laws violated but politically one-
sided judgments on hard practical issues which not only the
leadership of the Third Reich expected, but whose deterrent value the
man in the street would understand, for better or worse. This Freisler

and his predecessor did remorselessly and relentlessly.

During any trial the worst offence a defendant could commit was to try to wriggle his way out of a charge, especially when the case – and the defendant's guilt – were all too obvious. As Freisler had insisted before his appointment, what counted for him was one's frame of mind. To intend to commit a crime was tantamount to having committed one, Freisler asserted. Hence he virtually created a new penal code for political attitudes, a *Gesinnungsstrafrecht*.

That he was mentally abnormal cannot be medically substantiated.[17] He was, in a word, 'the true believer'. In spite of all the sources of information available to him he believed unconditionally in Hitler, National Socialism and Germany to his very end and defended them with an eloquence equal only to that of Goebbels. Goebbels, however, was worse, for he was not a believer, but a cynic. Freisler lived modestly[18] and lived and died a convinced National Socialist. If that makes him abnormal, then so be it, but in that case we must accept that any believer in a chiliastic faith is similarly abnormal. With Freisler, and for that matter with most Germans of the period, the fault lay in believing in the wrong Messiah, or, as many would say today, in believing in a Messiah at all. Any man with a *total* belief in something is bound to overstep the boundary of fanaticism, but fanaticism is the enthusiasm of the mentally limited, or an indication of a mental limitation, irrespective of an intellect that may show signs of brilliance otherwise. Freisler was limited by his National Socialist convictions.

His judgments show signs that his generally attested high intelligence ceased to function the moment the Führer, his ideas, his orders and his life were involved. '[W]ho gave you the *right* (author's emphasis) to know that the Führer was dead?' Freisler cuttingly asked General Hoepner – a question which, if not formulated in the tension of the moment, demonstrates Freisler's uncritical dependence on Hitler. Even the slightest doubt on anything touching his idol Hitler was in Freisler's view a mortal sacrilege. In contrast to Hitler, about whom we have several psychogrammes – which, however, do not reflect with any great credit upon psycho-history – no such psychogramme exists about Freisler. Whether this is a matter to be regretted seems somewhat doubtful when we consider those about Hitler. Nevertheless, the fact that defeatists with doubts about Germany's 'final victory', doubts which from early 1944 were certainly more than justified, were mercilessly persecuted and convicted, is perhaps explicable if we assume that Freisler projected his own doubts on others in a common process of resolving psychic conflicts by transposing feelings of guilt. There is some evidence, especially in Freisler's correspondence, which supports this hypothesis and points to the conclusion that Freisler may have punished in draconian manner doubts in others which he himself felt and repressed. Both the venom with which he addressed many of those standing accused before him, and the doubts mentioned in his correspondence, appear to give this hypothesis a certain degree of probability.

But this has nothing to do with any mental illness in the general sense; there are no notes, diaries or letters of the period which would charge Freisler with mental abnormality. It became a convenient excuse after 1945 for those who shared the burden of guilt. That burden of guilt consisted in eliminating the *active* opponents of the NS system with an excessively wide interpretation of the letter of the law, law such as existed in 1933 and was enacted thereafter on the basis of the Enabling Law which allowed laws to be enacted even if they deviated from the constitution.

At first Thierack and Freisler fulfilled the NSDAP programme and the demands of its leaders, who throughout the Weimar Republic had heavily criticized the judiciary for being too soft in its sentencing policy on crimes involving high treason and Landesverrat. As already noted, Freisler had written in one of his articles that he who was devoid of honour deserved to be excluded from the German *Volksgemeinschaft*, be he a professional criminal or a political criminal.

Under pressure from Hitler, who usurped the right to transform any sentence into the death sentence, the VGH passed and carried out death sentences in greater number and speed. This was done under the mounting and extreme pressures of war and the increasing radicalization of all spheres of German public life. On the domestic front, the VGH was considered a vital instrument to stave off defeat and achieve 'final victory', even at a time when it must have been clear to all that victory could no longer be achieved.

It has been alleged that during the twelve years of Hitler's rule 32,600 people were sentenced to death by the German judiciary.[19] Recent studies consider this figure, which includes the death sentences of other courts beside those of the VGH, considerably exaggerated and have put it at a more realistic 16,560. Whether the figure of 12,891 death sentences passed by the VGH between 1934 and 1944 is correct will never be conclusively verified. All one can say in general terms is that the number of death sentences passed by the VGH before the war was low, that they increased with the outbreak of war and that they rapidly accelerated as the tide of war turned against Germany. Any assessment of final figures rests on very shaky ground, but assuming the figures shown in Chapter 8 are approximately correct then the rate of acceleration can be seen by the contrast between the 53 death sentences of 1940 and the 2,097 death sentences carried out in 1944.

The figures are not without their ambiguities, however. Thus for the first half of 1942 one source cites 1,146 death sentences, among them those of 106 Czechs and 530 Poles. Yet for the whole year the official figure is 1,192.[20] This would mean that during the second half of 1942 only 46 death sentences were handed out, a highly improbable drop which puts a question mark against the total figure, especially since according to *Führerinformation* No. 123 241 death sentences were passed in July 1942 alone, 64 of them for high treason and 23 for Landesverrat.[21] The *Führerinformation* does not provide details on death sentences passed by other courts. Moreover, the figure does not include those death sentences for *Wehrkraft-zersetzung*, a crime for which the almost inevitable punishment was death. Similar discrepancies arise if one examines 1943 and 1944.

In other words, the figures cited so far are highly questionable. They become even more questionable when we compare them with Thierack's and Freisler's own reports on the sentences pronounced by the VGH between 1937 and 1944 in which the total of death sentences between 1937 and 1944, inclusive, is given as 5,173. This would mean that if the total figure of 12,891 is correct, a total of 7,678 death sentences were passed between 1934 and the end of 1937 and 5,213 between January 1938 and the end of December 1944. That both Thierack and Freisler should understate the number of death sentences in reports not intended for public consumption is highly unlikely considering that the VGH was an institution which Thierack and Freisler dearly treasured, whose interest Freisler promoted up to 1942 and whose reputation in Hitler's eyes he was determined to enhance on becoming its president late in the summer of that year. And, as we have seen, the death sentence did not in all cases mean execution.

But even the oft-assumed tendency towards radicalization with the outbreak of the Second World War is, in the light of these figures, in need of qualification, especially the frequently heard assertion that in VGH practice the sentence of death was the rule, that of

imprisonment the exception. True, the figures show a marked
preference for the death sentence over the life sentence. However, if
by terms of imprisonment we mean hard labour, prison and formal
imprisonment in a concentration camp then in 1942 we have 48 per
cent of VGH sentences for imprisonment, in 1943 42 per cent and in
1944 38 per cent. If we compare death sentences and acquittals we
see the following development expressed in percentages:

|      | Death | Acquittal |
|------|-------|-----------|
| 1940 | 4.8%  | 7.3%      |
| 1941 | 8.2%  | 5.4%      |
| 1942 | 46.3% | 4.7%      |
| 1943 | 49.8% | 5.4%      |
| 1944 | 47.4% | 11.7%     |

In other words the drastic rise in death sentences had already begun
under Thierack and increased only marginally under Freisler. Indeed
under Freisler in 1943 and 1944 we note a decline of 2.4% of those
sentenced to death and a more than doubling of the number of
acquittals. The enormous rise in the death sentence from 1942
onwards can probably be attributed to the *Nacht-und-Nebel* cases,
and that for 1944 to the putsch attempt.

Normally each death sentence passed by the VGH required Hitler's
assent. Judgments were submitted to the Führer either via the head of
the NSDAP Chancellery, Martin Bormann, or via the head of the
Reich Chancellery, Lammers. Obviously to examine each case would
have taken up too much time and impeded the speed with which the
VGH was always called upon to act. Up to the outbreak of war the
Reich Ministry of Justice submitted to Hitler a monthly list of death
sentences together with any pleas for clemency (which also had to be
submitted via Bormann). This practice changed during the war when
Hitler, informed that over 900 individuals under sentence of death
were still in prison, empowered Thierack to order immediate
executions in all cases the result of which he considered to be beyond
doubt.[22] In consequence Thierack, in a circular of 27 August 1943,
asked all prosecutors not to involve any other authorities in any pleas
of clemency; Hitler had in fact delegated the review of any case to
Thierack.[23]

In November 1944, Thierack tried to simplify the process even
further by pointing out to Dr Otto Meissner, head of the Chancellery
of the Presidency, that in the past two years Hitler had ordered only

one execution out of 290 clemency references, and that therefore the clemency policy as practised by his ministry was in full accord with that of Hitler.[24] Therefore submission of cases to Hitler should only take place when a case was particularly doubtful. Hitler agreed, with the reservation that all cases in which women from the occupied territories were concerned should be submitted to him.[25] Thierack himself interpreted this very widely. Death sentences passed for *Wehrkraftzersetzung* were not to be reviewed, even at the risk that on·occasion the innocent would suffer. This applied to cases in which the condemned were not of age. Pleas for clemency submitted by the defence counsel, or by the accused or his relations, were even at that stage sometimes successful,[26] though they only very rarely succeeded in cases in which the accused were involved, however marginally, in the July 1944 conspiracy.

Contrary to previous practice, the bodies of those executed were not handed over to the relatives of the victim. They were either cremated or given to the medical faculties of university institutes.[27]

Although, as already indicated, the evidence is scant and sketchy and reliable statistics are difficult to compile, we can say that the figures for death sentences pronounced by the individual senates of VGH down to and including 1941 are:[28]

| Senates: | 1 | 2 | 3 | 4 | 5 | 6 |
|---|---|---|---|---|---|---|
| 1937 | 7 | 9 | 7 | 9 | – | – |
| 1938 | – | 1 | 6 | 10 | – | – |
| 1939 | 11 | 6 | 11 | 8 | – | – |
| 1940 | 12 | 15 | 11 | 15 | – | – |
| 1941 | 41 | 25 | 18 | 16 | 2 | – |

For the year 1942 Freisler's report reveals the following figures:[29]

| Senates: | 1 | 2 | 3 | 4 | 5 | 6 |
|---|---|---|---|---|---|---|
| Number of accused | 1,373 | 593 | 148 | 183 | 257 | 18 |
| Death sentences | 649 | 327 | 37 | 45 | 120 | 14 |
| Life sentences | 27 | 23 | 12 | 9 | 8 | – |
| Hard labour 10–15 yrs | 221 | 87 | 14 | 11 | 29 | 1 |
| Hard labour 5–10 yrs | 258 | 55 | 34 | 23 | 34 | 1 |
| Hard labour less than 5 yrs | 122 | 24 | 6 | 20 | 19 | 6 |
| Prison | 58 | 31 | 28 | 44 | 22 | – |
| Concentration camp | 2 | 22 | 3 | 10 | 8 | – |
| Acquittal | 36 | 23 | 14 | 15 | 17 | 2 |

From these figures it emerges again very clearly that the major cases had already been handled by the First Senate when Thierack was president of the VGH and that its sentencing policy was harsher than that of the other senates. In other words, Freisler simply continued what Thierack had already begun. Although there were acquittals, many of the individuals concerned can be assumed to have been re-arrested, as already indicated, and transferred to concentration camps. However, a breakdown of figures of those acquitted and then re-arrested can no longer be offered, since most of the original records were destroyed before the end of the war or were lost.[30]

For 1943 the picture, according to Freisler, is:[31]

| Senates | 1 | 2 | 3 | 4 | 5 | 6 |
|---|---|---|---|---|---|---|
| Number of accused | 1,332 | 610 | 145 | 259 | 348 | 612 |
| Death sentence | 769 | 368 | 49 | 72 | 200 | 204 |
| Life sentence | 8 | 2 | 4 | 2 | – | 8 |
| Hard labour 10–15 yrs | 80 | 29 | 6 | 25 | 48 | 78 |
| Hard labour 5–10 yrs | 234 | 92 | 15 | 37 | 47 | 168 |
| Hard labour less than 5 yrs | 97 | 57 | 12 | 19 | 51 | 64 |
| Prison | 87 | 43 | 25 | 42 | 20 | 42 |
| Concentration camp | 6 | 3 | 10 | 7 | 3 | 13 |
| Acquittal | 50 | 10 | 12 | 47 | 14 | 42 |

Again we see the dominant role of the First Senate, although at this point the number of cases passing through the other five senates begins to rise dramatically.

It is interesting to compare the death sentences for 1943 (1,662) and 1944 (2,097) with the sentencing policy of the courts of the German armed forces and the Reichskriegsgericht.

These courts pronounced death sentences for desertion as follows:[32]

| | Number of cases | Imprisonment | Death |
|---|---|---|---|
| 1940 | 1,060 | 656 | 313 |
| 1941 | 865 | 548 | 272 |
| 1942 | 3,627 | 1,818 | 1,551 |
| 1943 (1st half) | 1,927 | 827 | 1,039 |
| 1944 (1st half) | ? | 1,209 | 1,645 |

Here it must be added that the figures for the third and the fourth quarters of 1943 do not include a breakdown between army court sentences of imprisonment and death sentences passed, so that it is impossible to say how many of the 2,731 accused were sentenced to death and how many were given terms of imprisonment. The same is true of the 2,131 cases in the third quarter of 1944, the last quarter for which figures are available. While the years 1940 and 1941 provide a detailed breakdown between private soldiers, non-commissioned officers and officers, this breakdown no longer exists for the years thereafter. For the period from October 1944 to May 1945 no figures are available. Moreover, the available statistics include only two officers, one in 1940 and another in 1942.[33] After Stalingrad and the virtual destruction of the Army Group Centre in June–July 1944, however, a number of German generals and officers made themselves available to Russian propaganda instruments like the BDO, creating a new wave of military defections and thus, for our purposes, distorting the picture presented by the statistics; they were all sentenced to death *in absentia*.[34] What the statistics do reflect approximately is that the death sentences pronounced between 1940 and the end of September, and certainly from 1942 onwards, reveal a drastic upward trend and do not bear out the argument that army courts and the Reichskriegsgericht acted much more humanely than the VGH.[35]

On the contrary, bearing in mind that the jurisdiction of the VGH applied to roughly 70 million Germans, plus the Czech population, the Poles in the German annexed territories and the Germans in Alsace-Lorraine and Eupen-Malmedy, the jurisdiction of the army courts extended at the peak of military mobilization to just over 10 million Wehrmacht and Waffen-SS personnel. In the light of these proportions the death sentences awarded by the army courts and the Reichskriegsgericht appear even higher in percentage terms than those handed down by the VGH.

Furthermore, the army courts treated desertion as a political offence; such judgments as have survived contain nothing about violations of military discipline, but are based instead on political and ideological reasoning.[36] Desertion included not only leaving the forces in order to escape the armed services but also absence without leave from one's unit.[37] Moreover, the armed forces statistics do not include the vital period from October 1944 to the end of May 1945, a period in which soldiers and officers caught without the necessary papers were shot or hanged on the next tree or lamppost on the basis of drum-head courts martial held by the roadside. Their number cannot be accurately estimated; in April 1945, one local source counted within a 10 kilometre radius of Munich over 200 soldiers

and officers thus executed and left on display to warn members of
the Wehrmacht against following their example.[38] Hence the total
figure of death sentences carried out by the Wehrmacht is bound to
be much higher than the figures recorded here.

Recent findings allege that the Wehrmacht judiciary in fact handed
down more than 40,000 death sentences.[39] However, the methodo-
logical approach of this study gives cause for serious reservations.
Taking the 116th Infantry Division stationed in Vienna as his
sample, Manfred Messerschmidt, the author of the study, takes the
death sentences pronounced for members of this low-grade division and
extrapolates from it, applying the results not only to the army, but to
the three services of the Wehrmacht as a whole, ignoring the
fundamental differences between them. Even if he had applied his
extrapolation only to the army, he would have ignored the profound
qualitative differences between individual divisions. To lump, for
instance, the Grossdeutschland Panzer, the Panzer Lehr Division or
other elite divisions together with divisions with high numbers is
methodologically unsound and inevitably produces a distorted
picture.

Nevertheless, for both the civilian and military sector, the
continuing rapid deterioration of Germany's military fortunes
expressed itself in an escalation of the number of harsh sentences
awarded for political and military offences. Death sentences became
the order of the day.

When the writing on the wall became unmistakable, NSDAP
functionaries were forced to choose between two options: to remain
faithful to the ever-more draconian war measures in Germany, to
close ranks come what may, or to attempt to distance themselves
from the NSDAP in order to begin building bridges to the post-war
world and establish their political alibis *vis-à-vis* the future rulers of
Germany, east and west.

Freisler clearly belonged to the first category. In a letter dated 26
October 1944 he wrote:

> In one's innermost thoughts one has to admit that it is no longer
> impossible that Germany could lose the war. The V-weapons have not
> yielded the success which we all expected. Even Reich Minister
> Goebbels shares this view,[40] but according to his information much
> more destructive weapons are being prepared which will surpass in
> their destructive power anything the world has seen hitherto.[41] Then

we must not forget the time factor. We must at all costs hold out, the longer we hold our positions, the sooner this unnatural alliance between the Anglo-Americans and the Soviets will break asunder. It cannot be in the interests of Anglo-Americans that the Russians should dominate Central Europe, least of all the Jewish capitalists of the west. I must admit that a review of the last few years has forced me to abandon the belief in a world-wide Jewish conspiracy against Germany. This I consider too crude an interpretation. There exists a deep unbridgeable gap between the Jewish proletariat of eastern Europe from which the Jewish intelligentsia is recruited and which does all it can to bring about the Bolshevik Revolution on a world-wide scale, and the Jews in England and America who, largely assimilated, have no interest in revolutions, least of all a Bolshevik one backed by the material power of Soviet Russia, and whose profit motive contradicts the aims of their eastern brethren.

But if we should lose this war, which I fervently hope the genius of our Führer and providence will prevent, then we must also ensure that we go down with flying colours. In 1815 it was believed that the ideas of the French Revolution had been defeated. What we have seen so far, and what we are witnessing in France again, is that this was far from being the case. They have survived and in spite of periods of terrible weakness have taken hold of the French and become part of their national fabric.

The idea of National Socialism was born in an environment of abject misery and it has triumphed contrary to all expectations. Yet one cannot change a nation and its social fabric overnight or in just over ten years. The present series of trials have amply demonstrated this to me. I too was surprised by the extent of the conspiracy. What I originally assumed to be only a small clique has drawn on much wider circles than I had expected. Yet it is precisely the cowardice of many of their leaders which will have shown to the German people the infinite superiority of the National Socialist idea, compared with a programme devoid of ideals and revolutionary *élan*. Men who in their mental attitude and aspirations belonged to the Wilhelmine epoch and to the Weimar system, tried to take over Germany, a bunch of backward-looking old men, some of whom, like that fellow Goerdeler, have nothing better to do after their conviction than to inundate us with memoranda and information implicating an almost countless number of others in the reactionary plot. In that way they may well extend their lives for a few months but they will not escape the fate they deserve. In view of the extent of the conspiracy of which the German people are of course also now aware, one hears that the revolution is now devouring its children. In my view there would be some truth in this saying if it were applied to that fateful year 1934. But nothing

could be more wrong than to view the present events in this light. The
revolution is not devouring its children; the National Socialist revolution
is spitting out those who had never been part of this revolution,
those who need to be eliminated before this revolution can be brought
to its ultimate and final conclusion. They did not belong to us, they
did not want to belong to us, they represented an alien substance
inside National Socialist Germany.[42] In this sense, as in 1792 in
France, so in Germany in 1944 the Volksgerichtshof has become
a truly revolutionary tribunal to purify the nation. What will remain
will all be National Socialist to the core, as most *Volksgenossen*
already are, and even if defeated by the enemy they will see to it that
they and their successors will be National Socialists irrespective of the
name and form they take until the moment when the swastika can be
unfurled again over our cities and across the whole of our fatherland.
Irrespective of what the future may bring, National Socialism will
triumph. National Socialism, the impact of this war, which was the
last thing our Führer desired, and the aftermath of this war, will prove
the great levellers in German society which have swept and continue to
sweep away the class barriers and differences. All Germans are now in
one boat and have to pull the oars in one direction in order to attain
victory, or if the worst should come about, to achieve recovery and with
it ultimate and final triumph. . . .[43]

In this letter Freisler also mentioned his increasing burden of work
and the extremely difficult circumstances under which he had to
work. Allied air raids kept interrupting his trials and because of the
raids on Berlin he had sent his wife and two sons to safety.[44]

After Freisler's death, there were still four major trials to come. On
24 April 1945, the VGH moved from Potsdam to Bayreuth, but no
further trials were held. The end of the war overtook the VGH, and
it was formally dissolved on 20 October 1945 by Proclamation No. 3
of the Allied Control Council for Germany.[45] The last instrument of
terror of the NS regime had ceased legally to exist. Instruments of
terror of another brand, however, continued, at least in Germany's
eastern half, where the first Soviet proceedings against Germans were
every ounce as arbitrary as those of the VGH, and where the
concentration camps of Buchenwald, Sachsenhausen, Oranienburg
and Bautzen continued to exist, now populated not simply by former
National Socialists but also by those who opposed Soviet totalitarianism as much as they had opposed that of National Socialism. In
the course of the five years to 1950, over 55,000 Germans perished
there.[46]

Germany has retained the legacy of the NS People's Court. As an institution it and its members were never indicted in the Nuremberg and successor trials. All that has been done so far is that the Bundestag of the Federal German Republic on 25 January 1985 has, by unanimous vote, declared all VGH judgments null and void,[47] a potentially dangerous precedent since this decision represents a gross violation of the principle of the separation of powers in a democracy. Within the confines of constitutional legality the Bundestag is only allowed to request the Federal Supreme Administrative Court (Bundesverwaltungsgerichtshof, or BVG) to review all available VGH judgments and decide case by case – an extremely arduous task, but legally the only valid one. Justice is not a cheap commodity.

Forty years too late all former VGH judges, professional as well as lay, were to be prosecuted by Berlin's Landgericht I. The indictment had already been drawn up and the first trial was to be held in 1985. It was cancelled because the accused, an 84-year-old man, committed suicide. The trials have now been (temporarily?) called off.

Whether coming to terms with one's past, *Vergangenheitsbewältigung*, can be successfully achieved in this way more than forty years after the end of Hilter's Germany, is open to doubt. Children and grandchildren would be the judges of their fathers and grandfathers. Yet one cannot cleanse oneself of the past. The record of 1939 to 1945 has become history, a history in which the barbarism of the NS regime speaks for itself.

However, it is not inconceivable that had Freisler survived he would, like Lautz,[48] have been leniently treated, or have gone underground for several years only to re-surface in the 1950s and, like many of his colleagues, resume a respectable career and become once again a valuable asset to the community in which he lived. This transformation – from executive instrument of terror to highly respectable citizen – has been achieved by many.

National Socialism as a phenomenon of mass discipline and control began to interest scientists more than twenty years ago. The American psychologist Stanley Milgram tried in 1963 to examine the roots of the respect and subordination to authority which he considered characteristic of the NSDAP.[49] He intended to select a random sample of Germans who were to act as teachers who were 'to drum' lessons into their disobedient and stupid pupils. Before leaving for Germany he conducted a test in his own institute with American candidates.

The 'teachers' were instructed to treat 'pupils', with whom they had contact only via loudspeakers, with shocks of electric current up to 450 volts in order to improve their performance. The experiment, so the 'teachers' were told, was of particular scientific importance and therefore the test subjects, i.e. the 'pupils', would have to put up with some pain if necessary. (The 'pupils' did not in fact suffer; they feigned pain by shouting loudly into a microphone when the meter before them registered particularly strong shocks of electric current.)

Milgram's 'test run' made his trip to Germany superfluous. No less than 85 per cent of the American 'teachers' were quite prepared to subject lazy or stupid 'pupils' to strong shocks of electric current, almost half of them in lethal strength ranging between 200 and 450 volts.

Professor Dr Dietrich Mantell of the Max Planck Institute in Munich repeated Milgram's experiment in 1970 with German 'teachers' and 'pupils' and came to the same conclusion: under authoritarian pressure, and for an 'ideal aim', almost half of human beings when relieved of any responsibility for their actions are prepared to inflict the most serious physical damage on other human beings. Milgram's own conclusions were that merciless torture, liquidations, even outright murder are not a specifically German but a general human problem; subject to strong pressure for obedience and for the sake of a 'high ideal', even the normal citizen can become the willing helper of those who enjoy a monopoly of power.

Hence it seems doubtful that any trial of former VGH professional and lay judges, the youngest by now 75, the oldest 97 years of age, would have either an educational or self-cleansing effect. With the end of the VGH in 1945, three strands of continuity that mark its origin, development and actions also came to their final conclusion: the popular belief in the stab in the back legend; Article 2 of the Enabling Act which empowered the NS regime to enact laws deviating from the constitution, and last, but by no means least, the *Führerprinzip*. The NS Volksgerichtshof is now part of history – an evil part, no doubt, but history nevertheless.

# Appendix
# The Structure of the German Judiciary

A knowledge of the structure of the German judiciary is essential to an understanding of the VGH. In Germany, to start with the broadest possible category, both judicial structure and judicial proceedings before proper courts are regulated by a whole series of laws. The most important of these are the Gerichtsverfassungsgesetz (GVG) of 27 January 1877, which provides a legal foundation for the courts and their proceedings; and the Strafprozessverordnung (StPO) of 1 February 1877, which provides for legal proceedings in criminal cases.[1] Cases concerning civil law are regulated by other legislation; we are concerned here only with criminal law.

At the bottom of the judicial structure is the Amtsgericht, a local court which may deal with criminal cases in which the sentence is not likely to exceed one year's imprisonment. It is presided over by one judge who acts either individually or with the assistance of Schöffen, lay judges, in cases where the penalty is not likely to exceed three years of imprisonment. However, the Schöffen do not act in a decisive role, such as in the case of the Anglo-Saxon jury, they act only in an advisory capacity. The Amtsgericht may be a local court within a district or *Land* (region), or within a district of a city. Depending on its size a city may contain several Amtsgerichte.

The next highest court is the Landgericht. It is a court of appeal against any sentence handed down by an Amtsgericht, but it is divided in cases of criminal law into two chambers, one the small penal chamber (*kleine Strafkammer*) the other the large penal chamber (*grosse Strafkammer*). Both deal with criminal cases which exceed the competence of the Amtsgericht. As long as the death sentence existed a Landgericht was able to impose it. (In Germany's western half, a provisional new constitution, the Basic Law, was introduced in 1949 which abolished capital punishment.) Beside the presiding judge, there are two professional judges who assist him. For a short time, during the Weimar Republic, trial by jury made its appearance within the framework of the Landgericht but it was a relatively short-lived experiment; instead the judiciary preferred to return to the Schöffengericht, which can also operate within the Landgericht.

Next in the hierarchy, and superior both to the Amtsgericht and the Landgericht comes the Oberlandesgericht, again a court of appeal against decisions made by the lower courts and one which has a small and a large penal senate when dealing with criminal cases. The small senate deals as court of appeal from Amtsgerichte and from small and large penal chambers of the Landgerichte, while the large senate deals with treasonable actions, both as first instance and as court of final jurisdiction.

Since both the Bismarckian and the Weimar Constitutions were essentially federal constitutions, there existed variations to this general pattern from *land* to *land*. For instance in Belin there was and there is no Oberlandesgericht but a Kammergericht whose functions are identical. During the Weimar Republic several of the individual *lands*, for instance, Prussia and Bavaria, had their own Staatsgerichtshof, a supreme court of appeal, very often dealing with problems concerning the interpretation of the constitution of the individual *Land*. However, during the Weimar Republic there was one Supreme Court, the Reichsstaatsgerichtshof (later called Reichsgericht) which was both a court of final appeal and one dealing with particularly serious cases of treason.[2] The Reichsgericht continued throughout the Third Reich. However, after 1934, with the foundation of the People's Court, the NS Volksgerichtshof (VGH), this court took exclusive control of cases of treasonable activity.

As far as the judicial procedure for treason is concerned, once treason has been prosecuted by the police, the prosecuting authority, the Staatsanwaltschaft, is entrusted with the power to investigate further in order to decide whether sufficient grounds exist to bring a formal indictment. The prosecuting counsel, or Staatsanwalt, is a civil servant employed by the Ministry of Justice. He is therefore bound by the instructions of his immediate superiors and does not enjoy the independence and liberty from interference which a judge enjoys. In particularly serious and difficult cases, upon the request of the prosecuting authorities, and investigating judge, an Ermittlungs-richter, can be appointed to carry out extensive investigations. The bulk of these investigating judges were recruited on secondment from those judges who normally presided over a Landgericht. However, in Hitler's Germany, the tendency developed to leave the investigating functions almost exclusively in the hands of the prosecuting authority, a tendency which in the German Federal Republic has continued to this day.[3]

Once the indictment has been drawn up it is formally handed to the accused and his defence counsel, and a date for the trial is set. Initially it was the Oberlandesgericht which acted as court, both at first instance and in ultimate jurisdiction in a treason case. That is to say, once the sentence had been passed, there was no right of appeal. The most serious and spectacular cases could be referred to the jurisdiction of the Reichsgericht by an initiative of this tribunal. However, members of the armed forces or civilian employees of the Reichswehr (and later the Wehrmacht) accused of treason could only be dealt with by the highest court of Germany's armed forces, the Reichskriegsgericht. The exception was when the accused such as the lieutenants of the Ulm garrison were expelled in 1930 from the Reichswehr before official proceedings for treason began. After the bomb plot of 20 July 1944, Hitler, taking note of Weimar's precedent, insisted that members of the Wehrmacht implicated in it were first expelled by a hastily convened 'Court of Honour' from the Wehrmacht so that they could be handed over to the VGH.

In judicial terms, Germany's legal system based itself on public law, the *jus publicum*, which regulated that part of the legal order derived from activities by and for the state. The judiciary's task was not the protection or preservation of the public interest, but the application of sovereign power. Thus German public law is something quite different from private law. While the state can participate in any action involving private law, in disputes over private agreements and the like, the main concern of public law was and is constitutional administrative law, i.e. public law in its most narrow sense, and, of course, private as well as criminal law. The differentiation between public law and private law is largely a legacy of Roman law which did not exist in medieval Germany, or in Anglo-Saxon law. This differentiation is particularly significant for the separation of lawsuits based on a collision of private interests from lawsuits emerging out of constitutional, administrative and criminal affairs.

For any interpretation of the public law the principle of *Treu und Glauben*, of loyalty and good faith, is fundamental. Actions ostensibly based on public law but illegal in intent and consequences are null and void. Legal subjects of public law in Germany are the state, i.e. the state itself, the individual *Lands*, public institutions such as state banks and public corporations such as regional communities as well as public foundations. The position of a public subject is granted, defined and determined by corresponding legislation. Subjective public law rulings in the area of public law can be obtained by the individual or a corporation by legislation from the state or such other institutions of the state which on its behalf exercise sovereign power. They can be granted in order to participate in public functions such as elections, or a positive status can be granted concerning the claims against the state such as damages, the receipt of salaries or social demands such as pensions. There also exists a negative aspect which protects the individual against interference in the sphere of personal liberty. State intervention into this sphere of basic rights can take place only if it has a proper legal foundation or when the interest of the welfare of the majority commands such a step. Measured by these criteria both the emergency legislation in the wake of the Reichstag fire of 28 February 1933 and the Enabling Act of 24 March 1933 were entirely legal. According to public law, illegal interference by the state makes it liable to damages and compensation. In Germany international law is also a further aspect of the existing public law.[4]

The entire German conception of law rests on a legal philosophy which concerns itself with the origins, nature, validity, values and principles of law, with the forms of realizing and applying the law and the methods of interpretation. Within this context several major problems emerge. One is the problem of validity because the law confronts the individual with the claim that it represents the yardstick according to which the individual should act. The question which this problem raises concerns the validity of the basis of any law: can the legislator in any given context translate general rulings into the form of law, or are there limitations based on natural law or imposed by ethical norms? A second problem concerns the question of the existence of the law. After all, positive law emerges, changes and vanishes. As long as it is generally accepted and followed, it influences and determines the behaviour of men and thus the social structure within which they live. And here the question is raised as to the basis upon which the effectiveness of the law rests and its specific characteristics. The problem of the law's *geistige*, its spiritual existence, prompts the question of whether this existence is directed towards unchangeable central values, and, if so, whether the law can in fact provide absolute justice.

These problems have occupied generations of jurists over centuries. Until the early nineteenth century, the history of occidental law coincided with the history of ethics and natural law. G. Hugo (1764–1844), one of the foremost legal brains of the University of Göttingen, published a work, *Naturrecht als Philosophie des positiven Rechts*,[5] and Hegel then entered the scene with terms like '*Wissenschaft des Naturrechts*' and his *Philosophie des Rechts*.[6] With the gradual decline of Hegel's philosophy, interest in legal philosophy also declined, to be replaced during the second half of the nineteenth century by a legal positivism (*Rechtspositivismus*), whose representatives (R. Stammler, K. Binding, and G. Dulckheit) claimed to have derived it from Kant's philosophy.[7] However, there were still other competing schools of legal philosophy. N. Hartmann, for example, argued strongly in favour of the natural Christian sources of all law.[8]

The school of legal thought which dominated until 1945, however, was that of legal positivism. It equated the law with the behavioural norms determined by state and society, and which therefore required no further justification, and rejected natural law, describing it as mere unproven speculation. In essence legal positivism is sceptical since it negates the possibility of the existence of generally acceptable, unchangeable ethical norms. From this viewpoint, questions about the content of justice are unanswerable. In actual practice, however, legal positivism demands from the judge absolute loyalty to the letter of the law even if he considers the law unjust. In its most extreme form, notably expressed by Carl Schmitt, legal positivism teaches that all law emanates from the state. The state as legislator could, as long as it had the power to do so, initiate any law irrespective of its content.[9]

This, crudely and summarily, represents the philosophic basis of the legal training of three to four generations of German law students who, after two university examinations and various spells as unpaid clerks and assistants to courts, became judges in their late twenties.

# Abbreviations

Abt.    Abteilung (section, department or unit)
AOK    Armeeoberkommando (Command of an Army)
BAKO    Bundesarchiv Koblenz (Federal Archive, Koblenz)
BAMA    Bundesarchiv-Militärarchiv Freiburg (Federal Military Archive, Freiburg)
BDE    Befehlshaber des Ersatzheeres (Commander of Reserve Army)
BGB    Bürgerliches Gesetzbuch (German Legal Code)
BGH    Bundesgerichtshof (Federal German Supreme Court)
BGHSt    Entscheidungen des Bundesgerichtshofes in Strafsachen (federal court verdicts in criminal cases)
BDC    Berlin Document Center
BDO    Bund Deutscher Offiziere (League of German Officers)
BNSDJ    Bund Nationalsozialistischer Deutscher Juristen (League of National Socialist Jurists)
DAF    Deutsche Arbeitsfront (German Labour Front)
DAP    Deutsche Arbeiterpartei (German Workers' Party)
DJ    *Deutsche Justiz* (German judiciary's journal)
DJZ    *Deutsche Juristenzeitung* (German law magazine)
DNVP    Deutsch-nationale Volkspartei (German National People's Party)
d. Res.    der Reserve (reserve officer)
    *Deutsches Recht* (German law journal)
DRZ    *Deutsche Richterzeitung* (legal journal for judges)
FAUD    Freie Arbeiter Union Deutschlands (Union of Free German Workers)
GG    Grundgesetz (statute for provisional constitution)
Gestapo    Geheime Staatspolizei (State Secret Police)
GSta    Generalstaatsanwalt (Prosecutor General)
HJ    Hitlerjugend (Hitler Youth)
i.G.    im Generalstab (member of the General Staff)
IMT    International Military Tribunal
IfZg    Institut für Zeitgeschichte (Institute for Contemporary History)
ISK    Internationaler Sozialistischer Kampfbund (International Socialist Combat League)
JWS    *Juristische Wochenschrift* (weekly law journal)
KPD    Kommunistische Partei Deutschlands (Communist Party of Germany)
KPDO    Kommunistische Partei Deutsche Opposition (Communist Party – German Opposition)
KPC    Kommunistische Partei der Tschechoslowakei (Communist Party of Czechoslovakia)
KSSVO    Kriegssonderstrafrechtsverordnung (Special Wartime Penal Code)

KStVO   Kriegsstrafverfahrensverordnung (War Penal Code Procedure)
KWVO   Kriegswirtschaftsverordnung (Regulation of the War Economy)
KZ, KL   Konzentrationslager (concentration camp)
LG   Landgericht (*Land*, or County, Court)
MDR   *Monatsschritt für deutsches Recht* (monthly journal on German law)
MGM   *Militärgeschichtliche Mitteilungen* (military history journal)
MilStGB   Militärstrafgesetzbuch (Military Penal Code)
MilStGO   Militärstrafgerichtsordnung (Military Penal Procedure)
MNN   Münchner Neueste Nachrichten
NJW   *Neue Juristische Wochenschrift* (weekly journal for jurists)
NSDAP   Nationalsozialistische Deutsche Arbeiterpartei (National Socialist German Workers Party)
NKFD   Nationalkommitee Freies Deutschland (National Committee for a Free Germany)
NSF   Nationalsozialistische Frauenschaft (National Socialist Women's League)
NSKK   Nationalsozialistische Kraftfahrkorps (National Socialist Union of Motorists)
NSRB   Nationalsozialistischer Rechtswahrerbund (National Socialist League of Lawyers)
NSV   Nationalsozialistische Volkswohlfahrt (National Socialist Public Welfare Organization)
OKH   Oberkommando des Heeres (Army Supreme Command)
OKW   Oberkommando der Wehrmacht (Supreme Command of Armed Forces)
OLG   Oberlandesgericht (High County Court)
ORA   Oberreichsanwalt (Supreme State Prosecutor)
OStA   Oberstaatsanwalt (State Prosecutor)
PRO   Public Record Office
RFSSuChdDtPol.   Reichsführer-SS und Chef der Deutschen Polizei (Chief of the SS and German Police)
RG   Reichsgericht (Supreme Court of Justice)
RGBl.   *Reichsgesetzblatt* (publication of German law)
RGDt.   Entscheidungen des Reichsgerichts in Strafsachen (Reichscourt judgments in criminal cases)
RAD   Reichsarbeitsdienst (National Socialist Labour Service)
RJM   Reichsjustizminister(ium) (Reich Minister of Justice/Ministry of Justice)
RKG   Reichskriegsgericht (Supreme Military Court)
RMI   Reichsministerium des Inneren (Reichs Ministry of Interior)
RSHA   Reichssicherheitshauptamt (Reich Security Main Office)
RStCB   Reichsstrafgesetzbuch (Reich Penal Code)
RMVP   Reichsministerium für Volksaufklärung und Propaganda (Reich Ministry of Popular Enlightenment and Propaganda)
RStPO   Reichsstrafprozessordnung (Reich Criminal Procedure)
SA   Sturmabteilung der NSDAP (Storm Troopers of the NSDAP)
SAP   Sozialistische Arbeiterpartei (Socialist Workers Party)
SD   Sicherheitsdienst des Reichsführer-SS (Security Service of the Reich Commander of the SS)
SG   Sondergericht (Special Court)
SPD   Sozialdemokratische Arbeiterpartei Deutschlands (Social Democratic Party of Germany)
SS   Schutzstaffeln der NSDAP (Protection Squads of the NSDAP, "black shirts")

| StA | Staatsanwalt (Public Prosecutor) |
|---|---|
| StGB | Strafgesetzbuch (penal code) |
| StPO | Strafprozessordnung (penal code decree) |
| SZ | *Süddeutsche Zeitung* |
| VB | *Völkischer Beobachter* (NSDAP daily newspaper) |
| VfZg | *Vierteljahrhefte für Zeitgeschichte* (quarterly journal of contemporary history) |
| VGH | Volksgerichtshof (People's Court) |
| VO | Verordnung (decree) |
| WBK | Wehrbezirkskommando (Army District Command) |
| WKr | Wehrkreis (army district) |
| ZAkDR | *Zeitschrift der Akademie für Deutsches Recht* (journal of the academy of German law) |
| ZfDR | *Zeitschrift für deutsches Recht* (journal of German law) |
| ZfP | *Zeitschrift für Politik* (journal of politics) |

# Notes

## Chapter 1: The Background

1. Personal account by one of the participants, interviewed by the author in June 1978.
2. Landesverrat together with high treason are contained in the special part of the penal code (StGB) which made conspiracy for Landesverrat punishable. Paragraph 87 dealt with Landesverrat and corresponded closely to that part of paragraph 84 dealing with high treason. Paragraph 88 also dealt with armed aid, i.e. serving in the military forces of one of Germany's enemies; 89 concerned active support of any enemy at war with Germany; 90 defined the various crimes which came under the heading of actions aiding the enemy. Punishments also applied to foreigners living in Germany. Actual Landesverrat was dealt with in paragraph 92. As in the act of high treason, for Landesverrat no capital punishment was threatened until after 30 January 1933. At the end of the nineteenth century the provisions of the StGB were already thought to contain too many gaps which new formulations were to close, such as the Decree of 3 June 1914 (*RGBl.* I, 1914, p. 195). But irrespective of these new formulations and amendments the death sentence did not become mandatory until after January 1933.
3. *RGBl.*, I, 3.6.1914, p. 195.
4. Freisler letter, 26.10.1944.
5. *Freisler Personalakte*, Thierack to Freisler, 9.9.1942.

## Chapter 2: A Political Judiciary

1. *Bürgerliches Gesetzbuch* (BGB), Berlin 1900.
2. *Strafgesetzbuch* (StGB), Berlin 1971.
3. E. Kehr, 'Das soziale System der Reaktion in Preussen unter dem Ministerium Puttkammer' in H.-U. Wehler (ed.) *Der Primate der Innenpolitik*, Berlin 1965, p. 64ff.
4. M.L. Anderson and K. Barkin, 'The Myth of the Puttkammer Purge and the Reality of the Kulturkampf: Some Reflections on the Historiography of Imperial Germany' in *Journal of Modern History*, Chicago 1982, p. 646ff.
5. See *Weimar: Sebstpreisgabe* . . . op. cit., especially H. Hottenbauer, 'Zur Lage der Justiz in der Weimarer Republik' p. 169ff.
6. K.D Bracher, *Die Auflösung der Weimarer Republik*, Villigen 1960, p. 191ff.
7. BAKO R 43 I/2703, Niederschrift über Besprechung am 22.11.1921 in der Reichskanzlei.

8. The Selbstschutz Oberschlesien is treated in detail by H.W. Koch, *Der Deutsche Bürgerkrieg: Geschichte der deutschen und österreichischen Freikorps 1918–1924*, Berlin 1978, p. 274ff; on the Black Reichswehr, see Th. Vogelsang, *Reichswehr, Staat und NSDAP*, Stuttgart, 1962, p. 31; and see *Die Weltbühne*, vol. 1923, issue 8, p. 23.

9. Bundesarchiv-Militärarchiv Freiburg i. Br. (BAMA), Nachlass Schleicher N 42/39, Vortragsnotz betr. Verfahren wegen Landesverrates gegen Redakteur der *Vorwärts* und Reichtagssitzung 18.6.1927. 27. Ausschuss: Femeorganisation und Fememord. Aussage Kurt v. Schleicher.

10. Dr W. Luetgebrune, 'Femeprozess und Recht' in *Völkischer Beobachter* (VB) Munich 9.10.1928 and *Frankfurter Zeitung* of the same date.

11. *ibid.*

12. See H. Hottenbauer, *op. cit.*, p. 175ff.

13. H. Hottenbauer, *Vom Reichsjutsizamt zum Bundesministerium der Justiz. Zum 100. jährigen Gründungstag des Reichsjustizamtes*, Cologne, 1977, p. 43ff; F.K. Kübler, 'Der deutsche Richter und das demokratische Gesetz' in *Archiv für civilistische Praxis*, vol. 162, 1963, p. 104f. See also D. Kolbe, *Reichsgerichtspräsident Dr Erwin Bumke. Studien zum Niedergang des Reichsgerichts und der deutschen Rechtspflege*, Karlsruhe 1975.

14. C. Schmitt, *Legalität und Legitimät*, Bonn 1932, p. 7ff.

15. *ibid.*, p. 23.

16. H. Schüler, *Auf der Flucht erschossen: Felix Fehrenbach 1894–1933*. Cologne 1981, p. 175.

17. Bayerisches Hauptstaasarchiv, Abt. II, Geheimes Staatsarchiv (BHSA Abt. II) Munich, Nachlass Epp, Vol. II, Regelungen der Volksgerichte.

18. Bayerisches Gesetzblatt, 13.7.1919, p. 3, Munich 1919.

19. Schüler, *Auf der Flucht . . . op. cit.*, p. 178.

20. E. Deuerlein (ed.) Der Hitler-Putsch: Bayerische Dokumente zum 8./9. November 1923, Stuttgart 1962; also *Der Hitlerprozess vor dem Volksgericht München*, Munich 1924, *passim*.

21. BAKO R 43 I/1020 Besprechung mit den Parteiführern vom 28.6.1922, speech quoted by Eyck, *Geschichte . . . op. cit.*, Vol. I, p. 292ff.

22. See G. Jasper, *Der Schutz der Republik*, Tübingen 1963.

23. Martin Hirsch, 'Juristen sind zu allem fähig', interview in *Der Spiegel*, No. 22, 1981, p. 88ff. Hirsch in this interview emerges as a serious critic of the present federal German judiciary.

24. From Hitler's point of view Joël had rendered the NSDAP great service by refusing to bend the law to apply it against the party. Such attempts had been frequent, coming mainly from the Prussian Social Democratic civil service and from Robert W. Kempner, a Prussian civil servant who later became US Deputy Prosecutor in the trial of major German war criminals in 1946, and a full prosecutor in later trials. Joël intervened first in 1931 over the issue of the 'Boxheim documents'. These were plans drawn up by Dr Werner Best, a young NSDAP intellectual, for an NS *coup d'état* in the event of a Communist takeover. Kempner argued that the documents could justify the proscribing of the NSDAP; Joël concluded that the only action which could be legally taken would be that against the author of the documents.

A year later Joël intervened again, this time to argue against the Reich Minister of the Interior, Wilhelm Groener, that NSDAP paramilitary formations should not be banned unless all paramilitary forces were; under Joël's urging, the ban was finally revoked. He received his full pension until his death, and although he was not allowed to travel he remained relatively untouched by the events around him. At least two other individuals of Jewish descent were similarly protected. Hans von Dohnany, another official of the Reich Ministry of Justice between 1929 and 1938, was 'Aryanized' according to Hitler's special orders and allowed to rise up the ladder of promotions although not to join the NSDAP. He was murdered in Dachau in April 1945 for his involvement in the conspiracy against Hitler. Erhard Milch, ultimately Field Marshal of the Luftwaffe and its armaments chief, was the beneficiary of a cover-up to disguise his Jewish origins. Göring (his immediate superior), Hitler and Himmler all knew of the deception. (On Joël, see K.-D. Goldau-Schüttge, *Rechtsverwalter des Reiches. Staatssekretär D. Curt Joël*, Frankfurt/Main 1981, *passim*; on Best, see Bracher in his *Auflösung . . . op. cit.*, he omits on p. 431ff. to mention that Best's plans were for a contingency which never arose, and, contrary to the evidence, asserts that these had official character. On von Dohnany, see R. Westrich, *Who's Who in Nazi Germany*, London 1982, p. 56; on Milch see *ibid.*, p. 209f; David Irving in *Tragödie der Deutschen Luftwaffe. Aus den Akten und Erinnerungen von Feldmarschall Milch*, Berlin 1970 maintains that this detail about Milch's origins is incorrect but fails to provide any evidence to the contrary.)

25. Kübler 'Der deutsche Richter . . .' *op. cit.*, p. 107.
26. *DRZ*, January 1932, leading article, 'Zum neuen Jahr!'.


## Chapter 3: The NSDAP and the Law

1. See H. Barmeyer, 'Geschichte als Überlieferung und Konstruktion – Das Beipsiel der der Dolchstosslegende' in *Geschichte, Wissenschaft und Unterricht*, Kiel 1977, p. 257ff.
2. W.S. Churchill, *The World Crisis*, London (n.d.), Vol. II, pp. 1370, 1398, 1399.
3. *ibid.*, Lloyd George, *Memoirs*, Vol. II, London 1938, p. 1980ff.; see also K. Schwabe, *Deutsche Revolution und Wilson Friede. Die amerikanische und deutsche Friedensstrategie zwischen Ideologie und Machtpolitik 1918/19*, Düsseldorf 1971. For a recently published contemporary assessment that as late as October 1918 the German army in the west had not been beaten see K. Jeffrey (ed.) *The Military Correspondence of Field Marshal Sir Henry Wilson 1918–1922*, London 1985.
4. G. Ritter, *The Sword and the Sceptre*, Coral Gables 1972, Vol. IV, p. 399ff.
5. K. Kosyck, *Deutsche Pressepolitik im Ersten Weltkrieg*, Düsseldorf 1968, p. 51ff.
6. *ibid.*, p. 124.
7. A. Thimme, *Flucht in den Mythos. Die deutschnationale Volkspartei und die Niederlage von 1918*, Göttingen 1968, p. 292; S.A. Kaehler, 'Über die Herkunft des Schlagwortes "Im Felde unbesiegt" ' in *Vier quellenkritische Untersuchungen zum Kriegsende. Studien zur Geschichte des 19. und 20. Jahrhunderts*, Göttingen 1961, p. 303ff.
8. F. Ebert, *Schriften, Aufzeichnungen und Reden. Mit unveröffentlichten Erinnerungen aus dem Nachlass*, Dresden 1926, Vol. II, p. 127.

9. *Neue Zürcher Zeitung*, 17.12.1918, p. 3; F. Frhr. Hiller v. Gaetringen, ' "Dolchstoss" – Die Diskussion und Dolchstosslegende im Wandel von vier Jahrzehnten' in *Festschrift für Hans Rothfels*, Göttingen 1962, p. 122ff.

10. Gaetringen *op. cit.*, p. 127; E. Nolte, *Der Faschismus in seiner Epoche*, Munich 1963, p. 379.

11. Document reprinted by H. Michaelis, E. Schraepler and G. Scheel (eds) in *Ursachen und Folgen: Vom deutschen Zusammenbruch bis zur staatlichen Neuordnung Deutschlands in der Gegenwart*, Berlin (n.d.) Vol. II.

12. For the most incisive recent analysis of the Versailles Treaty see A. Lentin, *Guilt at Versailles*, Leicester University Press, 1984.

13. Nolte, *op. cit.*, p. 413ff; R. Dahrendorf, *Democracy and Society in Germany*, London 1968, p. 311; D. Schoenbaum, *Hitler's Social Revolution*, London 1967, p. 59; T. Mason, *Arbeiterklasse . . . op. cit.*, p. 2ff.

14. M. Broszat, 'Nationalsozialistische Konzentrationslager 1933–1945' in H. Buchheim, M. Broszat, H.-A. Jacobsen and H. Krausnick (eds) *Anatomie des SS-Staates*, Vol. II, Munich 1967, p. 11ff.

15. Mason, *Arbeiterklasse . . . op. cit.*, p. 4ff; *Anatomie . . . op. cit.*, Vol. I, p. 166ff; G. Stein, *The Waffen-SS at War*, Oxford 1966, p. 15ff; H. Höhne, *The Order of the Death's Head*, London 1969, p. 438; G. Reitlinger, *SS – Alibi of a Nation*, London 1957, p. 75. For the most recent interpretation see B. Wegner, *Hitlers politische Soldaten: Die Waffen-SS 1933–1945*, Paderborn 1982, esp. Chapter 1, p. 25ff. See also A. Speer, *Inside the Third Reich*, London 1970, p. 230.

16. K.D. Bracher, W. Sauer and G. Schulz, *Die nationalsozialistische Machtergreifung*, Cologne 1962, p. 169ff.; E. Matthias and R. Morsey (eds) *Das Ende der Parteien*, Düsseldorf 1960 *passim*.

17. For different interpretations compare Mason *op. cit.* and Schoenbaum *op. cit.*, and most recently R. Zitelmann, *Hitler, Selbstverstandnis eines Revolutionärs*, Stuttgart 1987.

18. Bracher, *Auflössung . . . op. cit.*; Bracher, Sauer and Schulz, *Machtergreifung*, *op. cit*; Dahrendorf, *op. cit.*, and Schoenbaum, *op. cit.*; see also E. Nolte, 'Between Myth and Revisionism. The Third Reich in the Perspective of the 1980s' in H.W. Koch (ed.) *Aspects of the Third Reich*, London 1985.

19. P. Hoffmann, *Widerstand, Staatsstreich, Attentat*, Munich 1969, p. 15ff; p. 69ff.

20. See H. Boberach (ed.) *Meldungen aus dem Reich. Auswahl der geheimen agebeberichten des Sichterheitsdienstes der SS 1939–1944*, Neuwied 1965; the complete *Meldungen aus dem Reich 1938–1945* have now been published in 17 paperback volumes ed. by Boberach, Munich 1984. However an index volume is still outstanding. See also M. Steinert, *Hitlers Krieg und die Deutschen*, Düsseldorf 1970.

21. A. Hitler, *Mein Kampf*, Dünndruckausgabe, Munich 1936, p. 610ff.

22. Programme of the NSDAP, 24 February 1920, reprinted in W. Maser, *Die Frühgeschichte der NSDAP. Hitlers Weg bis 1924*, Frankfurt 1965, p. 468.

23. BAKO, Nachlass Luetgebrune, Vol. 18.

24. *ibid.*, Vol. 19; E.v. Salomon, *Die Geächteten*, Berlin 1929, p. 387; *idem.*, *Der Fragebogen*, Hamburg 1951, p. 371ff; BAKO, Nachlass Luetgebrune, Vol. 29; see also Deuerlein, *Hitlerputsch*, *op. cit.*

25. BAKO, Nachlass Luetgebrune, Vols 54 and 55; see also G. Stoltenberg, *Politische Strömungen im schleswig-holsteinschem Landvolk 1928–1933*, Düsseldorf 1962.

26. *ibid.*, Vol. 70; Berlin Document Center (BDC) File Luetgebrune, Dr Otto; Salomon, *Fragebogen, op. cit.*, p. 369.

27. *ibid.*, p. 367; also BDC, *op. cit.*

28. BAKO Nachlass Luetgebrune, Vol. 73.

29. For a fairly good assessment of Hans Frank see J. Fest, *Das Gesicht des Dritten Reiches*, Munich 1963, though Frank's diary was not accessible to Fest at the time. See W. Präg and W. Jacobmeyer (eds) *Das Diensttagebuch des deutschen Generalgouverneurs in Polen 1939–1945*, Stuttgart 1975, p. 7ff; see also H. Frank, *Im Angesicht des Galgens. Deutung Hitlers und seiner Zeit auf Grund eigener Erlebnisse und Erkenntnisse*, Neuhaus 1955, and also G.M. Gilbert, *Nuremberg Diary*, New York 1960.

30. Fest, *Gesicht . . . op. cit.*, p. 286ff; also Bracher, Sauer and Schulz, *Machtergreifung . . . op. cit.*, p. 516ff.

31. Fest, *ibid.*

32. J. Schädecke and P. Steinbach (eds) *Der Widerstand gegen den Nationalsozialismus*, Munich 1986, p. 537.

33. H. Picker, *Hitlers Tischgespräche im Führerhauptquartier*, Stuttgart 1976; though some doubts have emerged recently about the veracity of Picker's account in connection with the publication of the memoirs of Hitler's secretary Christa Schröder, as well as in connection of a conversation with this author.

34. A. Bullock, *Hitler: A Study in Tyranny*, London 1962, p. 391; Ch. Bewley, *Hermann Göring*, Göttingen 1956, p. 284; between 1933 and 1939 the author was Irish ambassador to Berlin.

35. P. Bucher, *Der Reichswehrprozess. Der Hochverrat der Ulmer Reichswehroffiziere 1929/1930*, Boppard/Rhein 1967. For details of the subsequent fate of these officers see Salomon, *Fragebogen . . . op. cit.*, p. 645ff; also R. Scheringer, *Der Weg eines Kämpfers: Reichswehrleutnant a.D. Scheringer zweimal wegen Hochverrats vor dem Reichsgericht*, Berlin 1932, *idem.*; *Das grosse Los: Unter Soldaten, Bauern und Rebellen*, Hamburg 1959, reprint 1986.

36. Bucher, *Reichswehrprozess . . . op. cit.*, p. 24ff.

37. Bracher, *Auflösung . . . op. cit.*, p. 364ff.

38. Protocol of Hitler's evidence in Bucher, *Reichswehrprozess . . . op. cit.*, p. 237ff; also *Ursachen und Folgen op. cit.*, Vol. VII, p. 529ff.

39. Bucher, *Reichswehrprozess . . . op. cit.*, pp. 240 and 242.

40. M. Domarus (ed.) *Hitlers Reden und Proklamationen 1932–1945*, 4 vols, Wiesbaden 1973, Vol. I, p. 229ff; 444 deputies voted for the bill including 101 who were not NSDAP members.

41. Archiv des Bundesjustizministeriums, Bonn, *Personalakte Freisler*. At present this file is held by the Staatsanwaltschaft of the Landgericht Berlin, which was kind enough to provide me with a photocopy.

42. *Personalakte Freisler*; Lebenslauf.

43. Thus Buchheit, *Richter . . . op. cit.*, p. 15.

44. Letter from the Czechoslovak Ministry of the Interior, Prague, 8.1.1980.

45. On Freisler's 'Jewish appearance', see Buchheit *op. cit*; author's own archive.

46. *ibid.*; also *Personalakte Freisler*, School report 1908, 1909, 1910, 1911.

47. *Personalakte Freisler*, Abiturzeugnis 1912.

48. *Personalakte Freisler*, Lebenslauf, copy of Soldbuch.

49. *ibid.*, Soldbuch; the award of both classes of the Iron Cross is also mentioned in *Der Grossdeutsche Reichstag, iV. Wahlperiode* ed. by Büro des Reichtages

Beginn am 10. April 1938, verlängert bis zum 30 Januar 1947, Berlin 1943.

50. Freisler: Lebenslauf. Both the German writers Bruno Brehm and Edmund Erich Dwinger were in identical position as POWs in Russia between 1915–1920. Information supplied by former to the author in July 1970, by the latter on 15.9.1980.

51. Contrary to Buchheit's assertion, p. 16ff.; nor did he ever learn Russian fluently.

52. *Personalakte Freisler*, Heerestruppenamt an Freisler 30 August 1920.

53. Dr Roland Freisler, *Grundsätzliches über die Betriebsorganisation*, published in *Schriftens des Instituts für Wirtschaftsrecht*, University of Jena, 1922.

54. *ibid.*

55. *ibid.*

56. *ibid.*

57. *ibid.*; NSDAP Mitgliedausweis Dr Roland Freisler.

58. *ibid.*; *Mitglieder des deutschen Reichstages*, Berlin 1930; *Führerlexikon der NSDAP*, Munich 1934.

59. *Personalakte Freisler*, Heiratszeugnis des Standesamtes Kassel 24.3.1928; author's own archive.

60. *Personalakte Freisler*, Taufzeugnisse von Harald und Roland Freisler.

61. *ibid.*; Zeugnis der Religionszugehörigkeit.

62. BAKO Nachlass Luetgebrune, Vol. 29, for example, Strafverfahren gegen Redde, Elsner und Gross, 1928.

63. D. Orlow, *Organisational History of the Nazi Party, op. cit.*, Vol. II, p. 20; he is mistaken when he asserts that the Gauleiter of the *Gau* Hessen-Nassau-Süd in 1927 was Karl Weinrich. The author of the derogatory report was indeed Weinrich, but he was *Gau* treasurer and not Gauleiter. See BDC, file Dr Freisler, Roland; letter by Gauschatzleiter Weinrich to Reichsleitung der NSDAP Munich, 16.1.1927.

64. Archiv des Instituts für Zeitgeschichte Munich (IfZg): Strafsachen vor dem Schöffengericht Kassel gegen Dr Roland Freisler, 24 November 1930.

65. This account is based on the judgment by the Schöffengericht Kassel in the case against Freisler lasting from 17 to 24 November 1930, *ibid.* See also Freisler's lengthy reply in the same file, which, however, in this account has been ignored. For Communist terrorist activities at that time see also Dr K.-J. Jannssen, 'Bomben, Bullen, Barrikaden' in *Die Zeit, Zeitmagazin* Nos 20 and 21, Hamburg 1981, which reproduces largely contemporary source material.

66. *Personalakte Freisler*: Lebenslauf; BAKO Nachlass Luetgebrune, Vol. 29; in 1931 and 1932 Freisler acted in nine different criminal cases on behalf of Luetgebrune.

67. Author's own archive.

68. See, for instance, the judgment by the Kleine Strafkammer des Landgerichtes Kassel, 2.7.1927, 5.P. 21/27–22, Stadtarchiv Kassel.

69. Oranienburger trial, March 1930; newspaper reports are in the Stadtarchiv Kassel together with photographs of Freisler and Gregor Strasser. As to the left wing of the NSDAP see R. Kühnl, *Die nationalsozialistische Linke 1925–1930*, Meisenheim/Glan 1966; also W. Horn, *Führerideologie und Parteiorganisation der NSDAP*, Düsseldorf 1972.

70. Reports of Freisler's speeches prior to 1933 are contained in the *Kasseler Volksanzeiger*, the *Kurhessische Landeszeitung*, the *Kasseler Landbote* and also in the *Völkischer Beobachter* such as the issue of 16.6.1932 which praises the

speech he had held in Berlin-Wedding, a working-class district known for its Communist sympathies, but one in which the SA managed to make considerable inroads between 1930 and 1933. The *VB* report does *not* contain the sentence which Buchheit, *Richter . . . op. cit.*, p. 20 quotes: 'War Pg. Freisler doch selbst einmal Kommunist.'

71. H. Pickjer, *Hitlers Tischgespräche . . . op. cit.*, p. 258ff; 260ff.
72. *ibid.*, p. 62.
73. C. Riess, *Das gab es nur einmal*, Munich 1977, p. 131; Picker, *op. cit.*, p. 103.
74. S. Kracauer, *From Caligari to Hitler*, Princeton 1947, p. 222ff.
75. Picker, *op. cit.*, p. 157.
76. *ibid.*, p. 267.
77. *ibid.*, pp. 423 and 451.
78. *Die Verfassung des Deutschen Reiches*, Berlin 1920, Article 76; see also F. Hartung, *Deutsche Verfassungsgeschichte*, Stuttgart 1968, p. 339ff; E.R. Huber, *Deutsche Verfassungsgeschichte seit 1789*, Stuttgart 1959–1985, 7 vols, particularly Vols 6 and 7.
79. Hartung, *Verfassungsgeschichte . . . op. cit.*, p. 344.
80. *Verordnung zur öffentlichen Sicherheit vom 30.1.1933*, Preussisches Gesetzblatt vom 31.1.1933; also contained in *Documents on German Foreign Policy* (DGFP) Series C, (The Third Reich's First Phase) Vol. I, p. 15, Washington 1957.
81. *RGBl.* I, 1933, p. 35ff.
82. See Göring's evidence at the Nuremberg Trial, *Trial of the Major War Criminals before the International Military Tribunal*, Vol. XXV, p. 372ff, Doc. No. PS–351. Also R. Diels, *Lucifer ante partas . . . Es spricht der erste Chef der Gestapo*, Stuttgart 1950, p. 171ff, p. 177ff. H. Bucheim has also analysed the impact of those various measures upon the German Lands, see *Gutachten des Instituts für Zeitgeschichte*, Munich 1958, p. 20ff, p. 294ff. and p. 336ff. Further see A. Weber, *Politische Polizei: Wesen und Begriff der politischen Polizei im Metternichschen System, in der Weimarer Republik und im nationalsozialistischen Staate*, Berlin 1937.
83. F. Tobias, *Der Reichtagsbrand. Legende und Wirklichkeit*, Rastatt 1962.
84. H. Mommsen, 'Der Reichstagsbrand und seine politische Folgen' in *VfZg*, Munich 1964, p. 351ff.
85. Mommsen, 'Reichtagsbrand . . .' *op. cit.*
86. Verordnung des Reichspräsidenten zum Schutze von Volk und Staat vom 28.2.1933, *RGBl.* I, 1933, No. 17.
87. *RGBl.* I, 1933, No. 28.
88. Gesetz gegen heimtückische Angriffe auf Staat und Partei und zum Schutz von Parteiuniformen vom 20.12.1934, *RGBl.* I, 1934, p. 1269.
89. See Bracher, Sauer and Schulz, *Machtergreifung . . . op. cit.*, *passim*; Matthias and Morsey, *Das Ende . . . op. cit.*, p. 696.
90. Niederschrift über Ministerbesprechung am 30. Januar 1933, 5 Uhr nachm. in der Reichskanzlei; Niederschrift über die Ministerbesprechung am 28. Februar 1933 vorm. 11 Uhr; Niederschrift über die Ministerialbesprechung am 7. März, nachm. 4.15 Uhr in der Reichskanzlei; Niederschrift über die Ministerbesprechung am 24. März vorm. 11.30 Uhr in der Reichskanzlei, all reprinted in Tobias *op. cit.*, pp. 613–630. See also Bracher, Sauer and Schulz, *Machtergreifung op. cit.*, p. 88ff.

91. Excerpt in Hofer, *Nationalsozialismus op. cit.*, p. 28, speech by Hitler held in Munich, 14.12.1930.
92. *VB*, 12.11.1930, p. 1ff.
93. Gesetz zur Behebung der Not von Volk und Reich, *RGBl.* I, 1933, p. 141.
94. R.S. Schäfer, 'Die Vorgänge um das Ermächtigungsgesetz von 1933' in *Frankfurter Hefte*, Frankfurt 1947, p. 948ff; Matthias and Morsey, *Das Ende ... op. cit.*, pp. 68ff, 116ff, 335ff; R. Morsey, 'Hitlers Verhandlungen mit der Zentrumsführung am 31. Januar 1933' in *VfZg*, 1961, p. 182ff; A. Brecht, *Vorspiel zum Schweigen. Das Ende der Weimarer Republik*, Vienna 1948, p. 170ff; *idem.*; 'Die Auflösung der Weimarer Republik und die politische Wissenschaft' in *Zeitschrift für Politik (ZfP)*, Munich 1955, p. 296ff; DGFP, Vol. I, p. 155ff; H. Brüning, *Memoiren*, Stuttgart 1970, p. 689ff; E. Matthias, 'Die Siztung der Reichstagsfraktion des Zentrums am 23. März 1933' in *VfZg*, 1961, p. 195ff; Bracher, Sauer and Schulz, *Machtergreifung ... op. cit.*, p. 273ff; Papen, *Memoirs op. cit.*, p. 273ff.
95. Domarus, *Reden ... op. cit.*, Vol. I, p. 229ff.
96. *Verhandlungen des Reichstages*, Berlin 1933, Vol. 457, p. 38ff; Matthias and Morsey, *Das Ende ... op. cit.*, Chapter 10; F. Stampfer, *Erfahrungen und Bekenntnisse*, Cologne 1957, p. 268.
97. H. Schacht, *76 Jahre meines Lebens*, Bad Wörishofen 1953, p. 221.
98. Kurt Tucholsky, *Gesammelte Werke op. cit.*, Vol. 3, Brief an Werner Hasenclever, 4.3.1933.
99. *Verordnung* (VO) 30.1.1937, *RGBl.* I, 1937, p. 105; *VO vom* 30.1.1939, *RGBl.* I, 1939, p. 95 and VO vom 10.5.1943, *RGBl.* I, 1943, p. 295; see also Bracher, Sauer and Schulz, *Machtergreifung ... op. cit.*, p. 53ff; 136ff; 169ff; 165ff; 186ff and 193ff.
100. *Vorläufiges Gesetz zur Gleichschaltung der Länder mit dem Reich* vom 31.3.1933, *RGBl.* I, 1933, p. 153; *Zweites Gesetz zur Gleichschaltung der Länder mit dem Reich* vom 7.4.1933, *RGBl.* I, 1933, p. 173, p. 736; *Reichsstatthaltergesetz* vom 30.1.1935, *RGBl.* I, 1935, p. 65; P. Hüttenberger, 'Nationalsozialistische Polykratie' in *Geschichte und Gesellschaft*, Göttingen 1976, p. 417ff; E. Fränkel, *The Dual State*, New York 1941 *passim*; K.D. Bracher, *Die deutsche Diktatur*, Frankfurt 1973, p. 553ff, M. Broszat, *Der Staat Hitlers*, Munich 1969, p. 24; E.M. Petersen, *The Limits of Hitler's Power*, Princeton 1969, *passim.*; H. Mommsen, *Beamtentum im Dritten Reich*, Stuttgart 1966, *passim*; see also Hitler's remarks in favour of greater decentralization in Picker, *Tischgespräche op. cit.*, p. 383.

## Chapter 4: The National Socialist State and the Law

1. H. Freyer, *Der Staat*, Leipzig 1925, p. 113ff.
2. M. Weber, 'Der Reichspräsident', 'Parlament und Regierung im neugeordneten Deutschland' in *Gesammelte Schriften* ed. by J. Winkelmann, Tübingen 1958, p. 294ff; H. Theisen, *Die Entwicklung zum nihilistischen Nationalismus in Deutschland 1918–1933*, Munich 1958, p. 24ff; D. Lerner, *The Nazi Elite*, Stanford 1951, p. 53ff; H.A. Winkler, 'Extremismus der Mitte? Sozialgeschichtliche Aspekte der nationalsozialistischen Machtergreifung' in *VfZg* 1972, p. 175ff.

3. Point 24 of the NSDAP programme does not demand specifically a dictatorship but 'for its execution (i.e. the party programme) we demand the creation of a strong central authority for the Reich.' Nor was such a demand contained in the Enabling Law.

4. K.D. Bracher, *Zeitgeschichtliche Kontroversen im Faschismus, Totalitarismus, Demokratie*, Munich 1976, pp. 28, 39, 53f.

5. E. Goldhagen, 'Weltanschauung und Erlösung' in *VfZg* 1976, p. 379ff, 281.

6. H. Herrfahrdt, 'Politische Verfassungslehre' in *Archiv für Rechts- und Staatsphilosphie*, Vol. XXXX, Marburg 1933; *idem. Die Verfassungsgesetze des Nationalsozialistischen Staates dem Text der Weimarer Republik gegenübergestellt*, Marburg 1935, *passim*.

7. *Mein Kampf, op. cit.*, p. 371ff; Freyer, *Staat, op. cit*; Fränkel, *Dual State, op. cit.*; 'Führung als Rechtsprinzip' in *DR*, 1934, p. 327ff. No author is given but style and diction suggest it to have been written by Freisler.

8. H.H. Lammers, 'Die Staatsführung im Dritten Reich' in *Deutsche Justiz (DJ)*, 1934, p. 1296; *idem.* 'Zum 30. Januar 1942' in *Reichsverwaltungsblatt*, Berlin 1942, p. 43.

9. For example, U. Scheuner, 'Die nationale Revolution' in *Archiv für öffentliches Recht*, 1934, Neue Folge 1933–4, p. 166ff, 261ff.

10. W. Hamel, 'Die Aufgabe der Polizei im nationalsozialistischen Staat' in *Deutsche Juristenzeitung (DJZ)*, 1936, p. 1469ff.

11. O. Koellreuter, *Zur Entwicklung der Rechtseinheit*, Jena 1935; *idem. Vom Sinn und Wesen der nationalen Revolution*, Tübingen 1933; *idem. Der Führerstaat*, Tübingen 1934, *idem. Volk und Staat in der Weltanschauung des Nationalsozialismus*, Berlin 1935, *idem. Grundlagen des völkischen und staatlichen Lebens im deutschen Volksstaat*, Berlin 1935; *idem. Deutsches Verfassungsrecht: Ein Grundriss*, Berlin 1936; *idem. Deutsches Verfassungsrecht*, Berlin 1938; H. Krüger, *Führer und Führung*, Breslau 1935, p. 5; C. Schmitt, *Staat, Bewegung, Volk, op. cit.*, pp. 33, 39, 41ff.

12. W. Sauer, 'Rechtssprechung und Regierung. Zur Frage der Unabhängigkeit des Richters' in *DJ*, 1935, p. 181ff.; F. Sauer, 'Das Reichsjustizministerium' in *Schriften der Hochschule für Politik*, issue 36/37, Berlin 1939, p. 23.

13. E.R. Huber, *Vom Sinne der Verfassung*, Hamburg 1935, p. 10, 20ff.

14. C. Schmitt, 'Neue Leitsätze für die Rechtspraxis' in *Juristische Wochenschrift (JWS)*, 1935, p. 273ff., and in *DR*, 1933, p. 201ff.

15. R. Freisler in *DR*, 1942, p. 145ff.; H. Frank, 'Leitsätze des Reichsjuristenführers zur richterlichen Unabhängigkeit' in *DJZ*, 1936, p. 179ff.

16. *RGBl.* I, 1933, p. 1016.

17. According to A. Krebs, *Tendenzen und Gestalten des NSDAP. Erinnerung an die Frühzeit der NSDAP*, Stuttgart 1959, p. 138, claimed by Hitler towards the end of 1930; *Mein Kampf, op. cit.*, p. 571ff.; H. Nocolai, *Grundlagen der kommenden Verfassung*, Berlin 1933, p. 23; also S. Neumann, *Permanent Revolution. The Total State in a World of War*, London 1942, p. 126ff.

18. Broszat, *Der Staat Hitlers op. cit.*, p. 328ff.; C. Schmitt, 'Nationalsozialistisches Rechtsdenken' in *DR*, 1934, p. 225ff, p. 228ff.

19. P.M. Merkl, *Political Violence under the Swastika*, Yale 1975 *passim.*, *idem.* 'Die alten Kämpfer in der NSDAP' in *Sozialwissenschafliches Jahrbuch für Politik*, Vol. II, Munich 1971. Both studies are based on 582 autobiographical sketches of old NSDAP members gathered from 1934 onwards by sociologists of Columbia

University, New York. However, the sample may be considered too small to allow wide sweeping generalizations.

20. Hitler's proclamation of 11.9.1935, *VB* No. 255, 12.9.1935.

21. As well as through the Gesetz gegen die Neubildung von Parteien, 14.7.1933, *RGBl.* I, 1933, p. 479.

22. Paragraph 6, *Gesetz zur Sicherung der Einheit von Partei und Staat* vom 1.12.1933, *RGBl.* I, 1933, p. 1016ff.

23. Deutsches Beamtengesetz vom 26.1.1937, *RGBl.* I, 1937, p. 41, see also paragraphs 1 and 3, the first emphasising the duty of loyalty, the second unconditional obedience to the Führer.

24. *loc. cit.*, paragraph 3.

25. Reichsgericht am 17.2.1933 in *Höchstricherliche Rechtsprechung* (*HRR*) No. 845/1939; see *Münchner Neueste Nachrichten* (*MNN*) Nov. 1938, quoted by F. Neumann, *Behemoth*, New York/London 1942, p. 73f.

26. P. Diel-Thiele, *Partei und Staat im Dritten Reich. Untersuchungen zum Verhältniss von NSDAP and allgemeiner Staatsverwaltung 1933–1945*, Munich 1969; see also *Mein Kampf, op. cit.*, p. 445 and Beamtengesetz, *op. cit.*, paragraph 26, section 1, No. 2.

27. Thus Dr Erwin Bumke, appointed in 1929, remained president of the Reichsgericht; Gürtner, appointed in 1932, remained in office until his death in 1941; and Schlegelberger, Secretary of State, remained in his post until his retirement in 1942. However, a definitive statement on judicial personnel will only be possible when all personnel files are available.

28. See *Handbuch der Justizverwaltung*, Berlin 1942; *Taschenkalender für Verwaltungsbeamte*, Berlin 1932 and 1934 edition. In Prussia changes appear more numerous than elsewhere in Germany. Of the OLG presidents and general state prosecutors there in 1931, only three were still in office by the end of 1934, though reasons for their departures are not indicated. See BAKO R 22/1462, listing the members of the judiciary for 1938 and BAKO R 22/4402 listing these for 1942 which show greater changes among OLG presidents and general state prosecutors than among the highest and lowest levels of the judiciary. But the evidence is too scant and fragmentary to allow quoting reliable figures and any firm conclusions.

29. Archiv des Bundesjustizministeriums, Bonn, based on personnel files of 25 OLG presidents and 19 general state prosecutors from 35 OLG districts.

30. Gesetz zur Wiederherstellung des Berufsbeamtentums vom 4.4.1933, *RGBl.* I, 1933, p. 409, which contained the infamous 'Aryan' paragraph.

31. Sitzung des Reichskabinetts which passed the *Gesetz über Staatsnotwehr*, 3.7.1934, *RGBl.* I, 1934, p. 529; also public communique on the cabinet session in Domarus, *Reden . . . op. cit.*, Vol. I, p. 406; *ibid.*, Hitler's Reichstag speech, 13.7.1934, p. 410ff.

32. Information supplied to author by Dr Lothar Gruchmann, IfZg in September 1973.

33. F. Petsch-Heffter, *Jahrbuch für öffentliches Recht*, Vol. 22, 1935, p. 1ff; p. 265; 'Sondergericht Hamburg' in *DRZ*, No. 553, 1935; 'Sondergericht Hamburg' in *Reichsverwaltungsblatt* (*RVerwBl*), 1935, p. 700; 'Badischer VGH' in *Deutsche Verwaltung*, 1938, p. 503.

34. E.R. Huber, 'Anmerkungen zur Entscheidung des Sondergerichts Darmstadt' in *Juristische Wochenschrift* (*JWS*), 1934, p. 1747.

35. 'Sondergericht Hamburg' in *DRZ*, 1935, p. 553.
36. W. Stuckart and H. Globke, 'Reichsbürgergesetz vom 15.9.1935. Gesetz zum Schutz der Erbgesundheit und der deutschen Ehre vom 18.10.1935' in *Kommentare zur deutschen Rassengesetzgebung*, Vol. I, Munich 1936, introduction p. 3, 13, 34.
37. See 'Sondergericht Hamburg' *op. cit.*
38. *DR*, 1934, p. 27, states: 'It is therefore self-evident that any discussion of the constitutional structure must begin with the simple sentence: "The Weimar Constitution is no longer valid." '
39. *VO*, über den Volksgerichtshof, 12.6.1934, *RGBl.* I, 1934, p. 492.
40. See *RGBl.* I, 1934, p. 529 *op. cit.*
41. H. Steffens, 'Die rechtliche Vertretung der Juden im Reich' in *DR*, 1942, p. 9ff. Initially no legislation to this extent had been planned, for 'economic reasons', as Steffens put it, but in practice pressure was exercised on German lawyers not to represent Jews. See F. Gürtner, 'Richter und Staatsanwalt im neuen Staat' in *DJ*, 1934, p. 369ff. Also F. Fritscher, 'Was ist ein Eingriff in die Berufsaufgaben des Rechtsanwalts?' in *JWS*, 1937, p. 525. However, in 1934 the prohibition was introduced applying to all lawyers not members of the NSDAP. See 'Anordnungen des Stellvertreters des Führers vom 16.8.1934 and 8.10.1934' as well as directive from the Reichrechtsamt der NSDAP quoted by Steffens in the article just cited. After the November 1939 pogrom positions further hardened. Shortly prior to it the 5. VO zum Reichbürgergesetz vom 27.9.1938 had excluded Jewish lawyers from practising law in Germany altogether. The 'Anordnung des Stellvertreters des Führers vom 19.12.1938' and 'Die Anordnung des Reichsleiters des Reichsrechtsamtes der NSDAP, Hans Frank, vom 2.1.1939' extended the 1934 prohibitions to all German lawyers. See *Verfügungen, Anordnungen, Bekanntmachungen*, ed. by the Parteikanzlei der NSDAP, Zenralverlag der NSDAP, Munich (n.d.), Vol. II, p. 405, *ibid.*, 'Anordnung XXX–I/39' p. 432. The prohibition was then extended to all lawyers on 31.12.1939 in 'Bekanntgabe des Präsidenten der Reichsrechtsanwaltkammer vom 31.12.1939' in *JWS*, 1939, p. 274; on the gypsies, see Steffens 'Die rechtliche Vertretung . . .' *op. cit.*, p. 11.
42. *loc. cit.*
43. *Personalakte Freisler op. cit.*
44. This account is derived from documents in the author's own archive.
45. Freisler letter 3.2.1934.
46. *Personalakte Freisler, op. cit.*, Beförderungen.
47. BAKO P 135/3147, Bericht des Regierungspräsidenten der Rheinprovinz, 24.11.1929.
48. W. Heuber, 'Der Bund Nationalsozialistischer Deutscher Juristen und die deutsche Rechtsfront' in *Nationalsozialistisches Jahrbuch 1933*, ed. by Reichsleitung der NSDAP, Munich (n.d.), pp. 1566ff.
49. Weinkauf, *Die deutsche Justiz . . . op. cit.*, p. 201.
50. R. Freisler, 'Rechtswahrergedanken zum Kriegsjahr 1940' in *DJ*, 1941, p. 9.
51. *RGBl.* I, 1933, p. 175.
52. *Berliner Tageblatt*, No. 38, 23.1.1934, contains an interesting survey supported by apparently reliable statistics.
53. BAKO P 135/89 Gesamtaufstellung über Rechtsanwälte und Notare in den preussischen Oberlandesgerichtsberzirken bei den Generalakten des preussischen

Justiz ministeriums. See also BAKO P 135/76 Statistiken über den Stand am 1.1.1933.

54. BAKO P 135/6334 Rundverfügung vom 27.6.1933 an den Kammergerichts-präsident und die Oberlandesgerichtspräsidenten.

55. VO des Reichspräsidenten zum Schutz von Volk und Staat vom 28.2.1933, RGBl. I, 1933, p. 83.

56. ibid., paragraph 5.

57. Gesetz über die Verhängung und den Vollzug der Todesstrafe vom 29.3.1933, RGBl. I, 1933, p. 151.

58. ibid., paragraph 2. Schlegelberger with considerable effort tried to prevent the introduction of retroactive legislation, but Hitler was not impressed. Nuremberg Doc. NG–2287 produced in IMT Case III, 1946–7.

59. For the complex of Reichswehr, Abwehr and treason see H. Höhne, Canaris, Gütersloh 1977, to date the best informative source. See also BAMA A54/1613 Truppenamt, Chefbesprechung vom (date illegible) Mai 1933 betr. Auswirkung der neuen Gesetzgebung in Spionage- bzw. Verratsfällen.

60. ibid., BAMA; see also Picker, Tischgespräche op. cit., p. 359.

61. Tobias op. cit., p. 305ff.

62. ibid., where excerpt is reprinted on p. 457.

63. DR, 1934, p. 19; further criticism came from DJ, 1933, p. 870.

64. Picker, Tischgespräche . . . op. cit., p. 278.

65. BAKO R 23/1115 Niederschrift der Ministerbesprechung vom 23.3.1934.

66. ibid.

67. BAKO R 23/1115, Gürtner's note, dated 25.4.1934, recording the decision and attached die Niederschrift.

68. VB, 19.11.1934; also DJ, 1935, p. 1709; DR, 1935, p. 518; Volkmar, Elster and Kückenhoff (eds) Handwörterbuch der Rechtswissenschaft, Berlin 1937, see under Volksgerichtshof.

69. F. Richter, 'Der Volksgerichtshof ist kein Revolutionstribunal' in Deutscher Reichs-Preussischer Staatsanzeiger, No. 146, 26.6.1934; see also G. Gribbohm 'Der Volksgerichtshof' in Juristische Schulung. Zeitschrift für Studium und Ausbildung, No. 2, 1969, p. 55.

70. VO über den Volksgerichtshof vom 12.6.1936, RGBl. I, 1936, p. 492; also paragraph 1 of the VO for the execution of the above and 'Die 25. Anderung des Besoldungsgesetzes vom 18.4.1936', RGBl. I, 1936, p. 398. Bestimmungen über die Eernennung und Entlassung von Reichsbeamten, 1.2.1935, RGBl. I, 1935, p. 74 und der Beamten in der Reichsjustizverwaltung, 20.3.1935, RGBl. I, 1935, p. 391 and DJ, 1935, p. 635 and 638. H. Frank (ed.) Nationalsozialistisches Handbuch für Recht und Gesetzgebung, Munich 1935, p. 1409.

71. The Reichsrat dissolved itself by decree, 14.2.1934, RGBl. I, 1934, p. 89.

72. Investigating judges had been introduced by the Reichsgericht according to paragraph of the VO des Reichspräsidenten gegen Verrat am Deutschen Volke und hochverräterische Umtriebe vom 28.2.1933, RGBl. I, 1933, p. 85. Ausführungsbestimmung of the RJM vom 12.6.1936, RGBl. I, 1936, p. 492. 3. VO zum Volksgerichtshof, RGBl. I, 1935, p. 1121.

73. RGBl. I, 1935, p. 398.

74. ibid.

75. ibid., paragraph 6.

76. RGBl. I, 1936, p. 503: Erlass des Führers und Reichskanzlers über die Amtstracht

in der Reichsjustizverwaltung vom 19.6.1936; *DJ*, 1936, p. 949; also *VO* über das Tragen von Amtstracht in der Justizverwaltung, 11.12.1937, *RGBl.* I, 1937, p. 1383.

77. *DJ*, 1934, p. 1013; *DJ*, 1935, p. 807; see also Chapters 10 and 11 below. Also IfZg Arno Weismann affidavit, 8.2.1947; NG–792; *ibid.*; NG–533 Rothaug affidavit, 2.1.1947.

78. *DJZ*, 1934, p. 979ff.; also 'Der Volksgerichtshof für das Deutsche Reich' in *JWS*, 1936, p. 1569; *DJ*, 1934, p. 1013.

79. BAKO R 43 II/1518, Volksgerichtshof 1934–1935: 'Vom Volksgericht des Deutschen Reiches' in *DJ*, 1935, p. 1709; *Deutsche Allgemeine Zeitung (DAZ)*, 22.4.1936; 'Juristische Rundschau' in *DJZ*, 1936, p. 561ff; R. Freisler, 'Die lebenswichtigen Aufgaben des Volksgerichtshofes' in *DJ*, 1936, p. 656; G. Thierack, 'Zwei Jahre Volksgerichtshof' in *DJ*, 1936, p. 1094; *idem*. 'Aufgaben und Tätigkeit des Volksgerichtshofes' in *Zeitschrift der Akademie des Deutschen Rechtes (ZAkDR)*, 1936, p. 855; *idem*. 'Der Volksgerichtshof – Das Reichsstrafgericht' in *ZAkDR*, 1935, p. 90; also O. Engert, 'Fünf Jahre Volksgerichtshof' in *VB*, 14.7.1939. The argument for fusing the VGH with the military judiciary and dissolving the latter is contained in *ZAkDR*, 1935, p. 242ff. Also BAKO Reichsjustizministerium Akten betreff Volksgerichtshof R 22/302, 1934/35; Gürtner letter to Ministry of Finance 30.11.1935; Memorandum of 23.7.1935.

80. BAKO R 43 II/1518 *op. cit.*, Gesetz über den Volksgerichtshof und über die 25. Änderung des Besoldumgsgesetzes vom 18.4.1936, *RGBl.* I, 1936, p. 386; *BDC*, NG–156, letter by Thierack to Lammers, 27.4.1936.

81. BAKO *ibid.*; *DJ*, 1936, p. 907.

82. See Freisler articles cited in Chapter 6 as well as BAKO 43 II/1518 *op. cit.*

83. *ibid.*, BAKO.

84. 'Deutsches Rechtsleben 1935 und 1936' in *DJ*, 1936, p. 50ff; 90ff; 219ff; and 433ff.

85. *ibid.*, p. 437.

86. See BAKO R 43 II/1518 *op. cit.*; also Thierack 'Reichstrafgericht . . .' *op. cit.*

87. Freisler 'Die lebenswichtigen Aufgaben . . .' *op. cit.*

88. *ibid.*

89. *DJ*, 1936, p. 907. On his introduction into office Gürtner described him as a 'temporary president'. Hans Frank in a letter to Hitler of 8.10.1934 proposed his own candidate, the lawyer Dr Schreer, Wuppertal, the General Inspector of the BNSDJ and an 'old fighter'. Hitler ignored the proposal; see BAKO R 43 II/1518 *op. cit.*: Volksgerichtshof 1934–1935.

90. For Thierack's *curriculum vitae* see *DJ*, 1942, p. 551; also IfZg, Bormann letter to Reichsschatzmeister Franz Xavier Schwarz, 9.2.1938. Thierack committed suicide in the British internment camp of Bad Nendorf.

91. As expressed in Bormann letter just cited; see also IfZg Schegelberger affidavit NG–097, 6.9.1946.

92. Freisler letter, 15 Nov. 1936. Into this period falls an acquaintanceship with a judge from southern Germany, whom he had apparently met at various conferences before. The relationship developed into a friendship which was bound to have been problematic for Freisler, because the judge's wife was half Jewish, being descended on her mother's side from an old established Alsacian Jewish family. Freisler was aware of this from the beginning and initially thought that the best protection could be provided by having the judge called to the VGH. The

judge was a member of the NSDAP and occupied a high SA rank. However, as it turned out, the judge's appointment would have involved close vetting by the Security Service (SD) of the SS, a fact which Freisler had at first ignored. But when the first enquiries started Freisler had the judge's appointment quickly withdrawn and told him that it was in his and his family's interest to stay where he was. Once war broke out, Freisler quickly established contact with the Supreme Command of the Luftwaffe who drafted the judge into the Signals and Communications Corps. In this position he was spared the attention of the SD and spent the war in fairly safe places. Nevertheless, irrespective of the somewhat problematical nature of this friendship, Freisler, by way of correspondence, maintained contact and Freisler's own letters reveal a rather surprising degree of openness of comment on Germany's internal as well as external situation until shortly before his death. Freisler's correspondence will be handed over to the archive of the Institut für Zeitgeschichte, Munich, but for reasons already mentioned, remain closed until the year 2010. Henceforth Freisler's correspondence will be cited as 'Freisler letter . . .'. Less than a year after completing this manuscript the author's attention was drawn to another batch of Freisler's correspondence, this time in the hands of a former VGH judge. This judge allowed the author to read the letters but not to make any excerpts from them, as they mention details concerning the practice of OLGs and the NS Special Courts. However, assurance was given to the author that this correspondence will be handed over to him after the judge's death.

93. See Chapter 7 below; also IfZg, NG–208B, Thierack 'Die Unabhängigkeit der Richter'.
94. Freisler 'Die lebenswichtige Aufgabe . . .' *op. cit.*
95. *ibid.*
96. Volkmar, Elster and Kückenhoff (eds) *Handwörterbuch . . . op. cit.*, p. 382.
97. R. Schraut (ed.) *Deutscher Juristentag 1933. 4. Reichstagung des Bundes Nationalsozialistischer Deutscher Juristen. Ansprachen und Fachvorträge*, Berlin 1933, p. 222ff; IfZg, NG–866, Rothenberger Bericht 'Sechzehn Monate Berlin. 4.4.1944'.


## Chapter 5: The National Socialist People's Court

1. StGB as of 30.1.1933.
2. *ibid.*, paragraphs 82, 83, 84 and 86.
3. *ibid.*, paragraphs 87, 88, 89 and 90.
4. *RGBl.* I, 1893, p. 205.
5. *ibid.*, 1914, p. 195.
6. At his trial in Munich in 1923 Hitler was accused of high treason. He admitted his actions, rejecting however that they represented high treason and argued that his actions were directed against those who in 1918 had committed Landesverrat, against the 'November criminals' and that he and his supporters wished only the best for Germany. The presiding judge raised no objections to this argument. See E. Deuerlein (ed.) *Der Aufstieg der NSDAP 1919–1933*, Düsseldorf 1968, p. 205; *idem. Der Hitlerputsch op. cit.*, p. 715ff.
7. See NSDAP programme, point 18 reprinted in Maser, *Frühgeschichte . . . op. cit.*, p. 468.
8. *RGBl.* I, 1933, p. 151.

9. *VO* des Reichspräsidenten zum Schutze von Volk und Staat vom 28.2.1933, *op. cit.*

10. *ibid.*

11. Gesetz über die Verhängung und den Vollzug der Todesstrafe vom 29.3.1933 *RGBl.* I, 1933, p. 151.

12. *RGBl.* I, 1933, p. 85, paragraphs 1–7; L. Schäfer, 'Die Verordnungen des Reichspräsidenten gegen Verrat am deutschen Volke und hochverräterische Umtriebe' in *JWS*, 1933, p. 873ff; *idem.* 'Änderungen des Verfahrens in Hoch- und Landesverratssachen' in *JWS*, 1933, p. 937ff.

13. Schäfer, '*Die Verordnungen . . .*' *op. cit.*

14. *RGBl.* as cited in ref. 12, paragraphs 2, 3, and 6.

15. *ibid.*, paragraph 5.

16. The Ulm officers accused were indicted under paragraph 83 of the StGB.

17. *RGBl.* I, 1933, p. 85, paragraph 4.

18. See also Gesetz zur Abänderung strafrechtlicher Vorschriften, 26.5.1933, *RGBl.* I, 1933, p. 295, especially paragraphs 92a and 92b of the StGB; also Gesetz zur Gewährleistung des Rechtsfriedens vom 13.10.1933, *RGBl.* I, 1933, p. 723.

19. Gesetz zur Abänderung . . . *op. cit.*, paragraph 11; also Volkmar, Elster and Kuckenhoff (eds) *Handwörterbuch . . . op. cit* under *Volksgerichtshof;* 'Das neue politische strafrecht' in *DR*, 1935, p. 12. Newly formulated were paragraphs 81, 88, 90, 90i of the StGB; see also Gesetz über die Gewährung von Straffreiheit vom 7.8.1934, *RGBl.* I, 1934, p. 769, new formulation of the same law on 30.4.1938; *RGBl.* I, 1938, p. 433; Artikel 1 der *VO* über den Geltungsberich der Strafrechte vom 6.5.1940, *RGBl.* I, 1940, p. 754.

20. *VO* über das Sonderstrafrecht im Kriege und bei besonderem Einsatz, *RGBl.* I, 1939, p. 213 which applied retroactively. The last supplementation of the KSSVO was made 5.5.1944, *RGBl.* I, 1944, p. 115.

21. *loc. cit.*

22. *RGBl.* I, 1934, p. 341.

23. *VO* des Reichspräsidenten zum Schutz von Volk und Staat *op. cit.*

24. *RGBl.* I, 1934, p. 341, article 3, paragraph 3, section 1.

25. *ibid.*, article 4, paragraph 2.

26. Freisler, 'Die lebenswichtige Aufgabe . . .' *op. cit.*

27. Vorschriften des Strafverfahrens und des GVG, 28.6.1935, *RGBl.* I, 1935, p. 844ff.

28. Gesetz gegen die Wirtschaftsspionage, 1.12.1935, *RGBl.* I, 1936, p. 999.

29. For details see *Richtlinien der Reichszentrale für Heimatdienst*, No. 219, *Wirtschaftskrise und öffentliche Finanzen*, Berlin, September 1931.

30. Among the legislation arising out of this territorial expansion are *VO* zur Überleitung der Rechtspflege im Saarland, 21.2.1935, *RGBl.* I, 1935, p. 248; *VO* über die Einführung der Vorschriften über Hochverrat und Landesverrat im Lande Österreich, 20.6.1938, *RGBl.* I, 1938, p. 640; *VO* über das Verfahren in Hochverrats- und Landesverratssachen in den sudetendeutschen Gebieten, 16.12.1938, *RGBl.* I, 1938, p. 1811; *VO* über die Ausübung der Strafgerichtsbarkeit im Protektorat Böhmen und Mähren vom 14.4.1939, *RGBl.* I, 1939, p. 745; Gesetz zur Angliederung des Memellandes, 23.3.1939, *RGBl.* I, 1939, p. 559; Erlass des Führers über die Wiedervereinigung der Gebiete von Eupen-Malmedy und Moresnet mit dem Deutschen Reich, 18.5.1940, *RGBl.* I, 1940, p. 777. As for the annexed territories of Poland see *VO* über die Einführung des

deutschen Strafrechts in den eingegliederten Ostgebieten, *RGBl.* I, 1939, p. 844.

31. All the *VOs* just cited contained provisions which made such prosecutions, indictments and trials possible.

32. A. Leber, *Das Gewissen entscheidet*, Berlin 1957, p. 118ff; see also the case cited in *DJ*, 1934, p. 1013.

33. VGH judgment 15.3.1935.

34. Virtually all sentences imposed by the VGH involved the suspension, in case of the death sentence, of civic rights. Consequently this author decided when citing or quoting VGH judgments to ignore the suspension or loss of civic rights since this is a fact to be taken for granted in each VGH conviction.

35. *DJ*, 1935, p. 909.

36. See NSDAP programme, point 18.

37. BAKO R 22/201113, Reichsjustizministerium R 22 Gr.5/XXIII–2, Vol. I.

38. Cited by E. Düsing, *Abschaffung der Todesstrafe*, Offenbach/Main 1952, p. 209.

39. Gesetz zur Änderung des StGB vom 28.6.1936, *RGBl.* I, 1936, p. 839; see also *Leipziger Kommentar zum Strafgesetzbuch*, Berlin 1944, paragraph 86, note 1.

40. BAKO R 43 II/1518, Thierack to Freisler, 9.9.1942.

41. BDC, NG–630 Schlegelberger circular to Generalstaatsanwälte und Oberstaatsanwälte, 20.7.1935.

42. *ibid.*

43. *ibid.*

44. See B.M. Kempner, *Priester vor Hitlers Tribunalen*, Munich 1966, *passim*.

45. See also J.S. Conway, *The Nazi Persecution of the Churches*, London 1968, p. 235ff; Bracher, Sauer and Schulz, *Machtergreifung . . . op. cit.*, p. 326ff.

46. BDC, NG–266, Rundschreiben des RJM an die Oberpräsidenten, Generalstaatsanwälte und Oberstaatsanwälte, 13.6.1936; also Dr. Kutzner's note, dated 12.8.1936, to the effect that at this conference the Gestapo's claim for more intensive interrogation would also have to be discussed.

47. This account of the conference is derived from *ibid.*; Besprechung über die Behandlung von Hochverratssachen, Tagung am 11. und 12. Nov. 1936.

48. BDC, NG–323, letter by Himmler to RJM, 18.2.1937, demanding the handing over of files 'politisch-polizeilicher Vorgänge' as well as the transfer to the Gestapo of individuals acquitted by the VGH or after having served their sentence.

49. The sources for this account are: BDC, NG–1566, Gürtner letter to prosecutors of the Reichsgericht, VGH and OLGs, 14.12.1938, informing them of the impending conference at the RJM on 23.1.1939; *ibid.*, Aus der Besprechung der Generalstaatsanwälte im Reichsjustizministerium 23.–26.1.1939.

50. *VB*, 17.1.1939, p. 2; also *VB*, 14.7.1939, Engert 'Fünf Jahre Volksgerichtshof'.

51. BDC, NG–254, Schlegelberger letter to Lammers, 14.7.1939; BAKO Reichsjustizministerium, Generalakten R 22/1039, letter by Freisler to Lammers, 12.8.1939; see also letters by Freisler to Lammers, 15.8.1939 and to Reichsgerichtpräsident, 25.11.1939 and by Reichsgerichtpräsident to Freisler, 1.12.1939.

52. *ibid.*, BDC, Schlegelberger letter.

53. *ibid.*, letter by Freisler to Lammers.

54. *ibid.*, Freisler to Reichsgerichtpräsident.

55. This emerges from the cases extracted from the files of the RJM and the Nuremberg documents.

56. BAKO, RJM, R 22 Gr.5/XXIII/1, Vol. 1, R 22/20062. Report by Lautz, 14.9.1936 in which such a case, VGH judgment of 10.7.1936, is discussed. See also VGH judgment in *DJ*, 1937, p. 198.

57. VGH judgments 30.10.1937 in *Leipziger Kommentare ... op. cit.*, 1938, paragraph 93, note 112; VGH judgment, 10.1.1939 in *DJ*, 1939, p. 479.

58. VGH judgment, 27.11.1938 in *DJ*, 1938, p. 114; VGH judgment, 10.11.1937 in *Leipziger Kommentare ... op. cit.*, 1938, paragraph 93, note 112; also in *DJ*, 1938, p. 114; VGH judgment, 3.1.1938, *DJ*, 1938, p. 113; VGH judgment 26.5.1937, *DJ*, 1938, p. 113.

59. VGH judgment, 12.2.1937 in *ZAkDR*, 1937, p. 570.

60. VGH judgment, 26.7.1937, *DJ*, 1938; p. 828; BAKO, RJM R 22/954, General-akten über Hochverrat 4012, Vol. II, letter by Oberreichsanwalt to Generalstaats-anwälte, 18.1.1937; also OLG-Karlruhe attitude to high treason; quote by Oberreichsanwalt Lautz.

61. *DJ*, 1941, p. 866.

62. BAKO, Entscheidungen des Reichsgerichtes in Strafsachen, pp. 71, 385 and 387–8.

63. VGH judgment, 23.8.1938 in *JWS*, 1939, p. 537.

64. VGH judgments 26.7.1936; 11.8.1937; 15.2.1938 and 8.3.1938 in *Leipziger Kommentare ... op. cit.*, paragraph 83, note 112, also *DR*, 1936, p. 448ff.

65. *Leipziger Kommentare loc. cit.*

66. BAKO R 22/20026, RJM Akten R. 22 Gr.5/XXIII, Vol. I, Az. 4021a; Az. IIIg 10a–1377/37g Gürtner Anweisung an Reichgericht und VGH, 27.12.1937.

67. Gesetz zur Verhinderung der Teilnahme am spanischen Bürgerkrieg, 18.7.1937, *RGBl.* I, 1937, p. 241.

68. BAKO, RJM R 22/20019, Lageberichte des Oberreichsanwalts vom 29.1.1941, 31.7.1941. According to those over 150 cases were subject to judicial investigation.

69. BAKO R 22/20062, RJM Akten R 22 Gr.5/XXIII, Vol. I, Az. IIIa/24/42g. Anweisung des RJM an das OKW vom 4.2.1942; Protokoll der Konferenz im Reichsaussenministerium vom 26.11.1941. The charge mentioned is raised by Ch. Streit in his book *Keine Kameraden*, Stuttgart 1978, but unsubstantiated. The archives of the Service Historique de l'Armée in the Château de Vincennes as well as the Bibliothèque du Ministère de la Guerre have the complete files on all French personnel who have fought with the Germans within the *Légion des Volontaires Français contre le Bolchevisme* (L.V.F.) as well as within the *33rd Waffen-Grenadier-Division der SS 'Charlemagne' (French No. 1)*. Although these files are not generally accessible copies of a substantial number of them have found their way outside. See also Saint-Loup (= Marc Augier) *Die Legion der Aufrechten*, Leoni 1977, p. 8ff.

70. See NSDAP programme cited above and *Mein Kampf passim*.

71. W. Hammer, *Hohes Haus in Henkers Hand: Rückschau auf die Hitlerzeit, auf Leidens- und Opfergang deutscher Parlamentarier*, Frankfurt 1956, pp. 87 and 94.

72. BAKO R 60 II/20, VGH judgment 25.6.1935; Hammer, *Hohes Haus ... op. cit.*, p. 36.

73. Hammer, *Hohes Haus ... op. cit.*, p. 67, for similar other cases see also pp. 49, 57.

74. *ibid.*, pp. 81 and 86.

75. BAKO R 60 II/9, VGH judgment 5.2.1936.

76. BDC, VGH judgment 4.6.1937; also Hammer, *Hohes Haus* . . . *op. cit.*, pp. 66 and 89.
77. IfZg, VGH judgment reprinted in NSDAP journal *Der Hoheitsträger*, 1943, p. 28.
78. BDC, VGH judgment 19.1.1938.
79. *ibid.*; thus Thierack in his judgment.
80. Reprinted in Hofer, *Nationalsozialismus* . . . *op. cit.*, p. 57ff.
81. Gesetz gegen die Neubildung von Parteien vom 14.7.1933, *RGBl.* I, 1933, p. 479.
82. BAKO, RJM R 22/20019, Lagebericht des Oberreichsanwalts vom 14.9.1936 in which reference is made to this Reichsgericht decision.
83. BAKO, RJM R 60 II/63, VGH indictment of 21.8.1935, judgment also in BDC.
84. O. Strasser, *Hitler und Ich*, Konstanz 1948, p. 148, see also Kühnl, *op. cit.*, *passim*.
85. See F.L. Carsten, *The Reichswehr in Politics*, Oxford 1966, p. 158ff; W. Abendroth, 'Das Problem der Widerstanstätigkeit der "Schwarzen Front" ' in *VfZg*, 1960, p. 181ff.
86. VGH judgment, 20.2.1935 in *Leipziger Kommentare* . . . *op. cit.*, Berlin 1935, paragraph 83, note 114.
87. Hoffman, *Widerstand* . . . *op. cit.*, p. 297; *Schriften des Bundes deutscher Jungenschaften*, No. 31, Bad Godesberg 1967: Helmut Hirsch 21.1.1916–4.6.1937; G.L. Weinberg in *The Foreign Policy of Hitler's Germany*, Vol. II, *1937–1939*, Chicago 1980, p. 10f. writes about the Hirsch case of 'the exceedingly dubious circumstances surrounding his arrest, trial, death sentence of an American citizen in Germany for supposedly having some anti-Nazi leaflets in his possession.' In the footnote he states 'The Germans claimed that one reason they could not release Hirsch, the person involved, was that a previously released prisoner had made unfriendly speeches about Germany after returning to the U.S.' Weinberg obviously confuses the Hirsch case with that of the US merchant navy sailor Simpson, a courier for the KPD in exile, who had distributed such leaflets. After being held in custody for 15 months he was tried on charges of high treason and Landesverrat and was sentenced to three years' imprisonment. Two months later, however, he was prematurely released and returned to the US. See *Foreign Relations of the United States 1936*, II, pp. 291–304; *ibid.*, 1937, pp. 395–405.
88. BDC, VGH judgment 20.11.1937.
89. *ibid.*, VGH judgment 5.7.1938.
90. *ibid.*, VGH judgment 2.11.1938, and VGH judgments of 23.1.1939, 18.3.1939; 21.9.1939 in *Leipziger Kommentare* . . . *op. cit.*, paragraph 83, note 114.
91. See K.v. Klemperer, *Germany's New Conservatism*, Princeton 1957; O.E. Schüddekopf, *Linke Leute von Rechts*, Stuttgart 1961; J. Petzold, *Wegbereiter des deutschen Faschismus: Die Jungkonservativen in der Weimarer Republik*, Berlin 1978; D. Stegmann, B.-J. Wendt and P.C. Witt (eds) *Deutscher Konservatismus im 19. und 20. Jahrhundert, Festschrift für Fritz Fischer*, Bonn 1983; A. Mohler, *Die konservative Revolution in Deutschland 1918–1932*, Darmstadt 1972.
92. BDC, VGH judgment 10.1.1939, also *DJ*, 1939, p. 479; *ibid.*, VGH judgment 18.2.1939.
93. VGH judgments of 5.11.1937 and 28.8.1938 in *Leipziger Kommentare* . . . *op. cit.*, paragraph 83, note 112.
94. BAKO, 8J 97/37, VGH judgment 9.10.1937; *ibid.*, VGH judgment 23.11.1938.
95. Wolfram Wette asserts in Vol. 1, p. 109 of *Das Deutsche Reich und der Zweite Weltkrieg*, published by the official *Militärgeschichtliches Forschungsamt* of the

West German forces, Freiburg, that this radio set was so constructed as to allow the listeners only to receive German stations. It is one of the many factual mistakes with which at least the first two volumes (four have appeared so far) is riddled. This author, then living in the heart of Munich in a groundfloor flat (hardly the most ideal place for long-range wireless reception!) remembers clearly when his parents and elder brother tuned in during times of crisis, such as for instance the Munich one, to listen to Swiss, French and British broadcasts, to which, during the later war years came also Radio Moscow. Towards the end of 1944 even the 'black propaganda' spread by the *Soldatensender Calais* operated by Sefton Delmer could be received which however this author's mother switched off because of the obscene vocabulary used in its broadcasts. She preferred the BBC.

96. G. Grosz, *Ein kleines Ja und ein grosses Nein*, Berlin 1955, p. 153.
97. G. Solo, 'Pinsel Faschismus' in *Die Zeit*, 18th Oct. 1984, p. 17f; 'Comeback der Nazikunst' by P. Sager and D. Reinartz in *Die Zeit, Zeit Magazin*, No. 44, 22 Oct. 1986, p. 66ff. Also the painter and graphic artist Max Beckmann emigrated – to neighbouring Belgium where he lived and worked undisturbed between 1940 and 1944 by the German occupation authorities, emigrating to the United States in 1947. Incidentally the NS term applied to most modern art, 'degenerate Art' was coined by Max Nordau, Theodor Herzl's successor as leader of the Zionist movement.
98. H.D. Schäfer, *Das gespaltene Bewusstsein: Deutsche Kultur und Lebenswirklichkeit 1933–1945*, Munich 1981, *passim*.

## Chapter 6: Freisler as Publicist

1. Elke Fröhlich (ed.) *Die Tagebücher von Joseph Goebbels. Sämtliche Fragmente*, Munich 1987, vol. 2, p. 667, entry for 26 August 1936.
2. *ibid.*, p. 757, entry for 15 Dec. 1936.
3. See H.W. Koch, *The Hitler Youth. Origins and Development 1922–1945*, p. 219. It is doubtful whether the charge was trumped up. After the war Roussaint was unfrocked and belonged to the extreme left of political spectrum in the Federal Republic on behalf of which he displayed great activity.
4. See ref. 1, vol. 3, p. 118 entry for 20 April 1937.
5. *ibid.*, p. 120, entry for 22 April 1937.
6. *ibid.*, p. 122, entry for 23 April 1937.
7. *ibid.*, p. 126, entry for 28 April 1937.
8. *ibid.*, p. 128, entry for 30 April 1937.
9. *ibid.*, p. 141, entry for 12 May 1937.
10. *ibid.*, p. 251, entry for 1 September 1937.
11. *ibid.*, p. 437, entry for 10 February 1938.
12. On Niemöller see J.S. Conway, *The Nazi Persecution of the Churches 1933–1945*, London 1968, *passim*. Niemöller was never exposed to the indignities of the normal concentration camp inmate but was treated as a 'privileged' prisoner, who within the confines of the camp could do as he pleased. At the outbreak of the Second World War he addressed a personal letter to Hitler offering his services for 'Grossdeutschlands' navy. Hitler did not reply.
13. *Personalakte Freisler, op. cit.* Auszeichnungen und sonstige Ehrenzeichen.

14. G.F.W. Hegel, *Grundlininien der Philosophie des Rechts*, *op. cit.*, p. 198ff.
15. Tönnies, *Gemeinschaft und Gesellschaft*, Darmstadt 163 passim.
16. J.G. Herder, *Ideen zur Philosophie des Gesshichte der Menschheit*, Textausgabe, Darmstadt 1966; one the best brief discussions of his is by Sir Isaiah Berlin, 'J.G. Herder' in *Encounter*, London, August 1967, p. 29ff, and September, p. 42ff, which stresses the democratic elements inherent in the concept of the Volk. For Herder Volk and race were mutually exclusive concepts.
17. M. Weber, *Gesammelte politische Schriften*, Tübingen 1959, p. 14.
18. E. Renan, *Que'st ce qu'une nation?*, Paris 1882; see also R. Johannet, *Le principe des nationalités*, Paris 1918.
19. R. Freisler, 'Der Rechtsstaat' in *DJ*, 1937, p. 151ff.
20. So in *DJ*, 1934, p. 43ff, and with direct reference to Schmitt the year before in *VB*, 13.12.1933, p. 3.
21. See ref. 4; also E. Lemberg, *Nationalismus I Psychologie und Geschichte*, Hamburg 1964, p. 171ff.; 'Nationalsozialistisches Strafrecht: Eine Erwiderung auf die Ausführungen von Prof. Gerland' in *DJ*, 1934, p. 417ff.
22. R. Freisler, 'Nationalsozialistisches Strafrecht: Erwiderung auf die Ausführungen von Prof. Gerland' in *DJ*, 1934, p. 417ff; *idem.*, 'Die Aufgaben der Reichsjustiz entwickelt aus der biologischen Rechtsauffassung' in *DJ*, 1935, p. 468ff; *idem.*, 'Der Schutz von Rasse und Erbgut im werdenden deutschen Strafrecht' in *ZAkDR*, 1936, p. 142ff.
23. R. Freisler, 'Einiges vom werdenden deutschen Blutbanngericht' in *DJZ*, 1935, p. 585ff; *idem.*, 'Das künftige Schwurgericht' in *DJ*, 1935, p. 151ff; *idem.*, 'Gedanken zum deutschen Rechtswahrertag 1939' in *DJ*, 1939, p. 821ff.
24. R. Freisler, 'Gedanken zur Vereinheitlichung der staatlichen Rechtswahrung des deutschen Volkes' in *DJ*, 1935, p. 82ff.
25. R. Freisler, 'Totaler Staat? – Nationalsozialistischer Staat' in *DJ*, 1934, p. 116ff.
26. R. Freisler, 'Aus Anarchie zur verantwortlichen Führung' in *DJ*, 1934, p. 1070ff.; it is doubtful that as far as 'irresponsible dead number' was concerned, Freisler was aware that in 1788 James Madison, for different reasons, had uttered similar sentiments. See *The Federalist Papers*, ed. by C. Rossiter, New York 1959, No. 36.
27. R. Freisler, 'Rechtserneuerung, Rückblick und Ausblick' in *DJ*, 1934, p. 5.
28. See E. Jäckel, *Hitlers Weltanschauung. Entwurf einer Herrschaft*, Stuttgart 1969, *passim.*; H.W. Koch, *Der Sozialdarwinismus. Seine Genese und Einfluss auf das imperialistische Denken*, Munich 1973, Chapter 12.
29. R. Freisler, 'Der Rechtsstaat' in *DJ*, 1937, p. 151ff.
30. R. Freisler, 'Rechtspflege und Verwaltung, Justizverwaltung und Richtertum' in *DJZ*, 1934, p. 168ff.
31. *ibid.*, p. 170.
32. *ibid.*, p. 172.
33. R. Freisler, 'Die Idee des Reiches und ihr Einfluss auf unser Rechtsdenken' in *DJ*, 1939, p. 937; *idem.*; 'Rechtswahrergedanken zum Kriegsjahr 1940' in *DJ*, 1941, p. 6ff.; *ibid.*, p. 13; *idem.*, 'Das deutsches Polenstrafrecht' in *DJ*, 1941, Teil I, p. 29ff.; Teil 2, *DJ*, 1942, p. 22ff., Teil III, *DJ*, 1942, p. 41ff.
34. R. Freisler, 'Der Führers Tat und unsere Pflicht' in *DJ*, 1934, p. 850ff. *idem.* 'Die Stellung des Richters zur kriminellen Erbschaft der November-republik' in *DJ*, 1934, p. 303ff.
35. BAKO R 42/315, Hans Frank to Gürtner 1.7.1934.

36. A. Dorpalen, *Hindenburg and the Weimar Republic*, Princeton 1964, p. 480.
37. Domarus, *Reden . . . op. cit.*, Vol. I, p. 216ff; 405ff.
38. Gesetz über Massnahmen der Staatsnotwehr vom 3.7.1934, *RGBl.* I, 1934, p. 529; Runderlass des Reichsministers der Justiz vom 3.7.1934, *ibid.*
39. Freisler, 'Der Führers Tat . . .' *op. cit.*, p. 852.
40. R. Freisler, 'Reich und Recht' in *DJ*, 1941, p. 478ff. I am indebted to my colleague J.W.D. Trythal for pointing this out to me.
41. R. Freisler, 'Richter, Recht und Gesetz' in *DJ*, 1934, p. 1333.
42. R. Freisler, 'Hier kämpft die Jugend: Die drei Eidgenossen' in *DJ*, 1934, p. 774ff.
43. See Chapter 10.
44. Felix Dahn, *Ein Kampf um Rom*, Stuttgart 1956, p. 700.
45. For a recent discussion of the 'Germanic' concept of *Treue* see Walther Kienast, 'Germanische Treue und "Königsheil"' in *Historische Zeitschrift*, vol. 227, Munich 1978, especially p. 320.
46. Cornelius Tacitus, *Sämtliche erhaltene Werke*, Esslingen 1976, *Germania*, p. 73ff, introduction by F. Baethge, p. 4.
47. *The Anglo-Saxon Chronicle*, London 1953, p. 48.
48. Fr. Graus, 'Über die sogenannte germanische Treue' in *Historica* I, Prague 1959, p. 307.
49. *Sachsenspiegel* III, paragraph 42, no. 6 cited by G. Franz, *Deutsches Bauerntum*, Vol. I, Darmstadt 1940, p. 164.
50. G. Franz, *Der deutsche Bauernkrieg*, Vol. I, Darmstadt 1977, p. 2.
51. See K. Kaczerowsky (ed.) *Flugschriften des Bauernkrieges*, Hamburg 1970; Weigandts Reichsreformentwurf vom 18. Mai 1525, p. 65ff.
52. R. Freisler, 'Der Volksverrat Hoch- und Landesverrat im Lichte des National-sozialismus' in *DJZ*, 1935, p. 907ff.; *idem.* 'Neues deutsches Strafrecht' in *DJZ*, 1935, p. 914ff.
53. 'Vom Majestätsverbrechen zum Volksverrat' in *DJZ*, 1935, p. 997ff.
54. See comments on this aspect by A. de Tocqueville, *The Old Regime and The French Revolution*, New York 1955, p. 226ff.
55. Freisler, 'Vom Majestätsverbrechen . . .' *op. cit.*, p. 1003.
56. *loc. cit.*
57. *ibid.*, p. 1005.
58. On this aspect see M. Boveri, *Verrat im 20. Jahrhundert*, 4 vols, Hamburg 1956–1960, especially Vol. I, p. 141ff. *Stichwort: Verrat – Kollaboration – Propaganda.*
59. Adolf Hitler, *Mein Kampf*, Munich 1937, p. 609.
60. Hitler cited by Arno Plack, *Wie oft wird Hitler noch besiegt?*, Düsseldorf 1982, p. 20.
61. *Duden*, Vol. 7, *Das Herkunftswörterbuch*, Mannheim 1980, under *Verrat*.
62. Boveri, *Verrat . . . op. cit.*, p. 143.
63. Not only individuals but minorities are potential traitors. Examples include the US citizens of Japanese descent in 1941, the Chinese minorities in Southeast Asia to this day, and, of course, in the context of this study, the Jews in Germany and occupied Europe.
64. BAKO, RJM, Generalakten R 22/899: R. Freisler: 'Materielles Strafrecht im Allgemeinen' 1. Lesung 1933/34; *ibid.* R 22/887 'Grundprobleme national-sozialistischer Strafrechtsreform' 1933/34.; 'Von der Arbeit am Volksgesetzbuch' in *ZAkDR*, 1941, p. 104ff. Also see ref. 40 'Der Volksverrat . . .' *op. cit.*

65. 'Das Verbrechen des Angriffs auf den Führer (Paragraph 94 StGB)' in *DJ*, 1938, p. 837ff; Landesverrat (Paragraphen 88–93a StGB) zuzüglich der dazu geschaffenen Ergänzungen. Verbrechen nach Paragraph 18 der VO zum Schutze des Deutschen Volkes vom 4.2.1933; Verbrechen gegen Paragraph 1 des Gesetzes gegen Wirtschaftssabotage vom 1.12.1936; Hochverrat (Paragraphen 80–87 StGB mit den dazu geschaffenen Ergänzungen: Vergehen nach Paragraph 5 der VO zur Erhaltung des inneren Friedens vom 19.12.1933. Vergehen gegen Paragraph 18 der VO zum Schutze des Deutschen Volkes vom 4.2.1933; Vergehen gegen Paragraph 20–21 derselben VO; Vergehen gegen Paragraph 4 der VO zum Schutze von Volk und Staat vom 28.2.1933. Verbrechen gegen den volks-schädigenden Kanzelmissbrauchs (Paragraph 130a StGB). This was a legacy from Bismarck's *Kulturkampf*. Verbrechen der Staatsverleumdung (Paragraph 131 StGB) und den dazu gehörigen Ergänzungen: Verbrechen gegen Paragraph 1 und 2 des Gesetzes gegen heimtückische Angriffe auf Staat und Partei vom 20.2.1934. Verbrechen der Beschimpfung von Staat und Partei (Paragraphen 134a und 134b StGB) nebst der dazu geschaffenen Ergänzung: des Schutzes von nationalen Symbolen vom 19.5.1933. Verbrechen gegen die Bestimmungen zum verstärken Schutz des Führers, der Minister und anderer leitender Männer (Paragraph 1 der VO zum Schutz von Volk und Staat vom 28.2.1933) in der Fassung des Artikels 4, Ziffer 4, des Gesetzes vom 28.6.1935 und dem Gesetz zur Gewährleistung des Rechtsfriedens vom 13.10.1933 gegen Angriffe auf bestimmte, der Sicherheit von Staat und Partei besonders dienenden Funktionsträgern. Verbrechen strafbar nach dem Gesetz zur Abwehr politischer Gewalttaten vom 4.4.1933 (enthaltend Strafverschärfungen für gewisse Sprengstoff- und Brandstiftungsverbrechen usw).

66. R. Freisler, 'Vom Schutzzweck der Strafrechtspflege gegenüber Volksschädlingen' in *DJ*, 1938, p. 365ff.

67. R. Freisler, 'Die Rasse als Träger und Ziel des deutschen Volksrechts, unter besonderer Berücksichtigung des Strafrechts' in *DJ*, 1936, p. 803ff.

68. R. Freisler, 'Die Aufgaben der Reichsjustz entwicket aus der biologischen Rechtsauffassung' in *DJ*, 1935, p. 573.

69. R. Freisler, 'Der Schutz der Rasse und Erbgut im werdenden deutschen Strafrecht' in *ZAkDR*, 1936, p. 142.

70. R. Freisler, 'Staatsnotwehr im Lichte des Nationalsozialismus' in *DJ*, 1935, p. 856ff; *idem.* 'Zur Reichstagung der deutschen Ärzte des öffentlichen Gesundheitsdienstes' in *DJ*, 1939, p. 946ff.

71. See Chapter 11 below.

72. R. Freisler, 'Aus Anarchie zur verantwortlichen Führung' in *DJ*, 1934, p. 1070ff.

73. V. Valentin, *Geschichte der deutschen Revolution 1848/49*, Cologne 1970, Vol. II, p. 588.

74. R. Freisler, 'Einiges vom vom werdenden deutschen Blutbanngericht' in *DJZ*, 1935, p. 585ff.

75. R. Freisler, 'Kriegsdienstappell deutscher Rechtswahrer' in *DJ*, 1941, p. 441.

76. R. Freisler, 'Der Versuch' in *ZAkDR*, 1934, p. 82.

77. R. Freisler, 'Nationalsozialistisches Strafrecht und aufbauende Kritik' in *DJ*, 1934, p. 223.

78. Freisler, 'Nationalsozialistisches Strafrecht . . .' *op. cit.*, p. 421.

79. R. Freisler, 'Aktive Rechtspflege' in *DJ*, 1934, p. 625ff.

80. *ibid.*, p. 627.

81. R. Freisler, 'Rechtspolitische Gedanken zur Wiederaufnahme eines Verfahrens' in *DJ*, 1937, p. 730ff.

82. *ibid.*, p. 733.

83. R. Freisler, 'Deutsche Rechtswahrerausbildung' in *DJ*, 1941, p. 833ff.; *idem.* 'Eignung zum Beruf des Rechtswahrers' in *DJ*, 1941, p. 645ff.

84. R. Freisler, 'Deutscher Osten' in *DJ*, 1941, p. 737.

85. R. Freisler, 'Gedanken zur Vereinheitlichung der staatlichen Rechtswahrung des deutschen Volkes' in *DJ*, 1935, p. 82ff.

86. R. Freisler, 'Rechtspflege und Verwaltung, Justizverwaltung und Richtertum' in *DJZ*, 1934, p. 171.

87. R. Freisler, 'Die Einheit von Partei und Staat in der Personalpolitik der Justiz' in *DJ*, 1935, p. 16687.

88. R. Freisler, 'Recht und Gesetz' in *DJ*, 1936, p. 151.

89. R. Freisler, 'Einfluss auf der Staatsauffassung auf den Geltungsbereich des Strafrechtes', *DJ*, 1940, p. 639.

90. Kriegssonderstrafrechtsverordnung (KSSVO), 17.8.1938, *RGBl.* I, 1939, p. 1457; Kriegsstrafverfahrondsordnung von 17.8.1938; *RGBl.* I, 1939, p. 1458; VO über Massnahmen auf dem Gebiet der Gerichtsverfassung und der Rechtspflege vom 1.9.1939, *RGBl.* I, 1939, p. 1609; VO über ausserordentliche Rundfunkmassnahmen vom 1.9.1939, *RGBl*, I, 1939, p. 1683; Kriegswirtschaftsverordnung vom 4.9.1939, *RGBl.* I, 1939, p. 1609; VO über Volksschädlinge vom 4.9.1939, *RGBl.* I, 1939, p. 1679; Gesetz zur Änderung von Vorschriften des Gerichts- verfahrens des Wehrmachtsstrafrechts und des Strafgesetzbuches vom 16.9.1939, *RGBl.* I, 1939, p. 1841; VO zum Schutz gegen jugendliche Schwerverbrecher vom 4.10.1939, *RGBl.* I, 1939, p. 2000; VO über eine Sondergerichtsbarkeit für Angehörige der SS und für Angehörige der Polizeiverbände bei besonderem Einsatz vom 17.9.1939, *RGBl.* I, 1939, p. 2107. On this see H. Grosscurth, *Tagebuch eines Abwehroffiziers*, Stuttgart 1970, p. 80ff.; G. Reitlinger, *SS – Alibi of a Nation*, London 1957, p. 134ff. VO zur Ergänzung der Strafvorschriften zum Schutze der Wehrkraft vom 25.11.1939, *RGBl.* I, 1939, p. 2319. VO gegen Gewaltverbrecher vom 5.12.1929, *RGBl.* I, 1939, p. 2390.

91. R. Freisler, 'Zur Verordnung über ausserordentliche Rundfunkmassnahmen' in *DJ*, 1940, p. 105ff.

92. Freisler, 'Kriegsdienstappell . . .' *op. cit.*, p. 449.

93. Gesetz des Srafrechtes gegen Polen und Juden, *RGBl.* I, 1941, p. 759; Freisler, 'Polenstafrecht . . .' *op. cit.* As to the activities of the *Einsatzgruppen* see H. Krausnick and H.-H. Wilhelm, *Die Truppe des Weltanschaungskrieges*, Stuttgart 1981.

94. Freisler on 'Polenstrafrecht . . .' *op. cit.*

95. R. Freisler, 'Deutsche Justiz in den Niederlanden' in *DJ*, 1942, p. 141ff.

96. Louis de Jong, *Het Koninkrijk der Nederlanden in de tweede wereldoorlog*, Vols I–IX, Xa and Xb, The Hague 1969–1982; Gerhard Hirschfeld, *Fremdherrschaft und Kollaboration, Die Niederlande unter deutscher Besatzung 1940–1945*, Stuttgart 1984; Paul Sérant, *Les vaincus de la libération*, Paris 1964.

97. R. Freisler, 'Der deutsche Rechtswahrer der deutschen Strafrechtspflege, denkt, spricht und schreibt deutsch!' in *DJ*, 1941, p. 1113ff.

## Chapter 7: Judiciary in Crisis 1939–1942

1. The author's attention was first drawn to the incident concerning Klausener by Hitler's former secretary Frau Christa Schröder. It was later fully reported in *Die Welt*, Bonn, 4 December 1985.
2. IfZg, NG–566, Freisler to Generalstaatsanwälte, 16.10.1939; NG–135 Schlegelberger to Lammers, 30.6.1941.
3. Broszat, *Staat* . . . *op. cit.*, p. 336ff, 403ff.
4. IfZg, NG–340, Lammers to Gürtner, 8.8.1939.
5. BAKO, Akten des RJM *op. cit.* Himmler to Gürtner, 18.2.1937.
6. *ibid.*, Thierack to Lammers, 21.1.1939.
7. *ibid.*, Lautz to Gürtner, 29.7.1940.
8. *ibid.*, Führerbefehl vom 26.7.1939.
9. R. Freisler, 'Arbeitseinsatz in Dienste des Vierjahresplanes' in *DJ*, 1938, p. 584ff.
10. See Himmler to Gürtner 28.2.1939.
11. *loc. cit.*
12. BAKO, Generalakten *op. cit.*, Freisler to Gürtner, 12.12.1939.
13. IfZg, NG–466, Freisler to Generalstaatsanwälte, 16.9.1939.
14. See ref. 12; also BDC, NG–729, Gürtner Anweisung vom 4.11.1939 and letter to Lammers of the same date.
15. *ibid.*; H. Boberach (ed.) *Meldungen aus dem Reich*, Hersching 1984, Vol. 4, p. 1146.
16. BAKO, RJM, Generalakten R 22/955, Freisler memorandum to Gürtner, 2.9.1940; BDC, NG–131, Lammers to RJN, 27.5.1941; NG–135, Freisler to Gauleiter Greiser, 27.6.1941.
17. *ibid.*, BAKO, Gürtner to Lammers, 17.9.1939.
18. IfZg, NG–135, Schlegelberger to Lammers, 30.1.1941; NG–665–PS, Hitler's directive, December 1941.
19. *ibid.*, BAKO Geschäftsverteilung für 1942; R. Freisler, 'Gedanken zum Deutschen Rechtswahrertag 1939' in *DJ*, 1939, p. 824.
20. Data extracted from personnel files in BDC and Archiv des Bundesjustizministeriums, Bonn; IfZg, NG–176, Laienrichter des VGH, Stand vom 29.5.1942.
21. *loc. cit.*
22. See M. Buber-Neumann, *Als Gefangene bei Stalin und Hitler*, Munich 1962, p. 145ff.
23. IfZg, NG–823, Lagebericht des Oberreichsanwalt vom 28.5.1942.
24. *loc. cit.*
25. BAKO, Akten des Oberreichsanwalts beim VGH R 60 II/84, *Führerinformation*, 1942, no. 21.
26. BAKO, RJM, Generalakten *op. cit.* Schlegelberger to Lammers 15.9.1942.
27. BAKO R 22/20019, RJM R 22 Gr.5./5–12, Lageberichte des Oberreichsanwalts vom 29.1.1941; 21.5.1941, 31.7.1941, 2.10.1941.
28. BAKO, VGH judgment 24.6.1942 – 9J 34/42–H–91/41, 25.6.1942; see also VGH judgment 25.7.1942 8 J 92/14–1 H 148/42; VGH judgment 28.7.1942 – 8 J 123/14–1 H 146/42.
29. BAKO, VGH judgment 25.7.1942 8 J 92/42–H 148/42.
30. The judgment admitted that the accused was a frail, infirm old man.

31. *loc. cit.*

32. BAKO, VGH judgment 12.7.1944 6 J 71/44–1 H 119/44.

33. *ibid.*, VGH judgment 18.7.1944 8 J 123/44–1 H 116/44.

34. IfZg, Fa 117/320 Indictment 23.2.1944; BDC VGH judgment, NG–435.

35. See VGH judgment BAKO R 60 II/9, 5.2.1936; BAKO, VGH judgment 25.11.1942 – 10 J 16/42g–1 H 247/42.

36. BAKO, VGH judgment 6.1.1943–9 J 206/42g – 1 H 302/42.

37. BAKO, *Führerinformation*, 19.6.1942, no. 49.

38. For the most detailed analysis of the 'Red Orchestra' see H. Höhne, *Kennwort Direktor*, Gütersloh 1967.

39. *ibid.*, p. 206ff.

40. BAKO, VGH judgment 4.12.1942. File signature illegible.

41. BDC, NG–926, VGH indictment and judgment.

42. BDC, BG–369, VGH judgment 26.7.1940; also Thierack letter, 6.8.1940, see BAKO R 60 II/9, VGH judgment 4.7.1940.

43. IfZg, NG–399; BAKO, VGH judgment 16.12.1943–10 J–1095/43–1 H 305/43.

44. BAKO, VGH judgment 26.6.1943–10 J 405/43g–1 H 158–/43.

45. See W. Laqueur, *Young Germany*, London 1961 *passim*.

46. See Arno Klönne, *Gegen den Strom*, Göttingen 1958, *passim*.

47. *ibid.*

48. H. Rothfels, *Die Deutsche Opposition gegen Hitler*, Krefeld 1951, p. 20; M.V. Hellfeld, *Edelweisspiraten in Köln*, Cologne 1982; K.-H. Janssen, 'Edelweisspiraten' in *Die Zeit*, Zeit Magazin, no. 16, Hamburg 1981.

49. On Sosnowski see Höhne, *Canaris, op. cit.*, p. 160; BDC, VGH judgment 16.2.1935 11 J 145/34–3 L 29/34.

50. *Leipziger Kommentare . . . op. cit.*, 1939, paragraph 49.

51. Gesetz für Änderung strafrechtlicher Vorschriften vom 26.5.1933, *RGBl.* I, 1933, p. 295.

52. Gesetz zur Ergänzung der Vorschriften gegen Landesverrat vom 22.11.1942, *RGBl.* I, 1942, p. 668. Retroactive legislation was subject to approval by the RJM, the Chief of the OKW and Reichsführer-SS Himmler.

53. BDC, NG–241, VGH judgment 18.10.1941; IfZg, NG–5404 Lautz affidavit.

54. Ergänzungen zum StGB, *RGBl.* I, 1940, p. 754.

55. *ibid.*

56. BAKO R 22/20019, RJM, R 22 Gr.5/5–12 Lagebericht des Oberreichsanwalts vom 29.1.1941.

57. BAKO R 22/20113, RJM, Akten 4020g, Schlegelberger note 17.2.1940.

58. *ibid.*, Gürtner Aktenvermerk vom 2.8.1940.

59. *ibid.*, Gürtner Aktenvermerk.

60. BAKO R 22/302, Generalakten des RJM 3270, Thierack to Lammers 18.12.1941.

61. BAKO, see ref. 56, Lagebericht vom 2.10.1941.

62. BAKO, VGH judgment 15.9.1942–1 J 11/42g–4 L 45/42.

63. BAKO, VGH judgment 25.2.1942–1 J 161/40g–3 L 114/41.

64. BAKO, VGH judgment 9.3.1943–11/3 J 295/406–1 L 36/42.

65. BAKO, VGH judgment 24.3.1944–7 (8) J 94/43g–1 32/449.

66. See for instance BAKO, VGH judgment 12.2.43–6 (5) J 91/42g–1 32/117.

67. BAKO, VGH judgment 15.7.1943, file signature illegible.

68. BAKO, VGH judgment 3.3.1942–4–L 2/42, *Leipziger Kommentare . . . op. cit.*,

1942, paragraph 91, note 3; VGH judgment 21.12.1942–8–J 362/42g–1 H 265/42; BDC, NG–642, VGH judgment 24.2.1942; *ibid.*, NG–352, VGH judgment 12.8.1942.

69. BAKO R 22/20019, RJM, R 22 Gr.5./5–12 Lautz report to Schlegelberger 1.8.1942.

70. Erlass des Führers und Reichskanzlers über die Gewährung von Straffreiheit vom 7.6.1939, *RGBl.* I, 1939, p. 1023; IfZg, NG–3539, Der Vertreter des Auswärtigen Amts bei dem Reichsprotektor in Prag vom 5.10.1940 an das Auswärtige Amt which contains these details as well as German plans for the future of Czechs. According to them they were neither to be resettled nor be granted autonomy, but they were to be 'Germanized'. See also BAKO R 22/4070, Gürtner Vermerke 6.9.1940 and 25.9.1940. In the latter Gürtner refers to Hitler's express wish not to create any 'martyrs' in the protectorate.

71. *ibid.*, Gürtner Vermerk 6.9.1940.

72. *ibid.*, Gürtner Vermerk 25.9.1940; BAKO R 22/4070 Hochverratsverfahren gegen Protektoratsangehörige 1939–1942; RJM Bericht vom 4.4.1940 und 1.6.1940; IfZg, NG–682 Schlegelberger Vermerk vom 1.10.1940, Thierack to RJM 4.12.1941.

73. So Heiber 'Der Fall Elias' *op. cit.*

74. Mástny, *op. cit.*, p. 180.

75. For the Eliáš case see H. Heiber, 'Der Fall Elias' in *VfZg*, 1955, p. 275ff. V. Mástny, *The Czechs under German Rule. The Failure of National Resistance*, New York 1971, p. 189ff.

76. IfZg, NG–801 and NG–147 indictment and judgment of Eliáš.

77. ibid., indictment.

78. BAKO R 22/4060 *op. cit.* Lautz Vermerk vom 26.9.1941.

79. *ibid.*, Thierack Vermerk vom 27.9.1941.

80. Thus Heiber's correct assessment *op. cit.*

81. Thus Lautz's complaint to Schlegelberger 1.10.1931 *loc. cit.*

82. For the account of the trial see Heiber 'Der Fall . . .' *op. cit.*; also IfZg, NG–081.

83. See ref. 76, indictment.

84. As expressed in judgment, IfZg, NG–147.

85. *loc. cit.*; the text of the judgment against Klapka can no longer be traced.

86. BAKO R 22/4060 *op. cit.*, Heydrich to Bormann 1.10.1941.

87. *ibid.*, report of speech by Vertreter des Auswärtigen Amts beim Reichsprotektor in Prag, 2.10.1941.

88. *ibid.*, Schlegelberger to Heydrich 5.10.1941; Heydrich Fernschreiben to Bormann 7.10.1941, Schlegelberger to Lammers 7.10.1941.

89. *ibid.*, Thierack to Lammers 10.10.1941 but his assertion 'Herr Staatssekretär Dr. Freisler wurde über alle Einzelheiten von mir unterrichtet' seems to be far from the truth.

90. *loc. cit.*

91. BAKO, R 43 II/1145a, RJM, Personalangelegenheiten des Ministers 1933–1943 Gratifikationszahlung für besondere Leistungen des Herrn Staatssekretärs a.D. Dr. Franz Schlegelberger.

92. For a detailed analysis of the pogrom see L. Kochan, *Pogrom*, London 1957.

93. H. Heiber, 'Der Fall Grynsoan' in *VfZg*, 1963, p. 267ff.

94. Lautz to IfZg 28.3.1955, Zeugenschrifttum.

95. BDC, NG–971, Diewerge to Krümer. Ministry of Propaganda, 22.12.1942:

Propagandistische Vorbereitung des Mordprozesses Grynspan. See also L.P. Lochner (ed.) *The Goebbels Diaries*, London 1948, but unpublished excerpts such as the quote just cited are held by the IfZg.

96. *Goebbels Diaries loc. cit.*
97. *ibid.,* p. 41.
98. Lautz *op. cit.*
99. BDC, NG–971 *op. cit.* Propagandistische Vorbereitungen.
100. *loc. cit.*
101. *loc. cit.*
102. Schlegelberger Vermerk of letter (undated) in NG–971 *op. cit.*
103. Konferenznotiz (undated and unsigned) vom 22.1.1942 in NG–971 *op. cit.*
104. Schlegelberger Aktennotiz betr. Führeranweisung in NG–971 *op. cit.*
105. BAKO, *Führerinformation*, 1942, No. 118.
106. BAKO, *Führerinformation*, 1942, No. 160.
107. *loc. cit.*
108. IfZg, Archiv: Adressenkartei.
109. Picker, *Tischgespräche . . . op. cit.,* p. 62.
110. *ibid.,* p. 104.
111. *ibid.,* p. 131.
112. *ibid.,* p. 267.
113. *ibid.,* p. 278.
114. *ibid.,* p. 332.
115. *ibid.,* p. 343.
116. R. Freisler, 'Deutsche Rechtswahrerausbildung . . .' *op. cit.,* see chapter 6, ref. 72.
117. Picker, *Tischgespräche . . . op. cit.,* p. 359ff.
118. BDC, NG–287, Lammers to Schlegelberger, 25.10.1941.
119. BAMA, N 51/7, Verabschiedung des Generaloberst Hoepner.
120. *loc. cit.*
121. IfZg, photostat copies of unpublished Goebbels diaries.
122. Picker, *Tischgespräche . . . op. cit.,* p. 158ff.
123. BDC, NG–221, Schlegelberger Vermerk zum Fall Schlitt und Führertelefonat vom 17.4.1942.
124. *loc. cit.,* also Domarus, *Reden . . . op. cit.,* Vol. 4, p. 1856ff.
125. As expounded in his book *Hitler's War*, London 1977 *passim.*
126. H. Linge, *Bis zum Untergang: Als Chef des Persönlichen Dienstes bei Hitler*, Munich 1982, p. 201.
127. As already indicated in a previous reference, *Meldungen aus dem Reich* are now available complete, 17 vols. Munich 1984.
128. Domarus, *Reden . . . op. cit.,* Vol. 4, p. 1874ff.
129. *Goebbels Diaries, op. cit.,* p. 141.
130. Boberach, *Meldungen . . . op. cit.,* p. 249, 27.4.1942.
131. *loc. cit.*
132. Imperial War Museum, London, FD 332/46, 27.4.1942.
133. BAKO R 22/3380 Generalstaatsanwalt Naumburg (Saale) 26.5.1942.
134. BAKO R 22/3357 Generalstaatsanwalt Braunschweig, 31.5.1942.
135. Goerdeler's proposed radio proclamation after a successful coup against Hitler. In Archiv Peter (ed.) *Spiegelbild einer Verschwörung*, Stuttgart 1961, p. 213.
136. Freisler letter of 5 May 1942.

137. BAKO R 22/3366, Der Präsident des Hanseatischen Oberlandesgerichtes 11.5.1942.

138. *Goebbels Diaries*, *op. cit.*, p. 158.

139. BAKO, Generalaktren, RJM, R 22/4070, Schlegelberger to Bormann 28.4.1942; Frank to Goebbels 1.5.1942.

140. *Das Schwarze Korps*, 16.7.1942, 'nabhängig – wovon?', p. 3.

141. H. Heiber and H.v. Koke (eds) Facsimilie *Querschnitt durch das Schwarze Korps*, (Munich n.d.) introduction, p. 8.

142. Freisler letters 31.5.1942; 18.6.1942; 5.7.1942.

143. H. Höhne in *Der Spiegel*, no. 51, 1984, p. 76.

144. The author's own search for the original has been in vain. Dr Kempner has ignored the author's specific questions as the whereabouts of the original document though he was ready enough to answer other queries. Those participants who have survived have surprisingly little to say about the conference. But even the Secretary of State in the Foreign Office, Ernst v. Weizsäcker, does not mention the conference at all. There are no diary entries between 16 January and 25 January 1942. See L.E. Hill (ed.) *Die Weizsäcker Papiere 1933–1950*, Berlin 1974. But Hill's editorial practice is open to challenge beause in Vol. I, published in 1982, on p. 442, he blandly states: 'Within the framework of this collection it has not been possible to indicate contents of letters, diary entries and passages omitted.' Whether this applies also to the period 1933–1950 is an open question.

145. Freisler's own phrase, see Chapter 10; his attendance at the Wannsee conference is attested in BAKO, Akten betr. Volksgerichtshof 1934–1945; list of attendants at the Wannsee conference.

146. Freisler in his letter 5.7.1942 cautiously speculated that the choice might perhaps go his way: 'Thierack hat doch unnötigerweise sehr viele Feinde im Justizwesen geschaffen'.

147. BDC, NG–1243, Vortrag beim Reichsminister (Lammers) 17.8.1942.

148. BDC, NG–1243, Personalveränderungen im Reichsjustizministerium 17.8.1942.

149. *ibid.*; also BAKO R 43 II/1145a, RJM, Personalangelegenheiten des Ministers 1933–1943.

150. *ibid.*; see also Bormanns Rundschreiben No. 131/42 vom 27.8.1942, BDC, NG–541 copy of Freisler's appointment as president of the VGH; also contained in BAKO *Personalakte Freisler*, undated, as well as undated prepared press releases of the new appointments.

151. See ref. 148 containing Schlegelberger's letter of resignation on the grounds of 'ill health'.

152. Erlass des Führers vom 26.8.1942 is contained in files under ref. 149; it does not appear to have been printed in the *Reichsgesetzblatt*.

153. Broszat, *Der Staat . . . op. cit.*, p. 260.

154. W. Präg and W. Jacobmeyer (eds) *Das Diensttagebuch des deutschen Generalgouverneurs in Polen*, Stuttgart 1975, p. 446.

155. *ibid.*, p. 517.

156. *Münchner Neueste Nachrichten*, 20.7.1942, p. 3.

157. *Dienstagebuch . . . op. cit.*, p. 552.

158. *ibid.*, p. 553ff.

159. *loc. cit.*

160. *ibid.*, p. 555.

161. See R. Westrich's *Who's Who* ... *op. cit.*, p. 225ff; Ohlendorf's own papers have until 1985 been in the hands of his widow and those of Herr Herbert Taege. I am grateful to Herr Taege for supplying me with details from them. In 1985 the papers were transferred to the archive of the Institut für Zeitgeschichte, Munich. As to the disproportional overrepresentation of jurists within the SS see G.C. Boehnert 'The Jurists in the NS-Führerkorps 1925–1939' in G. Hirschfeld and L. Kettenacker (eds) *Der Führerstaat: Mythos und Realität*, Stuttgart 1981, p. 361ff. The almost excessive degree of administrative conscientiousness of Himmler, for whom no detail was too trivial, is best reflected in his correspondence. See H. Heiber (ed.) *Reichsführer! Briefe von und an Himmler*, Munich 1970. As to the *Einsatzgruppen* see Kausnick and Wilhelm, *Die Truppe des Weltanschauungskrieges*, *op. cit.* Ohlendorf's short-lived career under Dönitz is dealt with by Marli Steinert, *Die 23 Tage der Regierungs Dönitz*, Düsseldorf 1967 *passim*. The facsimile reproductions of the two secret orders of 1940 are contained in Paul Hausser, *Soldaten wie andere auch* (a book title borrowed from Konrad Adenauer's description of the Waffen-SS), Osnabrück 1966, p. 293; p. 298. See also p. 301ff.

162. BAKO, R 43 II/1145a, undated copy of Ohlendorf's exposition; see also P. Schneider 'Rechtssicherheit und richterliche Unabhängigkeit aus der Sicht des SD' in *VfZg*, 1961, p. 236ff.

163. *ibid.*; BAKO, p. 3.

164. *ibid.*, p. 6.

165. *ibid.*, p. 12.

166. See Boehnert.

167. *ibid.*, Heiber.

## Chapter 8: Freisler as VGH President

1. Freisler letter 5.9.1942.

2. *Personalakte Freisler*, Freisler to Thierack 28.8.1942.

3. *ibid.*, Thierack to Freisler, 30.9.1942.

4. BAKO R 43 II/1145a, RJM, Personalangelegenheiten des Ministers 1933–1943 which also contains copies of the documents cited in refs. 1, 2, and 3.

5. BAKO, Generalakten RJM R 22/4070 Kommunistische Aktionen in Skandinavien.

6. *Freisler Personalakte, op. cit.*, Freisler to Thierack 9.9.1942.

7. *ibid.*, Thierack to Freisler 9.9.1942.

8. For this table the StGB, 1943, has been used.

9. Archiv des Bundesjustizministeriums, Bonn, 'Jahresstatistiken des VGH'.

10. *ibid.*

11. *ibid.*, Geschäftsbericht der Reichsanwaltschaft, File 564, Vol. II.

12. *ibid.*

13. *ibid.*

14. *ibid.*, File 566. For France see Sérant, *Les vaincus* ... *op. cit.*, p. 140ff; H. Amouroux, *La grande histoire des Français sous l'occupation*, Paris 1978 *passim.*; M. Dank, *The French against the French*, London 1978, p. 139ff.; *The Sorrow and the Pity*, London 1975 (The English text of Ophuls' TV documentary *Le Chagrin et la Pitié*).

15. BAKO *op. cit.*

16. Compiled from Thierack's and Freisler's annual reports; see also Geschäftsbericht der Reichsanwaltschaft, files 564, Vol. II and file 566 as well as figures cited in *DJ*, 1939, p. 1185.

17. *ibid.*; the figures for these death sentences passed by the VGH been extracted from the *Leipziger Kommentare . . . op. cit.* of these years and vary only very marginally with those contained in the BAKO files. Although clemency practice on death sentences did exist, records concerning this aspect appear to have been destroyed.

18. *ibid.*

19. BAKO, Generalakten RJM R 22/4070 *op. cit.*, copy of Richterbrief 12.10.1942.

20. VO zur Ergänzung und Änderung der Zuständigkeitsverordnung vom 29.1.1943, *RGBl.* I, 1943, p. 76.

21. Tagungsbericht der Generalstaatsanwälte 3.2–4.2.1944, Generalakten 313, Bayerisches Staatsministerium der Justiz.

22. BAKO R 22/20040, Ausführungen auf der Tagung der Arbeitsgemeinschaft für Straf- Wirtschaftsstraf- und Ordnungsstrafrecht 14.7.1944.

23. BAKO, VGH judgment 20.4.1943–9 J 411/43–1 L 40/43.

24. BAKO, VGH judgment 21.5.1943–5 J 33/43–1 H 106/43.

25. *12-Uhr-Blatt*, Berlin, 20 Sep. 1943. Höfer was also contributor to Goebbels' weekly *Das Reich*, as were the first president of the Federal Republic, Theodor Heuss, Rudolf Augstein, editor of *Der Spiegel* and a host of others, past and present luminaries of the Federal Republic's political and intellectual life. Prof Dr. Theodor Eschburg, renowned political scientist, asserts in *Die Geschichte der Bundesrepublik Deutschland. Jahre des Besatzung 1945–1949*, Stuttgart 1983, p. 148 that the US authorities vetted particularly journalists for their zone of occupation. This assertion at best is based on ignorance or worse. But then Eschenburg himself had himself been a member – of the SS!

26. BAKO, VGH judgment 8.9.1943–1 J 473/43–1 L 78/43; that NSDAP members were tried before the VGH numerous cases attest to this fact such as BAKO VGH judgment 1.9.1943–9 J 660/43–1 L 68/43.

27. BAKO, VGH judgment 6.9.1943–1 J 458/43–1 L 73/43.

28. BAKO, VGH judgment 6.9.1943–7 J 365/4–1 H 20/43; VGH judgment 29.9.1943–2 J 522/43–1 L 102/43; VGH judgment 5.10.1943–1 J 529/43–1 L 109/43.

29. For the Scholl case see I. Scholl, *Die Weisse Rose*, Frankfurt 1955. Some of the files are still in existence (the majority are destroyed) and are held by the BHSA, Abt. 1 Allgemeines Staatsarchiv. However at the time of research and writing the files were put at the disposal of a film team producing a documentary on the Scholls and their friends for the 40th anniversary of their deaths.

30. The author has been given access to read the circular, but due to circumstances referred to already in the preface, both persons, he who established the contact in the first place, and the present owner of the circular withdrew their permission to be named. Nor was the author allowed to make a photocopy of it.

31. U.v. Hassel, *Vom anderen Deutschland*, Frankfurt 1964, p. 270.

32. Scholl *op. cit.*, p. 90ff. as to the case.

33. *loc. cit.*

34. See Kempner, *Priester vor Hitlers Tribunalen op. cit. passim.*

35. BAKO, *Führerinformation* 1943, no. 139.

36. BAKO, VGH judgment 23.6.1943–8 J 382/426–2 H 65/43.

37. BAKO, VGH judgment 2.7.1943–1 J 147/43g–1 50/43.

38. BAKO, VGH judgment 1.10.1943–2 J 518/43–1 L 104/43.

39. BAKO, VGH judgment 14.10.1943–8 J 190/43g–1 H 253/43; VGH judgment 3.11.1943 3 J 249/43g–1 L261/43; VGH judgment 15.12.1943 3 J 301/43–1 1270/43; VGH judgment 3.1.1944–3 J–617/43g–1 1310/44; BAKO, VGH judgment 18.4.1944–8 J 168/43–1 L 79/44; BAKO, VGH judgment 28.7.1944–5 J 170/44–1 L 234/44.

40. BAKO, VGH judgment 9.8.1944–5 J 179/44–1 L 263/44.

41. See Kempner, *Priester . . . op. cit.*, p. 135.

42. BAKO R 22/20198, RJM, R 22 Gr.5./XXIII–3, Vols 1–3, copy of Keitel's directive of 12.12.1941 based on Hitler's instructions of 7.12.1941.

43. *ibid.*, also in IMT judgment, Case III, *op. cit.*, p. 92.

44. *ibid.*, Vermerk der Rechtsabteilung des OKW, 15.1.1942.

45. In IMT judgment, Case III, *op. cit. loc. cit.*

46. See ref. 42 containing this correspondence.

47. IfZg,NG–665–PS, Hitler's directive of 7.12.1941; NG–232 Rundverfügung vom 6.2.1942 bei Freisler; NG–223 Thierack in *ZAkDR*, 1943, p. 997; BAKO, RJM Archiv, Thierack to Freisler 9.9.1942; BDC, NG–628 Thierack 13.10.1942 betr. Lenkung der Kriegsrechtsprechung im Kriege; BDC, NG–226 Freisler to Thierack 14.10.1942 accepting Nacht-und-Nebel trials for VGH, also RJM directive concerning crimes against the Reich and the occupied territories 28.10.1942; BDC, NG–256 Thierack to Freisler emphasising that Germans are not subject to the Nacht-und-Nebel directive; BDC, NG–272 Kaltenbrunner to Thierack 20.9.1943 claiming SD participation.

48. As stated in Keitel's directive cited in ref. 42.

49. *ibid.*

50. *ibid.*

51. See ref. 47, RJM directive 14.10.1942.

52. *ibid.*, 13. VO zum Reichsbürgergesetz vom 1.7.1943, *RGBl.* I, 1943, p. 372.

53. IfZg, NG–1007 Behling affidavit.

54. IfZg, NG–792 Weimann affidavit; NG–7373 Hecker affidavit; NG–950 Bodden affidavit; NG–696 Wettenberg affidavit; NG–404 Ziegler affidavit. In several of the affidavits (Weimann, Bodden, Ziegler) the complaint is raised that when questioned by the Allies they were not allowed to answer vital questions; see also NG–659, NG–312 Barnickel affidavits; NG–535 Grünwald affidavit.

55. IfZg, NG–535 Grünwald affidavit.

56. Case III, *op. cit.*, pp. 96, 189f, 195, 199.

57. *ibid.*, p. 195; see also ref. 47, RJM directive of 28.10.1942; Thierack Rundschreiben vom 21.1.1944.

58. Case III, *op. cit.*, evidence of Chief of the Wehrmacht judiciary Rudolf Lehmann, p. 94f, 149.

59. BAKO R 22/20198 *op. cit.* Berichte der OLG-Generalstaatsanwaltschaften Köln, Essen und Kiel vom 1.6.1942.

60. *ibid.*, Freisler Bericht: Nacht-und-Nebel Fälle vor dem Ersten Senat des VGH, 20.12.1944.

61. *ibid.*; OLG München Bericht vom 30.12.1944; IfZg Zeugenschrifttum: Kriegs- und politische Gefangene in München-Stadelheim. Stand 30.4.1945.

62. IfZg, NG–792 Weimann affidavit.
63. BAKO, Bericht des Oberreichsanwalts vom 9.4.1944 und 27.6.1944 in R 22/20198, *op. cit.*
64. BAKO, VGH judgment 21.1.1943–1 J 1003/42g–2 325/42; VGH judgment 25.2.1943–3 J 1012/42g–1 L 10/43; VGH judgment 5.1.1944–11 J 1012/43g–1 L 42/43; VGH judgment 15.10.1943–1 J 1041/42g–2 L 126/43; VGH judgment 27.5.1943–2 J 1014/42g–2 L 743; VGH judgment 28.5.1943–2 J 1014/43g–2 79/43; VGH judgment 28.8.1943 1 J 1052/42g–2 L 119/43; VGH judgment 12.3.1944 321–6/60; VGH judgment 18.1.1944–3 J 1009/43–1 L 27/47; VGH judgment 12.10.1943–3 J 1016/43g–2 L 201/43; VGH judgment 28.10.1944–2 384/44g–1 L 391/44. Also see IMT Case III, *op. cit.*, p. 112, 192; IfZg, NG–599, Dr Poelchau affidavit.
65. BDC, NG–247, Thierack to Bormann 14.6.1944.
66. BAKO, R 22/956 Generalakten 4021, vol. IV des BJM; R 22/20019 Gr.5/5–12 H des RJM, Lageberichte des ORA especially those dated 4.4.1940; 30.7.1940; 31.7.1941; 2.10.1941; 3.10.1942; 1.6.1943 and 10.2.1944.
67. BDC, VGH judgment 9.6.1942–8 J 257/41–2 H 19/42.
68. *ibid.*; also BAKO, *Führerinformation* 1942, No. 51.
69. BDC, VGH judgments of 16.11.1943 8 J 70/43–5 H 128/43 and 8 J 75/43–5 H 134/34; judgment 9.12.1943–8 J 324/39g–5 H 110/43; VGH judgment 1.3.1944–7 (8) J 203/41–2 H 168/44; VGH judgment 23.2.1944–8 J 7/41–2 168/44.
70. BDC, VGH judgment 29.10.1942–8 J 214/42g–5 H 94/42.
71. BAKO, VGH judgment 17.10.1942–6 J 130/44–1 H 236/44.
72. See ref. 66, ORA Lagebericht 10.2.1944.
73. Information from Frau Karla Zapf, Munich, whose testimony is supported by that of numerous other visitors to Vienna at the time.
74. BAKO, VGH judgment 12.2.1943–7 J 572/42–1 H 336/42; VGH judgment 10.5.1943–1 J 169/43–1 H 92/43; VGH judgment 7.12.1944, file reference illegible; IfZg Fa 117/302, indictment 25.1.1945–7 645 corresponding with VGH judgment in BDC but without file reference.
75. Erlass des Führers Und Reichkanzlers über die Gewährung von Straffreiheit, 7.6.1939 *RGBl.* I, 1939, p. 1032; see also BAKO R 22/20113, Akten R 22 Gr.5/XXIII–2, RJM, Vol. 2.
76. *ibid.*
77. IfZg, NG–5359.
78. BAKO, Archiv des RJM, Akten Allg. Prozesse 1 XVII B/28.
79. *ibid.*, Archiv des RJM, R 22/957, Generalakten 4021 Su des RJM, betreffend Hoch- und Landesverrat in den sudetendeutschen Gebieten.
80. *ibid.*
81. *ibid.*
82. BAKO, VGH judgment, 8.7.1943–12 J 53/43–1 H 152/43.
83. *ibid.*, VGH judgment, 27.8.1943–12 J 97/43–1 H 184/43.
84. *ibid.*, Archiv des RJM, R 22/957, Generalakten 4021 des RJM betr. Hoch- und Landesverrat in den sudetendeutschen Gebieten und im Reichsprotektorat. Staatssekretär Karl-Hermann Frank and RJM 22.10.1942; BDC, VGH judgment 4.9.1942–12 J 335/41g–1 H71/42.
85. *ibid.*, VGH judgment 15.6.1944–12 J 43/44g–1 H 63/44.
86. *ibid.*, VGH judgment 14.8.1941–12 J 50/41–1 H 80/41.

87. Mastny, *op. cit. passim.* as well as personal recollections by the author at that time.

88. The most detailed report of this event and its background is to be found in A. Burgess, *Seven Men at Daybreak*, London 1960, *passim*.

89. H. Blau, 'Die Kriminalität in Deutschland während des Zweiten Weltkrieges' in: *Zeitschrift für die gesamte Strafrechtsweissenschaft*, 1952, p. 37ff.

90. Stanislav E. Berton, 'Das Attentat auf Reinhard Heydrich vom 27. Mai 1942. Ein Bericht des Kriminalrats Heinz Pannwitz' in: *VfZg*, Munich 1985, p. 668f and especially pp. 674 and 688ff.

91. BAKO, VGH judgment 28.3.1944–13 J 46/44–1 H 34/44.

92. The author is recalling his personal experience on the staff of Radio Free Europe in Munich and London.

93. BAKO, VGH judgment 16.6.1944–12 J 37/44–1 H 107/44; VGH judgment 8.7.1943–12 J 71/43g–1 H 153/43; VGH judgment 18.3.1942–8a J 248/40g–1 27/42; VGH judgment 13.1.1942–12 34/41–1 H 167/42; VGH judgment 16.7.1943–J 595/42–1 H 7/43; VGH judgment 25.1.1944–J 84/43–1 H 7/43.

94. See H. Böhme, *Der deutsch-französische Waffenstillstand im Zweiten Weltkrieg*, Stuttgart 1966, *passim*.

95. E. Jaeckel, *Frankreich in Hitlers Europa*, Stuttgart 1966, p. 75ff.

96. BAKO, VGH judgment 7.7.1943–5 J 80/43–1 H 142/43.

97. BAKO, VGH judgment 4.5.1943–1 J 42/43g–2 L 43/43; VGH judgment 25.1.1944–6 J 41/44–1 H 284/83; VGH judgment 27.4.1944–9 J 161/42g.

98. Vo über die vorläufige Gerichtsbarkeit in den wiedereingegliederten deutschen Ostgebiete vom 15.10.1939, *RGBl.* I, 1939, p. 916.

99. For details see Franks *Dienstagebuch . . . op. cit. passim*.

100. See N. Rich, *Hitler's War Aims*, Vol. II, London 1974, p. 84ff.

101. *Anatomie des SS-Staates*, *op. cit.*, Vol. I, p. 153ff, 182ff; Vol. II, p. 235ff.

102. BAKO, Lagebericht des ORA 2.10.1941.

103. BDC, Handakten des ORA 8 J 214/41; VGH judgment 18.12.1941–8 J 149/41–2 H 145/41; BAKO, VGH judgment 26.11.1940–8 J 408/40g–2 H 87/40; VGH judgment 6.1.1942, file signature illegible; see also Lagebericht des ORA vom 8.10.1943.

104. BAKO R 22/4062, RJM Akten R 22 Gr.5/535, Reichsstatthalter und Gauleiter Dr. Friedrich Rainer to RJM, 4.2.1943.

105. *ibid.*, Gauleiter Siegfried Uibereither to RJM, 16.3.1943.

106. BAKO Generalakten des RJM R 22/302, also 4021 which show that Rothenberger seems to have favoured the establishment of VGH branches but met with firm opposition from both Thierack and Freisler.

107. BAKO, VGH judgment 9.4.1943–J 142–45–1 H83, 84, 85, 86/43 and judgment of the same day 6 J 18/43g–1 H 8743.

108. BDC, NG–417, Bericht über die Rede des Reichsministers Dr Goebbels vor den Mitgliedern des Volksgerichtshofes vom 22.7.1942.

109. BDC, NG–130, Strafrecht gegen Polen und Juden in den eingegliederterten Ostgebieten 28.4.1941; NG–131 Lammers to Gürtner 27.5.1941; NG–744 Freisler to OLGs und Generalstaatsanwälte 'Polen und Juden in Verfahren gegen Deutsche' vom 7.8.1942; IfZg, NG–412 OKW to RJM 17.8.1942; NG–151, RJM to all ministries 13.9.1942: Rechtsmittelbeschränkung für Juden. Zweite VO zur Ergänzung der VO über die Strafrechtspflege gegen Polen und Juden in den eingegliederten Ostegieten vom 21.4.1943, *RGBl.* I, 1943, p. 252.

110. BDC, NG–199 Thierack Erlass über Personaländerungen im RJM und im Richterstand 20.10.1942; VO vom 31.3.1943 über Personalmassnahmen zum Neuaufbau der Justiz, *RGBl.* I, 1943, p. 359.

111. See ref. 108, Thierack to Goebbels 2.10.1942.

112. ORA Lagebreicht vom 3.10.1942 *op. cit.*, see also BAKO, *Führerinformation* 1942, No. 131.

113. IfZg, NG–097 Schlegelberger affidavit.

114. BDC, NG–631 Thierack an die höheren Justizbehörden 20.10.1942.

115. See *Personalakte Freisler op. cit.* which contains ample evidence of this.

116. BDC, NG–108, Freisler to Thierack 5.11.1942.

117. BDC, NG–322, Evangelisch-Lutherischer Kirchenrat to Thierack 28.12.1942 and RJM rejection 13.1.1943.

118. BDC, NG–235, Vorsitzender des Sondergerichts Essen to Landesgerichtspräsident 4.1.1943; RJM response on 18.1.1943 and 1.2.1943 respectively.

119. BDC, NG–439, Der SS-Richter beim Reichsführer-SS und Chef der Deutschen Polizei, SS-Obersturmbannführer Munder, an Staatssekretär Rothenberger 19.1.1943; NG–330 to GStA Vienna, 5.3.1943; NG–269 Thierack to VGH and OLGs demanding that specific executions be kept secret and not be published; NG–302 Lammers to Thierack, 17.8.1943 urging upon him Hitler's demand for speedy executions because of the excessive numbers of prisoners in prison; Thierack to Justizbehörden, 8.9.1943, ordering speedy executions.

120. BDC, NG–316, Freisler to Lautz, 9.2.1943; see also contradictory affidavits ref. 54 above.

121. BDC, see ref. 119, Thierack to Justizbehörden.

122. BDC, NG–310, Richtlinien und Auswahl von Laienreichtern und Richtern, 5.5.1943.

123. BAKO, ORA Lageberichte *op. cit.*, also in BDC, NG–671, ORA Lautz Lagebericht vom 19.2.1944. Thierack forwarded it to Freisler on 15.3.1944 together with note on 'confessionally orientated' actions against the state.

124. As the Plan of Business Distribution operated from the beginning of each year it would include indictments that had been drawn up from 1 January, or cases that were left over from the previous year.

125. BAKO Generalakten RJM, *op. cit.*, Geschäftsverteilungsplan des VGH für 1944.

126. BDC, NG–783, Gauleitung Kärnten an RJM. 3.6.1944.

127. BDC, NG–646, Erlass des Führers über die Verfolgung politischer Straftaten. von Angehörigen der Wehrmacht, Waffen-SS und Polizei vom 20.9.1944. This decree was *not* published in the *Reichsgesetzblatt.*

128. BDC, NG–260, 'Rechtsanwaltbriefe', 1.10.1944.

129. BDC, NG–252, Freisler, 'Die Strafrechtspflege im fünften Kriegsjahr' undated.

130. BAKO, Generalakten RJM, *op. cit.*, Thierack to Freisler, 18.10.1944.

131. BAKO, Generalakten RJM, *op. cit.*, RJM to SS-*Obersturmbannführer* Bender, 17.12.1942 in which RJM rejects complaints from Vienna NSDAP that VGH sessions are conducted by 'Berliners'; Thierack to Freisler, 19.9.1943, in which Thierack objects to Freisler's extremely narrow interpretation of 'public' (Öffentlichkeit) to which Freisler replied on 28.9.1943 defending his attitude on the grounds of the inherent danger of *Wehrkraftzersetzung*; see also letter by Melitta Wiedemann to Thierack, 16.11.1943, details on p. 172ff and below); Thierack to Freisler, 22.11.1943 complaining about Freisler's excessive concentration of important cases in his own Senate; Thierack to Freisler, 18.10.1944,

asking him to emphasise more strongly the political valuation of a crime.

132. W.v. Seydlitz-Kurzbach, *Stalingrad*, Berlin 1977, p. 273ff.; H. Graf von Einsiedel, *Tagebuch einer Versuchung*, Berlin 1950, *passim.*; Autorenkollektiv, *Sie kämpften für Deutschland*, Berlin 1955 *passim.*; K.-H. Friesner, *Krieg hinter Stacheldraht*, Mainz 1981, *passim.*

133. On this complex, though not always accurate on detail, see H. Rothfels, *Die deutsche Opposition gegen Hitler*, Frankfurt 1958, p. 59ff; G. Ritter, *Carl Goerdeler und die deutsche Widerstandsbewegung*, Munich 1964, pp. 110ff, 407, 527ff; P. Hoffmann, *Widerstand, Staatsstreich, Attentat*, Munich 1969, pp. 40, 50ff, 284, 290, 429, 747, 748, 773, 790 and 791.

134. *Deutschland im Zweiten Weltkrieg*, Autorenkollektiv der Akademie der DDR, Berlin 1978, Vol. 3, p. 307ff.

135. BAKO, *Führerinformation* 1945, no. 190.

136. Freisler letter, 2.10.1943.

137. *ibid.*, 4.2.1944.

138. BDC, NG–3999, Lammers to Thierack, 29.7.1944, with unsigned copy of the letter.

139. *ibid.*; the precise date when VGH sessions were closed to the general public can no longer be established with any certainty. Possibly with the beginnings of the bomb plot trials.

140. See ref. 131, Freisler reply to Thierack 28.9.1943.

141. *ibid.*; Melitta Wiedemann letter, 16.11.1943.

142. *loc. cit.*

143. BAKO, Generalakten RJM, *op. cit.* Fernschreiben Thieracks an Bormann 18.4.1944.

144. *ibid.*; Thierack to Freisler 19.4.1944.

145. BDC, NG–3999 undated and unsigned copy of a member of the RSHA.

146. BAKO, Generalakten RJM, *op. cit.*, report by unnamed RJM official on a Freisler lecture and forwarded to Thierack.

## Chapter 9: Conspiracies Against Hitler and the NS Regime

1. About this attempt no other documents exist than BAKO, *Führerinformation*, 1942, no. 132.

2. For this and the following see L. Gruchmann (ed.) *Autobiographie eines Attentäters: Johann Elser*, Stuttgart 1970, p. 7ff.

3. *ibid.*, p. 9.

4. On Best and Payne see H. Höhne, *Der Orden unter dem Totenkopf*, Gütersloh 1967, p. 267, and *Autobiographie . . . op. cit.*, p. 18ff.

5. *Autobiographie . . .* p. 20.

6. *VB*, 22.11.1939, p. 2.

7. *loc. cit.*

8. Boberach, *Meldungen . . . op. cit.*, p. 18, SD reports 10.11.1939, 13.11.1939, 22.11.1939; also BAKO, Misch. 1792, 'Stimmungsgemässer Überblick über die gesamtpolitische Lage im Kreis Wiesbaden', also BAKO, 58/144; R/58/145.

9. Boberach, *Meldungen . . . op. cit.* SD Report 10.11.1939.

10. BAKO R 22 Gr.5./5–12 VGH judgment 25.9.1944 10 J 26/44; for literature on

Römer see Rothfels, *Opposition* . . . *op. cit.*, p. 57; Hoffmann, *Widerstand* . . . *op. cit.*, pp. 36, 49, 50, 53, 299, 676, and 677.

11. Rothfels, *Opposition* . . . *op. cit.*, p. 51, 70, 120; Ritter, *Goerdeler*, *op. cit.*, p. 91ff; Hoffmann, *Widerstand* . . . *op. cit.*, p. 34, 240, 247.

12. K.-J. Müller, *Das Heer und Hitler*, Stuttgart 1969, p. 593ff.

13. H. Mommsen, 'Hitlers Stellung im nationalsozialistischen Herrschaftssystem' in G. Hirschfeld and L. Kettenacker (eds) *Der 'Führerstaat'* . . . *op. cit.*, p. 55ff.

14. Ch. Dipper, 'Der deutsche Widerstand und die Juden' in *Geschichte und Gesellschaft*, Göttingen 1983, pp. 349ff.

15. Hans Adolf Jacobsen (ed.) *Spiegelbild einer Verschwörung*, Stuttgart 1984, Vol. 1, p. 449ff. This is, but for editorial commentary and a few further documents, the same version as that of Archiv Peter published under the same title in 1961, the previous one-volume edition now expanded into two volumes by using a larger typeface.

16. K. Schwabe and R. Reichardt (eds) *Gerhard Ritter. Ein politischer Historiker in seinen Briefen*, Boppard/Rhein 1984, p. 769ff.

17. Müller, *Das Heer* . . . *op. cit.*, p. 198ff.

18. *ibid.*, p. 255ff; H.C. Deutsch, *Hitler and his Generals*, Minnesota 1974, p. 78ff; N.v. Below, *Als Luftwaffenadjudant bei Hitler*, Mainz 1980, p. 238ff.

19. Müller, *Das Heer* . . . *op. cit.*, p. 198ff.

20. *ibid.*, *loc. cit.*; Deutsch, *Hitler* . . . *op. cit.*, p. 190.

21. Müller, *Das Heer* . . . *op. cit.*, p. 104; Rothfels, *Opposition* . . . *op. cit.*, p. 63, p. 70ff; Ritter, *Goerdeler* . . . *op. cit.*, p. 132ff; p. 158ff; Hoffmann, *Widerstand* . . . *op. cit.*, p. 69ff; K.-J. Müller, *General Ludwig Beck*, Boppard/Rhein 1980, p. 272ff.

22. Public Record Office, London, (PRO) FO 371/29733, C.5933 Vansittart Memorandum 6 July 1937; FO 371/21665, C.14809 Goerdeler Memorandum, 22 November 1938. These are but a few of many examples. See also I. Colvin, *Vansittart in Office*, London 1965, p. 150ff.

23. Rothfels, *Opposition* . . . *op. cit.*, p. 64ff.; Ritter, *Goerdeler* . . . *op. cit.*, p. 200ff; Hoffmann, *Widerstand* . . . *op. cit.*, p. 94ff.

24. K. Feiling, *Life of Neville Chamberlain*, London 1947, p. 418; *Documents on British Foreign Policy* (DBFP), Third Series, Vol. VII, no. 597, Lipski's assessment of German morale; B. Martin, *Friedensinitiativen und Machtpolitik im Zweiten Weltkrieg*, Düsseldorf 1973, p. 49ff, p. 207ff. The PRO file PREMIER 1–333 'Germany 1939' is closed to the historian until 1990, the file concerning Best and Payne until 2017.

25. Ritter, *Goerdeler* . . . *op. cit.*, p. 245ff; Hoffmann, *Widerstand* . . . *op. cit.*, p. 146ff; I. Colvin, *Hitler's Secret Enemy*, London 1951, p. 98f; H. Höhne, *Canaris*, Gütersloh 1977, p. 365ff.

26. BAKO R 58/214, Ereignismeldung No. 26, 18.7.1941; International Military Tribunal, Trial of the Major German War Criminals (IMT) Vol. XXXVIII, p. 712, Doc. 108–L.

27. *ibid.*, (IMT) p. 671; Gesamtbericht vom 15.10.1941.

28. BAMA, AOK 17/14499/51; OKH/GenStH/HWesAbt (Abw.) No. 2111/41, 12.7.1941.

29. As cited by Ch. Streit, *Keine Kameraden*, Stuttgart 1978, p. 312.

30. For Nebe see Krausnick and Wilhelm, *Die Truppe des Weltanschauungskrieges op. cit. passim.*; Rothfels, *Opposition* . . . *op. cit.*, p. 183, does not mention

Nebe's activities as head of an *Einsatzgruppe* at all; see the highly unreliable memoirs of H.B. Gisevius, *Bis zum bitteren Ende*, Zürich 1954, p. 497; Ritter, *Goerdeler* . . . *op. cit.*, p. 198 claims Nebe to have been a member of resistance since 1938 but gives no source. Hoffmann, *Widerstand* . . . *op. cit.* relies largely on Gisevius, see p. 63, and on p. 316 asserts Nebe had joined the Einsatzgruppen on the urging of Gisevius, a claim which even Gisevius does not make. See also ref. 20, Ereignismeldung vom 30.6.1941, Streit, *Keine Kameraden op. cit.*, p. 535.

31. W. Görlitz, *Kleine Geschichte des deutschen Generalstabs*, Berlin 1967, p. 400; Ritter, *Goerdeler* . . . *op. cit.*, p. 360ff.; H.A. Jacobsen and J. Rohwer, (eds) *Decisive Battles of World War II*, London 1965, p. 137ff.

32. Jacobsen and Rohwer, *Battles* . . . *op. cit. loc. cit.*

33. Ritter, *Goerdeler* . . . *op. cit.*, p. 357ff, p. 519, note 362.

34. W.S. Churchill, *The Second World War*, Vol. 4, London 1951, p. 541ff.

35. F.v. Schlabrendorff, *Offiziere gegen Hitler*, Frankfurt 1959, pp. 94, 99; R.Ch.v. Gersdorff, *Soldat im Untergang*, Berlin 1977, p. 132.

36. For Stauffenberg's biography see Ch. Müller, *Oberst i.G. von Stauffenberg*, Düsseldorf 1971.

37. General a.D. Johann Adolf Graf Kielmansegg on p. IX of his introduction to M. Messerschmidt, *Die Wehrmacht im NS-Staat*, Hamburg 1969.

38. See E. Bethge, *Dietrich Bonnhoefer*, Munich 1967, *passim*.

39. For an assessment of the *Kreisau* circle, see Rothfels, *Opposition* . . . *op. cit.*, p. 120ff; Hoffmann, *Widerstand* . . . *op. cit.*, p. 247.

40. Hoffmann, *op. cit.*, p. 249.

41. Hoffmann, *Widerstand* . . . *op. cit.*, p. 249; see also H. Mommsen, 'Fritz-Dietlof Graf von der Schulenberg und die preussische Tradition' in *VfZg*, 1984, p. 213ff.

42. Hoffmann, *op. cit.*, p. 253.

43. *ibid.*, p. 252.

44. For Moltke's biography see M. Balfour and J. Frisby, *Helmuth von Moltke: A leader against Hitler*, London 1972, *passim*.

45. Ritter, *Goerdeler* . . . *op. cit.*, p. 316.

46. Hoffmann, *Widerstand* . . . *op. cit.*, p. 240.

47. Rothfels, *Opposition* . . . *op. cit.*, p. 122ff.

48. *ibid.*, pp. 126, 131.

49. *ibid.*, p. 133f.

50. Hoffmann, *Widerstand* . . . *op. cit.*, p. 231.

51. Archiv Peter, *Spiegelbild* . . . *op. cit.*, p. 389, 390ff.

52. Rothfels, *Opposition* . . . *op. cit.*, p. 37; Ritter, *Goerdeler* . . . *op. cit.*, p. 389; Hoffmann, *Widerstand* . . . *op. cit.*, p. 299, 448; *Spiegelbild* . . . *op. cit.*, p. 351, 421, 547.

53. Hoffmann, *Opposition* . . . *op. cit.*, p. 448.

54. *loc. cit.*

55. Ritter, *Goerdeler* . . . *op. cit.*, p. 416ff; Hoffmann, *Widerstand* . . . *op. cit.*, p. 415. But in view of the sources cited by Ritter and Hoffmann there is still ample room for doubt whether Rommel belonged to the conspirators. He agreed with the view that victory for Germany was out of reach, once and for all, and that *something* needed to be done. It is about the something that no clarity exists. Nevertheless Rommel has been appropriated by the German resistance since 1945.

56. This applies to von Kluge, von Manstein, Guderian as well as Waffen-SS Generals Hausser and Sepp Dietrich. See ref. 30 Gersdorf, *Soldat* . . . *op. cit.*, p. 123ff,

134ff, and 155ff; Ritter, *Goerdeler, op. cit.*, p. 379. H. Lehmann, *Die Leibstandarte*, Vol. N/1, p. 318, Osnabrück 1987.

57. See the indications contained in Ritter, *Goerdeler ... op. cit.*, p. 450; Salomon, *Fragebogen op. cit.*, p. 396.

58. Information supplied by Oberstleutnant a.D. F.W. Heinz to author, August 1968; also Salomon, *Fragebogen loc. cit.*; on Popitz's role see Ritter, *Goerdeler ... op. cit.*, p. 451ff; G. Reitlinger, *SS – Alibi of a Nation, op. cit.*, p. 298ff.

59. H.W. Hagen, *Zwischen Eid und Befehl*, Munich 1958, p. 21; *Spiegelbild ... op. cit.*, pp. 12, 14, 15.

60. Hagen, *... Eid ..., op. cit.*, p. 24.

61. *ibid.*, p. 54; for Remer's own account see O.E. Remer, *Verschwörung und Verrat um Hitler*, Preussisch Oldendorf 1981, p. 24ff, p. 40ff.

62. Remer, *Verschwörung ... op. cit.*, p. 55; Hoffmann, *Widerstand ... op. cit.*, p. 602ff.

63. See the SD reports referred to below.

64. *Spiegelbild ... op. cit.*, pp. 1–3, Der Chef der Sicherheitspolizei und des SD, 21.7.1944 'Erste stimmungsmässige Auswirkungen des Anschlags auf den Führer'.

65. *ibid.*, pp. 4–5.

66. BAKO R 55/614; Berichte der Regierungspräsidenten Braunschweig, Hannover, Stuttgart, Stettin, Nürnberg, Königsberg; BAKO R 22/3369, OLG-Präsident Jena. For army response see BAMA R 55/575 Feldpostbriefe: Bericht des SD vom 30.10.1944 'Die Verschwörer vom 20. Juli und die Wehrmacht', also in *Spiegelbild ... op. cit.*, pp. 475–476; Militärgeschichtliches Forschungsamt Freiburg i. Br. (MGFA) H 34/1 Zensurberichte der Wehrmacht.

67. *ibid.*, Feldpostbriefe.

68. *Spiegelbild ... op. cit.*, p. 6.

69. G.C. Zahn, *Die deutschen Katholiken und Hitlers Krieg*, Cologne 1965, p. 185.

70. *ibid.*, *loc. cit.*

71. M.J. Gruffein and M. Janowitz, 'Trends in Wehrmacht Morale' in *Public Opinion Quarterly*, 1946, p. 81ff.

72. BAKO NS Misch/1634, Stimmungsbericht für den Kreis Schlüchtern 27.11.1944, see also *Spiegelbild ... op. cit.*, p. 10.

73. *Spiegelbild ... op. cit.*, p. 10.

74. On Robert Bosch see Ritter, *Goerdeler ... op. cit.*, pp. 158–160, 336ff and *passim.*; Hoffmann, *Widerstand ... op. cit.*, pp. 53, 76, 245, 685.

75. BAKO NS 19/Neu 830: SS-Sturmbannführer Backhaus an den persönlichen Referenten des Reichsführers-SS, Standartenführer Brandt, 26.8.1944.

76. BAKO R 55/164: Treuekundgebungen für den Führer; BAKO, Generalakten RJM, Der Chef der deutschen Sicherheitspolizei und des SD an RJM 31.8. 1944.

77. *Spiegelbild ... op. cit.*, p. 5.

78. *ibid.*, p. 7.

79. *ibid.*, pp. 10–11; BAKO R 55/601 Tätigkeitsbericht der Leiters der Propaganda-abteilung des RMVP, 7.8.1944.

80. W.v. Oven, *Finale Furioso*, Tübingen 1974, p. 36ff.

81. BAKO NS 6/vorl. 347, Bormann Rundschreiben vom 24.7.1944.

82. H. Heiber (ed.) *Reichsführer! ... op. cit.*, letter to SS-Gruppenführer Hermann Fegelein, 26.7.1944, p. 274.

83. BAKO NS 1/544, Sonderbericht des SD sent by Kaltenbrunner to Reichsschatz-meister Franz Xavier Schwarz, 7.8.1944.

84. Freisler letter, 1.8.1944.

85. See ref. 80, Sonderbericht des SD.

86. BAKO NS 6/411 Meldungen über die Entwicklung der öffentlichen Meinungs-bildung 12.8.1944.

87. BAKO R 55/601 Wöchentlicher Tätigkeitsbericht des stellvertrenden Leiters der Abt. Propaganda im RMVP, 18.9.1944; *ibid*. Führungsbericht vom 8.9.1944.

## Chapter 10: The Trial of the Conspirators

1. Hoffmann, *Widerstand . . . op. cit.*, p. 623. At this point it should be made clear that within the limits of this chapter only the most important, or perhaps significant cases before the VGH will be dealt with. It does not and cannot claim a comprehensive treatment of all cases which in terms of number of accused and number of court sessions would fill another book.

2. BAKO, Generalakten RJM *op. cit.*, Thierack to Bormann and Himmler, 24.7.1944.

3. H. Guderian, *Erinnerungen eines Soldaten*, Heidelberg 1950, p. 313.

4. Decree published in full in Domarus, *Reden, op. cit.*, Vol. 4, p. 2137ff.

5. See p. 155, refs. 51, 52; IfZg, *Führerinformation* 1944, No. 181; VGH judgment 2 J 243/44gRs. vom 18.7.1944.

6. Hoffmann, *Widerstand . . . op. cit.*, pp. 229, 448.

7. W. Wagner, *Die deutsche Justiz . . . op. cit.* (Chapter 1, ref. 3), p. 66.

8. *loc. cit.*

9. The author's attention was drawn to this by the last NS government deputy spokesman Helmut Sündermann in 1971. The author has carried out a corresponding experiment and finds Sündermann's observations confirmed.

10. A reprint of the full transcript of the first major trial would be desirable since the majority of versions, printed, filmed or recorded on records since 1945 omit vital sections. For instance Witzleben's attempt at offering the Hitler salute is cut from virtually every film clipping shown since 1945, although the complete film is available in BAKO, Film Archiv, Festung Ehrenbreitstein. The author follows in this first trial the Nuremberg Document 3881–PS, *Verhandlung vor dem Volksgerichtshof des Grossdeutschen Reiches gegen Witzleben und Genossen. Am 7. und 8. August 1944 im Grossen Plenarsaal des Kammergerichts Berlin*, pp. 300–530. Misspellings of names, etc., have been corrected.

11. Doc. 3881–PS, p. 305–306.

12. *ibid.*, p. 306.

13. It is worth noting that in the trial of British civil servant Clive Ponting, accused of violating the Official Secrets Act, the judge explicitly directed the jury to disregard Ponting's motives but to consider the points of law; see *The Times*, 9.2.1985; *Daily Telegraph*, 9.2.1985.

14. Doc. 3881–PS, p. 307.

15. *loc. cit.*

16. *ibid.*, p. 308.

17. *ibid.*, p. 309.

18. *loc. cit.*

19. *loc. cit.*
20. *ibid.*, p. 310.
21. *ibid.*, p. 313.
22. *ibid.*, p. 322.
23. *ibid.*, p. 348.
24. *ibid.*, p. 350.
25. *ibid.*, p. 351.
26. *ibid.*, p. 351.
27. *ibid.*, p. 356ff.
28. *ibid.*, p. 368.
29. *ibid.*, p. 370.
30. *ibid.*, p. 372.
31. *loc. cit.*
32. *ibid.*, p. 375.
33. *ibid.*, p. 377; E.v. Manstein, *Verlorene Siege*, Bonn, 1955, p. 614ff.
34. *ibid.*, p. 379.
35. *ibid.*, p. 380.
36. *ibid.*, p. 381.
37. *ibid.*, pp. 383ff.
38. *ibid.*, p. 384ff.
39. *ibid.*, p. 388.
40. *ibid.*, pp. 388, 392.
41. *ibid.*, p. 397.
42. *loc. cit.*
43. *ibid.*, p. 399.
44. *ibid.*, p. 405.
45. *ibid.*, p. 418.
46. *ibid.*, p. 420.
47. *ibid.*, p. 424.
48. Hoffmann, *Widerstand*, *op. cit.*, p. 869.
49. Lautarchiv des Deutschen Rundfunks, Frankfurt, VGH Verhandlung gegen Graf Hans-Bernd v. Haeften, Adam von Trott zu Solz vom 10.8.1944; see also BAKO NS 6/20, Prozessbericht an Bormann which contains v. Haeften's description of Hitler.
50. W. Wagner, *Die deutsche Justiz* . . . *op. cit.*, p. 676.
51. Doc. 3881–PS, p. 424.
52. *loc. cit.*
53. *ibid.*, pp. 424–425.
54. *ibid.*, p. 426.
55. *ibid.*, p. 428.
56. Freisler letter, 11.8.1944.
57. W. Wagner, *Die deutsche Justiz* . . . *op. cit.*, p. 676.
58. See for example A. Leber, *Das Gewissen entscheidet*, Berlin 1958, *passim.*; idem., *Das Gewissen steht auf: 64 Lebensbilder Aus dem deutschen Widerstand 1933–1945*, Berlin 1960; G. Weissenborn, *Der lautlose Aufstand*, Hamburg 1962; F.v. Schlabrendorff, *Offiziere gegen Hitler*, *op. cit.*
59. H.J. v. Moltke, *Letzte Briefe aus dem Gefängnis Tegel*, Berlin 1963, p. 68; also reproduced in *Germans against Hitler*, ed. by H.A. Jacobson, Bonn 1969, p. 252; see also Balfour and Frisby, *Moltke* . . . *op. cit.*, the German original is

contained in the German translation of the work, Stuttgart 1975, p. 313, and runs as follows: 'Dieser Brief ist in vielem auch eine Ergänzung zu meinem gestern geschriebenen Brief, der viel nüchterner ist. Aus beiden müsst Ihr eine Legende machen . . .'.

60. *Spiegelbild* . . . . *op. cit.*, p. 180.

61. *ibid.*, p. 182.

62. Schlabrendorff, *Offiziere* . . . *op. cit.*, p. 180ff, provides rather a gruesome picture, whether accurate is another matter. Though several of the Gestapo and Criminal Police Commission interrogators are still alive and their addresses known, neither Schlabrendorff, as long as he lived, nor anyone else in the Federal Republic has ever taken out criminal proceedings against any of them. Even Ritter, *Goerdeler* . . . *op. cit.* expresses his doubts about alleged torture as far as Goerdeler was concerned. Ritter himself, although imprisoned for belonging to Goerdeler's circle, was never subjected to torture. In fact he continued with his historical studies.

63. W. Wagner, *Die deutsche Justiz* . . . *op. cit.*, p. 681.

64. IfZg, NG–403 Wergin affidavit.

65. BDC, NG–5405 Lautz affidavit.

66. Doc. 3881–PS, p. 468.

67. *ibid.*, p. 454.

68. *ibid.*, p. 529.

69. Salomon, *Die Geächteten op. cit.*, p. 397; *idem.*, *Fragebogen op. cit.*, p. 113.

70. P. Sérant, *Les vaincus de la libération*, Paris 1965, p. 140ff; Boveri, *Der Verrat* . . . *op. cit.*, 4 vols, *passim*.

71. G. Buchheit, *Soldatentum und Rebellion*, Rastatt 1961, p. 430, who provides no source for this assertion. Also he maintains that the film of the executions was shown in Hitler's headquarters. Neither Albert Speer, nor anyone of Hitler's surroundings, has ever seen this film. Buchheit's assertion is based on hearsay.

72. Author's own recollection.

73. BAKO NS Misch/1832, Kreisleitung Säckingen, 10.8.1944; Bericht von Kielpinski, 20.8.1944: 'Stimmungsmässige Auswirkungen der Verhandlungen vor dem Volksgerichtshof gegen die Attentäter vom 20.7.1944'. The report also records the existence of a dissenting minority opinion.

74. See Reitlinger, *SS – Alibi* . . . *op. cit.*, p. 298ff.

75. G. Reitlinger, *The Final Solution*, London 1961, p. 456ff; R. Hilger, *The Destruction of European Jews*, New York 1961, p. 631.

76. IfZg, Terminkalender des Reichsführers-SS 1.7.–31.12.1944.

77. J.W. Wheeler-Bennet, *The Nemesis of Power*, London 1954, p. 684; W.L. Shirer, *The Rise and Fall of the Third Reich*, London 1960, p. 1071.

78. *Germans against Hitler*, *op. cit.*, p. 211. Reports of the cameramen Erich Stoll and Sasse; BDC, NG–435 Strelow affidavit states, 'The execution was carried out in a manner that . . . stood on a stool and put the condemned man the noose around the neck. The assistants then lifted him up and the rope was fastened to a hook, after which the body was dropped.' In all cases the men were immediately unconscious, 'I am well informed from talks with higher officials that this kind of execution corresponded with the express wish of Hitler. At all costs he wanted to avoid the imitation of the British method, whereby the condemned falls through a trap door.' On the nature of the executions see also Hoffmann, *Widerstand* . . . *op. cit.*, p. 629. He states that individual executions lasted

between 7 and 20 seconds, but his knowledge is also based on hearsay.

79. IfZg, Mitteilung von Landesgerichtspräsident a.D. v. Molte Kiel.

80. BDC, Reichskommissar für die Festigung deutschen Volkstums, Staatshauptamt an Thierack, 22.10.1944.

81. *loc. cit.*

82. *ibid.*, Thierack and Himmler, 24.10.1944.

83. BDC, Feldkommandantur Himmler an RJM Thierack, 7.11.1944.

84. On this point see Hoffmann, *Widerstand . . . op. cit.*, p. 619ff, though the list of names he provides fails to mention any of those who had already been released late 1944, early 1945. The small group remaining was first interned in Dachau, though not within the main KZ compound, where they wore their civilian clothes or Wehrmacht uniforms. Early in April 1945 they were transferred to the Tyrol where they were liberated by German army units.

85. *Lautarchiv des Deutschen Rundfunks*, Frankfurt/Main, Verhandlung vom 10.8.1944 vor dem VGH.

86. *Spiegelbild . . . op. cit.*, p. 515.

87. *loc. cit.*

88. *loc. cit.*

89. *loc. cit.*

90. *loc. cit.*

91. *loc. cit.*

92. *ibid.*, p. 514.

93. For Helldorf's career, see Rothfels, *Opposition . . . op. cit.*, pp. 64f; Ritter, *Goerdeler . . . op. cit.*, p. 198, 243, 410, 426; Hoffmann, *Widerstand . . . op. cit.*, p. 65, 105ff; R. Wistrich, *Who's Who in Nazi Germany*, London 1982, p. 129 contains the most concise summary of his career. See also H.B. Gisevius, *Bis zum bitteren Ende*, *op. cit.*, although its reliability is doubtful.

94. See E.v. Weizsäcker, *Erinnerungen*, 2 vols, Munich 1950 *passim.*; Ritter, *Goerdeler . . . op. cit.*, pp. 237, 266, 356; Hoffmann, *Widerstand . . . op. cit.*, pp. 87, 135, 195ff, 266ff, 276ff, 287ff; Rothfels, *Opposition . . . op. cit.*, pp. 141–5.

95. *Spiegelbild . . . op. cit.*, p. 515.

96. BAKO NS6/20 *op. cit.* Prozessbericht an Bormann vom 11.8.1944; contrary to Hoffmann, *Widerstand . . . op. cit.*, p. 627, the report does not contain the slightest criticism of Freisler's conduct of the trial. But in this instance Hoffmann relies not on primary sources but on post-1945 publications such as memoirs, etc.

97. BAKO Z Sg 1–197/2(12) Aufzeichnungen der Gräfin Hardenberg aus Neuhardenburg; Staatsarchiv Hannover, Zeugenschrifttum, evidence of Scharfrichter Rüttger, 2.9.1949.

98. *Lautarchiv, op. cit.*

99. *ibid.*; Hoffmann, *Widerstand . . . op. cit.*, p. 627, again on the basis of post-1945 accounts and citing remarks that are not contained on the recording. The great merits which Hoffmann's study possesses are diminished by his treatment of the VGH trials which he manages to compress into three pages consisting almost exclusively of defiant remarks allegedly made by the accused but nowhere substantiated in the primary sources.

100. *Lautarchiv, op. cit.* VGH Verhandlung vom 21.8.1944; on Wehrle see B.M. Kempner, *Priester . . . op. cit.*, p. 453ff.

101. About Lindemann's death, see E. Wagner, *Der Generalquartiermeister. Briefe und Tagebuchaufzeichnungen des Generalquartiermeister des Heeres General der Artillerie Eduard Wagner*, Munich 1963, p. 614.

102. BAKO NS 6/19 Anklageschrift O J 43/44, reports of trial to Bormann dated 29.11.1944 and 2.12.1944.

103. *Spiegelbild* ... *op. cit.*, p. 570, reprint of VGH judgment 27.11.1944.

104. BAKO NS 6/21 Verhandlungsbericht.

105. See ref. 102.

106. BAKO NS 6/20 Verhandlungsbericht vom 12.1.1945.

107. Schlabrendorff, *Offiziere* ... *op. cit.*, p. 43.

108. BAKO NS 6/32 Verhandlungsbericht vom 16.3.1945 contain nothing which Schlabrendorff according to Hoffmann, *Widerstand* ... *op. cit.* is supposed to have said to the court, p. 627.

109. Hoffmann, *Widerstand* ... *op. cit.*, p. 628, for Fromm's 'Heil Hitler' salute he quotes the obscure *Rhein-Neckar-Zeitung*, 17.9.1946. The article quoted is by an anonymous author, no name is given.

110. See J. Kimche, *Spying for Peace*, London 1961, p. 111.

111. PRO FO 371/21665 Goerdeler Memorandum 22.11.1938; also FO 371/22961 and FO 371/22960 C.113; see also Lord Vansittart, *Mist Procession*, London 1958, p. 512ff.

112. Ritter, *Goerdeler* ... *op. cit.*, p. 343ff; 557ff; 572ff.

113. IfZg, Gestapo Leitstelle Berlin an RSHA 10.8.1944.

114. *Lautarchiv, op. cit.* VGH Verhandlung vom 7. und 8.9.1944.

115. BAKO NS 6/28, Prozessbericht an Bormann vom 9.9.1944.

116. *ibid.*

117. BDC, NG–5405 Lautz affidavit.

118. P. Kleist, *Zwischen Hitler und Stalin*, Munich 1950, p. 207ff; H.W. Koch, 'The Spectre of a Separate Peace in the East: Russo-German Peace-Feelers 1942–1944' in *Journal of Contemporary History*, London 1975, p. 531ff.

119. *ibid.*, see also Reitlinger, *SS – Alibi* ... *op. cit.*, p. 412.

120. *loc. cit.*

121. See J. Leber, *Ein Mann geht seinen Weg. Briefe und Reden*, Frankfurt 1952 *passim.*; W.G. Oschilewski, *Gustav Dahrendorf. Ein Kämpferleben*, Berlin 1955 *passim.*; IfZg, NG–798 Erklärung Gustav Dahrendorfs vom 17.10.1946; *Lautarchiv, op. cit.* VGH Verhandlung vom 20.10.1944; BAKO NS 6/35 Verhandlungsbericht.

122. H. Lüdemann, *In schweren Zeiten*, Hannover 1948, *passim.*

123. Hoffmann, *Widerstand* ... *op. cit.*, p. 635.

124. W. Hammer, *Hohes Haus* ... *op. cit.*, p. 40.

125. BAKO NS 6/20, Verhandlungsbericht an Bormann.

126. *ibid.*, Verhandlungsbericht an Bormann, 13.1.1945.

127. *ibid.*, Verhandlungsbericht an Bormann vom 18. und 19.1.1944.

128. *loc. cit.*

129. *loc. cit.*

130. IfZg, MB 11, Auszug aus dem VGH Urteil vom 3.10.1944 O J 26/44gRs–1 L 349/33; see also H. Maier, 'Die SS und der 20. Juli 1944' in *VfZg*, 1966, p. 299ff.

131. Ritter, *Goerdeler* ... *op. cit.*, p. 396ff.

132. BAKO NS 6/21, Verhandlungsbericht vom 9. und 10.1.1945; the report contains

also a summary of the judgment.

133. Hoffmann, *Widerstand* . . . *op. cit.*, p. 426.

134. See ref. 132, *loc. cit.*

135. BAKO, Archiv des RJM, Telex message by Secretary of State Rothenberger to Bormann reporting Freisler's death; *ibid.*, Bormann instructions that on Hitler's orders no state funeral was to be held. See obituary in *DJ*, 16.2.1945 and *DR*, 1945, p. 73.

136. *ibid.*

137. *ibid.*

138. Ritter, *Goerdeler* . . . *op. cit.*, p. 463, in prison Ritter was the neighbour of Fritz Goerdeler.

139. This is omitted by Wagner, *Deutſche Justiz* . . . *op. cit.*; for Nebe's activities see Krausnick and Wilhelm, *Die Truppe* . . . *op. cit. passim*; Reitlinger, *SS – Alibi* . . . *op. cit.*, p. 182. Giservius, *op. cit.* states that Nebe 'served a few months on the eastern front'.

140. See Chapter 9, ref. 28.

141. Ritter, *Goerdeler* . . . *op. cit.*, p. 428; Hoffmann, *Widerstand* . . . *op. cit.*, p. 572ff.

142. BAKO NS 6/20 Verhandlungsbericht, VGH judgment 3.3.1945.

143. See PRO files mentioned in ref. 111.

144. BAKO NS 6/22 Verhandlungsbericht vom 23.2.1945; see also B. Scheurig, *Ewald v. Kleist-Schmenzin. Ein Konservativer gegen Hitler*, Oldeburg 1968, *passim*.

145. Scheurig, *Ewald v. Kleist* . . . *op. cit.*, p. 198.

146. One historiographer of the German resistance movement asserts that no one dared to include a 'provocative utterance' in the official protocol. Why, then, was von Haeften's characterization of Hitler as 'the executor of evil' included? Another asserts that Freisler's reference to the extermination of the Jews 'escaped him', since this was kept strictly secret from the German people. Surely if the protocol had been manipulated this could have been eliminated in a 'cleaned up' version. There is nothing which the protocol adds or omits; it is a reliable source.

## Chapter 11: The Final Days of the VGH

1. BAKO R 22/302, Generalakten 3204 des RJM, Geschäftsverteilung für 1945.

2. J. Goebbels, *Tagebücher 1945. Ltzte Aufzeichnungen*, Hamburg 1977, p. 115.

3. BDC, Personnel file Dr Haffner, Harry.

4. Zentrale Stelle der Landesjustizverwaltung zur Aufklärung nationalsozialistischer Verbrechen, Ludwigsburg, Ord. No. 184, picture frame No. 124–131.

5. Ernst Klee, *Was sie taten – Was sue wurden. Ärzte, Juristen und andere Beteiligte am Krakken- oder Judenmord*, Frankfurt/Main 1987, p. 268ff.

6. *ibid.*, *loc. cit.*

7. Goebbels, *Tagebücher* . . . *op. cit.*, p. 241.

8. Figures extracted from personnel files at BDC and BAKO R 22/303, Generalakten des RJM.

9. Freisler in *DJ*, 1936, p. 656.

10. *ibid.*

11. BDC, Geschäftsverteilung für das Jahr 1936.

12. BDC, Geschäftsverteilung für das Jahr 1942 und Geschäftsverteiling des VGH für das Jahr 1943.

13. Compare Geschäftsverteilung für 1942 with that for 1943.

14. In spite of the scarcity of VGH documents the BAKO holds a substantial number of acquittals, in which, however, name and personal data have been erased. Also there are a number of judgments still classified because those formerly indicted are still alive.

15. IfZg, NG–555 Weimann affidavit; NG–400 Boden affidavit; NG–535 Grünwald affidavit, to mention but a few.

16. So OLG-Rat Dr Günter Gribbohm in a review of Buchheit's *Richter . . . op. cit. Deutsche Richterzeitung*, 1970, p. 87, who does not quote Hitler himself but Dr Werner Scheidt, a subaltern officer at Hitler's headquarters, who, however, on the basis of recent evidence of his former secretary, saw Hitler only once.

17. So Gribbohm, *op. cit.*

18. Author's archive.

19. Hammer, *Hohes Haus . . . op. cit.*, p. 118.

20. W. Wagner, *Deutsche Justiz . . . op. cit.*, p. 800.

21. BAKO, Generalakten, *Führerinformation* 1942, no. 123.

22. BDC, NG–302, Thierack to Justizbehörden, 8.9.1943, ordering speedy executions.

23. BAKO, Generalakten RJM, Thierack Rundschreiben vom 27.8.1943.

24. *ibid.*

25. *ibid.*

26. *ibid.*

27. *ibid.*

28. Archiv des Bundesjustizministeriums, Bonn, File I, p. 5.

29. *ibid.*; according to reports compiled by Thierack and Freisler; also in BAKO Archiv des RJM.

30. Letter by BAKO to author, 9.5.1981.

31. See ref. 23.

32. F.W. Seidler, 'Die Fahnenflucht in der deutschen Wehrmacht während des Zweiten Weltkrieges' in *Militärgeschichtliche Mitteilungen* (*MGM*), Freiburg 1977, issue 2, p. 23ff.

33. *ibid.*

34. For NKFD and BDO see Chapter 8 above and notes.

35. As asserted by Buchheit, *Richter . . . op. cit.*, p. 125ff.

36. See ref. 20.

37. *ibid.*

38. Herr Max Pfäffle, sen. Munich to author.

39. Manfred Messerschmidt and Fritz Wüllner, *Die Wehrmachtsjustiz im Dienste des Nationalsozialismus*, Baden-Baden 1987, *passim*. After having aborted a legal career, Prof Messerschmidt turned to history and he is now the 'leading historian' (*Leitender Historiker*) of the Militägeschichteliches Forschungsamt der Bundeswehr in Freiburg i. Br., an institution which in recent years has become so scandal-ridden that the Federal Ministry of Defence found itself compelled to intervene. It is highly significant that this study was published without the imprint of the MGFA.

40. Confirmed by Oven, *Finale . . . op. cit.*, p. 206ff.

41. *ibid.*; Goebbels not only propagandized the new V-weapons but firmly believed they would become available. For Goebbel's outbursts when their completion was delayed time and again see Oven, *op. cit.*, confirmed also by the relevant sections of Goebbel's hitherto unpublished diaries, photocopies of which are held by the IfZg.

42. Hitler himself is said to have commented to Luftwaffe General K.H. Bodenschatz: 'I know that Stauffenberg, Goerdeler and Witzleben have acted in the belief that they would save the German people through my death. But so far one thing has clearly emerged: These people did not have any plan as to what to do afterwards. They had no idea which of the armies would support them, which of the defence districts. Even the most immediate thing, to establish contact with the enemy they failed to achieve, yes, I have even been told that their offers of negotiation have been rejected by the enemy. Think about it, Bodenschatz, on the eastern front German soldiers are engaged in bitter battle. Almost 9 million. And imagine the effect! It would have become a war of everybody against anybody, a civil war within the German army. The Russians would have been the laughing third. They would have captured immense booty. Look, Bodenschatz, this in my view constitutes the crime of the assassins.' Bodenschatz interview in *Hausfreund für Stadt und Land*, Nuremberg, 26.6.1954.

43. Freisler letter, 26.10.1944.

44. *ibid.*

45. BAKO, Amtsblatt des Kontrollrats, no. 1, p. 22.

46. Gebhardt, *Handbuch der deutschen Geschichte* ed. by K.D. Erdmann, dtv-edition, Vol. 22, *Das Ende des Reiches und die Neubildung deutscher Staaten*, p. 189.

47. *Süddeutsche Zeitung* vom 26/27, January 1985, p. 3.

48. *IMT Case III, Das Nürnberger Juristenurteil, 3–4 Dezember 1947*, Hamburg 1948, p. 78.

49. S. Milgram, 'Behavioural Study of Obedience' in: *Journal of Abnormal and Social Psychology*, New York 1963, Vol. 67, part 4, p. 371ff; *idem.* 'Group Pressure and Actions against a Person' in: *ibid.*, 1964, Vol. 69, part 2, p. 137ff. The reference to Dr Mantell's experiment I owe to Dr Hans Meissner, Munich.

## Appendix: The Structure of the German Judiciary

1. *Gerichtsverfassungsgesetz* (GVG), Berlin 27 January 1977; *Strafprozessordnung* (StPO), Berlin 1 February 1877.

2. All these details are contained in both GVG and StPO.

3. *ibid.*

4. See *dtv*-Lexikon, Munich 1981, Vol. 7, p. 204.

5. G. Hugo, *Naturrecht als Philosophie des positivien Rechts*, Göttingen/Berlin 1819.

6. G.F.W. Hegel, *Grundlinien der Philosophie des Rechts*, Göttingen 1821; H. Glockner (ed.) *G.F.W. Hegel: Sämtliche Werke*, 26 vols, Berlin 1927, Vol. IX. For recent discussion of these points see E. Bloch, *Subjekt-Objekt*, Tübingen 1962; Th.W. Adorno, *Drei Studien zu Hegel*, Frankfurt 1976; H. Marcuse, *Vernunft und Revolution*, Cologne 1971.

7. R. Stamller, *Die Lehre vom richtigen Recht*, Göttingen 102; K. Binding, *Die Normen und ihre Übertretung*, 4 vols, Leipzig 1872; and G. Dulckheit, *Die Philosophie der Rechtsgeschichte*, Berlin 1901.

8. N. Hartmann, *Ethik*, Marburg 1910.
9. C. Schmitt, *Verfassungslehre*, Cologne 1957 (2nd and revised edition of the 1927 edition). By the same author, *Legalität und Legitimität*, Bonn 1932; *Über die drei Arten rechtswissenschaftlichen Denkens*, Berlin 1936; *Staat, Bewegung, Volk*, Berlin 1934. I want to express my gratitude for the advice given on these legal and theoretical questions by Herr Rechtsanwalt Dr Wilhelm Lotze, Soest, Germany.

# Sources

## UNPRINTED PRIMARY SOURCES

### Bundesarchiv Koblenz

*File Numbers*

R 22/302  R 22/3270  R 22/4693  R 22/4693  R 22/885  R 22/887  R 22/899
R 22/951  R 22/952  R 22/953  R 22/954  R 22/955  R 22/956  R 22/957
R 22/1032  R 22/1039  R 22/1044  R 22/1074  R 22/1099  R 22/1127
R 22/1462  R 22/3356  R 22/3357  R 22/3359  R 22/3366  R 22/3369
R 22/3380  R 22/4070  R 22/4088  R 22/4402  R 22/4694  R 22/5001
R 22/5003  R 22/5007  R 22/5011  R 22/20019  R 22/20026  R 22/20040
R 22/20113  R 22/20198  R 22 Nr. 3355–3389  R 58 Nr. 144–214  NS Misch.
NS 1  NS 5  NS 6  NS 19/246  NS 19/neu 830  NS 22  R 55 Nr. 600–614, 620
R 55 Nr. 570–599, 610/18  Z Sg 1–197
R 60 I  R 60 II/9  R 60 II/20  R 60 II/63  R 60 II/83  R 60 II/84  All. Proz. 1,
XVII B 2, B 5, B 6, B 19, B 20, B 24, B 28, B 33, B 42, B 44, B 98, F 2, F 4.
R 43 I/213  R 43 I/1020  R 43 I/2703  R 43 II/1145  R 43 II/1145a
R 43 II/1145b  R 43 II/1518  R 43 II/1517b  R 43 II/1517c  R 43 II/1130
R 54 II/1561  Nachlass Luetgebrune: 28, 29, 54, 55, 69, 70, 73, 142, 143, 145.
P 135/76  P 135/80  P 135/3147  P 135/6334  Kl. Erw. 379–4  NG–157
NG–176  NG–400  NG–401  NG–402  NG–471  NG–533  NG–535
NG–541  NG–555  NG–862  NG–866  NG–914  NG–954  NG–1007
NG–1103  NG–1243

### Bundesarchiv-Militärarchiv Freiburg

N 42/39  N 51/7  Wi I F 5/3211  AOK 17/14499/51  OKH/GenStH/HWesAbt.
(Abw.) Nr. 2111/41

### Archiv des Bundesjustizministeriums Bonn

Personalakte Freisler
Jahrestatistiken des Volksgerichtshofes
Geschäftsberichte der Reichsanwaltschaft

### Institut für Zeitgeschichte, Munich

Fa 117/302  Fa 117/308  Fa 117/320  MB 11
  Nuremberg Documents: 3881–B, NG–077, 097, 135, 147, 151, 156, 160, 186,

208B, 211, 223, 235, 254, 259, 276, 289, 232, 312, 333, 340, 351, 362, 393, 386,
399, 400, 401, 402, 403, 404, 408, 412, 434, 466, 470, 471, 486, 495, 175, 362, 316,
533, 535, 555, 566, 599, 656, 659, 665–PS, 682, 696, 737, 792, 798, 801, 823, 858,
862, 866, 912, 919, 950, 954, 973, 1005, 1007, 1307, 1343, 1474, 1483, 1485, 1540,
1566, 2150, 2217, 5359, 5405, 7373

## Berlin Document Center

ORA 8 J 214/41
  Nuremberg Documents: NG–071, 130, 131, 135, 157, 159, 176, 177, 190, 198,
199, 200, 244, 252, 253, 254, 247, 226, 256, 241, 228, 266, 269, 272, 287, 260, 226,
276, 302, 303, 235, 322, 323, 329, 330, 310, 316, 363, 369, 412, 417, 355, 352, 427,
435, 439, 473, 474, 470, 541, 555, 628, 630, 631, 642, 646, 671, 683, 659, 729, 737,
744, 783, 791, 792, 813, 817, 896, 912, 926, 937, 954, 971, 1243, 1307, 1474, 1483,
1566, 2929

## Militärgeschichtliches Forschungsamt Freiburg

H 34/1

## Bayerisches Hauptstaatsarchiv Abt. II (Geheimes Staatsarchiv)

MA 106 671    MA 106 673    MA 106 674    MA 106 676    MA 106 678
MA 106 679    MA 106 681    MA 106 683

## Hessisches Hauptstaatsarchiv Wiesbaden

Zug. 68/67

## Hauptstaatsarchiv Stuttgart

K. 750

## Staatsarchiv Hannover

Zeugenschrifttum
277

## Geheimes Preussisches Staatsarchiv Berlin-Dahlem

Rep. 90/2326

## Stadtarchiv Kassel

Akten des Einwohnermeldeamtes
Gerichtsakte S P. 21/27–22 (part of this file is also contained in Personalakte Freisler)
Zeitungsarchiv

## Public Record Office, London

FO 371/29733 C 5933    FO 371/21665 C 14809    FO 371/22961 C 173
FO 371/22960    PREMIER I – 333.

**Imperial War Museum, London**

Foreign Documents Centre: 271/46 C10S 4233, FD 332/46

**Author's archives**

Freisler correspondence, interviews


# PERIODICALS AND NEWSPAPERS

Archiv für Öffentliches Recht
Archiv für Rechts- und Staatsphilosophie
Archiv für zivilistische Praxis
Berliner Tageblatt
Civitas
Deutsche Richterzeitung
Deutsches Recht
Deutsche Justiz
Deutsche Juristenzeitung
Deutscher Reichs- und Preussischer Staatsanzeiger
Deutsche Allgemeine Zeitung
L'Europe Nouvelle
Frankfurter Hefte
Frankfurter Zeitung
Geschichte, Wissenschaft und Unterricht
Der Hoheitsträger
Juristische Wochenschrift
Juristische Schulung, Zeitschrift für Studium und Ausbildung
Kassoler Stadtzeitung
Kassoler Landbote
Kurhessische Landeszeitung
Münchner Neueste Nachrichten
Militärgeschichtliche Mitteilungen
Manchester Guardian
Neue Juristische Wochenschrift
Neue Zürcher Zeitung
Das Parlament
Public Opinion Quarterly
Reichsverwaltungsblatt
Das Schwarze Korps
Schriften der Hochschule für Politik
Süddeutsche Zeitung
The Times
Verwaltungsarchiv
Vierteljahrhefte für Zeitgeschichte
Völkischer Beobachter
Die Weltbühne
Die Zeit

Zeitschrift der Akademie des Deutschen Rechtes
Zeitschrift für Deutsches Recht
Zeitschrift für Politik

# PRINTED SOURCES

Abendroth, W., 'Das Problem der Widerstandstätigkeit der "Schwarzen Front" ' in
    *VfZg*, 1960, p. 188ff.
Adorno, Th.W., *Drei Studien zu Hegel*, Frankfurt, 1976.
*Amtsblatt des Kontrollrats* No. 1, Berlin, 1945.
Arendt, H., *Eichmann in Jerusalem*, Munich, 1964.

Bader, K.S., 'Die deutsche Justiz im Selbstzeugnis' in *Juristentag*, Issue 15, 1960, p. 1.
——, 'Strafverteidigung vor deutschen Gerichten im Dritten Reich' in *Juristentag*, Issue
    27, 1972.
'Badischer Volksgerichtshof' in *Deutsche Verwaltung*, 1938, p. 503ff.
Balfour, M. and Frisby, J., *Helmuth von Moltke: A leader against Hitler*, London,
    1972.
——, *Propaganda in War 1939–45*, London, 1979.
Barmeyer, H., 'Geschichte als Uberlieferung und Konstruktion – Das Beispiel der
    Dolchstosslegende' in *Geschichte, Wissenschaft und Unterricht*, Kiel, 1977,
    p. 257ff.
*Bayerisches Gesetzblatt*, Munich, 1919.
Becker, J., 'Zentrum und Ermächtigungsgesetz' in *VfZg*, Munich, 1961, p. 195ff.
Below, N.v., *Als Luftwaffenadjudant bei Hitler*, Mainz, 1980.
Bethge, E., *Dietrich Bonnhoeffer*, Munich, 1967.
Bewley, Ch., *Hermann Göring*, Göttingen, 1956.
Binding, K., *Die Normen und ihre Übertretung*, 4 vols., Leipzig, 1872.
Blau, H., 'Die Kriminalität in Deutschland während des Zweiten Weltkrieges' in
    *Zeitschrift für die gesamte Strafrechtswissenschaft*, 1952, p. 37ff.
Bloch, E., *Subjekt-Objekt*, Tübingen, 1962.
Boberach, H., *Meldungen aus dem Reich. Auswahl aus den geheimen Lageberichten
    des Sicher heitsdienstes der SS 1939–1944*, Neuwied, 1965; *ibid.*, 17 vols,
    Herrsching 1984.
Böhme, H., *Der deutsch-französische Waffenstillstand im 2. Weltkrieg*, Stuttgart,
    1966.
Bovarie, M., *Der Verrat im 20. Jahrhundert*, 4 vols., Hamburg, 1958–63.
Bracher, K.D., *Die Auflösung der Weimarer Republik*, Villingen, 1960.
Bracher, K.D., Sauer, W. and Schulz, G., *Die Nationalsozialistische Machtc greifung*,
    Cologne, 1962.
——, *Die deutsche Diktatur*, Frankfurt, 1973.
——, *Zeitgeschichtliche Kontroversen im Faschismus, Totalitarismus, Demokratie*,
    Munich, 1976.
Brandes, W., *Die Tschechen unter deutschem Protektorat*, Munich, 1964.
Brecht, A., *Vorspiel zum Schweigen. Das Ende der Weimarer Republik*, Vienna, 1948.
——, 'Die Auflösung der Weimarer Republik und die politische Wissenschaft' in *ZfP*,
    Munich, 1955, p. 296ff.

Broszat, M., 'Zur Perversion der Strafjustiz im Dritten Reich' in *VfZg*, 1958, p. 358ff.
——, 'Nationalsozialistische Konzentrationslager 1933–1945' in Buchheim, H., Broszat, M., Jacobsen, H.A. and Krausnick (eds) *Anatomie des SS-Staates*, Vol. II, Munich, 1967, p. 11ff.
——, *Der Staat Hitlers*, Munich, 1969.
Brüning, H., *Memoiren*, Stuttgart, 1967.
Buber-Neumann, M., *Als Gefangene bei Hitler und Stalin*, Munich, 1962.
Bucher, P., *Der Reichswehrprozess. Der Hochverrat der Ulmer Reichswehroffiziere 1929/1930*, Boppard/Rhein, 1967.
Buchheit, G., *Richter in roter Robe*, Munich, 1968.
*Bundesgesetzblatt*, Bonn, 1949–81.
*Bürgerliches Gesetzbuch*, Berlin, 1900.
Burgess, A., *Seven Men at Daybreak*, London, 1960.

Carsten, F.L., *The Reichswehr and Politics*, Oxford, 1966.
Celovsky, B., *Das Münchner Abkommen*, Stuttgart, 1958.
Colvin, I., *Hitler's Secret Enemy*, London, 1951.
——, *Vansittart in Office*, London, 1965.
Conway, J.S., *The Nazi Persecution of the Churches*, London, 1968.
Churchill, W.S., *The World Crisis*, 2 vols, London (n.d.).
——, *The Second World War*, 6 vols, London, 1947–53.

Dahrendorf, R., *Democracy and Society in Germany*, London, 1968.
Deist, W., 'Die Aufrüstung der Wehrmacht' in *Deutschland im Zweiten Weltkrieg*, ed. by Militärwissenschaftliches Forschungsamt, Freiburg, Vol. I, p. 371ff, Freiburg, 1981.
Delmer, S., *Black Boomerang*, London, 1962.
*Denkschrift des Reichsanwalts über den Hochverrat in der Rechtsprechung des Reichsgerichtes und des Staatsgerichtshofes zum Schutz der Republik*, Drucksache des Reichstages IV. Wahlperiode, Berlin, 1928.
Deuerlein, E., *Der Hitler-Putsch: Bayerische Dokumente zum 8./9. November 1923*, Stuttgart, 1962.
*Deutsche Richterzeitung*, January, 1932, 'Zum neuen Jahr!'
*Deutschland im Zweiten Weltkrieg*, Autorenkollektiv der Akademie der DDR, 6 vols, Berlin, 1978.
Diels, R., *Lucifer ante portas . . . es spricht der erste Chef der Gestapo*, Stuttgart, 1950.
Diehl-Thiele, P., *Partei und Staat im Dritten Reich. Untersuchungen zum Verhältnis von NSDAP und allgemeiner Staatsverwaltung 1933–1945*, Munich, 1969.
*Documents on German Foreign Policy*, Series C, (The Third Reich's First Phase) Vol. I, Washington D.C., 1957.
Domarus, M., *Hitlers Reden und Proklamationen 1932–1945*, 4 vols, Wiesbaden, 1973.
Dunke, H., *Die KPD von 1933 bis 1945*, Cologne, 1972.
Düsing, E., *Abschaffung der Todesstrafe*, Offenbach/Main, 1952.

Ebert, F., *Schriften, Aufzeichnungen und Reden. Mit unveröffentlichten Erinnerungen aus dem Nachlass*, 2 vols, Dresden, 1926.
Einsiedel, H. Graf v., *Tagebuch der Versuchung*, Berlin, 1950.

Ehrt, A., *Bewaffneter Aufstand*, Berlin, 1933.

Engert, O., 'Fünf Jahre Volksgerichtshof' in *VB*, 14 July 1939.

Erdmann, K.D. and Schulze, H. (eds) *Weimar: Selbstpreisgabe einer Demokratie*, Düsseldorf, 1980.

Eschenburg, Th., 'Systemzusammenbruch als historisches Phänomen – Weimar' in Hennis, W., Kielmannsegg, P. Graf, and Matz, U. (eds) *Regierbarkeit*, Vol. 2, Stuttgart, 1979, p. 47ff.

Eyck, E., *Geschichte der Weimarer Republik*, 2 vols, Zürich, 1956.


Fallada, H., *Bauern, Bonzen, Bomben*, Hamburg, 1965 (reprint of the 1931 edition).

Feiling, K., *Life of Neville Chamberlain*, London, 1947.

Fenske, H., 'Monarchisches Beamtentum und demokratischer Staat' in *Demokratie und Verwaltung. Schriftenreihe der Hochschule für Verwaltungswissenschaften Speyer*, Vol. 50, Berlin, 1972, p. 118ff.

——, 'Beamtenpolitik der Weimarer Republik' in *Verwaltungsarchiv*, Bonn, 1973.

——, 'Radikale im öffentlichen Dienst' in *Civitas*, Bonn, 1976, p. 121ff.

Fest, J., *Das Gesicht des Dritten Reiches*, Munich, 1963.

——, *Hitler*, Berlin, 1973.

Finer, H., *The Theory and Practice of Government*, Chicago, 1956.

Frank, H., (ed.) *Nationalsozialistisches Handbuch für Recht und Gesetzgebung*, Munich, 1935.

——, 'Leitsätze des Reichsjuristenführers zur richterlichen Unabhängigkeit' in *DJZ*, 1936, p. 179ff.

——, *Im Angesicht des Galgens. Deutung Hitlers und seiner Zeit auf Grund eigener Erlebnisse und Erkenntnisse*, Neuhaus, 1955.

Frankel, E., *The Dual State*, New York, 1941.

Freisler, R., *Grundsätzliches über die Betriebsorganisation*, Jena, 1922.

——, 'Rechtserneuerung, Rückblick und Ausblick' in *DJ*, 1934, p. 5ff.

——, 'Nationalsozialistisches Strafrecht und aufbauende Kritik' in *DJ*, 1934, p. 223ff.

——, 'Die Stellungs des Richters zur kriminellen Erbschaft der Novemberrepublik' in *DJ*, 1934, p. 303ff.

——, 'Hier kämpft die Jugend: Die drei Eidgenossen' in *DJ*, 1934, p.774ff.

——, 'Des Führers Tat und unsere Pflicht' in *DJ*, 1934, p. 850ff.

——, 'Aus Anarchie zur verantwortlichen Führung' in *DJ*, 1934, p. 1070ff.

——, 'Nationalsozialistisches Strafrecht: Erwiderung auf die Ausführungen von Prof. Gerland' in *DJ*, 1934, p. 417ff.

——, 'Aktive Rechtspflege' in *DJ*, 1934, p. 625ff.

——, 'Richter, Recht und Gesetz' in *DJ*, 1934, p. 1333ff.

Freisler, R., Luetgebrune, W., *et al.* Denkschrift des Zentralausschusses der Strafrechtsabteilung der Akademie für Deutsches Recht über die Grundzüge eines allgemeinen Deutschen Strafrechts, Berlin, 1935.

——, 'Grundzüge eines allgemeinen Deutschen Strafrechts' in *ZAkDR*, 1934, p. 161ff.

——, 'Der Versuch' in *ZAkDR*, 1934, p. 251ff.

Freisler, R., 'Rechtspflege und Verwaltung, Justizverwaltung und Richtertum' in *DJZ*, 1934, p. 168ff.

——, 'Das künftige Schwurgericht' in *DJ*, 1935, p. 151ff.

——, 'Gedanken zur Vereinheitlichung der staatlichen Rechtswahrung des deutschen Volkes', in *DJ*, 1935, p. 82ff.

——, 'Die Aufgaben der Reichsjustiz entwickelt aus der biologischen Rechtsauffassung' in *DJ*, 1935, p. 468ff.

——, 'Neue Grundsätze für die Auslese von Rechtswahrern' in *DJ*, 1935, p. 856ff.

——, 'Staatsnotwehr im Lichte des Nationalsozialismus' in *DJ*, 1935, p. 956ff.

——, 'Der Wandel der politschen Grundanschauungen in Deutschland und sein Einfluss auf die Erneuerung von Strafrecht, Strafprozess und Strafvollzug' in *DJ*, 1935, p. 1247ff.

——, 'Die Einheit von Partei und Staat in der Personalpolitik der Justiz' in *DJ*, 1935, p. 1685ff.

——, 'Der Volksverrat, Hoch- und Landesverrat im Lichte des Nationalsozialismus' in *DJZ*, 1935, p. 907ff.

——, 'Neues deutsches Strafrecht' in *DJZ*, 1935, p. 914ff.

——, 'Vom Majestätsverbrechen zum Volksverrat' in *DJZ*, 1935, p. 997ff.

——, 'Einiges vom werdenden deutschen Blutbanngericht', *DJZ*, 1935, p. 585ff.

——, 'Der Volksgerichtshof – das Reichsstrafgericht?' in *ZAkDR*, 1935, p. 90ff.

——, 'Strafprozessrecht' in *ZAkDR*, 1935, p. 33ff.

——, (ed.) *Der Volksrichter im neuen deutschen Strafrecht*, Berlin, 1936.

——, 'Deutsches Rechtsleben 1935 und 1936' in *DJ*, 1936, p. 50ff.

——, 'Die neuen Gesetze zur Behebung der Not des Rechtsanwaltstandes' in *DJ*, 1935, p. 1790ff.

——, 'Recht und Gesetz' in *DJ*, 1936, p. 151ff.

——, 'Die lebenswichtigen Aufgaben des Volksgerichtshofes' in *DJ*, 1936, p. 656ff.

——, 'Rasse als Träger und Ziel des deutschen Volksrechts, unter Berücksichtigung des Strafrechts' in *DJ*, 1936, p. 803ff.

——, 'Unser Hoheitszeichen' in *DJ*, 1936, p. 950ff.

——, 'Der Schutz von Rasse und Erbgut im werdenden deutschen Strafrecht' in *ZAkDR*, 1936, p. 142ff.

——, 'Der Rechtsstaat' in *DJ*, 1937, p. 151ff.

——, 'Einige Gedanken zu den ersten vier Jahren nationalsozialistischer Rechtsarbeit' in *DJ*, 1937, p. 212ff.

——, 'Rechtspolitische Gedanken zur Wiederaufnahme des Verfahrens' in *DJ*, 1937, p. 730ff.

——, 'Vom Schutzzweck der Strafrechtspflege gegenüber Volksschädlingen' in *DJ*, 1938, p. 365ff.

——, 'Arbeitseinsatz im Dienste des Vierjahresplanes' in *DJ*, 1938, p. 584ff.

——, 'Das Verbrechen des Angriffs auf den Führer (Paragraph 94 StGB)' in *DJ*, 1938, p. 837.

——, 'Zur neuen Justizausbildungsordnung' in *DJ*, 1939, p. 116ff.

——, 'Gedanken zum Gesetz gegen das räuberische Stellen von Autofallen' in *DJ*, 1939, p. 344.

——, 'Reich und Recht' in *DJ*, 1939, p. 444ff.

——, 'Zur Reichstagung der deutschen Ärzte des öffentlichen Gesundheitsdienstes' in *DJ*, 1939, p. 946ff.

——, 'Gedanken zum Deutschen Rechtswahrertag 1939' in *DJ*, 1939, p. 821ff.

——, 'Die Idee des Reiches und ihr Einfluss auf unser Rechtsdenken' in *DJ*, 1939, p. 937ff.

——, 'Gedanken zum nationalsozialistischen Arbeitsrecht' in *DJ*, 1939, p. 1110ff.

——, 'Zur Verordnung über ausserordentliche Rundfunkmassnahmen' in *DJ*, 1940, p. 41ff.

——, 'Justiz im Zeitgeschehen' in *DJ*, 1940, p. 105ff.

——, 'Die neue Methode der strafrechtlichen Zuständigkeitsbestimmung' in *DJ*, 1940, p. 281ff.

——, 'Nichtigkeitsbeschwerde' in *DJ*, 1940, p. 341ff.

——, 'Psychische Grundlage der Polengreuel, dargestellt an der Entwicklung des polnischen Volksgeistes' in *DJ*, 1940, p. 557.

——, 'Einfluss der Staatsauffassung auf den Geltungsbereich des Strafrechtes' in *DJ*, 1940, p. 637ff.

——, 'Verantwortungsauslastung' in *DJ*, 1940, p. 1058ff.

——, 'Rechtswahrergedanken zum Kriegsjahr 1940' in *DJ*, 1941, p. 6ff.

——, 'Das deutsche Polenstrafrecht' in *DJ*, 1941, Teil I, p. 29ff; Teil II, *DJ*, 1942, p. 22ff; Teil III, *DJ*, 1942, p. 41ff.

——, 'Preisgestaltung und Strafrecht' in *DJ*, 1941, p. 147ff.

——, '. . . noch kein vollwertiger Mitarbeiter . . .' in *DJ*, 1941, p. 422ff.

——, 'Kriegsdienstappeli deutscher Rechtswahrer' in *DJ*, 1941, p. 441ff.

——, 'Eignung zum Beruf des deutschen Rechtswahrers' in *DJ*, 1941, p. 645ff.

——, 'Deutscher Osten' in *DJ*, 1941, p. 737ff.

——, 'Deutsche Rechtswahrerausbildung' in *DJ*, 1941, p. 833ff.

——, 'Gedanken über das Gesetz zur Änderung des Reichsstrafgesetzbuches' in *DJ*, 1941, p. 929ff.

——, 'Der Rechtswahrer denkt, spricht und schreibt deutsch!' in *DJ*, 1941, p. 1113ff.

——, 'Von der Arbeit am Volksgesetzbuch' in *ZAkDR*, 1941, p. 104ff.

——, 'Ein Reich – ein Recht' in *DJ*, 1941, p. 478ff.

——, 'Deutsche Justiz in den Niederlanden' in *DJ*, 1942, p. 141ff.

Freyer, H., *Der Staat*, Leipzig, 1925.

Fritscher, F., 'Was ist ein Eingriff in die Berufsaufgaben des Rechtsanwalts?' in *JWS*, 1937, p. 525ff.

*Führerlexikon der NSDAP*, Munich, 1934.


Gaetringen, F. Frhr. Hiller v., ' "Dolchstoss" – Diskussion und "Dolchstosslegende" im Wandel von vier Jahrzehnten' in *Festschrift für Hans Rothfels*, Göttingen, 1962, p. 122ff.

George, Lloyd, *Memoirs*, 2 vols, London, 1938.

Gerland, Prof. Dr, 'Einige Anmerkungen zu der Denkschrift des Preussischen Justiz ministers' in *DJ*, 1934, p. 224ff.

*Gebhardt, Handbuch der deutschen Geschichte*, ed. by K.D. Erdmann, dtv-edition, Vol. 22, 'Das Ende des Reiches und die Neubildung deutscher Staaten', Munich, 1980.

Gersdorf, R. Chr. v., *Soldat im Untergang*, Berlin, 1977.

Gilbert, G.M., *Nuremberg Diary*, New York, 1960.

Gisevius, H.B., *Bis zum bitteren Ende*, Zürich, 1946.

Goebbels, J., *Tagebücher 1945. Die letzten Aufzeichnungen*, Hamburg, 1977.

Goldau-Schüttke, K.-D., *Staatssekretär Curt Joel*, Frankfurt/Main, 1981.

Goldhagen, E., 'Weltanschauung und Erlösung' in *VfZg*, 1976, p. 379ff.

Görlitz, W., *Kleine Geschichte des deutschen Generalstabes*, Berlin, 1967.

Gostomski-Loch, E.v., *Der Tod von Plötzensee*, Freising, 1966.

Greil, L., *Die Wahrheit über Malmedy*, Munich, 1958.

Gribbohm, G., 'Der Volksgerichtshof' in *Juristische Schulung. Zeitschrift für Studium und Ausbildung*, No. 2, 1969, p. 55ff.

Grimm, H., *Woher, Warum und Wohin?*, Lippoldsberg, 1954.

Grosscurth, H., *Tagebuch eines Abwehroffiziers*, Stuttgart, 1970.

Gruchmann, L. (ed.) *Autobiographie eines Attentäters: Johann Elser*, Stuttgart, 1970.

*Der Grossdeutsche Reichstag, IV. Wahlperiode. Beginn am 10. April 1938, verlängert bis zum 30. Januar 1947*, ed. by Büro des Reichstages, Berlin, 1943.

Gruchmann, L. 'Hitler über die Justiz. Das Tischgespräch vom 20. August 1942' in *VfZg*, 1964, p. 86ff.

Gruffein, M.J. and Janowitz, M., 'Trends in Wehrmacht Morale' in *Public Opinion Quarterly*, 1946, p. 81ff.

Guderian, H., *Erinnerungen eines Soldaten*, Heidelberg, 1950.

Gutman, Y., *The Jews of Warsaw 1939–1943*, Brighton, 1982.

Gumbel, J., 'La Psychologie du Meurte Politique en Allemagne' in *L'Europe Nouvelle*, Vol. V, Paris, 1922, p. 1066ff.

——, *Vier Jahre politischer Mord*, Berlin, 1922.

——, *Verschwörer: Beiträge zur Geschichte und Soziologie der deutschen nationalistischen Geheimbünde seit 1918*, Vienna, 1924.

——, *Verräter verfallen der Feme. Opfer, Mörder, Richter 1919–1920*, Berlin, 1929.

Gürtner, F. (ed.) *Das kommende deutsche Strafrecht. Allgemeiner Teil. Bericht über die Arbeit der amtlichen Strafrechtskommission*, Berlin, 1934.

——, 'Richter und Staatsanwalt im neuen Staat' in *DJ*, 1934, p. 369ff.


Hagen, H.W., *Zwischen Eid und Befehl*, Munich, 1958.

Hammer, W., *Hohes Haus in Henkers Hand: Rückschau auf die Hitlerzeit, auf Leidensweg und Opfergang deutscher Parlamentarier*, Frankfurt/Main, 1956.

Hamel, W., 'Die Aufgabe der Polizei im nationalsozialistischen Staat' in *DJZ*, 1936, p. 1465ff.

*Handbuch der Justizverwaltung*, Berlin, 1942.

Hartmann, N., *Ethik*, Marburg, 1910.

Hartung, F., *Deutsche Verfassungsgeschichte*, Stuttgart, 1968.

Hassel, U.v., *Vom anderern Deutschland*, Frankfurt, 1964.

Hegel, G.F.W., *Grundlinien der Philosophie des Rechts*, Göttingen, 1821.

——, *Sämtliche Werke*, ed. by H. Glockner, 26 vols, Berlin, 1927.

Heiber, H., 'Der Fall Elias' in *VfZg*, 1955, p. 275ff.

——, 'Der Fall Grynspan' in *VfZg*, 1963, p. 267ff.

——, (ed.) *Lagebesprechungen im Führerhauptquartier*, Munich, 1963.

——, (ed.) *Reichsführer!*, Munich, 1972.

Heiber, H. and Koke, H.v. (eds) *Facsimilie Querschnitt durch das Schwarze Korps*, Munich (n.d.).

Heims, H. and Jochmann, W., *Monologe im Führerhauptquartier 1941–1944*, Hamburg, 1980.

Hellfeld, M.v., *Edelweisspiraten in Köln*, Cologne, 1982.

Hellmer, J., *Der Gewohnheitsverbrecher und die Sicherheitsverwahrung 1934–1945*, Berlin, 1945.

Hempel, M., *Richterbilder in der Weimarer Republik*, Frankfurt, 1978.

Hempfer, W., *Die nationalsozialistische Staatsauffassung in der Rechtssprechung des Preussischen Oberverwaltungsgerichts. Dargestellt an ausgewählten Beispielen rechtsstaatlicher Grundsätze*, Berlin, 1974.

Herrfahrdt, H., 'Politische Verfassungslehre' in *Archiv für Rechts- und Staatsphilosophie*, Vol. XXX, Marburg, 1933.

——, *Die Verfassungsgesetze des Nationalsozialistischen Staates dem Text der Weimarer Republik gegenübergestellt*, Marburg, 1935.

Heuber, W., 'Der Bund Nationalsozialistischer Deutscher Juristen und die Deutsche Rechts-front' in *Nationalsozialistisches Jahrbuch 1933*, ed. by Reichsleitung der NSDAP, Munich, 1934, p. 1566ff.

Hilger, R., *The Destruction of the European Jews*, New York, 1961.

Hill, L.E., *Die Weizsäcker Papiere 1933–1945*, Berlin, 1977.

Hillermeier, H. (ed.) *In Namen des Volkes*, Neuwied, 1980.

Hintze, O., *Die Hohenzollern und ihr Werk*, Berlin, 1915.

Hirsch, M., 'Juristen sind zu allem fähig', interview in *Der Spiegel*, No. 22, 1981, p. 88ff.

*Der Hitlerprozess vor dem Volksgericht München*, Munich, 1924.

Hitler, A., *Mein Kampf*, Dünndruckausgabe, Munich, 1936.

Höhne, H., *The Order of the Death's Head*, London, 1969.

——, *Kennwort Direktor*, Gütersloh, 1967.

——, *Canaris*, Gütersloh, 1977.

Hofer, W., *Der Nationalsozialismus: Dokumente 1933–1945*, Frankfurt, 1957.

Hoffmann, G., *Sozialdemokratie und Berufsbeamtentum*, Hamburg, 1972.

Hoffmann, P., *Widerstand, Staatsstreich, Attentat*, Munich, 1969.

Hohenstein, A., *Wartheländisches Tagebuch*, Stuttgart, 1959.

Hönig, H., *Das Zentrum in Preussen in der Weimarer Republik*, Mainz, 1979.

Honnecker, E., *My Life*, London, 1980.

Horn, W., *Führerideologie und Parteiorganisation in der NSDAP*, Düsseldorf, 1972.

Hottenbauer, H., *Vom Reichsjustizamt zum Bundesministerium der Justiz. Zum 100-jährigen Gründungstag des des Reichsjustizamtes*, Cologne, 1977.

——, 'Zur Lage des Justiz in der Weimarer Republik' in *Weimar: Selbstpreisgabe einer Demokratie*, ed. by K.D. Erdmann and H. Schulze, Düsseldorf, 1980, p. 169ff.

Huber, E.R., 'Anmerkungen zur Entscheidung der Sondergerichts Darmstadt' in *JWS*, 1934, p. 1747ff.

——, *Vom Sinne der Verfassung*, Hamburg, 1935.

——, *Deutsche Verfassungsgeschichte seit 1789*, 7 vols, Stuttgart, 1957–1980.

Hugo, G., *Naturrecht als Philosophie des positiven Rechts*, Göttingen/Berlin, 1819.

Hüttenberger, P., 'Nationalsozialistische Polykratie' in *Geschichte und Gesellschaft*, 1976, p. 417ff.

International Military Tribunal, *Case III, 3–4 December 1947*, Washington D.C., 1948; in German *Das Nürnberger Juristenurteil*, 3–4 December 1947, Hamburg, 1948.

Irving, D., *The Trail of the Fox*, London, 1980.

Jacobsen, H.A. and Rohwer, J. (eds) *Decisive Battles of World War II*, London, 1967.

——, *Germans against Hitler*, Bonn, 1969.

Jäckel, E., *Frankreich in Hitlers Europa*, Stuttgart, 1966.

Jasper, G., *Der Schutz der Republik*, Tübingen, 1963.

Janssen, K.-H., 'Bomben, Bullen, Barrikaden' in *Die Zeit*, Zeitmagazin Nos. 20 and 21, Hamburg, 1981.

Johe, W., *Die gleichgeschaltete Justiz. Organisation des Rechtswesens und Politisierung der Rechtssprechung 1933–1945 dargestellt am Beispiel des Oberlandesgerichtes Hamburg*, Frankfurt/Main, 1971.

Johnston, D., *Nine Rivers from Jordan*, London, 1955.

*Judgment at Nuremberg*, HMSO, London, 1946.

Jünger, E., *Strahlungen*, Munich, 1955.

——, Interview with *Der Spiegel*, No. 22, Hamburg, 1982, p. 154ff.

Kaehler, S.A., 'Über die Herkunft des Schlagwortes "Im Felde unbesiegt" ' in *Vier quellenkritische Untersuchungen zum Kriegsende: Studien zur Geschichte des 19. und 20. Jahrhunderts*, Göttingen, 1961.

Kalbhen, U., *Die NS – Rechtstheorie als Herrschaftsideologie. Logische Struktur und soziale Funktion naturrechtlicher Konstruktionen im Nationalsozialismus*, Heidelberg, 1969.

Kehr, E., 'Zur Genesis der preussischen Bürokratie und des Rechtsstaats' in *Der Primat der Innenpolitik*, ed. by H.-U. Wehler, Berlin, 1965.

——, 'Das soziale System der Reaktion in Preussen unter dem Ministerium Puttkammer' in *Der Primat der Innenpolitik*.

Kempner, B.M., *Priester vor Hitlers Tribunalen*, Munich, 1966.

Kimche, J., *Spying for Peace*, London, 1961.

Klein, B.H., *Germany's Economic Preparations for War*, Cambridge, Mass., 1959.

Kleist, P., *Zwischen Hitler und Stalin*, Munich, 1950.

Klemperer, K.v., *Germany's New Conservatives*, Princeton, 1957.

Klose, W., *Generation im Gleichschritt*, Oldenburg, 1964.

Koch, H.W., 'Hitler and the Origins of the Second World War – Second Thoughts on the Status of some of the Documents' in *Historical Journal*, Cambridge, 1968, p. 125ff.

——, 'The Spectre of a Separate Peace in the East – Russo-German Peace Feelers 1942–1944' in *Journal of Contemporary History*, London, 1975, p. 331ff.

——, *The Hitler Youth: Origins and Development 1922–1945*, London, 1975.

——, *Der Deutsche Bürgerkrieg 1918–1924*, Berlin, 1978.

——, *A History of Prussia*, London, 1978.

Kochan, L., *Pogrom*, London, 1957.

Kolbe, D., *Reichsgerichtspräsident Dr. Erwin Bumke. Studien zum Niedergang des Reichsgerichts und der deutschen Rechtspflege*, Karlsruhe, 1975.

Koselleck, R., 'Staat und Gesellschaft in Preussen' in *Staat und Gesellschaft in deutschen Vormärz*, Stuttgart, 1962.

Kosyck, K., *Deutsche Pressepolitik im Ersten Weltkrieg*, Düsseldorf, 1968.

Kotowski, G., 'Preussen in der Weimarer Republik' in *Preussen: Epochen und Probleme seiner Geschichte*, ed. by R. Dietrich, Berlin, 1964.

Koellreuter, O., *Zur Entwicklung der Rechtseinheit*, Jena, 1935.

——, *Vom Sinn und Wesen der nationalen Revolution*, Tübingen, 1933.

——, *Der Führerstaat*, Tübingen, 1934.

——, *Volk und Staat in der Weltanschauung des Nationalsozialismus*, Berlin, 1935.

——, *Grundlagen des völkischen und staatlichen Lebens im deutschen Volksstaat*, Berlin, 1935.

——, *Deutsches Verfassungsrecht: Ein Grundriss*, Berlin, 1936.

——, *Deutsches Verfassungsrecht*, Berlin, 1938.

Kracauer, S., *From Caligari to Hitler*, Princeton, 1947.

Krausnick, H. and Wilhelm, H.-H., *Die Truppe des Weltanschauungskrieges*, Stuttgart, 1981.

Krebs, A., *Tendenzen und Gestalten der NSDAP. Erinnerungen an die Frühzeit der NSDAP*, Stuttgart, 1959.

Krebs, A., *Fritz-Dietlof Graf von der Schulenburg – Zwischen Staatsraison und Hochverrat*, Hamburg, 1964.

Krüger, H., *Führer und Führung*, Breslau, 1935.

Kübler, F.K., 'Der deutsche Richter und das demokratische Gesetz' in *Archiv für civilistische Praxis*, Vol. 162, 1963, p. 104ff.

Kühnl, R., *Die nationalsozialistische Linke 1925–1930*, Meisenheim/Glan, 1966.

Laqueur, W., *Young Germany*, London, 1961.

Lammers, H.H., 'Die Staatsführung im Dritten Reich' in *DJ*, 1934, p. 1296ff.

——, 'Zum 30. Januar 1942' in *Reichsverwaltungsblatt*, 1942, p. 43ff.

Leber, A., *Das Gewissen entschidef*, Berlin, 1957.

——, *Das Gewissen steht auf: 64 Lebensbilder aus dem deutschen Widerstand 1933–1945*, Berlin, 1954.

Leber, J., *Ein Mann geht seinen Weg. Briefe und Reden*, Frankfurt, 1952.

*Leipziger Kommentar zum Strafgesetzbuch*, Berlin, 1934–1944.

Lenin, W.I., *Ausgewählte Werke*, Berlin, 1955.

Lerner, D., *The Nazi Elite*, Stanford, 1951.

Lochner, L.P. (ed.) *The Goebbels Diaries*, London, 1948.

Luetgebrune, W., 'Femeprozess und Recht' in *VB*, Munich, 9 October 1928.

Marcuse, H., *Vernunft und Revolution*, Cologne, 1972.

Martin, B., *Friedensinitiativen und Machtpolitik im Zweiten Weltkrieg*, Düsseldorf, 1973.

Maser, W., *Die Frühgeschichte der NSDAP. Hitlers Weg bis 1924*, Frankfurt/Main, 1965.

Mason, T.W., *Arbeiterklasse und Volksgemeinschaft*, Cologne, 1975.

Mastny, V., *The Czechs under German Rule. The Failure of National Resistance*, New York, 1971.

Matthias, E., 'Die Sitzung der Reichstagsfraktion des Zentrums am 23. März 1933' in *VfZg*, 1956, p. 302ff.

Matthias, E. and Morsey, R., *Das Ende der Parteien*, Düsseldorf, 1960.

Merkl, P.H., *Violence under the Swastika*, Yale, 1975.

——, 'Die alten Kämpfer der NSDAP' in *Sozialwissenschaftliches Jahrbuch für Politik*, Vol. II, Munich, 1971.

Michaelis, H., Schraepler, E. and Scheel, G. (eds) *Ursachen und Folgen: Vom deutschen Zusammenbruch bis zur staatlichen Neuordnung Deutschlands in der Gegenwart*, 12 vols, Berlin (n.d.).

*Mitglieder des deutschen Reichstages 1930*, Berlin, 1930.

Mohler, A., *Die konservative Revolution*, Darmstadt, 1978.

——, *Von rechts gesehen*, Stuttgart, 1979.

Moltke, H.J. Graf v., *Letzte Briefe aus dem Gefängnis Tegel*, Berlin, 1953.

Mommsen, H., 'Der Reichstagsbrand und seine politischen Folgen' in *VfZg*, Munich, 1964, p. 351ff.

——, *Beamtentum in Dritten Reich*, Stuttgart, 1966.

——, 'Die Stellung der Beamtenschaft in Reich, Ländern und Gemeinden in der Ära Brüning' in *VfZg*, 1973, p. 119ff.

Morsey, R., 'Hitlers Verhandlung mit der Zentrumsführung am 31. Januar 1933' in *VfZg*, 1961, p. 182ff.

——, 'Zur Beamtenpolitik des Reiches von Bismarck bis Brüning' in *Demokratie und Verwaltung*, Vol. 50, *Schriftenreihe der Hochschule für Verwaltungswissenschaften Speyer*, Berlin, 1972, p. 109ff.

——, 'Staatsfeinde im öffentlichen Dienst (1929–1933). Die Beamtenpolitik gegenüber NSDAP Mitgliedern' in *Öffentlicher Dienst. Festschrift für G.H. Ule*, ed. by K. König, H.-W. Laubinger and F. Wagener, Cologne, 1977, p. 111ff.

Müller, Ch., *Oberst i.G. von Stauffenberg*, Düsseldorf, 1971.

Müller, K.-J., *Das Heer und Hitler*, Stuttgart, 1969.

——, *Armee, Politik und Gesellschaft in Deutschland 1933–1945*, Paderborn, 1979.

——, *Generaloberst Beck*, Boppard/Rhein, 1980.

*Nationalsozialistisches Strafrecht. Denkschrift des preussischen Innenministers*, Berlin, 1933.

*Neue Zürcher Zeitung*, 17 December 1918.

Neumann, F., *Behemoth*, New York and London, 1942.

Neumann, S., *Permanent Revolution. The Total State in a World of War*, London, 1942.

Nicolai, H., *Grundlagen der kommenden Verfassung*, Berlin, 1933.

Niethammer, L., *Entnazifizierung in Bayern*, Frankfurt, 1972.

Nolte, E., *Der Faschismus in seiner Epoche*, Munich, 1963.

*Das Nürnberger Juristenurteil, 3–4 December 1947*, Hamburg, 1948.

*Das Nürnberger Juristenurteil, Ergänzende Angaben über die Angeklagten im Fall III (IMT)*, Hamburg, 1948.

Orlow, D., *The History of the Nazi Party*, 2 vols, Pittsburgh, 1973.

Papen, F.v., *Memoirs*, London, 1952.

*Das Parlament*, Bonn, 1979.

Pechel, R., *Deutscher Widerstand*, Zürich, 1947.

Peter, E., *Der Lübecker Christenprozess 1943*, Mainz, 1960.

Peterson, E.N., *The Limits of Hitler's Power*, Princeton, 1969.

Petzold, J., *Wegbereiter des deutschen Faschismus: Die Jungkonservativen in der Weimarer Republik*, Berlin, 1978.

Picker, H., *Hitlers Tischgespräche im Führerhauptquartier*, Stuttgart, 1976.

Poetsch-Heffter, F. (ed.) *Jahrbuch für öffentliches Recht*, Berlin, 1935.

Präg, W. and Jacobmeyer, W., *Das Diensttagebuch des deutschen Generalgouverneurs in Polen 1939–1945*, Stuttgart, 1975.

*Preussisches Gesetzblatt*, Berlin 1919–1932.

Peter (Archiv), *Spiegelbild einer Verschwörung*, Stuttgart, 1961.

Reichardt, F., *Andreas Hermes: Eine Biographie*, Neuwied, 1953.

*Reichsgesetzblatt*, Berlin 1918–1944.

*Reichsjustizministerium, Denkschrift des Reichsjustizministers zu 'Vier Jahren politischer Mord'*, Berlin, 1924.

Reitlinger, G., *SS – Alibi of a Nation*, London, 1957.

——, *The Final Solution*, London, 1961.

Remer, E., *Verschwörung und Verrat um Hitler*, Göttingen, 1982.

Rendulic, L., 'Der Partisanenkrieg' in *Bilanz des Zweiten Weltkrieges*, Hamburg, 1953.

Rich, N., *Hitler's War Aims*, 2 vols, London, 1973–4.

Richter, F., 'Der Volksgerichtshof ist kein Revolutionstribunal' in *Deutscher ReichsPreussischer Staatsanzeiger*, No. 146, 26 June 1934.

Riess, C., *Das gab es nur einmal*, Munich, 1977.

Ritter, G., *Carl Goerdeler und die deutsche Widerstandsbewegung*, Stuttgart, 1956.

——, *The Sword and the Sceptre*, 4 vols, Coral Gables, 1969–72.

Roon, G. van, 'Oberst Wilhelm Staehle. Ein Beitrag zu den Auslandskontakten des deutschen Widerstandes' in *VfZg*, 1966, p. 209ff.

Rosenberg, H., *Bureaucracy, Aristocracy and Autocracy: The Prussian Experience 1660–1815*, Boston, 1966.

Rossiter, C. (ed.) *The Federalist Papers*, New York, 1959.

Rösler, I., *Anteil und Rolle der politischen Justiz bei der Entstehung des Hitlerfaschismus*, 1956.

Roszychi-von Hoewel, Dr. jur., *Justiz am Scheideweg! – Heute*, Berlin, 1940.

Rothfels, H., *Die deutsche Opposition gegen Hitler*, Krefeld, 1951.


Salomon, E.v., *Die Geächteten*, Berlin, 1929.

——, *Der Fragebogen*, Hamburg, 1951.

Sauer, F., 'Das Reichsjustizministerium' in *Schriften der Hoschule für Politik*, Issue 36–37, Berlin, 1939.

Sauer, W., 'Rechtsprechung und Regierung. Zur Frage der Unabhängigkeit des Richters' in *DJ*, 1935, p. 181ff.

Seidler, F.W., 'Die Fahnenflucht in der deutschen Wehrmacht während des Zweiten Welt-Krieges' in *Militärgeschichtliche Mitteilungen*, Freiburg, 1977, Issue 2, p. 23ff.

Sérant, P., *Les vaincus de la liberation*, Paris, 1965.

Seydlitz, W.v., *Stalingrad*, Berlin, 1977.

*Sie kämpften für Deutschland*, Ministerium für nationale Verteidigung, Berlin, 1959.

'*Sondergericht Hamburg*' in *DRZ*, No. 553, Berlin, 1935.

'*Sondergericht Hamburg*' in *Reichsverwaltungsblatt*, Berlin, 1935, p. 700ff.

Sontheimer, K., *Antidemokratisches Denken in der Weimarer Republik*, Munich, 1962.

Speer, A., *Inside the Third Reich*, London, 1970.

——, *Spandauer Tagebuch*, Berlin, 1978.

*Spiegelbild einer Verschwörung. Die Kaltenbrunnerberichte*, Stuttgart, 1961.

Schacht, H., *76 Jahre meines Lebens*, Bad Wörishofen, 1953.

Schaefer, R.S., 'Die Vorgänge um das Ermächtigungsgesetz von 1933' in *Frankfurter Hefte*, Frankfurt/Main, 1947, p. 984ff.

Schäfer, W., *Die NSDAP*, Hannover, 1956.

Schäfer, H., 'Die Verordnungen des Reichspräsidenten gegen Verrat am deutschen Volke und hochverräterische Umtriebe' in *JWS*, 1933, p. 873ff.

——, 'Änderungen des Verfahrens in Hoch- und Landesverratssachen' in *JWS*, 1933, p. 937ff.

Scheuner, U., 'Die nationale Revolution' in *Archiv für öffentliches, Recht*, 1934, Neue Folge 1933–4, p. 166ff, p. 261ff.

Scheurig, B., *Ewald von Kleist-Schmenzin. Ein Konservativer gegen Hitler*, Oldenburg, 1968.

——, (ed.) *Verrat hinter Stacheldraht?*, Munich, 1965.

Schier, W., 'Die Justiz im totalitären Staat. Erläuterungen an der Strafrechtsauffassung des nationalsozialistischen Staates' in *Geschichte, Wissenschaft und Unterricht*, 1960, p. 661ff.

Schneider, P., 'Rechtssicherheit und richterliche Unabhängigkeit aus der Sicht des SD' in *VfZg*, 1961, p. 237ff.

Schoenbaum, D., *Hitler's Social Revolution*, London, 1967.

Scholl, I., *Die weisse Rose*, Frankfurt, 1955.

Schlabrendorff, F.v., *Offiziere gegen Hitler*, Frankfurt/Main, 1964.

Schorn, H., *Der Richter im 3. Reich*, Frankfurt/Main, 1959.

Schmahl, H., *Disziplinarrecht und politische Betätigung der Beamten in der Weimarer Republik*, Berlin, 1977.

Schmitt, C., *Verfassungslehre*, Cologne, 1957 (revised version of the 1928 edition).

——, *Legalität und Legitimität*, Bonn, 1932.

——, 'Neue Leitsätze für die Rechtspraxis' in *JWS*, 1933, p. 273ff and in *DR*, 1933, p. 201ff.

——, 'Nationalsozialistisches Rechtsdenken' in *DR*, 1934, p. 225ff.

——, *Staat, Bewegung, Volk*, Berlin, 1934.

——, *Über die drei Arten rechtswissenschaftlichen Denkens*, Berlin, 1936.

Schramm, P.E. (ed.) *Kriegstagebuch des Oberkommandos der Wehrmacht*, Studienausgabe, 8 vols, Munich, 1982.

Schramm, R.v., *Aufstand der Generale: Der 20. Juli in Paris*, Munich, 1964.

*Schriften des Bundes deutscher Jungenschaften*, No. 31, Bad Godesberg, 1967, 'Helmut Hirsch 21.1.1916–4.6.1937'.

Schraut, R. (ed.) *Deutscher Juristentag 1933. 4. Reichstagung des Bundes Nationalsozialistischer Deutscher Juristen. Ansprachen und Fachvorträge*, Berlin, 1933.

Schüddekopf, E., *Linke Leute von Rechts*, Stuttgart, 1961.

Schüler, H., *Auf der Flucht erschossen: Felix Fehrenbach 1894–1933*, Cologne, 1981.

Schulz, G., *Aufstieg des Nationalsozialismus*, Frankfurt, 1975.

——, 'Rechtliche Grundlagen im Parteienstaat' in *Staat und NSDAP 1930–1932*, ed. by Maurer, I. and Wengst, U., Düsseldorf, 1977, p. XIff.

Schulze, H., *Otto Braun oder Preussens demokratische Sendung*, Berlin, 1979.

——, *Weimar, Deutschland 1917–1933*, Berlin, 1982.

Schwabe, K., *Deutsche Revolution und Wilson Friede. Die amerikanische und deutsche Friedensstrategie zwischen Ideologie und Machtpolitik*, Düsseldorf, 1971.

*Das Schwarze Korps*, volume for 1942.

Staff, I. (ed.) *Justiz im Dritten Reich*, Frankfurt, 1978.

Stammler, R., *Die Lehre vom richtigen Recht*, Göttingen, 1902.

Stampfer, F., *Erfahrungen und Bekenntnisse*, Cologne, 1957.

Steffens, H., 'Die rechtliche Vertretung der Juden im Reich' in *DR*, 1942, p. 9ff.

Stein, G.S., *The Waffen-SS at War*, Oxford, 1966.

Steinert, M., *Hitlers Krieg und die Deutschen*, Düsseldorf, 1962.

Stern, F., *The Politics of Cultural Despair*, New York, 1965.

Stoltenberg, G., *Politische Strömungen im schleswig-holsteinischem Landvolk 1918–1933*, Düsseldorf, 1962.

*Strafgesetzbuch*, Berlin 1871 and supplements to 1943.

*Strafprozessordnung*, Berlin, 1877.

Strasser, O., *Hitler und Ich*, Konstanz, 1948.

Streit, Chr., *Keine Kameraden*, Stuttgart, 1978.

Stuckart, W. and Globke, G., 'Reichsbürgergesetz vom 15.9.1935. Gesetz zum Schutz der Erbgesundheit und der deutschen Ehre vom 18.10.1935' in *Kommentare zur deutschen Rassengesetzgebung*, Vol. I, Munich, 1936.

*Taschenkalender für Verwaltungsbeamte*, Berlin, 1932 and 1934.

Theisen, H., *Die Entwicklung zum nihilistischen Nationalismus in Deutschland 1918–1933*, Munich, 1958.

Thimme, A., *Flucht in den Mythos. Die deutschnationale Volkspartei und die Niederlage von 1918*, Göttingen, 1968.

Thierack, G., 'Aufgaben und Tätigkeit des Volksgerichtshofes' in *ZAkDR*, 1936, p. 855ff.

Tobias, F., *Der Reichstagsbrand. Legende und Wirklichkeit*, Rastatt, 1962.

Tocqueville, A. de, *The Old Regime and the French Revolution*, New York, 1955.

*Trial of the Major German War Criminals before the International Military Tribunal*, Vol. XXV, London, 1947.

Tucholsky, K., *Gesammelte Werke*, ed. by Mary Tucholsky, Hamburg, 1965.

Tyrell, A., *Vom Trommler zum Führer*, Munich, 1975.

United States Senate Committee on Armed Forces. *Malmedy Massacre Investigation Hearing 1949*, Washington D.C., 1949.

Vansittart, Sir R., *Mist Procession*, London, 1958.

*Die Verfassung des Deutschen Reiches*, Berlin, 1920.

*Verfügungen, Anordnungen, Bekanntmachungen*, ed. by the Parteikanzlei des NSDAP, Munich (n.d.).

*Verhandlungen des Reichstages*, Vol. 457, Berlin, 1933.

Vogelsang, Th., *Reichswehr, Staat und NSDAP*, Stuttgart, 1962.

Volkmann, H.-E., 'Die NS-Wirtschaft in Vorbereitung des Krieges' in *Deutschland im Zweiten Weltkrieg*, Vol. 1, Freiburg, 1981.

Volkmar, Elster and Küchenhoff (eds) *Handwörterbuch der Rechtswissenschaft*, Berlin, 1937.

'Vom Volksgericht des Deutschen Reiches' in *DJ*, 1935, p. 1709ff.

'Der Volksgerichtshof für das Deutsche Reich' in *JWS*, 1936, p. 1569ff.

Wagner, W., 'Braune Rechtsprechung, Politische Justiz im "Dritten Reich" ' in *Politische Meinung*, 1961, p. 41ff.

——, *Die deutsche Justiz und der Nationalsozialismus*, Vol. 3, *Der Volksgerichtshof im nationalsozialistischen Staat*, Stuttgart, 1974.

Watt, D.C., 'Die bayerischen Bemühungen um die Ausweisung Hitlers 1924' in *VfZg*, 1972, p. 375ff.

Weber, A., *Politische Polizei: Wesen und Begriff der politischen Polizei im Metternichschen System, in der Weimarer Republik und im nationalsozialistischen Staate*, Berlin, 1937.

Weber, M., 'Der Reichspräsident' and 'Parlament und Regierung im neugeordneten Deutschland' in *Gesammelte Schriften*, ed. by Winkelmann, J., Tübingen, 1958.

Wegner, B., *Hitlers politische Soldaten: Die Waffen-SS 1933–1945*, Paderborn, 1982.

Weinkauff, H., *Die deutsche Justiz und der Nationalsozialismus: Ein Überblick*, Stuttgart, 1968.

Weingartner, J.J., *Hitler's Guard: The Story of the Leibstandarte-SS Adolf Hitler, 1933–1945*, Southern Illinois University Press, 1968.

Weisenborn, G., *Der lautlose Aufstand*, Hamburg, 1962.

Weizsäcker, E.v., *Erinnerungen*, 2 vols, Munich, 1951.

West, R., *A Train of Powder*, London, 1954.

*Die Weltbühne*, 1918–1933, 16 vols, reprint, Berlin, 1978.

Wheeler-Bennet, J.W., *The Nemesis of Power*, London, 1954.

White, L.D. (ed.) *The Civil Service in the Modern State. A Collection of Documents*, Chicago, 1930.

Winkler, H.A., 'Extremismus der Mitte? Sozialgeschichtliche Aspekte der national-sozialistischen Machtergreifung' in *VfZg*, 1972, p. 175ff.

Wolff, W., *An der Seite der Roten Armee*, Berlin (n.d.).

Young, D., *Rommel*, London, 1950.

Zahn, G.C., *Die deutschen Katholiken und Hitlers Krieg*, Cologne, 1965.

Ziemessen, D., *Der Malmedy Prozess*, Munich, 1952.

Ziesel, K., *Das verlorene Gewissen*, Munich, 1956.

# Index